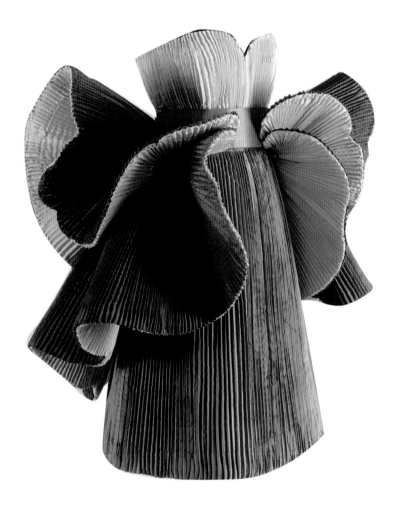

# THE DRESS

*To Ruth Wass Wright (1924–2014)*

Published in 2021 by Welbeck
An imprint of Welbeck Non-fiction Limited, part of
Welbeck Publishing Group
20 Mortimer Street
London
W1T 3JW

First published in 2014 by Goodman

10 9 8 7 6 5 4 3 2 1

A CIP catalogue record for this book is available
from the British Library.

ISBN  978 1 78739 923 5

Printed in China

**PREVIOUS PAGE:** Roberto Capucci's
peplum petal dress, see also page
187. He referred to his work as
"a study in form" inspired by art,
architecture and nature.

**OPPOSITE:** Spinal Column Dress
by Helen and Kate Storey from
the "Primitive Streak" collection,
1997. The fashion/textile
collection chronicled the first
1,000 hours of human life, from
fertilization to the recognizable
human form.

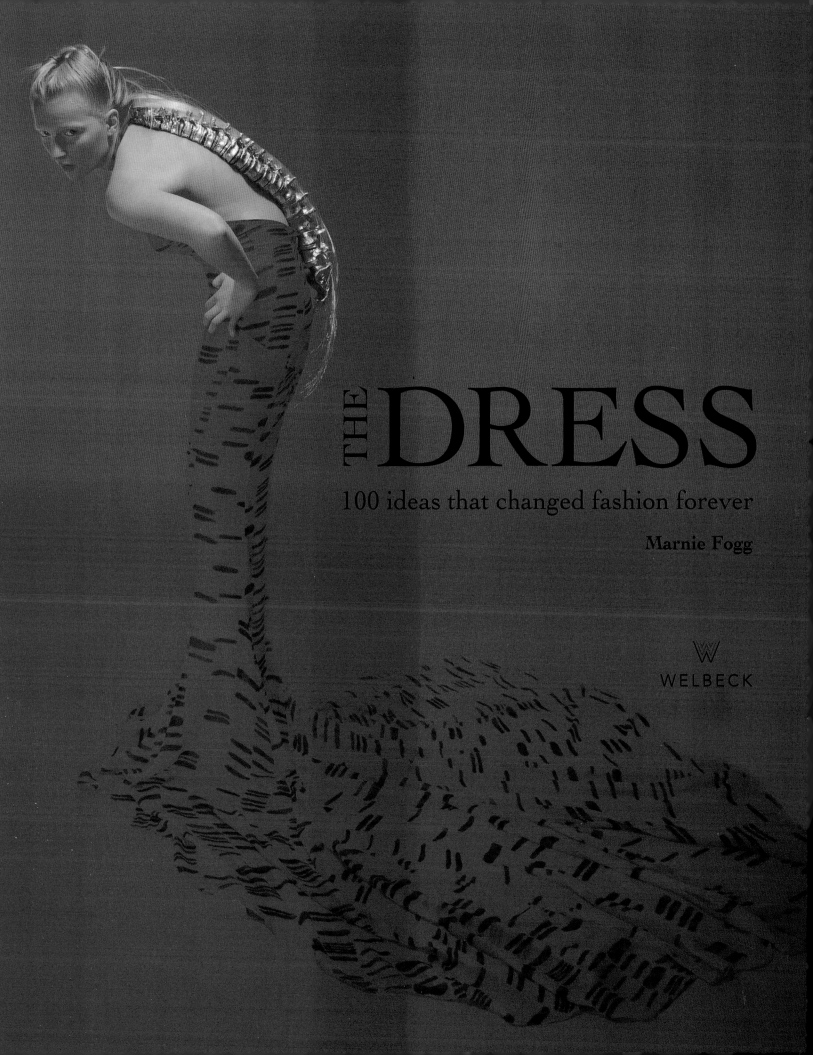

# THE DRESS

## 100 ideas that changed fashion forever

Marnie Fogg

W
WELBECK

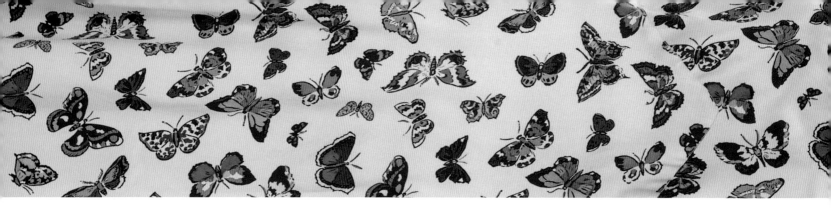

# Contents

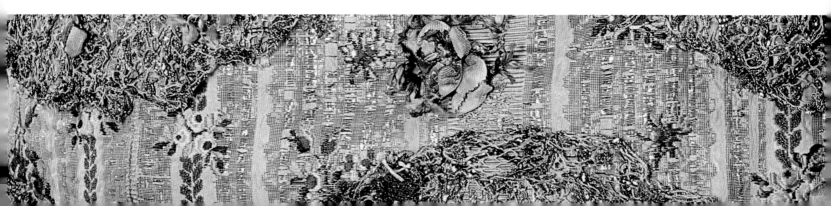

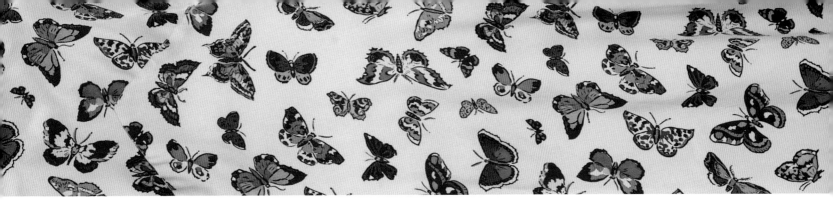

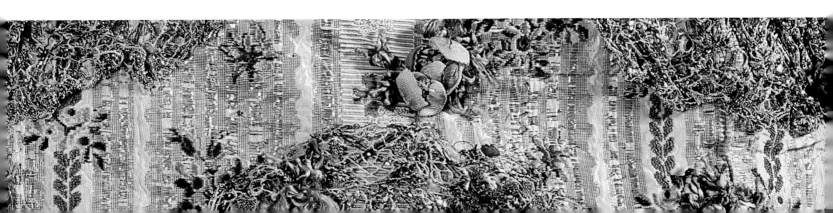

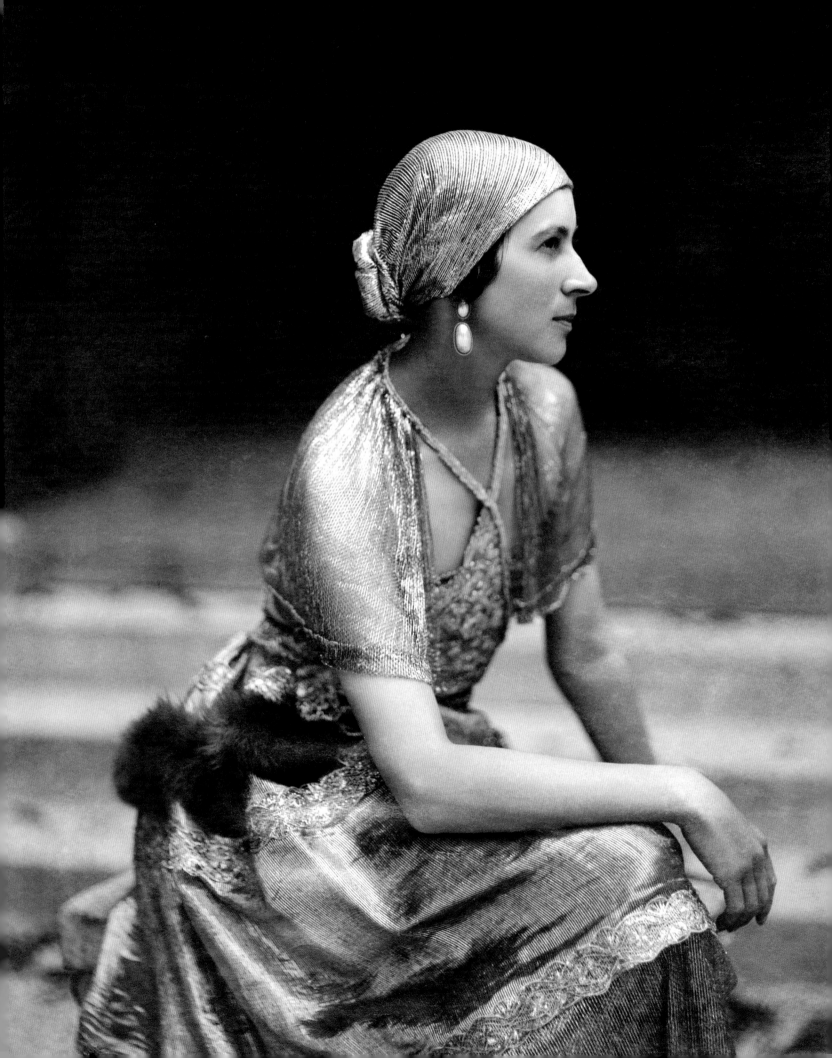

# Introduction

At the core of fashion is the dress; it is the litmus paper of fashion change and the first garment in the wardrobe to signpost new and sometimes startling directions. Innovation is the unifying attribute of the iconic examples of fashionable dress featured in this book, a characteristic that resides in either technical virtuosity, in the denial of the dominant taste of the era or is the result of the singular vision of the designer – a notion first associated with dressmaker Louis Hyppolite Leroy. In defining the style of Empress Joséphine and the Napoleonic court in the early nineteenth century, Leroy promulgated the fashion for the columnar high-waisted gown throughout Europe's monarchies and aristocracies. Paris was first formalized as the centre of western fashion in the seventeenth century with Louis XIV's regulation of the French textile trade, and this was consolidated in 1868 with the formation of what would subsequently be known as the Chambre Syndicale de la Haute Couture. This body promoted the activities of the couturiers and constituted a mannered backdrop of experimental theatricality and unimaginable luxury that was instrumental in creating influential and innovative ideas.

Fashion is often analyzed as a cyclical phenomenon, with the implication of a predictable rotation, but it acts more in the manner of a complex orbital system of interactions subject to the arrival and departure of preceding influences, modulated by wider culture. For example, Charles Frederick Worth's mid-nineteenth century crinoline was to be reimagined in the mid twentieth century by both Charles James and Christian Dior in his New Look, and has since been referenced on the catwalk by Alexander McQueen and John Galliano. Conversely, changes in fashion are often reactive – in an inevitable contrast to the periods when the corseted, full-skirted hourglass figure prevails, sartorial emancipation follows, allowing the designer to introduce a game-changing silhouette, most notably expressed by French couturiers Jean Patou and Coco Chanel in the 1920s with the introduction of the tubular chemise, a simplicity of outline that was subsequently adopted by Mary Quant in the 1960s. The trajectory of these and other groundbreaking designs is charted on the following pages, from their first diverse introduction into fashion to their subsequent reinterpretations, providing a vivid picture of radical changes in style over the years.

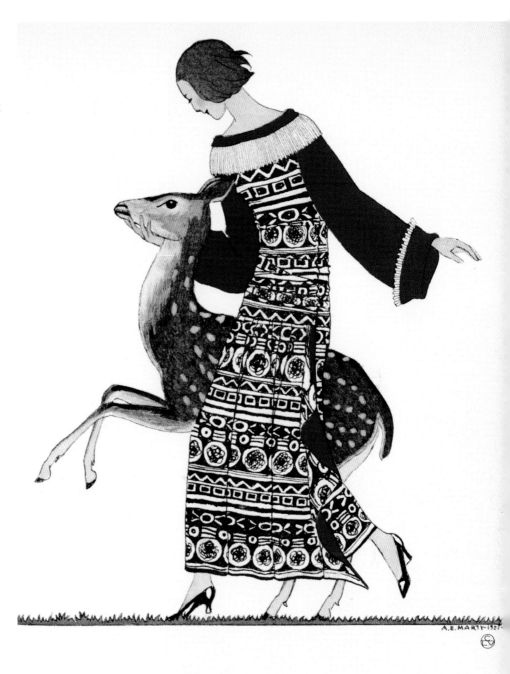

## LA BICHE APPRIVOISÉE
ROBE, DE PAUL POIRET

**OPPOSITE:** One of the first initiators of twentieth-century haute bohème and credited with changing the course of fashion history, Parisian couturier Paul Poiret created designs that freed women from the limiting corset, as seen here in a *toilette de soirée* modelled by his wife in 1921.

**ABOVE:** Poiret combined "exotic" textiles with an unstructured silhouette, as illustrated here in a 1922 edition of *Gazette du Bon Ton*, entitled *La Biche Apprivoisée – The Tame Doe –* by A. É. Marty (1882–1974), a Parisian artist who worked mainly in the Art Deco style.

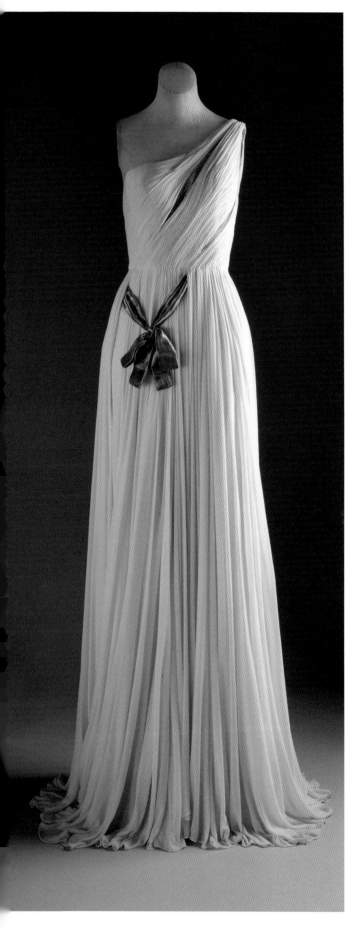

# The Amazonian Dress

Legendary for their fearless physical prowess, the Amazons, a race of female warriors, reputedly severed their right breasts to concentrate all their power in their right arms and shoulders in order to draw more effectively on a bow. One-shouldered gowns are frequently described as "Amazonian", but the term has also come to mean any high-achieving woman in the arena of physical daring or accomplishment. The importance of physical fitness for women was first recognized in the 1920s when the streamlined body represented modernity. Vigorous sports were undertaken to this end, such as tennis, swimming and mass bicycle rides. Callisthenics, a form of movement popularized by the American pioneer of modern dance Isadora Duncan, represented the awakening desire for physical strength and freedom.

The classical form of ancient Greece is uniquely associated with bodily perfection. Madame Alix Grès, one of the foremost couturiers of the twentieth century, employed innovative construction techniques in the pursuit of a classical aesthetic. In 1954 she combined fluidity in the form of minutely pleated jersey, attached to a boned corselette beneath, for a one-shouldered gown that exemplified statuesque beauty.

The 1980s heralded the arrival of the gym-toned "glamazon", the contemporary businesswoman who dressed for success in a series of sharp-shouldered suits and stiletto heels. Women were instructed to "feel the burn" by film actress Jane Fonda in her work-out videos, and gym membership was a prerequisite for the quintessential yuppie. The late Princess Diana, an über-glamazon, continually favoured a one-shouldered gown to emphasize her toned physique, including a white gown embroidered with translucent glass beads and crystals worn to a state visit in Japan in 1984 and a Catherine Walker gown of silk taffeta printed with red roses in 1988. It was only with her burgeoning confidence in her own style, however, that the one-shouldered gown came to epitomize a woman at the height of her powers, in a peacock-blue gown by Italian designer Gianni Versace that she wore in 1996.

The one-shouldered gown is not always confined to eveningwear. Not surprisingly influenced by her role as creative designer for the 2012 British Olympic Team, UK designer Stella McCartney introduced the one-sleeve style into her Spring/Summer collection of the same year, mixing Aertex-inspired power-mesh sports fabric with a foulard print into a thigh-high minidress. The cutaway halter-top also referenced the sporting racer-back vest.

**LEFT:** Dating from 1954, the evening gown designed by Madame Grès (Alix Barton) (1903–93) exemplifies the couturier's deft use of pleating and draping. The gold lamé sash, threaded diagonally across the breasts and ending in the flourish of a bow, is redolent of celebratory regalia.

**OPPOSITE:** This one-shouldered gown, worn by supermodel Naomi Campbell, is resonant of the style of Greek sculpture copied by the Roman sculptor Pasiteles in his figure of a victorious Atalanta – known as the *Barberini Atalanta* – the fierce virgin huntress of the first century BCE.

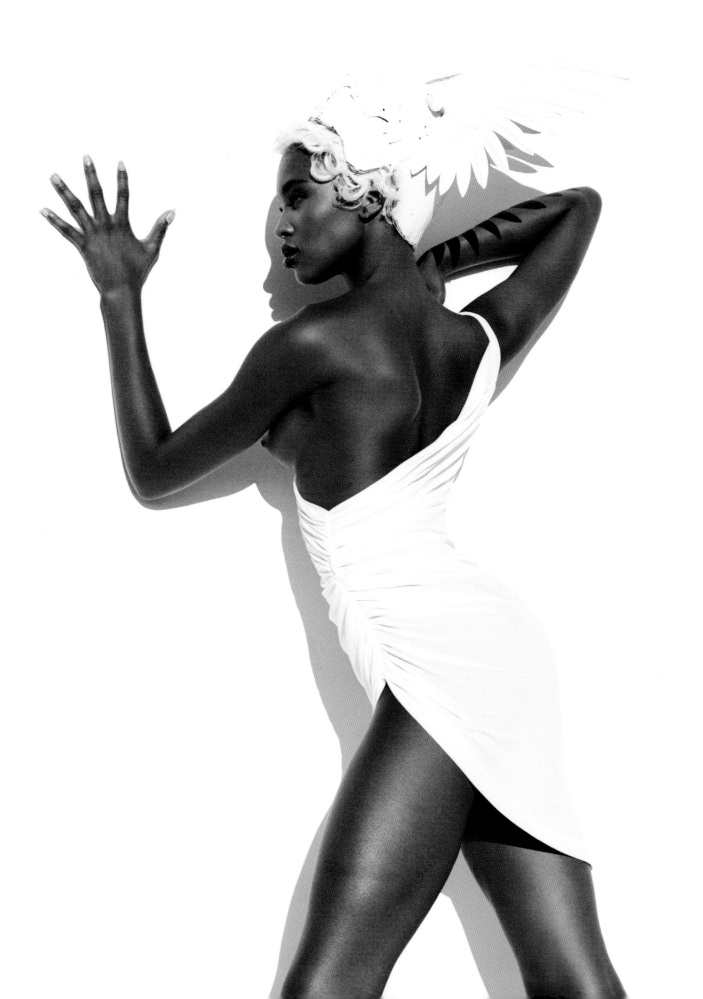

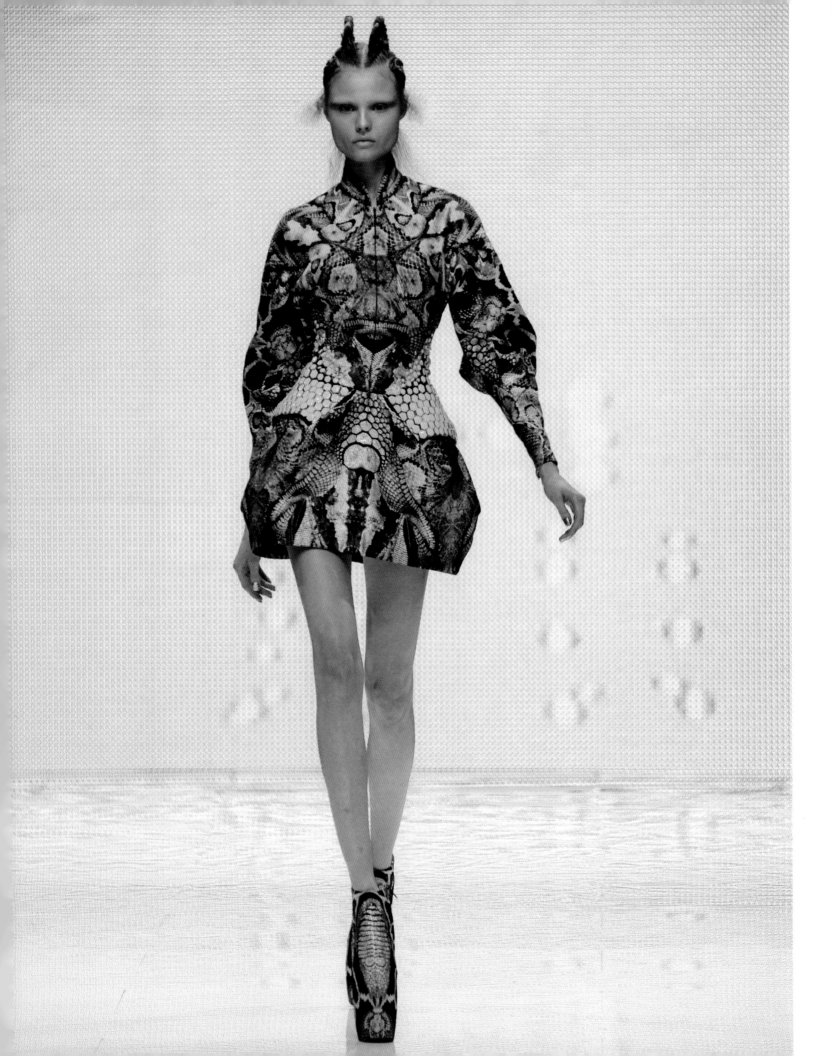

# The Snake Goddess

Wearing the skin of reptiles is imbued with both an alarming sensuality and an awareness of the potential for imminent danger, owing to the sinuous lines of the snake and the suddenness of its deadly attack. It also evokes notions of the Minoan "snake goddess", the foremost figure of worship in ancient Crete, and of the Greco-Roman Medusa, the femme fatale with hair of hissing snakes whose stare turned all who looked on her to stone, the protector of the most ancient ritual secrets.

The serpentine woman has been considered a fatal temptress since the snake tempted Eve to taste the Garden's apple, and from the Pre-Raphaelites to the *fin-de-siècle* decadents, snakes have been associated with wild, tumbling hair that ensnares the unsuspecting male victim. Conversely, as snakes shed their skin through sloughing, they are symbols of rebirth and transformation. The coiled serpent embroidered on the sleeve of the gown with a heart-shaped ruby in its mouth – worn by Elizabeth I in the *Rainbow Portrait* and attributed to Isaac Oliver – is thought to represent wisdom, and the ruby Elizabeth's heart, implying that the Queen's wisdom controls her emotions.

Unlike fur and animal skins, the skin of the reptile traditionally offered no practical protection from the elements, and was used historically purely for the visually dynamic patterning of its skin. Interpreting the scales of the reptile with a pavé of silver embroidery in his 1998 collection for Givenchy Haute Couture, Alexander McQueen created a second-skin silhouette of serpentine curves that represented the snake itself. The designer also engineered digitally printed mythological sea serpents for his post-apocalyptic "Plato's Atlantis" collection, where he fashioned the fabric into a corseted body with pannier-like skirts.

A constant visual reference for designers, snakeskin was used by Erdem Moralioglu when he patchworked his signature lace with pastel-coloured faux python for his Spring/Summer collection of 2013.

Along with crocodile and lizard leathers, snakeskin is considered an "exotic" skin and belongs to the category of reptile leathers, and all types of skin have been crafted into fashionable garments in the past, most notably by Ossie Clark in the 1970s, with his signature python-skin biker jackets. However, modern sensibilities are understandably ambivalent about the use of real skins in the manufacture of garments, and it is a practice condemned by animal rights activists.

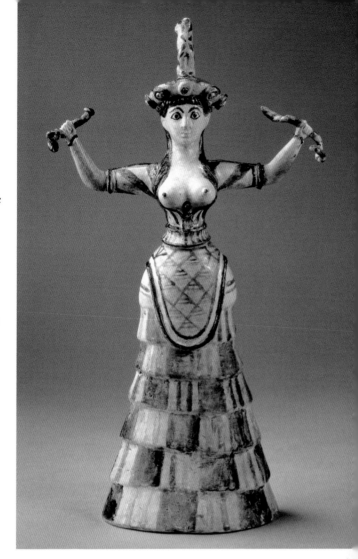

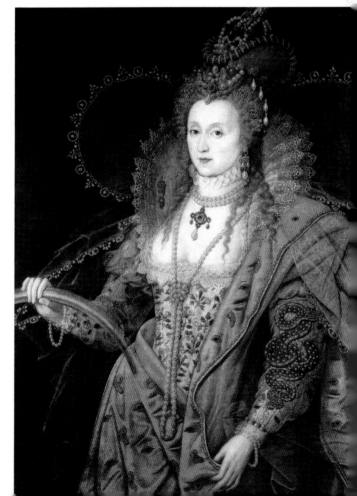

**OPPOSITE:** Iconoclastic designer Alexander McQueen (1969–2010) combines his renowned technical skills of cut and construction with the drama of an apocalyptic vision in his S/S "Plato's Atlantis" collection of 2010, mediated through the imagery of mythical sea serpents.

**ABOVE RIGHT:** Representing powers of destruction and regeneration, the ancient Cretan idol of the Minoan "snake goddess" (a term coined by archaeologist Arthur Evans in 1903) was imbued with reverence for the snake. The emphasis on her breasts and hips denotes fertility.

**RIGHT:** Known as the *Rainbow Portrait* (c.1600), owing to its Latin inscription *non sine sole iris*, which translates as "No rainbow without a sun", the painting shows Elizabeth I dressed with great formality in opulent garments ablaze with symbolic emblems.

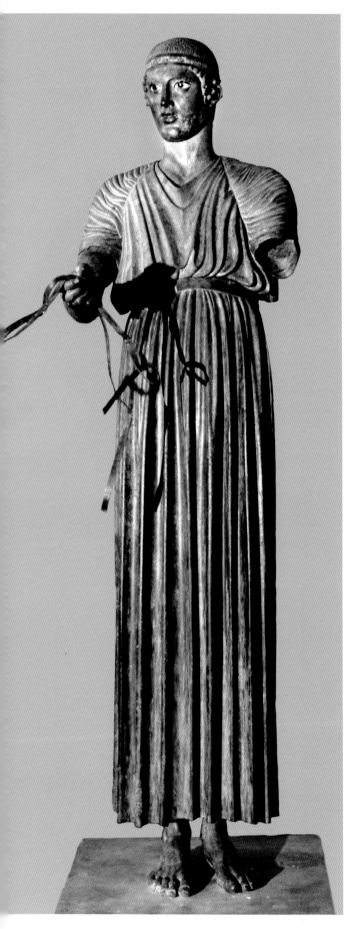

# Classical Style

Exploring the sculptural possibilities of controlling fabric to create the look of classical antiquity, Parisian couturière Alix Barton, later known as Madame Grès (*see also page* 8), created "goddess gowns" by deploying intricate pleating, gathering and draping techniques. With a silhouette that replicates the fluted Greek and Roman columns, the gown also references the Hellenic Greek *chiton* worn by both men and women to denote high status, communicating wealth and prestige through its amplitude, as seen in the bas-relief sculpture *The Charioteer of Delphi* dating from 475 BCE.

Grès constructed the gown with the deceptive simplicity of garments created around the loom width. She was expert at seaming together the fabric vertically to create a continuous line from hem to neckline, pleating and tucking the materials to shape them to the body in a single fluid outline. The sculptural qualities of the silhouette, inspired by statues and images found on pictorial vases, are enhanced by the draping qualities of the material used, the adoption of neutral colours such as cream, stone and grey, and the overlong length – the fabric is allowed to pool in sculptural folds around the hem.

Classical revivals usually occur as an alternative to ordinary dress, but during the 1930s the classically draped gown – occasionally one-shouldered, deploying ties or drawstrings to gather in the fabric – was the norm for evening, providing a glamorous relief from the austere daywear of a recession-hit economy. Although Madeleine Vionnet's gowns were somewhat removed from authentic classical reconstruction, she nevertheless deployed draping to great effect, extending the spirit of the classical originals with her innovations in cut. Since the 1930s, the classical mode is one that has been a consistent favourite with designers, and more recently the go-to style for fail-safe red-carpet dressing, providing a statuesque grandeur without ostentation or near-nudity.

Although a timeless design, slight adjustments to the classical style are evident, depending on the prevailing style. In 1973, American designer Halston (Roy Halston Frowick), renowned for his modern minimalism, introduced a toga-like pleated cape composed of yards of chiffon for his evening gown with wrap. French couturier Emanuel Ungaro's classical gown from 1990 suspends the fabric of the *himation*-inspired draped bodice from a shoulder line supported by pads, in keeping with the wide-shouldered silhouette of the era, and in 2003 Tom Ford for Gucci introduced a body-exposing drape to the neoclassicism of twenty-first-century clothing.

**LEFT:** Dating from the fifth century BCE, this life-size sculpture *The Charioteer of Delphi*, is made of cast bronze. Also known as *Iniohos* – meaning "he who holds the reins" – the figure is wearing the athletic version of the long *chiton*, the *xystis*. The perpendicular flow of fabric is emphasized by the high waist.

**OPPOSITE:** Couturier Madame Grès continued to utilize unbroken lengths of fabric throughout her career, as in this evening dress from 1965, which replicates the classical Greek *himation* – a shawl-like garment – here draped across the body in light silk chiffon.

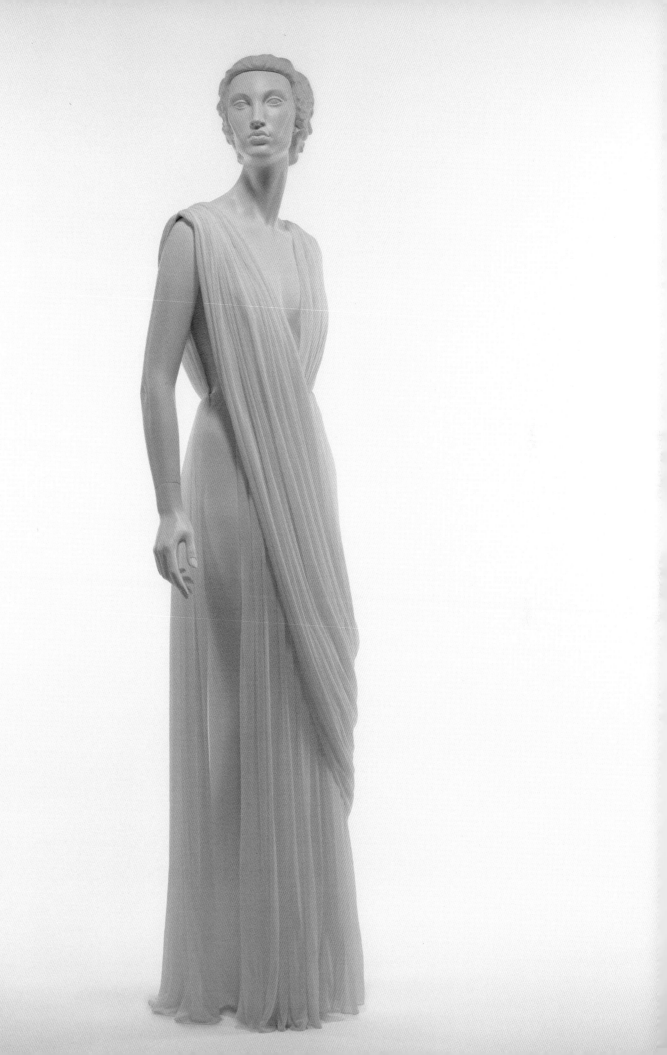

# Egyptian Dress

Egyptian clothing is fused with the general idea of antiquity, although the similarities between the *chiton* of ancient Greece and the *kalasiris* worn during the era of the New Kingdom – between 1500 and 332 BCE – were restricted to the use of the loom width to create simple garments. The long-fringed semi-transparent *kalasiris* was worn by both men (who wore it over a *schenti*, a pleated loin cloth fastened with a belt) and women. The sheath-like dress in fine, lightweight linen, with well-defined pleating, reached to just under the breasts, where it was secured with shoulder straps. Elaborate beaded collars in silver and gold, inset with semi-precious stones such as amethyst, turquoise, lapis lazuli and green and red jasper formed a yoke that covered the top of the shoulders. A taste for ancient Egypt within the framework of neo-classicism was manifest following Napoleon Bonaparte's Egyptian campaign of 1788–89. Napoleon documented the antiquities, architecture and natural history of the country, and eventually published the findings in *Description de l'Egypte*, leading to a period of Egyptmania, in which pleating and drapery modified the vertical line of the neo-classical dress of the era.

A fantasy version of Egyptian costume was mediated through film, first with screen vamp Theda Bara in the title role of Cleopatra in 1917, followed by Claudette Colbert in 1934 in Cecil B. DeMille's epic film of the last pharaoh of ancient Egypt. Colbert combines a version of the *kalasiris* with the silhouette of the 1930s, a trailing bias-cut gown in sumptuous satin.

The most outstanding revival of Egyptmania occurred after the discovery by Howard Carter of the tomb of the boy-pharaoh Tutankhamun in 1922, when interest was fuelled by newsreel footage of the archaeological digs and numerous biblical epics. Egyptian iconography pervaded modern culture, and Egyptian motifs became inextricably linked to the vocabulary of Art Deco, a style that would dominate the decorative arts until the mid-1930s. In addition to adorning architecture and furniture, the highly stylized aesthetic meshed well with the simplicity of the prevailing silhouette, and Egyptian motifs such as palm trees, hieroglyphs and scarabs, along with geometric renderings of plants, were incorporated into the decorative arts of the day.

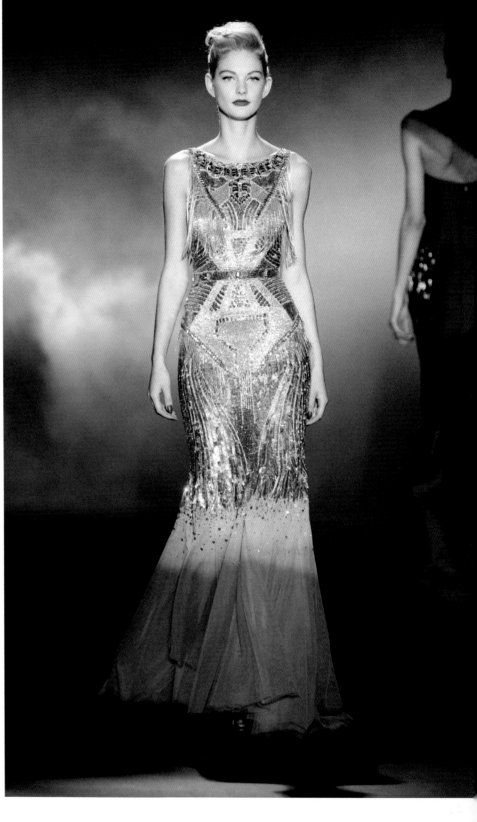

**ABOVE:** Mark Badgley and James Mischka, of US label Badgley Mischka, translate the rigid symmetry of the tied folds of the pharaoh's robe, with its decorated bands of pattern and colour, into richly textured brocade that has much of the impact of the mosaic jewellery of Tutankhamun.

**OPPOSITE:** Starring as the eponymous heroine of Cecil B. DeMille's film *Cleopatra*, actress Claudette Colbert offered a fantasy version of Egyptian dress in costumes designed by Travis Banton (1894–1958), renowned head costumier at Paramount Pictures during the 1930s.

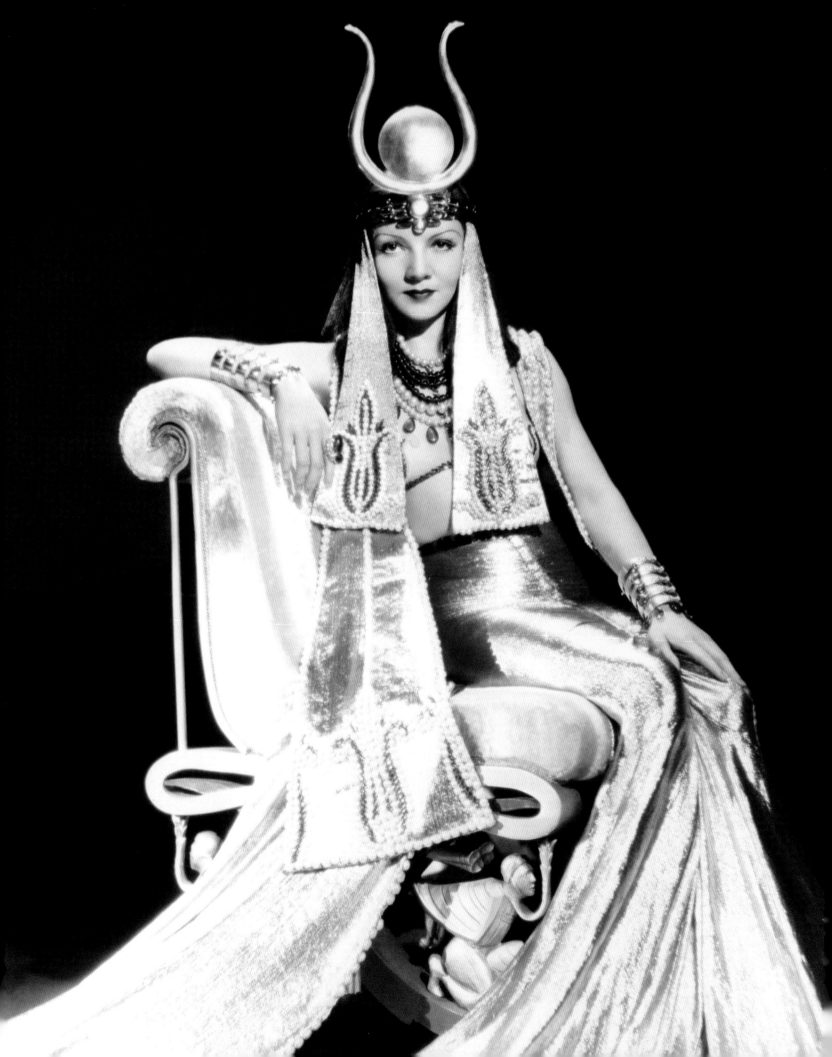

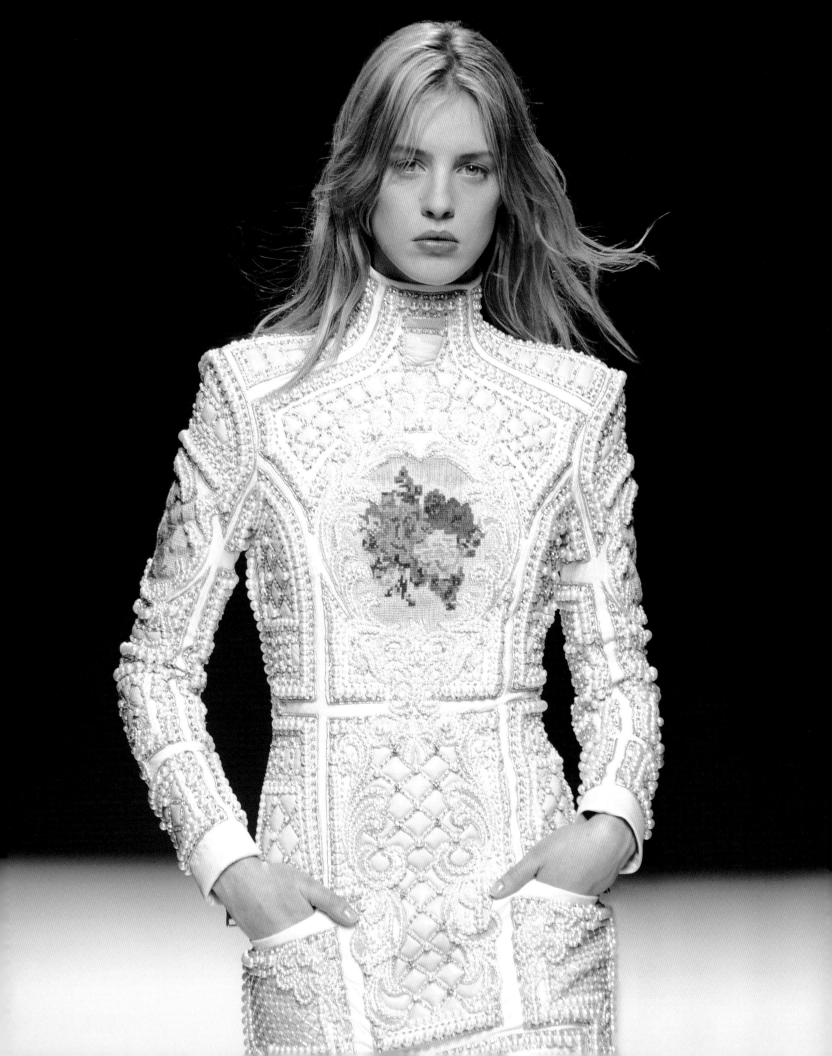

# The Embroidered Dress

In cultures across the globe, lavish embroidery has been used to indicate wealth and status for at least 2,500 years. Exquisite fragments of chain-stitched silk gauze survive from ritual garments of the late Zhou Dynasty of fifth–third century BCE. Every stage of the artisan creation of richly coloured embroidered silk cloth is beset with painstaking, labour-intensive processes – from the conversion of raw material into woven cloth, to the coloration and application of threads and other precious components to form decorative patterning. In this way, the embroidered material is invested with high value, positioning it at a premium in the hierarchy of luxury.

Either by court decree or simply through market forces, sumptuous hand-embellished fabrics were placed alongside jewellery amidst the exotic treasures accruing to plutocrats, monarchs and aristocrats. Appetites for high-value luxury goods added considerable momentum to global trade, to exploration and to the expansion of trading hubs such as Venice and Byzantium. In medieval England, embroidery skills flourished in professional workshops, controlled by guilds, gaining a reputation across Europe for English Work or *Opus Anglicanum*.

In Nicholas Hilliard's portrait of Queen Elizabeth I (*c*.1575) we are confronted with an extravagant level of saturated sumptuary pomp, embodying thousands of hours of handiwork and framing an elaborate declaration of the unequivocal status of the sitter as Gloriana. The textiles have the opulence of the treasure chest – finest punto embroidery in aria lace at neck and cuff; raised goldwork on the slashed bodice, patterned in oak leaves studded with pearls and banded with massive gemstones; and freestitch blackwork lace at the shoulder, making graphic reference to regal heritage with Tudor roses.

At a remove of four centuries, Olivier Rousteing employed similar resonances to produce embroidered dresses of unabashed richness in his second collection for Balmain in Autumn/Winter 2012–13. His touchstone is the artist-jeweller of the Russia Imperial court, Peter Carl Fabergé. Rousteing took inspiration from the exquisite formality of the illustrious bejewelled Easter eggs, produced annually by Fabergé for his patrons, the family of the Czar. The intricate and carefully balanced Imperial Baroque style of Fabergé is translated with a degree of reverence by Rousteing into an encrusted leather shell economically formed to the body as a severe, heavily embroidered, long-sleeved dress, patterned with metal beads, costume pearls, quilting and cross-stitch. Imbued with the essential manner of majestic display, the Balmain dress carries the collar erect and the shoulder emphasized, while the overall surface lacks little in the way of competition with the extravagance of Tudor and Czarist precedent.

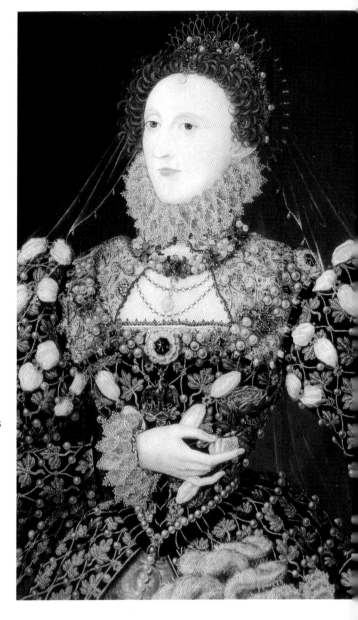

**OPPOSITE:** French designer Olivier Rousteing (1986–) at the couture house of Balmain enriches the surface of the severely structured dress with a multiplicity of traditional and contemporary embroidery techniques. These include laser-cut perforated leather and pearl and crystal embellishment.

**ABOVE:** Painted by miniaturist Nicholas Hilliard in 1572, and known as *The Phoenix Portrait* owing to the pendant brooch Elizabeth I wears at her breast, the painting portrays the Queen as a religious icon. The elaborate detailing of her costume signifies her status and achievements.

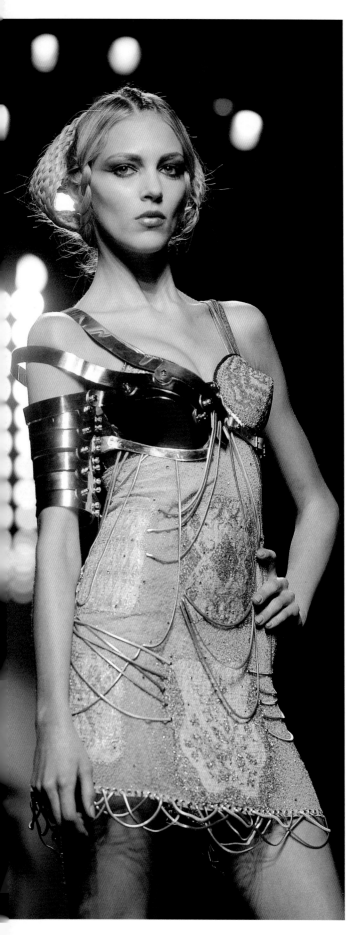

# Armoured Dress

Body armour has a direct connection with costume; it both conforms to the prevailing civilian fashion and inspires it, although this naturally occurs more with men's fashions than with women's.

Early armour included hardened leather, overlapping scales, padded linen and metal plates to protect the belly. Lamellar – armour composed of interconnected plaques or hoops – first appeared in eighth-century BCE Assyria, and is seen in the figure of a terracotta warrior from Emperor Qin Shi Huang's tomb, China *c.*210 BCE, which shows armour made of laced plates made from either bronze or hardened leather. Roman armour included a leather cuirass – torso armour embossed with musculature – which proved a popular costume in the pageants and masquerades of the nineteenth century and created an effect not unfamiliar to the superhero costumes of contemporary cinema. Mail armour, a series of riveted rings – the name deriving from the French *maille*, or "mesh" – continued to be worn throughout the Middle Ages, and was combined with plate armour, introduced in the early thirteenth century in response to changes in warfare and the use of the crossbow.

Heraldic devices on shields, banners and crests were designed as a means of identification in battle, made up of a combination of tinctures (colours) and charges (symbols). During the Renaissance, a full suit of body armour provided complete protection, although it was not worn by infantry troops such as the Swiss mercenaries, who wore elaborate bicoloured doublets and hose. The army set the trend for slashing cuts into garments, with the contrasting white linen undergarment worn beneath pulled through to create decorative puffs. The Swiss troops were copied by the German mercenaries known as *Landsknecht*, and were in turn copied by the French court, a fashion that was subsequently introduced into England with the marriage of Henry VII's sister Mary to Louis XII of France. A similar effect was seen in the seventeenth-century custom of clasping together the sleeve and bodice seams at regular wide-spaced intervals to show the chemise or shirt beneath, inspired by the military vest. Interest in armour was reanimated in the nineteenth century, in part sparked by a reorganization of the London's Tower armoury in 1824 and also owing to a revival in medievalism, which included re-enactments of sixteenth-century tournaments, resulting in the pageantry of the costume ball replacing the earlier masquerades.

**LEFT:** Jean Paul Gaultier (1952–) hybridizes his customary fetishism of the bra with warrior-like armour for S/S Haute Couture 2010. The studded and articulated metal straps of the one-sided sleeve and bra cup are offset by the fragility of the metallic lace dress.

**OPPOSITE:** Designed for A/W 2006–7 by John Galliano (1960–) for Christian Dior Haute Couture, the metallic evening dress combines a mesh headdress with the raised pauldron, a device originating in Renaissance armour, worn to protect the shoulder.

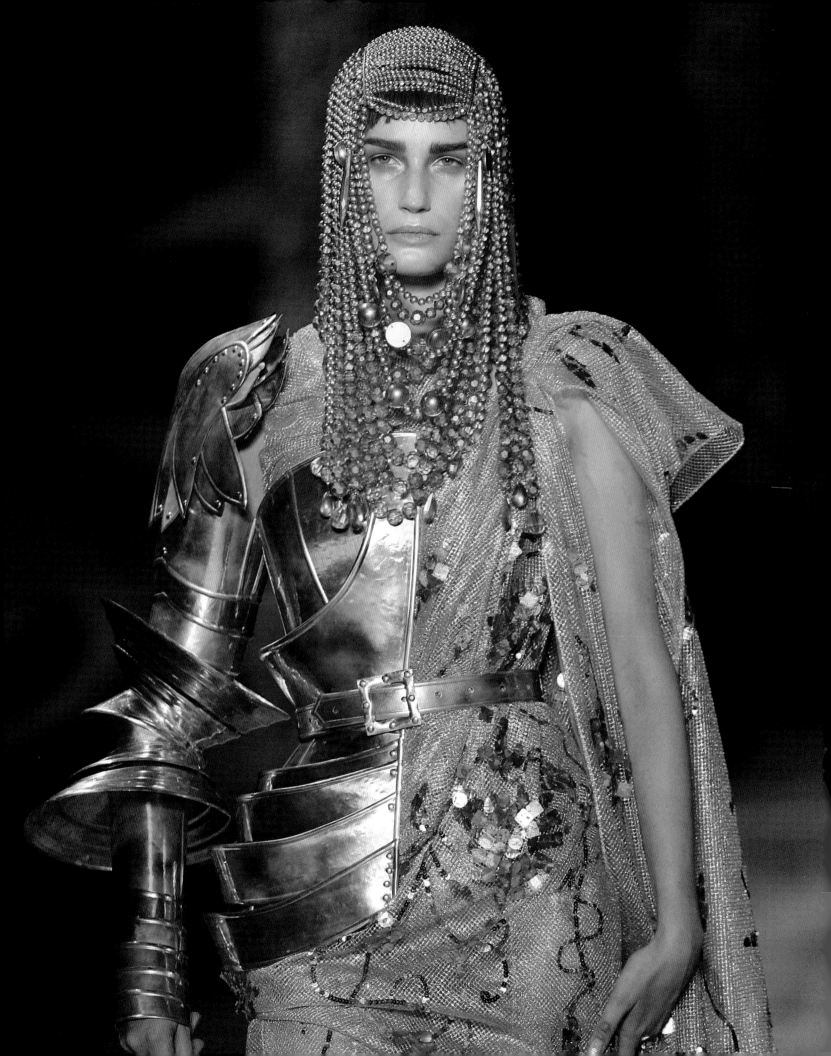

# The Chainmail Dress

Combining the bravura of a medieval knight complete with a flourish of feathers, and the experimental futurism of the 1960s, radical designer Paco Rabanne brought his experience of industrial design to his chain-link dress of 1969. Rejecting traditional couture techniques and textiles, the designer established the use of rigid materials held together by metallic rings or rivets with his first collection; this appeared in 1966 and was labelled with the provocative manifesto "Twelve Unwearable Dresses in Contemporary Materials". The collection established Rabanne's reputation as a revolutionary; he constructed his garments from plastic, aluminium and rhodoid – a cellulose acetate – with a pair of metal cutters, pliers and a blowtorch rather than a sewing machine and thread. One of the defining progenitors of 1960s modernism, alongside André Courrèges and Pierre Cardin, Rabanne epitomized the preoccupation of the era with technological advances and methods of assemblage.

Athough associated with the 1960s, the provenance of the chainmail dress derives from mail armour, commonly credited to the Celts and later adopted by the Romans. Constructed from a series of flexible riveted rings, chainmail continued to be worn throughout the Middle Ages, and was introduced in the early thirteenth century in response to changes in warfare and the use of the crossbow. The abbreviated tabard of Rabanne's dress is based on the hauberk, a thigh-length steel-resistant tunic of chainmail, and is constructed from a metallic knitted mesh, worn over a skirt of overlaid metal discs. The chainmail hood extends into a mail coif, or neck gorget, armour for the neck, below which three-dimensional metal discs join together to form a camail, or mail collar.

Modern techniques are capable of producing similar effects to chainmail without the drawbacks of the inflexibility and weight of the original. Manish Arora took over the helm at Paco Rabanne in 2011 and introduced a contemporary version of the rhodoid dresses of 1966, made with a digital body scan to ensure a close fit, creating an impression less of armour and more of reptile skin, with no single square of silvery painted python the same shape as the next. Equally observing of the heritage of the house, Lydia Maurer's debut show for Paco Rabanne introduced a finer, lighter textile mesh that combined fabric with metal for Spring/Summer 2013.

**RIGHT AND ABOVE RIGHT:** For his 1967 "Body Jewellery" collection, Spanish-born Francisco "Paco" Rabaneda Cuervo (1934–) applied his experience as a jewellery designer to create a futuristic, vest-shaped minidress, constructed from light-reflecting iridescent rhodoid discs, which were linked by metal rings.

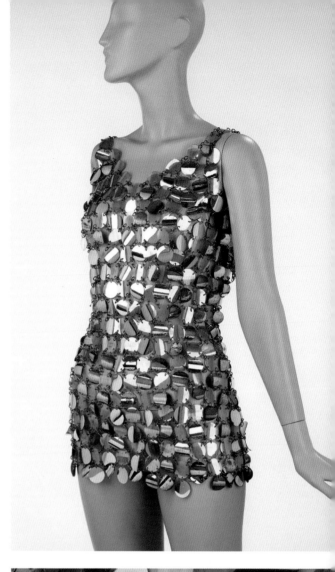

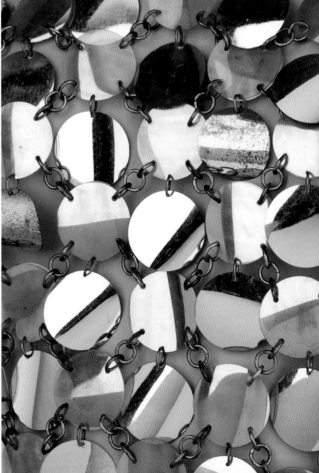

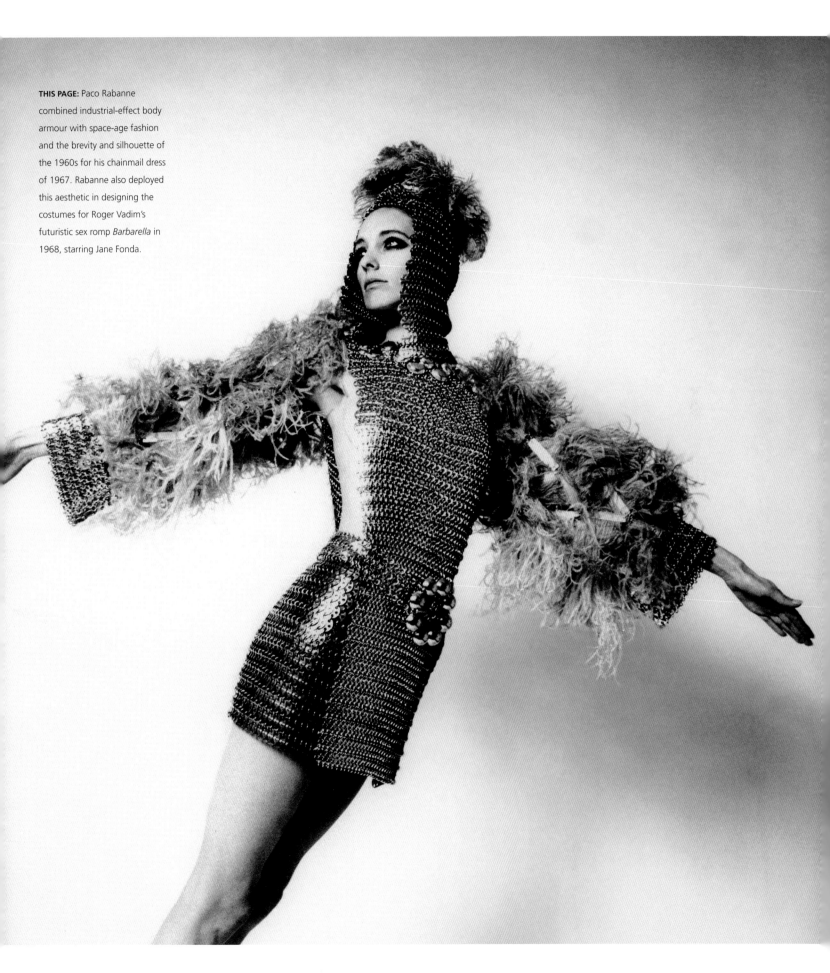

**THIS PAGE:** Paco Rabanne combined industrial-effect body armour with space-age fashion and the brevity and silhouette of the 1960s for his chainmail dress of 1967. Rabanne also deployed this aesthetic in designing the costumes for Roger Vadim's futuristic sex romp *Barbarella* in 1968, starring Jane Fonda.

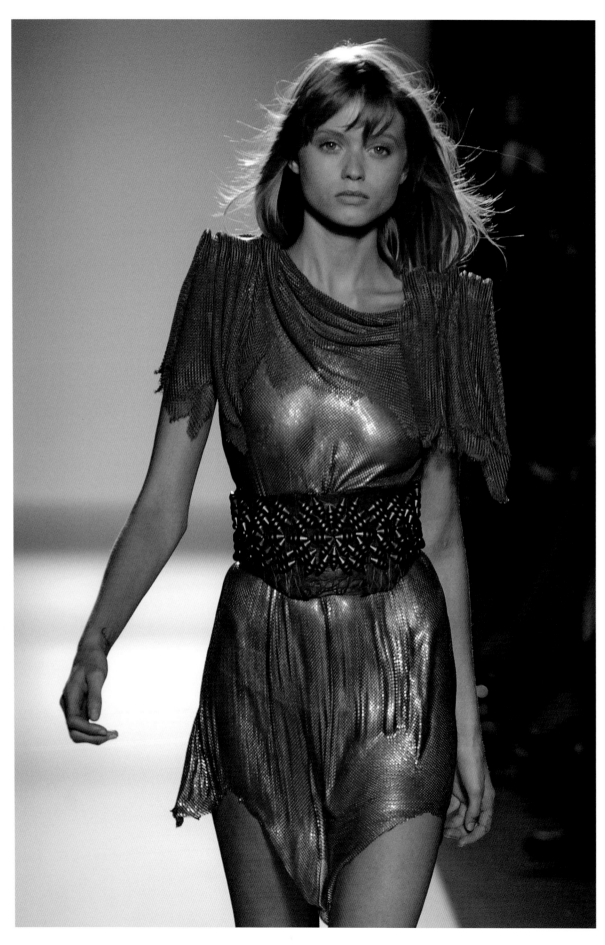

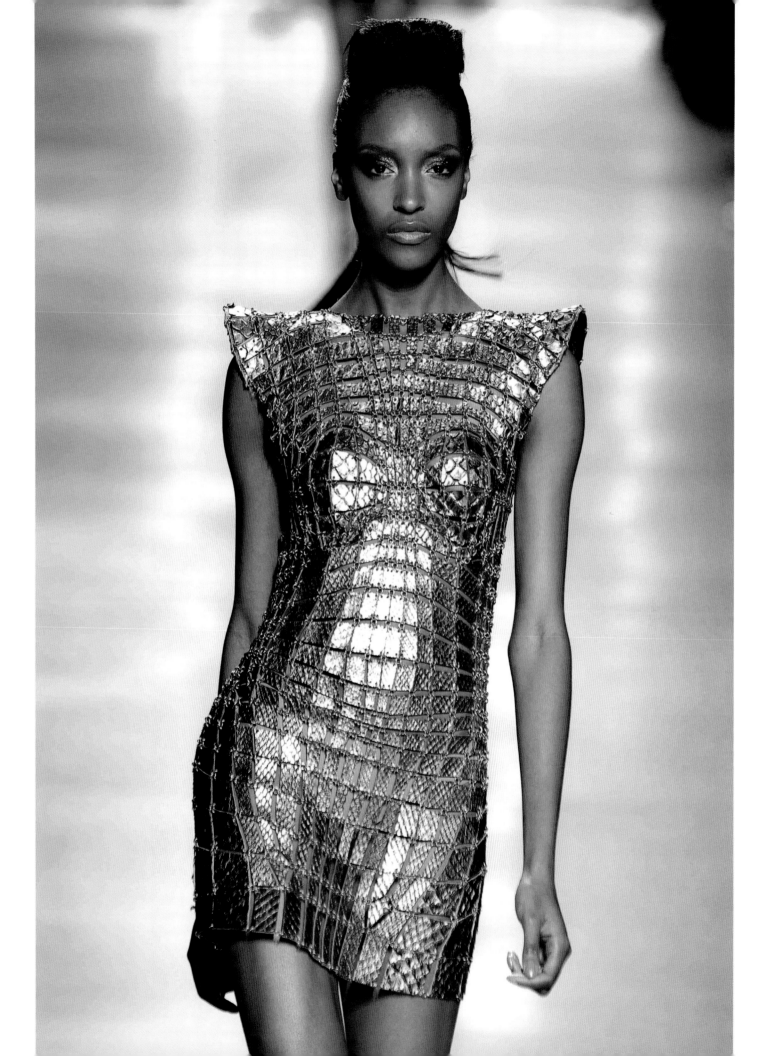

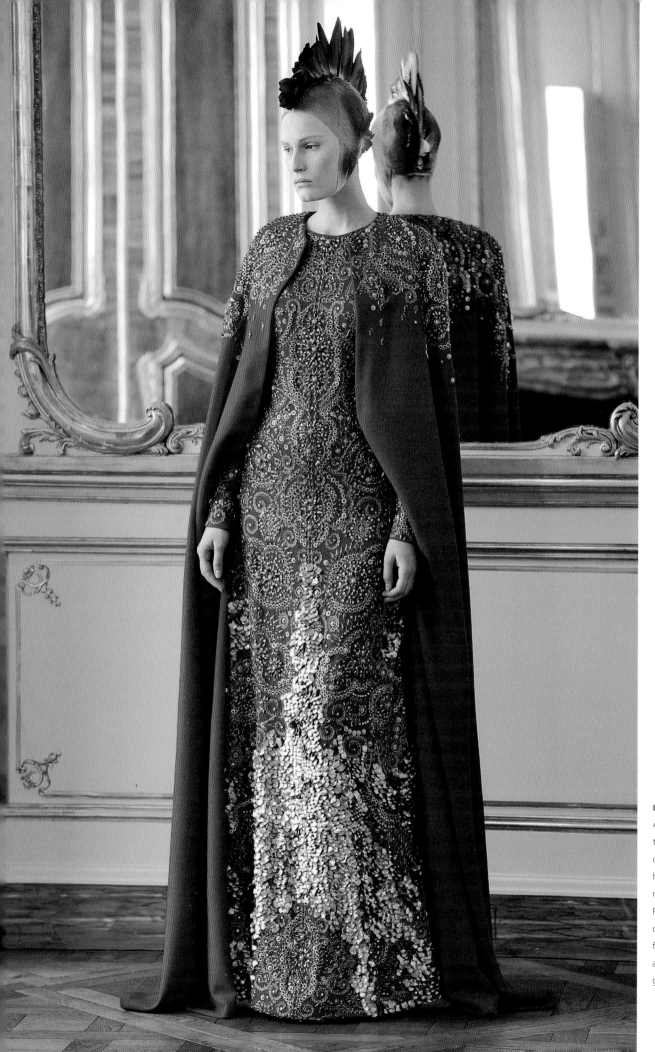

**LEFT:** In his final collection, Alexander McQueen (1969–2010) translated digital photography of Byzantine iconography into hand-loomed jacquards and rich gold-on-red embellishment. Promulgating his intensive craft-based ethos and exemplary form-fitting tailoring, he created an evening dress that combines glamour with simplicity.

# Byzantine Dress

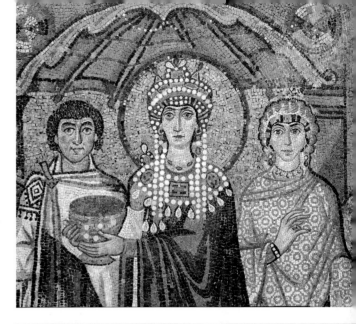

Throughout the Middle Ages, Constantinople (now Istanbul) was the largest and wealthiest city in the world. Founded in the seventh century BCE by the Greeks, who named it Byzantium, it was established as the second capital of the Roman Empire in AD 330 by Constantine the Great, who named it after himself. Following the fall of Rome in AD 476, Constantinople flourished, becoming the world's leading commercial centre, thanks to its location astride the Bosporus, the strait separating Europe and Asia. With the rise of the Empire, the commercial success of the city was closely linked to the manufacture and deployment of silks, and acted as a conduit for designs and weaving practices characterized by their brilliance of colour and use of gold threads. The patterns emanating from the Byzantine workshops were emblematic of power, incorporating winged horses, lions and other imagined and real animals, characteristically organized within a decorative roundel. These rich silks were solely for the use and disposal of the court, as were certain colours such as the expensive shellfish dye Tyrian purple, and both became especially associated with the splendour of the garments worn by Emperor Justinian I and his consort Theodora.

These loose-fitting robes were richly patterned and bejewelled, having evolved from the Roman aristocratic toga with the additional influence of Asiatic decorative textiles. Mosaics – a durable medium which allows the creation of images from the assemblage of small pieces of coloured glass or stone known as *tesserae* – became an essential element of both religious and secular art in the Byzantine Empire as the production of three-dimensional sculpture declined. As complex patterned objects of private devotion featuring sacred images representing the saints, Christ and the Virgin, these images are known as icons – from the Greek *eikones* – and became the inspiration for Italian designers Domenico Dolce and Stefano Gabbana in their Autumn/Winter 2013–14 collection.

One of the portable arts of the Byzantine Empire, the icon could also be of a more permanent character such as fresco and mosaic images decorating church interiors. The D&G design partnership looked to the Byzantine mosaics of the twelfth-century cathedral in the city of Monreale and used them to create elaborately gilded and embroidered dresses. Chanel's pre-Autumn 2011 collection was clearly inspired by the Empress Theodora, with draped toga-like dresses in rich purple with lavish gold embellishment. As premium global brands, with markets rooted in many cultures, both Chanel and Dolce & Gabbana knowingly make subtle allusion to the traditions of luxuriant drapery of the Near and Middle East, as well as of Asia.

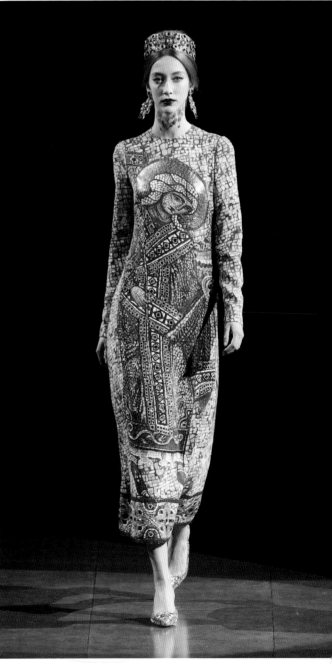

**ABOVE RIGHT:** The lavish and ostentatious dress worn by Empress Theodora, wife of Emperor Justinian I, was commensurate with her wealth and status. Strings of pearls, known as *praipendula*, or *kataseista*, are incorporated into her face-framing headdress.

**RIGHT:** Capturing religious iconography and referencing the Empress Theodora, Domenico Dolce (1958–) and Stefano Gabbana (1962–) hand-beaded evening dresses for A/W 2013–14 that are equal in embellishment to those worn at the height of the Byzantine Empire.

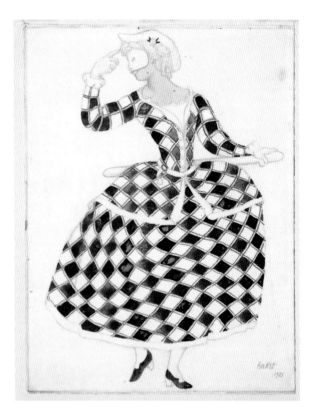

# L'Arlecchino – The Harlequin

Folkloric precursors of the motley Harlequin are found across Europe from as early as the twelfth century. In Italy, Alichino appears at the outset of the fourteenth century as a demonic character in Dante's *Divine Comedy*, forming an enduring template of knavish, infernal delinquency. Later reincarnating as Arlecchino in the Commedia dell'arte with a decidedly devil-may-care outlook, the model became identified by the vibrant graphic patterning of the liveried court fool. As a group of travelling players, the Commedia dell'arte was one of the first forms of professional theatre, evolving from improvisational street performances to delineated acts featuring stock characters. First seen in Rome in the sixteenth century, the Commedia were more usually associated with Venice and the carnival, although the group toured throughout Europe.

Aristocratic revellers came to adopt the theatrical dress of Commedia dell'arte for the purposes of rococo costume parties, exploiting inferences of decadence and urbanity. The timeless characters each represent an archetype identified by their costume, in turn elaborations of fashions of the Renaissance: Pantalone, the miserly Venetian merchant whose tight-fitting hose gave their name to the close-fitting trousers worn by men in the nineteenth century; Dottore Graziano, the pedant from Bologna; Petrolino (Pierrot), the sad clown and his face-framing floppy pie-crust frill attached to a baggy, smocked top and loose trousers; Colombina in servant attire; the swaggering Scaramuccia (Scaramouche) in his striped black and white costume; and Pulcinella, on which the puppet character Punch of the eponymous Punch and Judy shows is based.

Arlecchino – the Harlequin – the mischievous servant from Bergamo, is probably the best-known character, identified by his distinctive costume of diamond-patterned jacket and trousers in contrasting colours. These were initially brightly coloured patches that were later formalized into diamond shapes. The Commedia appeared as popular entertainment at the masquerades enjoyed in the late seventeenth and eighteenth centuries, captured on canvas by Jean-Antoine Watteau in a series of paintings featuring figures in aristocratic and theatrical dress in lush pastoral landscapes known as *une fête galante*. The artist's interpretation of *The Embarkation for Cythera*, painted in 1717, directly inspired Vivienne Westwood's 1989 "Voyage to Cythera" collection, one of the "Britain Must Go Pagan" series. The designer transposes the short tailored jacket and hose of the Harlequin into her favoured silhouette, the mini crini attached to a boned corset (*see also page 85*).

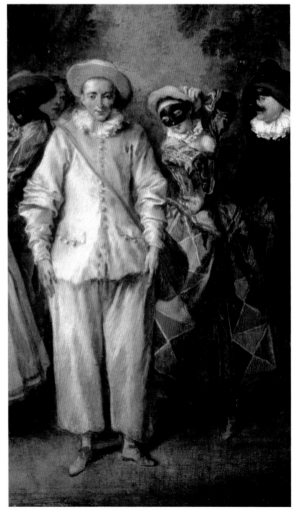

**ABOVE LEFT:** Dating from 1921, the pencil and watercolour sketch by Léon Bakst (1866–1924) – the costume and set designer for the revolutionary dance company Ballets Russes – is of a costume for Columbine in the ballet *Sleeping Princess*. It features the diamond pattern more usually associated with the Harlequin.

**LEFT:** The buffoonish Pierrot takes centre stage in the painting entitled *The Actors of the Commedia dell'Arte* by French artist Nicolas Lancret (1690–1743). Recognized by his front-buttoned, loose white blouse, wide white pantaloons and frilled collar, Pierrot was later also identified by a black skullcap.

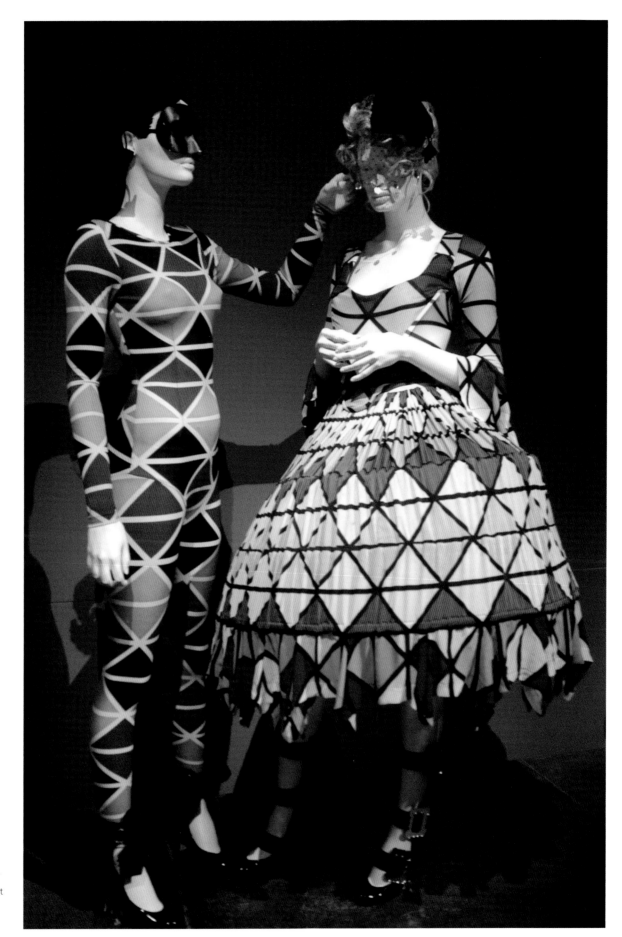

RIGHT: Providing a graphic interpretation of the harlequin pattern in printed jersey for both Columbine and her lover Arlecchino, London-based designer Vivienne Westwood (1941–) makes a direct reference to the painting by Nicolas Lancret in her "Voyage to Cythera" collection of 1989.

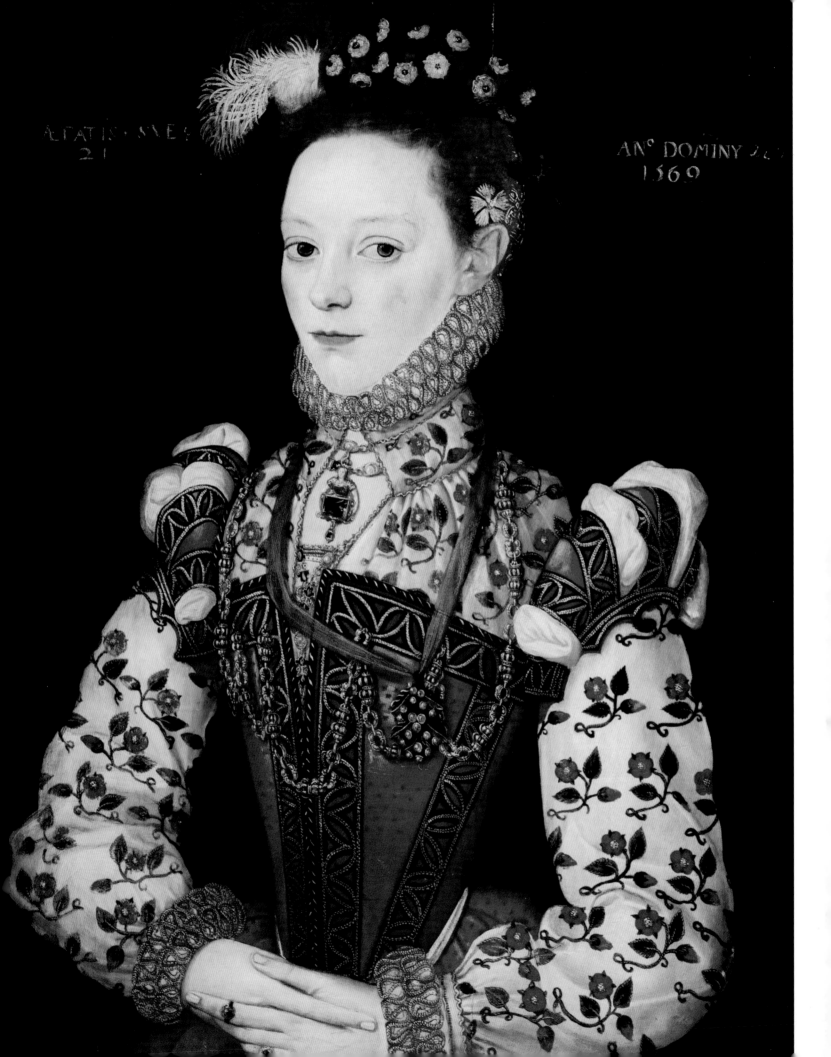

ÆTATIS SVE
21

AN° DOMINY
1569

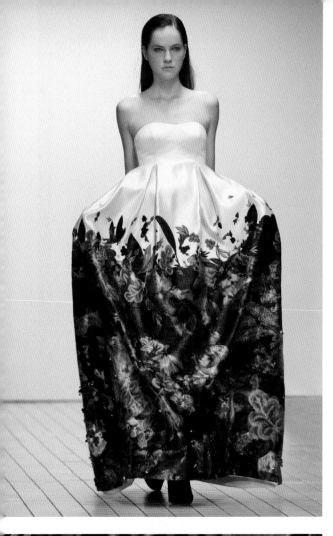

# Floral Print

Human beings have an innate desire to replicate the natural world. From flowers, animals and landscapes, the organic continues to animate and inspire designers in a universal desire to evoke a pastoral idyll. The sartorial passion for flower-strewn clothes reached its apotheosis in England's Elizabethan era, with a love of flowers espoused in the literature of Spenser, Sydney and Shakespeare. The English embroiderers of the heavily embellished robes strove for representation, copying their designs from printed herbals such as Collaert's *Florilegium*, published in 1590. In contrast, small-scale stylized floral prints became popular with the importing of patterned, block-printed "calicoes" derived from the Indian port Calicut, in the seventeenth century, providing a cheaper facsimile of brocades and silks. Once the London East India Company was granted their charter in 1600, Western merchants were able to commission their own versions of floral designs, bringing a European sensibility to the Indian craft. During the Rococo period, floral imagery, naturalistic in design, was combined with the cartouche, an asymmetrical or shell-shaped space incorporating serpentine garlands or ribbons.

Victorian Britain was the world's first urbanized society, and as a reaction to the mechanization of the Industrial Revolution and the stiff, stylized floral motifs intrinsic to Victorian design, William Morris reintroduced the notion of the artist/craftsman, producing block-printed floral designs that emphasized the natural growth of the plant. The potent relationship between floral imagery and high fashion was usually conveyed through the medium of print in the mid-twentieth century, particularly in the 1960s when "flower-power" came to symbolize the force of nature against the power of authority.

Twenty-first-century fashion designers such as Mary Katrantzou, Erdem and Jonathan Saunders deploy new technologies in print, laser cutting and embellishment to convey the allure of flowers. Raf Simons presented his first collection for the couture house of Dior for Spring/Summer 2013 with beaded, embroidered and appliquéd blooms in homage to his predecessor. Christian Dior inherited his mother's passion for flowers, confessing in his autobiography that it was his great pleasure to learn their names and descriptions by heart. It was not surprising that his first acclaimed fashion collection was named "Corolla", which means many-petalled.

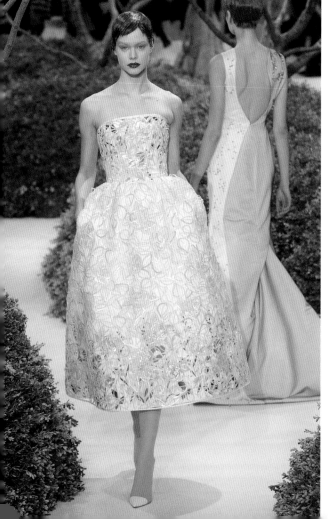

**OPPOSITE:** Painted c.1569, this portrait – possibly of Elin Ulfsdotter Snakenborg, Marchioness of Northampton, a Maid of Honour at the court of Queen Elizabeth I – wears a gown embroidered with the Tudor rose (sometimes called the Union rose), the traditional floral heraldic emblem of England.

**ABOVE LEFT:** Canadian-born designer Erdem Moralioglu (1977–) employs a bold colour palette of jewel-like tones, including citrus yellow, ruby and amethyst, with chlorophyll green, to create an herbaceous border of a digitally engineered floral print that borders a bell-like, box-pleated skirt.

**LEFT:** For his debut collection for Christian Dior, Belgian designer Raf Simons (1968–) produced a celebration of spring blooms, created from three-dimensional hand embroidery including beads, crystals, silk flowers and threads. The patterning is anchored at the hem and bodice with richer, intensified colour.

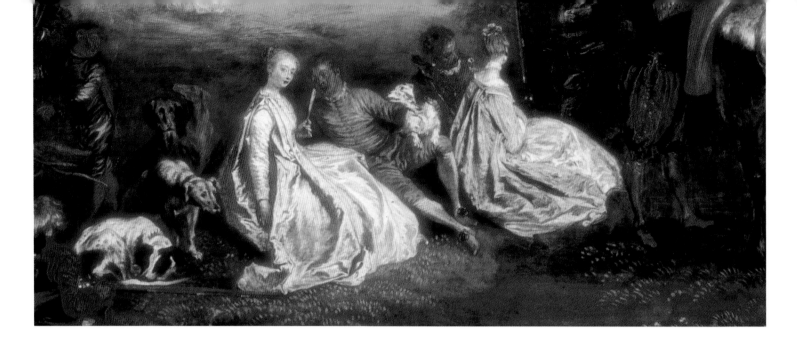

# The Sack

The revolutionary chemise or sack dress introduced by Parisian couturier Hubert de Givenchy in 1957 defined a new fashion ideal, one in which he controversially eschewed the prevailing hourglass silhouette for an innovative "waistless" line. The silhouette of the sack dress owes its origins to the sacque, or sack-back, gown also known as the *robe volante*, which first appeared around 1705 and was distinguished by a fall of unbroken stiffened pleats from the back of the neck. The robe provided a more informal female dress than the restrictive grand habit worn at the French court at the time of Louis XV and was representative of the more relaxed social mores and libertarianism of the period. Later, the gown also became known as the Watteau robe, after the painter Jean-Antoine Watteau (1660–1721), who depicted the garment on many of his sitters, including in the 1720 painting *The Halt During the Chase*. From *c.*1710 to 1760, the style of the *robe volante* was adopted by all social levels, although fabrics varied depending on class, with silk and satin for the aristocracy and more humble fabrics for the servant class. Although the *robe volante* was too informal for court dress, the pleated cape of the gown evolved into a train and became a feature of the *robe à la française*, where it was combined with a rounded pannier or "basket" petticoat to create a rectangular silhouette.

The sack dress attributed to Givenchy was initially perceived as avant-garde and was also associated with the desire of women for greater freedom of movement than that allowed by the corseted silhouette of the era. The look was deemed "ungainly" by a fashion press reluctant to endorse a garment that deliberately obscured the female form, but the dress was nevertheless copied extensively and was popular with the working woman, who enjoyed the ease of fit and freedom bestowed by its tubular shape. Hanging from a strong shoulder seam, the dress bypassed the waist and narrowed towards the hem, resulting in a modified barrel-shaped skirt. It marked the change in emphasis in fashion from the mature elegance of the 1950s to the youthful ingénue that was to follow. The sack dress was modified with a slight indentation to the waist and became a precursor to the sheath dress, which then evolved into the prevailing style of the 1960s, one suited to the pre-pubertal silhouette typified by models such as Twiggy.

**ABOVE:** Recording the fashions of the day in his painting *A Halt During the Chase*, Jean-Antoine Watteau (1684–1721) is best known for his invention of a new genre, the *fête galante*, in which elegant people are depicted in conversation or music-making in a secluded parkland setting.

**OPPOSITE:** Distinguished by its tubular line and "waistless" silhouette, the sack-look dress in fluid jersey received male opprobrium for its deliberate denial of female sexual attractiveness in place of the more conventional appeal of the tightwaisted dress and the hourglass figure. This is a 1957 copy of the Givenchy Sack dress.

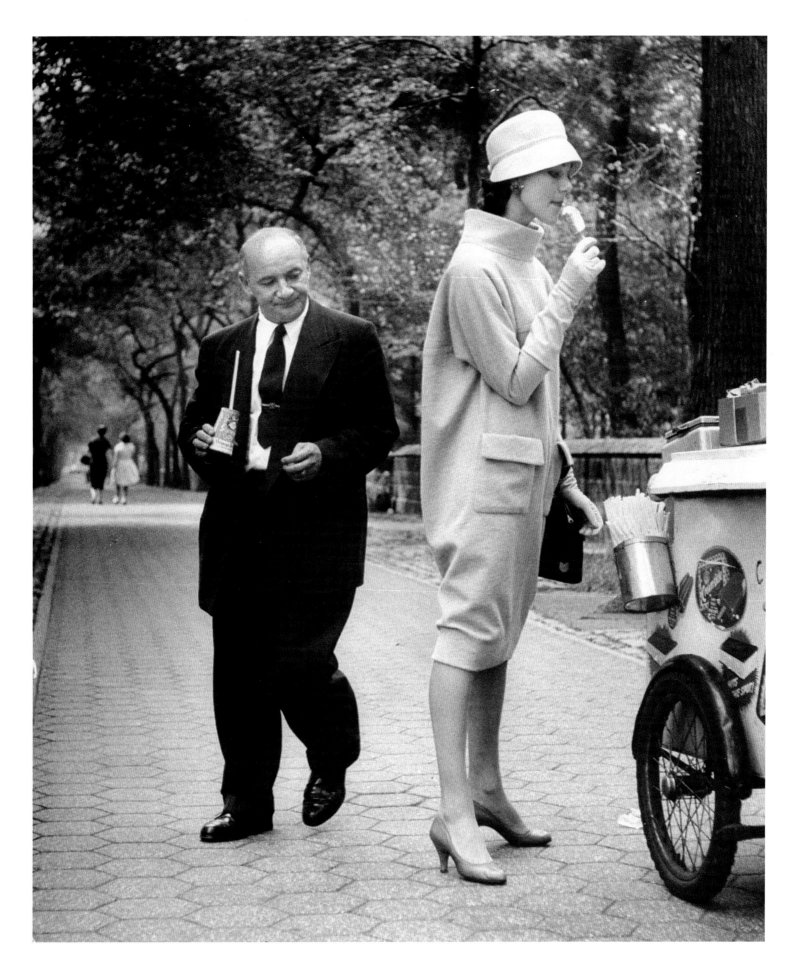

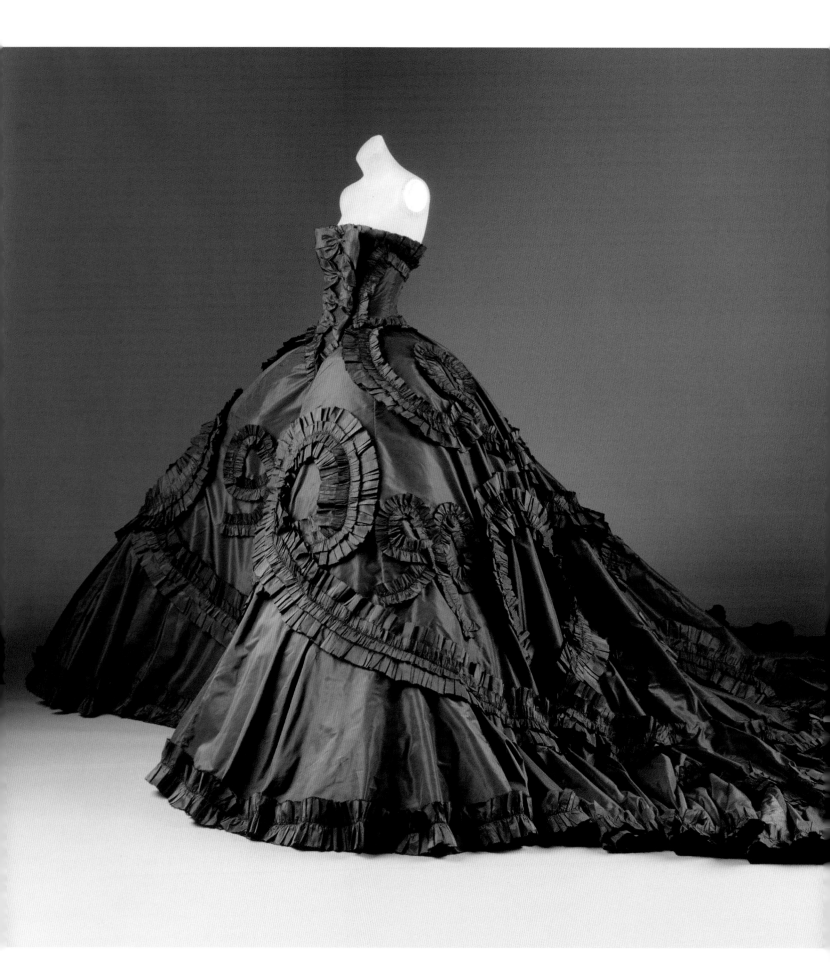

# The Train

The attachment or incorporation of a train into a garment identifies it immediately as one worn by an elite class for whom mobility is not an issue. Dresses with trains are usually attached to garments where the bodice and shoulders are structured with minimal detail – any exaggeration of the shoulders tends to mean a shorter hemline. First seen in the medieval clothing influenced by the court of France, with the development and subsequently the availability of textiles, the train was evidence of wealth, rank and title. As gowns gradually lengthened in the mid-fifteenth century, the extra fabric was caught up in a belt and left to fall in complex folds of fabric, often lined in fur. Trains generally appeared as an extension of an existing style. Towards the end of the seventeenth century, the train on the mantua – a full-length coat-like garment worn over a stiffened bodice and skirt – became much longer, with the sides intricately folded and pinned up at the back to reveal elaborate linings.

In the eighteenth century, the double pleats falling from the shoulders of the French *saque* (sack-back gown, *see page* 30) were extended into stiffened folds, affording maximum exposure for luxurious textiles. As skirts grew in circumference from 1840, the distinctive bustled silhouette created by Charles Frederick Worth in the nineteenth century emerged as a way of managing the copious amounts of material used in the crinoline. The drapery of the bustle was fashioned into a splayed "fishtail" train for both day- and eveningwear, with a ribbon device finishing the end of the train that could be attached to the wrist to facilitate walking. Later in the century, the couturier simply added length from the back waist to create a sweeping semi-circular train.

The romantic revivalism of the 1950s and the return to glamour reintroduced the train to eveningwear, exemplified by couturiers such as Charles James, Christian Dior and Jacques Fath, where the train was more usually structured from folds of duchesse satin or created from an asymmetrical side drape. Red-carpet dressing has made the train an effective tool of Hollywood glamour, usually fashioned into a boned, strapless bodice or one-shouldered gown. The train reoccurs in the historicism of John Galliano, who frequently introduced elements of eighteenth- and nineteenth-century dress into his collections.

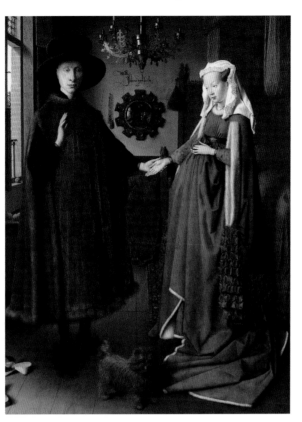

**ABOVE:** The floor-sweeping train of the woman's *houppelande* – an all-purpose gown worn by both men and women – in the painting *Giovanni Arnolfini and His Bride* (1360) by Jan Van Eyck is evidence of the wealth of the prosperous mercantile couple.

**LEFT:** The Maria-Luisa (dite Coré) gown designed by John Galliano, dating from 1998, combines the stomacher of the *robe à la française* with the crinolined excess of the mid-nineteenth century, featuring a voluminous skirt lavishly garlanded in overscale rosette ribbons.

# Equestrian Dress

Equestrian-inspired fashion has a universal appeal. In addition to immaculate tailoring and heritage fabrics, the accoutrements of saddlery – finely honed leather, strappings, harnesses, belts and buckles – have their own subversive attraction. The riding habit for women was first introduced in France in the seventeenth century with the *devantière* – a skirt split up the back to enable astride riding – but by the early eighteenth century, riding habits were made for riding side saddle, as it being deemed unseemly for women to sit astride. These were tailored in a masculine style throughout the seventeenth and eighteenth centuries and into the early nineteenth century.

During the fashionable Regency period, the riding habit was composed of a coat-dress, or redingote, which featured military detailing such as piping, braid, epaulettes and frogging, in imitation of hussar and other regimental uniforms, but as the eighteenth century progressed, the English hunting country gentleman became a major inspiration, and habits became plainer in cut and more functional. The skirt of the habit featured a train that ensured the legs were completely covered when riding side saddle, and from 1850 until the beginning of the twentieth century, the riding skirt hung on the left side to the length of the spur. On the right side it was much longer and when the rider dismounted the skirt was buttoned high on the waistline to even up the length. There was usually a loop or tie of some kind inside the skirt to hold up the long train while walking.

In the early twentieth century, it became socially acceptable for women to ride astride while wearing split skirts, and eventually breeches, and the riding habit generally was no longer worn. However, the juxtaposition of the severely tailored bodice, corseted waist and draped skirt has featured in the collections of contemporary designers including John Galliano at Christian Dior. French luxury house Hermès diversified from its equestrian roots – Thierry Hermès first opened a workshop in Paris supplying horse harnesses for calèches and carriages in 1837 – with a couture collection in 1929, and in 2008 avant-garde designer Jean Paul Gaultier became creative director of the company. Throughout his tenureship, the designer engaged with Hermès meticulous craftsmanship and long-held specialist skills in the use of leather, combining the house's horsey heritage with a fetishistic edge that incorporated body harnesses, jodhpur shorts, and whips and waist cinchers, all with more than a hint of bondage.

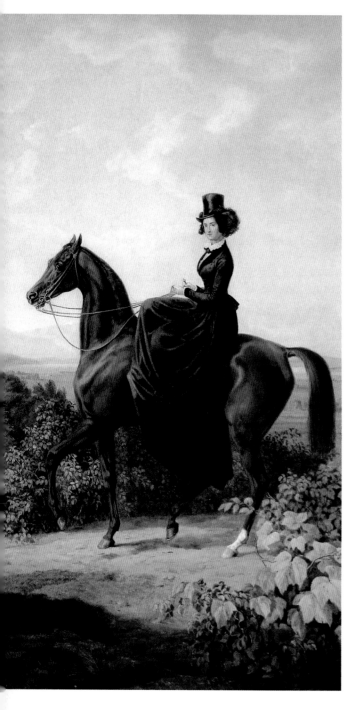

**ABOVE:** A portrait of the renowned Bavarian beauty Caroline von Waldbott-Bassenheim, painted by the equestrian artist Albrecht Adam (1786–1862) in 1850, shows the horsewoman wearing a facsimile of male hunting attire, with a tailored bodice with lapels, white stock and a top hat.

**OPPOSITE:** Jean Paul Gaultier harnesses the distinctive saddle stitch used in saddlery by heritage leather company Hermès – a process whereby two needles work two waxed threads in tensile opposition – for his black leather riding habit for A/W 2010–11.

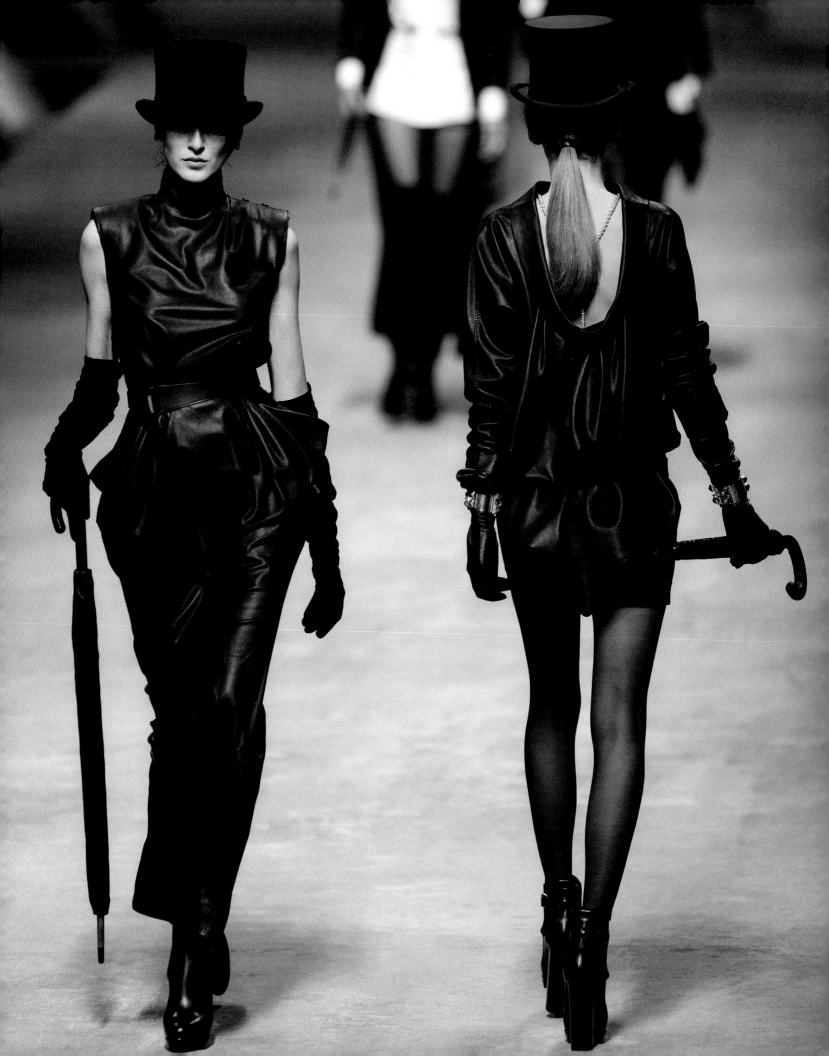

# Toile de Jouy Print

Denoting a single-colour image of a pastoral scene generally presented on a white background, the printed textile toile de Jouy – the word *toile* is French for cloth, and *Jouy* comes from the name of the town of its manufacture – perfectly complemented the neo-classical vogue of Napoleonic France for garments constructed from light cotton muslin. The cloth was woven in India, and the printed fabric was then imported into France via England, as the Indian fabric was banned by the French government in 1686 for fear of the financial impact the imported cloth would have on the French manufacture of silk, wool and cloth. The ban was finally lifted in 1759, and French factories sprang up to satisfy the demand for printed cotton, one of which was the Oberkampf factory founded by Bavarian engraver and colourist Christophe-Philippe Oberkampf in Jouy-en-Josas, near Versailles, France, in 1760.

During the first ten years, the design was printed using the wood block method, followed by etched copperplates from 1770 onwards. The technique had been used abroad in England and Ireland for a number of years but Oberkampf was the first cotton manufacturer to bring copperplate printing technology into France. Engraved copperplates resulted in finer lines than those produced by the wood block printing method, introducing the effects of light and shade into the image and also enabling the execution of a larger repeating pattern. This technique marked the beginning of monochrome printed scenes of rural landscapes, which depicted characters seen through the eyes of French aristocracy in the eighteenth century, for which the fabric is known. In 1797, the copper roller was introduced into the printing process, speeding up manufacture, and Oberkampf commissioned the foremost artists of the day to design these pastoral scenes with human figures, appointing the well-known painter Jean-Baptiste Huet as head designer in 1783, the same year that the Oberkampf factory was granted the title "Manufacture Royale" by Louis XVI. In 1806, the factory reached its peak but, paradoxically, the modernization of printing techniques directly contributed to the demise of toile de Jouy, and the factory was closed in 1843.

Contemporary versions of toile de Jouy fabrics are generally confined to interiors, and Vivienne Westwood is one of the few designers to incorporate the monochrome pattern in fashion, as seen in her Spring/Summer collection of 1995, which featured toile de Jouy fashioned into her signature crinoline silhouette.

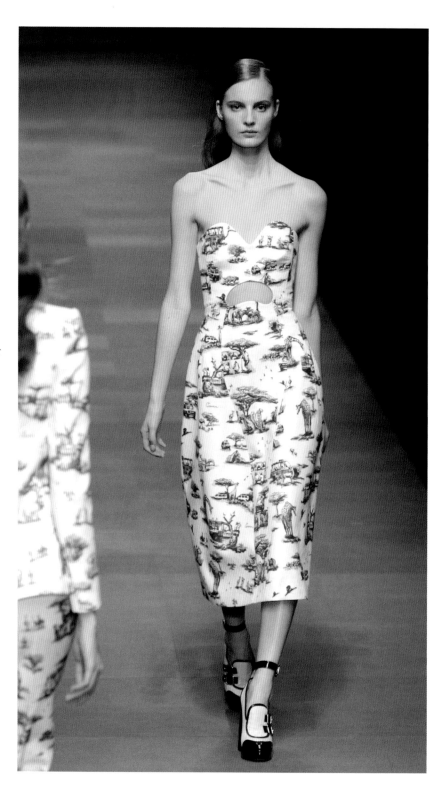

**ABOVE:** Rather than the usual European pastoral images, scenes of an animal safari, including giraffes and tigers, feature in the monochrome toile de Jouy used by Guillaume Henry, creative director of the 70-year-old Parisian house Carven, for S/S 2013.

**OPPOSITE:** From her "Erotic Zones" collection for S/S 1995, Vivienne Westwood employed a traditional pink-on-white toile de Jouy for the upthrust corseted bosom and the draped and padded pannier skirt, inspired by pre-Revolutionary France.

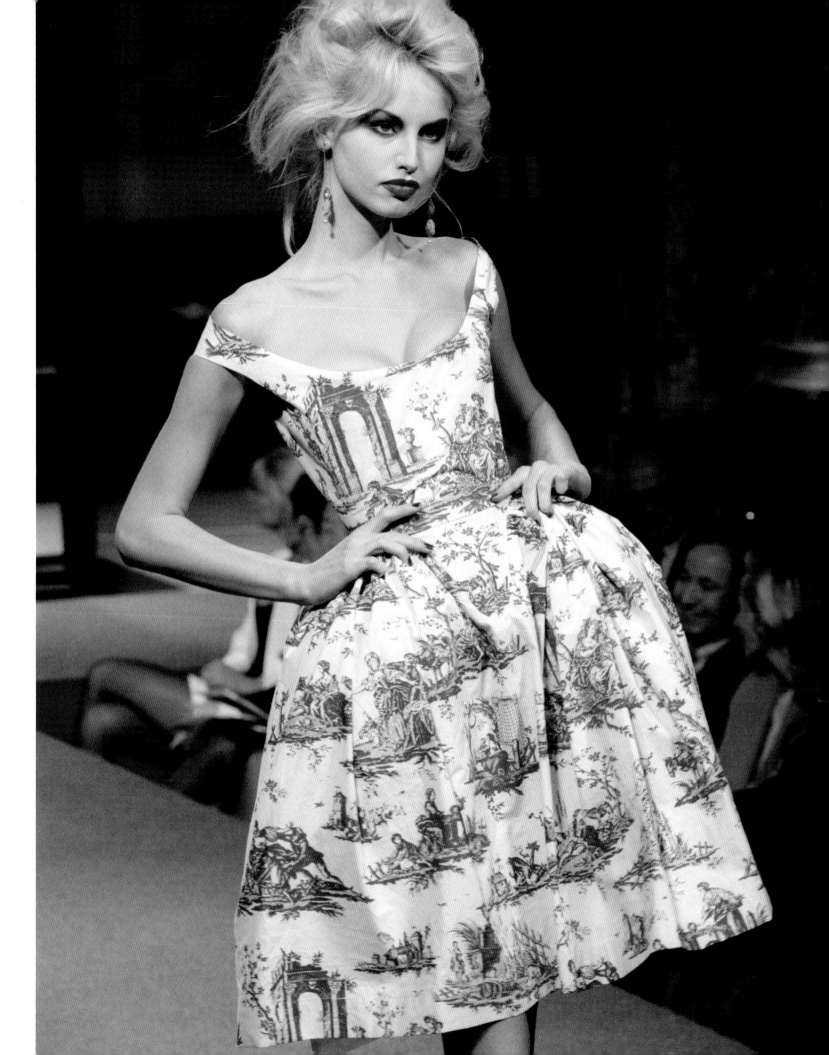

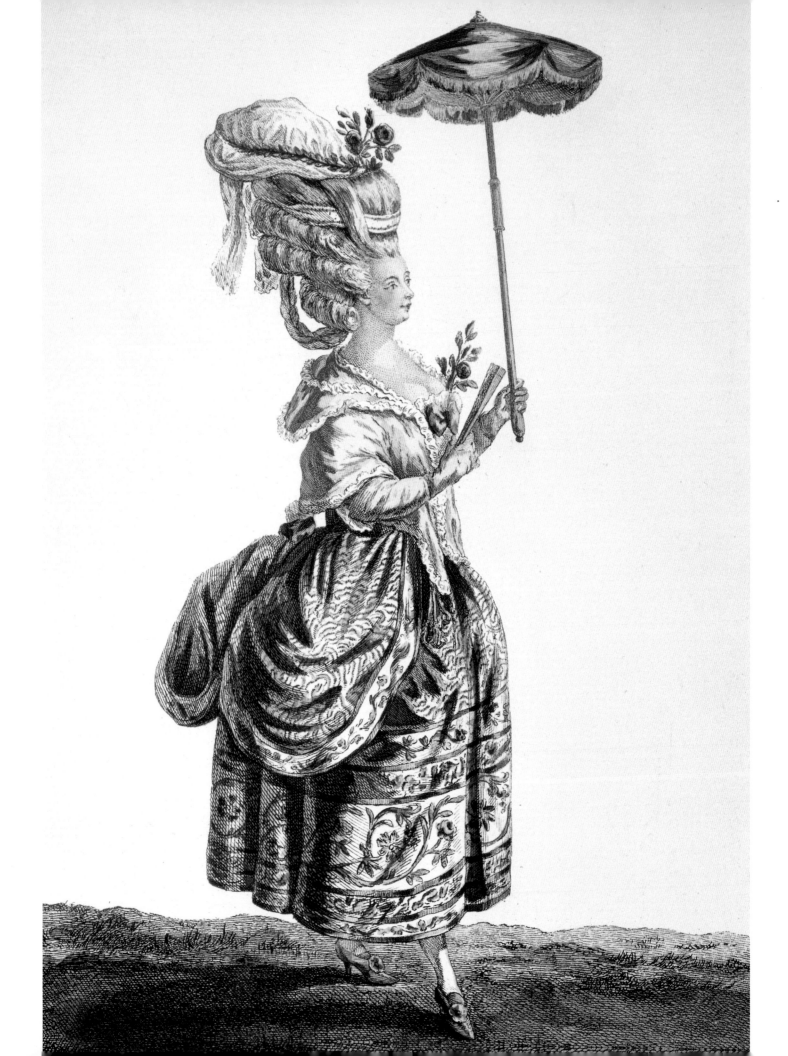

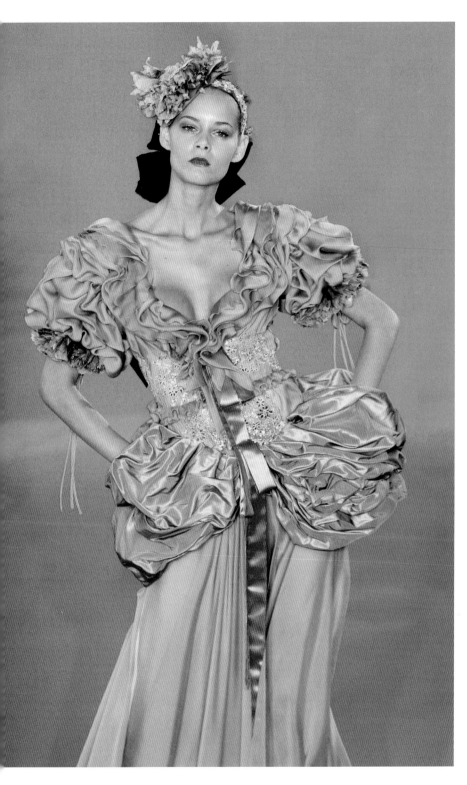

# The Polonaise

The mid-eighteenth-century Rococo period, an era of flamboyant excess before the fashions of the *ancien régime* were swept away by the French Revolution, included considerable variation in fashionable attire. The word Rococo, a derivation of the French words *rocailles* (loose stones) and *coquilles* (shells), referred to the shell and serpentine pattern that characterized the aesthetic, and France, with its opulent court at Versailles, dictated an emphasis on surface decoration, with an importance placed on trimmings such as ruffles, ribbons, shawls and towering headdresses. Court dress included the panniered *robe à la française*, with the *robe à l'anglaise* (*see also page* 40) worn on less formal occasions. From 1776, the fullness of the overskirt at the back waist of the open-fronted *robe à l'anglaise* was looped and bustled onto the hips in three sections, with the middle section longer than the two side sections. These were held by exterior silk cords and buttons or tassels, creating the *robe à la polonaise*. The style was thought to allude to the partition of Poland between three neighbouring countries – Austria, Prussia and Russia – in 1772, but it was more likely to have evolved from tucking the overskirt into pocket openings, which were worn beneath the gown and tied with ribbon around the waist – *retroussé dans les poches* – to facilitate walking.

During the nineteenth century, the polonaise style was revived with the popularity of the "Dolly Varden" dress, a character in the widely read 1839 novel by Charles Dickens, *Barnaby Rudge*, set in the eighteenth century. Favoured by English gentlewomen, it was a version of the Princess line, cut without a waist seam and typically made from patterned chintz or flowered cretonne worn over a plain, brightly coloured skirt of walking length. A straw hat, perched forward on the high coiffure, emphasized the informality of the gown.

Extravagant occasion-wear was worn by the fashionable elite in the 1980s, an era equal in flamboyance to pre-Revolutionary France. Christian Lacroix established a new couture house in 1987 following his success with *le pouf* (*see page* 191), when he headed the house of Patou. Taking inspiration from the eighteenth and early nineteenth centuries, Lacroix fashioned duchesse satin, lace, figured brocades and embellished fabrics over broad supported skirts. These were combined with luxurious hand-worked effects to form swagged overskirts *à la polonaise*.

**OPPOSITE:** Featured in this illustration from 1779, the polonaise of blue and white vermicelée-patterned linen is trimmed with bands of multicoloured painted flowers. The skirt appears specially cut to form the three rounded "petals".

**ABOVE:** From a collection entitled "An Angel Passing By", French couturier Christian Lacroix (1951–) featured a version of the polonaise skirt, created by the puffed-up volume of a silk taffeta overskirt attached to a bodice inspired by the eighteenth century.

# Anglomania

A surge of interest in all things English gripped Europe during the mid- to late eighteenth century. Initially a political and intellectual phenomenon, channelled through the works of Voltaire and his writing on English culture, Anglomania found its full expression when the privileges of the French nobility had been swept away by the French Revolution. Anglomania represented an idealized version of an Arcadian England, captured by English landscape and portrait painter Thomas Gainsborough and Swiss-born Angela Kauffmann, who both portrayed the English aristocracy posed within the settings of their country estates. The decreasing emphasis on French court style gave way to the adoption of English "country" clothes by the fashionable elite, with the emphasis placed on simplicity and practicality, evidenced by the adoption of the *robe à l'anglaise* and the *robe chemise* or *bastite*.

The *robe à l'anglaise* eschewed panniers and boning in favour of a less structured, although still corseted, silhouette, which provided greater ease of movement. The distinctive feature of the gown was the closely fitted back, the result of pleats stitched down before the fullness was released into the skirt in tiny pleats from a V-shaped waist, from where it fell into a small train. The single-piece robe was open in front to reveal a matching or contrasting petticoat beneath, and featured narrow elbow-length sleeves, which were finished with separate frills called *engageantes*. The fullness of the hips was obtained with the aid of padding worn beneath the petticoats. A silk gauze fichu – a three-cornered cape worn over the shoulders and crossed on the breast – was worn to hide the low décolleté of the gown. Utopian longings and a yearning for the imagined pursuits and occupations of the countryside were evident in the accompanying accoutrements – wide-brimmed straw hats, a plethora of artificial flowers worn as trimmings and artlessly tied ribbon sashes. Printed and woven floral designs reflected this pastoral fantasy.

Vivienne Westwood's "Anglomania" collection of Autumn/Winter 1993–94 referenced the French passion for English tailoring in the 1780s, which the designer combined with her interpretations of an eclectic mix of eighteenth-century aristocratic dress styles, from the sack-back dresses depicted in Jean-Antoine Watteau's paintings of the 1720s to François Boucher's shepherdesses' corsets, bringing the dress codes of the Enlightenment to a contemporary audience. Westwood also created a diffusion line, "Anglomania", a less expensive collection that reinterprets various pieces from her earlier collections.

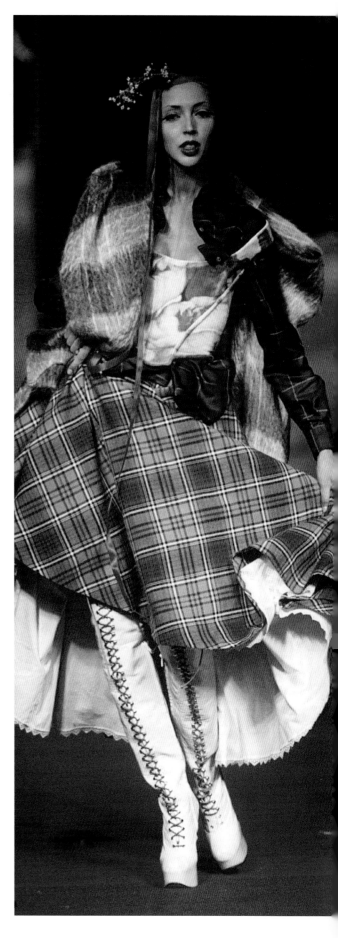

**RIGHT:** Vivienne Westwood (1941–) plunders the past and reinterprets history, engaging with the heritage and traditions of British tailoring and textiles, including Scottish tartan, as in this offering from the A/W 1993–94 "Anglomania" collection.

**OPPOSITE:** The *robe à l'anglaise*, described in the illustration from *Galerie des Modes et Costumes Français* in 1778, displays the closely fitting back and open-fronted robe with contrasting petticoat beneath, typical of the all pervading, more informal "English style" of the era.

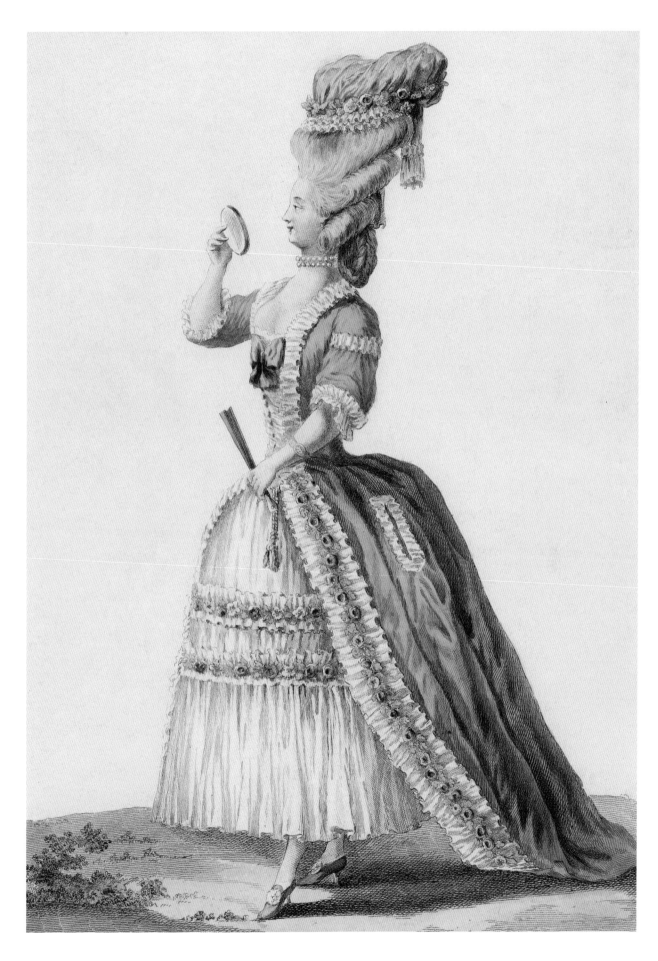

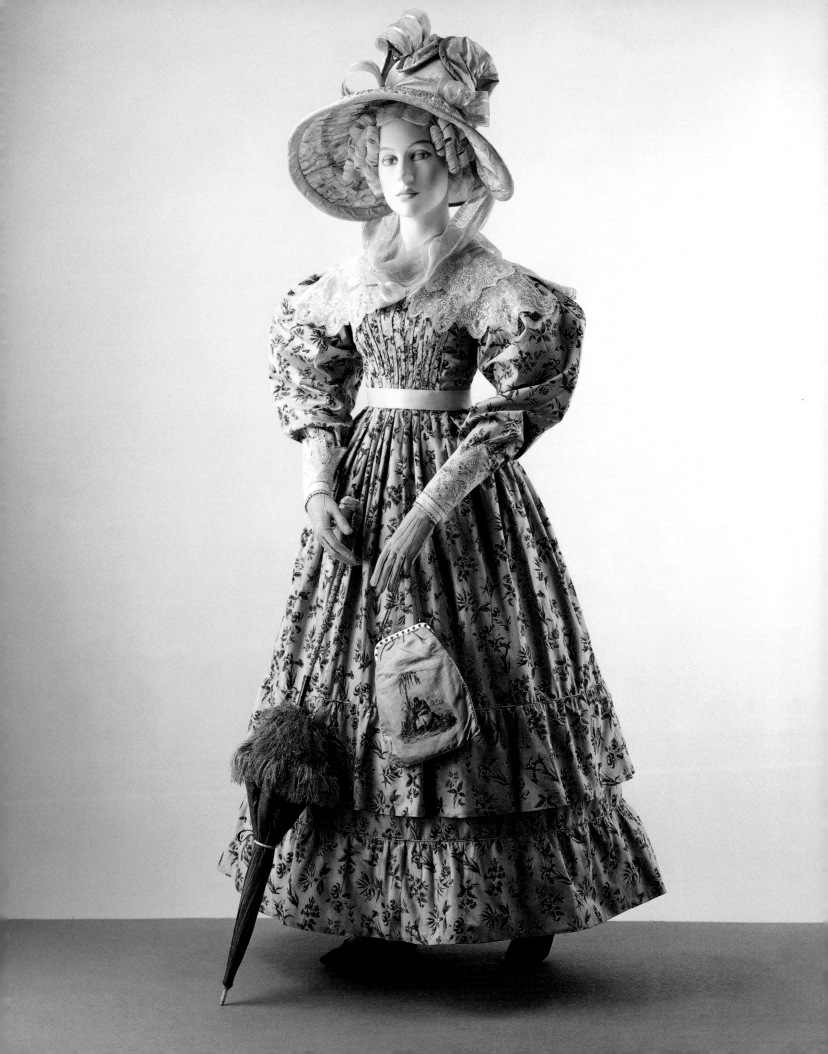

# Romantic Dress

The Romantic era of 1780–1850 originated in Europe and was inspired in part as a reaction against the scientific rationalization of nature, the encroachment of the Industrial Revolution – which began in the 1760s – and the collapse of the *ancien régime* in France. The vertical high-waisted Empire-style dress of the Directoire period was discarded in favour of fashion that offered an idealized view of country life, one that incorporated floral-sprigged cottons, rural accoutrements such as straw bonnets and parasols, and in 1825, a return to the natural waistline. Emphasizing the smallness of the waist were sleeves of an extraordinary width, as the short puff sleeves of the 1820s developed into full-blown balloon shapes – known as *gigot d'agneau* in French, due to their resemblance in shape to a leg of mutton – supported by a small whalebone pannier tied to the shoulder. These balanced the width of the A-line skirt at the hem, which was supplemented with gored panels over layers of petticoats, finishing at just above the ankle.

By the 1830s many advances had been made in printing techniques, which led to a fashion for simple printed cotton fabrics featuring small-scale floral designs. These often required no trimmings other than a silk-satin ribbon to mark the waist, a lace collar – which further widened the silhouette at the shoulder – or a double frill at the hem. Necklines varied from wide and shallow to a V-shape, but were invariably worn off the shoulder. Sleeves were short for eveningwear, still with the emphasis on the width, and long for day.

A similar desire for escapism, this time from the realities of the Great Depression in the US and the likelihood of war, prompted a revival of romantic fashion in the 1930s, which included the fashion phenomenon of the dress worn by Joan Crawford in the title role of Clarence Brown's feature film *Letty Lynton* (1932). The abundantly frilled long, white evening dress in *mousseline de soi* – a fine silk fabric – with extravagantly frilled sleeves and full skirt was designed by Hollywood costumier Adrian, and prompted numerous copies known as "butterfly-sleeve" dresses. Post-war eveningwear by Mainbocher, an exponent of discreet luxury, included a pink silk faille and black patterned silk satin evening ensemble replicating the silhouette of the 1820s, with large puffed gigot sleeves and sloping shoulders.

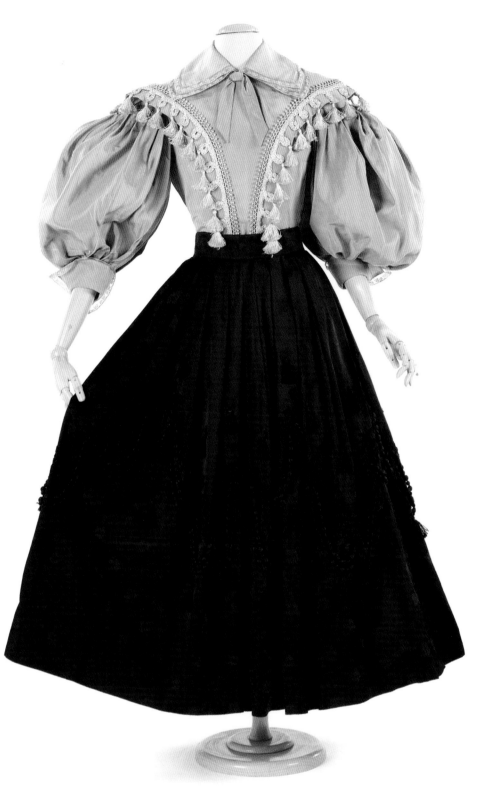

**OPPOSITE:** Following the Empire line of the classic chemise, a wide waistband helped to lower the waist, changing proportions to give a wider, shorter skirt and emphasizing the gigot sleeves. This 1828 floral-sprigged cotton dress represented a pastoral simplicity.

**ABOVE:** Inspired by the Biedermeier period of the 1830s – a simplified interpretation of the influential French Empire style of Napoleon I – this 1949 gown by Mainbocher (1890–1976) features a contemporary version of the gigot sleeve.

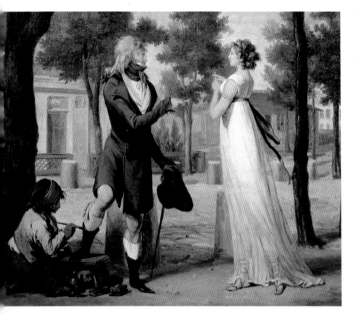

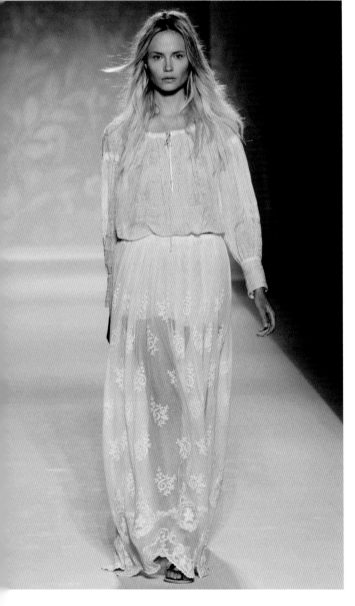

# The Transparent Dress

Attitudes to near-nudity in dress have varied over the centuries, veering between collective outrage and a relaxation of moral vigilance, depending on the social mores of the era. In ancient Egypt, the pleated linen of the *kalasiris* – a sheath-like dress – was so fine that it was semi-transparent, and the simple *chiton* worn by the Hellenic Greeks and the *stola* worn by Roman women were both constructed from fine textiles that revealed the body. Classicism became the principle style of fashion at the end of the eighteenth and the beginning of the nineteenth centuries, when women adopted the white, undecorated tubular high-waisted chemise dress constructed from semi-transparent fabrics such as imported calicos and muslins, making nudity *à la grecque* publicly acceptable. Nudity becomes an expression of modernity rather than overt sensuality when fashion is preoccupied with youthful attributes, as in the 1960s when see-through dresses featuring lace, crochet and clear plastic and transparent fabrics such as organza and tulle appeared on the catwalk of couturiers such as Yves Saint Laurent and Dior, as well as on the rails of avant-garde boutiques. Nudity and near-nudity may also be perceived as a political act, used by the hippies as a potent symbol of personal freedom and as an anti-war protest in the "Summer of Love" of 1968, when transparent maxidresses and cheesecloth smocks were worn over a braless body.

Since Robert Herrick wrote his ode in 1648 to *déshabillé* dress, "*A Sweet disorder in the dress, Kindles in clothes a wantonness*", it is universally accepted that a partially clothed body is more seductive than nakedness, and that transparency and dishevelment are potent symbols of arousal. Lace, chiffon, silk and satin conceal and reveal the contours of the body in boudoir couture, such as the bias-cut slip dresses of John Galliano. Among the designer's Autumn/Winter 2009–10 collection of Russian-inspired folk costume and the pannier-hipped, full-skirted coats and balloon-sleeved peasant blouses, Galliano introduced a sequence of bias-cut dresses in sheerest spangled tulle worn over the briefest bejewelled underwear. In the symbiosis between fashion and celebrity, transparency is also the currency of the celebrity seeker when unveiling is less to do with sexual display and more to do with commerce. One of the most famous transparent garments of the twenty-first century is the see-through dress worn by Kate Middleton, now Duchess of Cambridge, to a charity fashion show at the University of St Andrews in 2002.

**ABOVE LEFT:** In Louis-Léopold Boilly's *Incroyable et Merveilleuse* (1797), an exaggerated dandy, or *incroyable*, of the French Directoire is accompanied by a *merveilleuse* dressed *à l'Athénienne* in a high-waisted, semi-transparent muslin gown that looks back to the dress of the ancient Greeks and Romans (hence the sandals), celebrating the natural, untrammelled beauty of the body.

**LEFT:** Alberta Ferretti's feminine signature is expressed in this embroidered white-on-white transparent dress from S/S 2011. It is partly inspired by the *chemise à la reine*, the transparent muslin gown made fashionable by Marie Antoinette in 1783.

**OPPOSITE:** A 1968 Christian Dior transparent white lace shirt-dress worn by model Veruschka, photographed in Santo Domingo. Nudity and semi-transparency in dress at this time were natural counterparts of the uninhibited free-love decade.

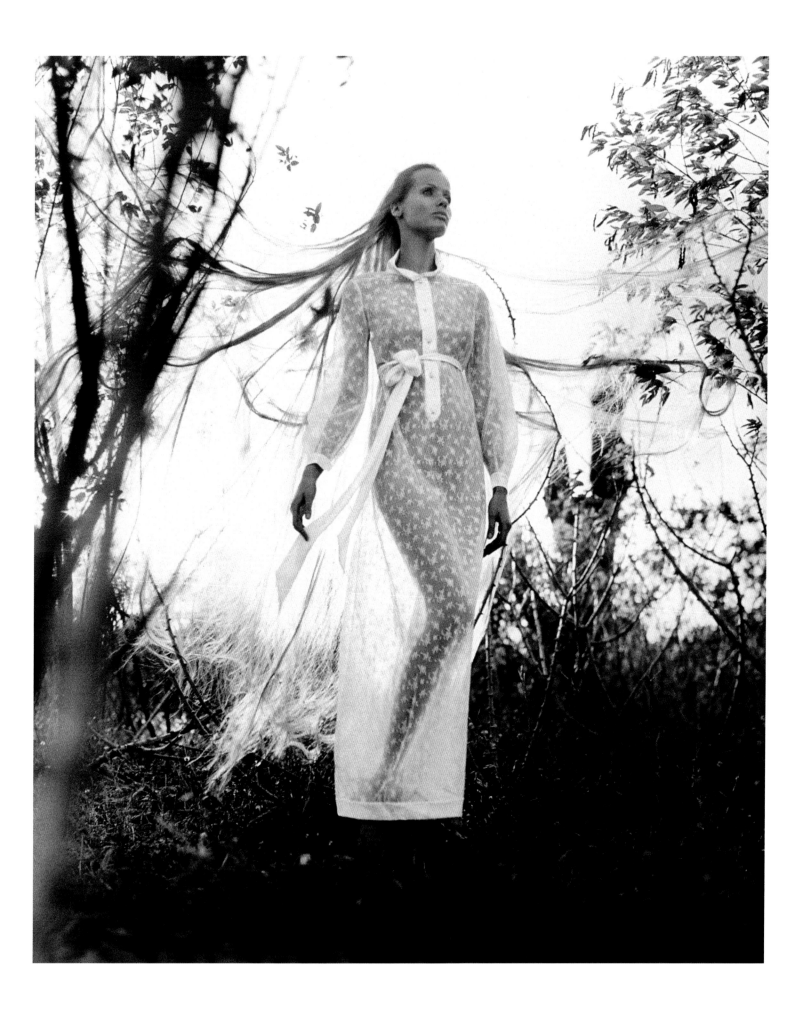

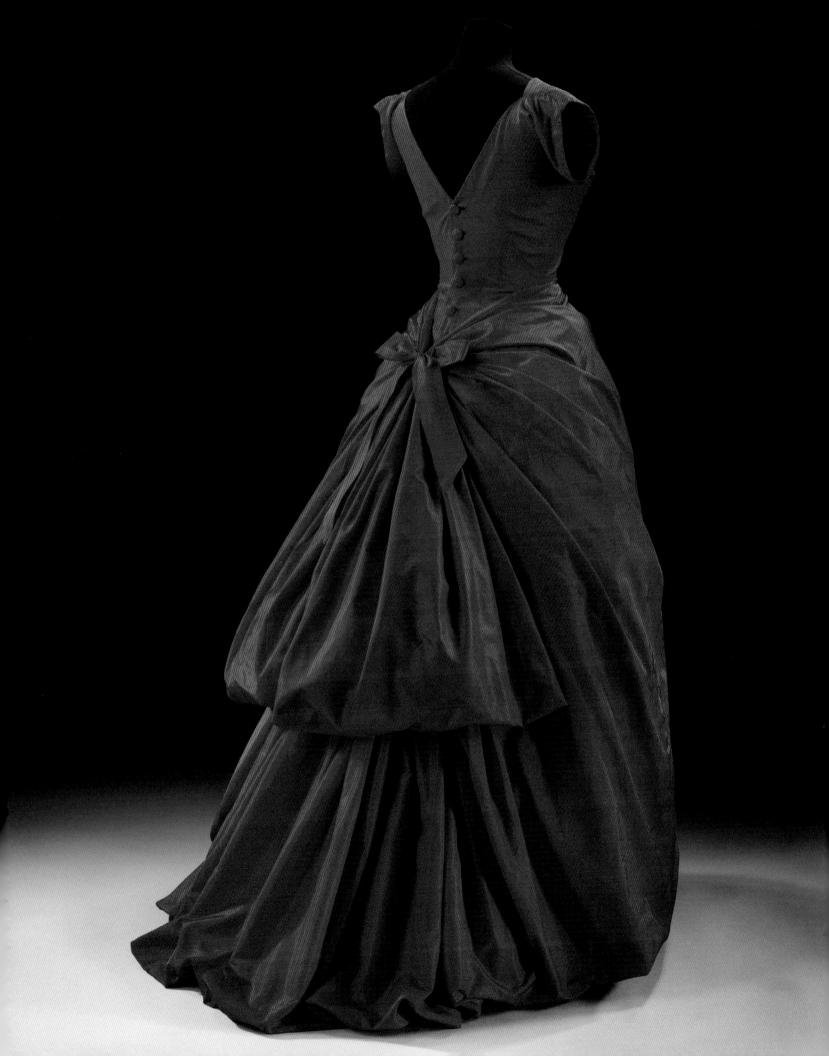

# The Bustle

The evolution of the crinoline (*see page* 85) into the bustle in the 1870s and 1880s was a sartorial development by couturier Charles Frederick Worth in response to women's attempts to pull back the excessive volume of the skirt to facilitate walking. He was also prompted in part by the necessity to sustain the same level of yardage required by the crinoline for his designs in his self-appointed role as promoter of the French textile industry. Worth achieved this by moving the fullness of the material to the back of the dress and adding a multiplicity of draped overskirts and trains in a variety of styles. Initially, the fullness of the skirt was dropped to the back of the knees, with the excess fabric creating a long train. Waists were emphasized by the external shaping of the bodice to a "V" that extended over the horizontal draping of the skirt. In the mid-1880s, the bustle moved upwards to the small of the back, which at its most extreme created a shelf-like protuberance. To support the weight of the bustle, light and flexible infrastructures were created with wire, cane or whalebone, held together by canvas tapes or inserted into quilted pockets.

Working closely with textile manufacturers such as A. Gourd et Cie and Tassinari et Chatel, Worth utilized luxurious fabrics and "upholstered" the gown with heavy embellishment in the form of *passimenterie* – tassels, braids and fringing – more usually employed in interiors. After reaching its most exaggerated shape in the 1880s, the bustle suddenly deflated to become little more than a small pad at the centre-back of the waist, and the silhouette evolved into the hourglass shape associated with the 1890s.

The impractical nature and extreme silhouette of the later shelf-like horizontal bustled gown has never been replicated since its disappearance at the end of the nineteenth century. However, the softer draping of the "puffed" bustle from the 1860s is frequently interpreted by the avant-garde and in haute couture, although it is also seen in wedding gowns, where the bustle is incorporated into the train to create an effective back view. The playful historicism of John Galliano included a deconstruction of the bustle in his "Creation" ensemble for Autumn/Winter 2005–6, which exposed the interior details and infrastructure of the garment, while Japanese designer Yohji Yamamoto combined the froufrou of the bustle with his signature strict tailoring in Autumn/Winter 1986–87.

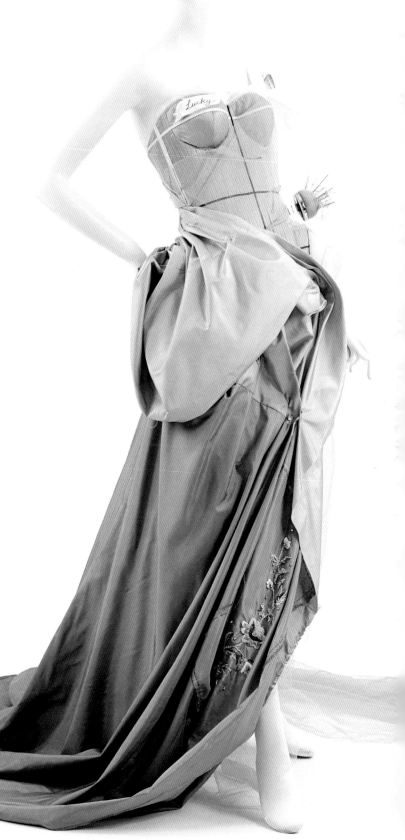

**OPPOSITE:** Renowned for the simple architectural volumes of his designs, Spanish-born couturier Cristóbal Balenciaga (1895–1972) controlled his favoured stiff material of silk taffeta to create an hourglass silhouette for an evening gown in 1953, featuring a two-tiered bustle anchored by a flat bow.

**RIGHT:** The "Creation" ensemble by John Galliano for the House of Dior displays the usually concealed details of the couture process – the implication of the tailors' mannequin and the construction of the toile – for a draped and bustled evening gown for A/W 2005–6.

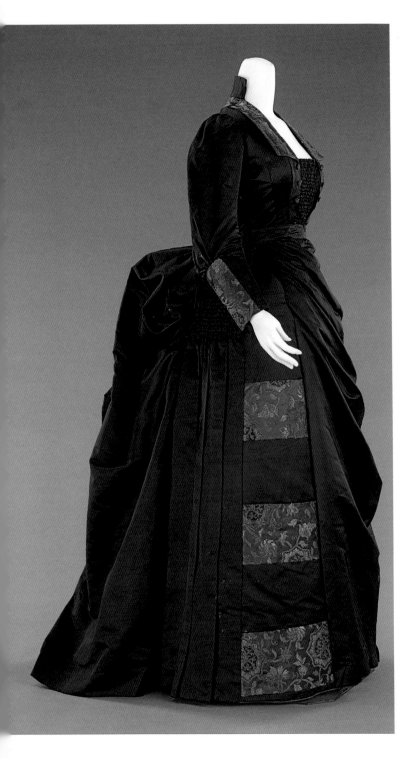

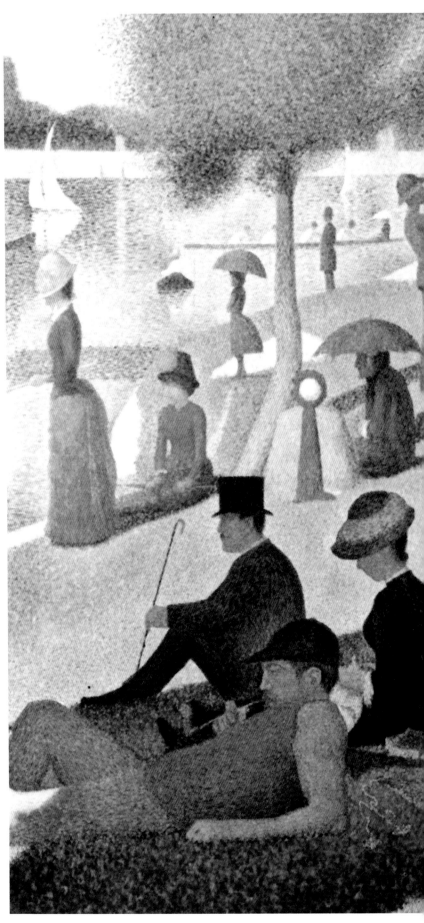

**ABOVE:** Positioned at the small of the back and supported by a flexible infrastructure, the exaggerated form of the shelf-like bustle, with a draped front and rectangular insertions of floral brocade, reached its most extreme form in this American afternoon ensemble dating from 1885–88.

**RIGHT:** The gowns depicted by post-Impressionist artist Georges Seurat (1859–91) in his painting *A Sunday Afternoon on the Island of La Grande Jatte* show the development of the heavily draped and embellished bustle into the pared-down and flat-fronted silhouette of 1884.

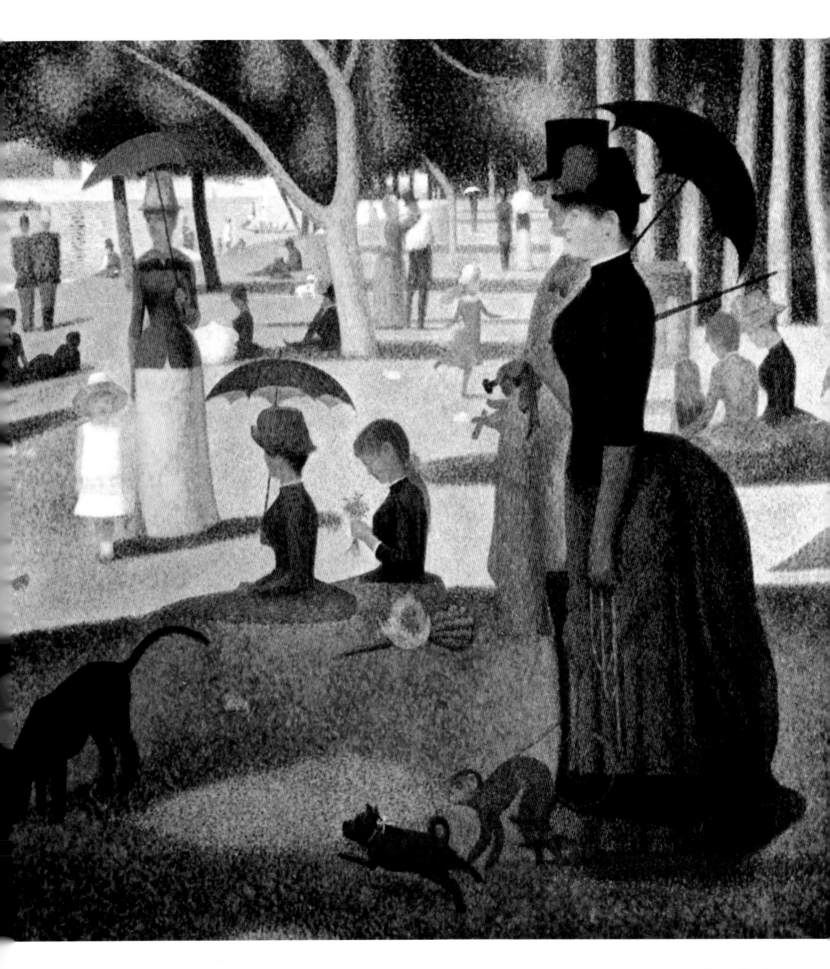

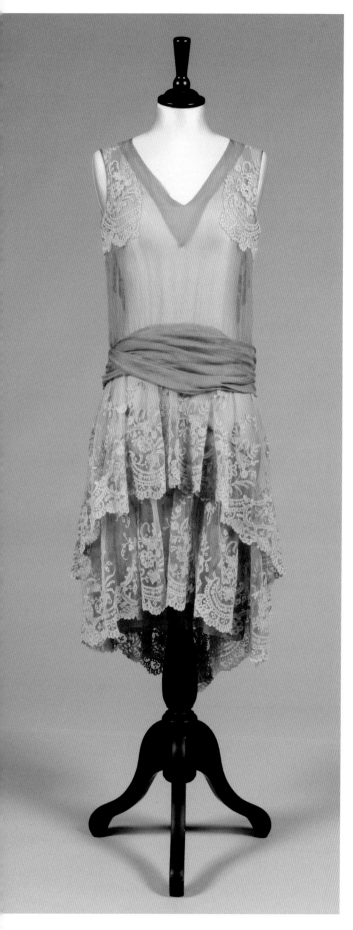

# The Chemise

The 1920s brought a series of significant changes to the lives of women in a society bereft of a generation of young men killed in World War I. Rejecting the norms of lady-like behaviour, the flapper went out unchaperoned, smoked in public, painted her face and hoicked up her skirts, the better to dance the Charleston or the Turkey Trot, an athletic and uninhibited dance popularized by Josephine Baker in *La Revue Nègre*. Visually, women transformed themselves into only slightly feminized versions of their male cohorts by wearing the tubular-shaped chemise dress or wide palazzo pants, with hair cropped into a short-back-and-sides with a side parting or cropped into a bob in imitation of film star Louise Brooks. The active lifestyles of the 1920s woman demanded clothes that allowed freedom of movement, and the radically simpler garments of the decade, such as jersey suits, golf ensembles and the chemise, brought into prominence new designers such as Coco Chanel, Jean Patou and Edward Molyneux.

The chemise dress, initially the prime female undergarment in the eighteenth century, was popularized as outerwear by Queen Marie Antoinette of France. It dominated fashion in the 1800s, and again in the 1920s, when it evolved into a sleeveless dress, skimming the contours of the body, bypassing the waist and falling straight to the hem, with the hipline marked with a belt or some form of decorative detailing. Necklines were simple round or "V" necks, often with the addition of a triangular scarf, the points hanging down in the daytime. Usually constructed from silk jersey, georgette or crepe de Chine, the chemise was worn over a combination of camisole and knickers known as cami-knickers, with the breasts bandaged flat for the desirable *la garçonne* look. Without suspenders, stockings were rolled down to the knee.

A version of the chemise dress reappeared in the 1950s when both Cristóbal Balenciaga and Christian Dior introduced straight, unfitted sheath dresses, sometimes called sack dresses in reference to its origins to the sack-back gown (*see page* 30). The counterpart of the free-spirited flapper was to be found in the 1960s: equally unencumbered by the constraints of structured clothes, young women enjoyed the freedom of the chemise, called the shift dress by now, cropped to mid-thigh and worn without a bra, creating a flapper-like androgynous silhouette.

**LEFT:** Presumed to be designed by British-born, Paris-based couturier Edward Molyneux, the chemise dress in pale tan-coloured silk chiffon features a transitional dipped hemline – a move from the shorter length of the mid-1920s to the mid-calf seen later in the decade.

**OPPOSITE:** In the portrait of Charlotte du Val d'Ognes, entitled *Young Woman Drawing* (1801), painted by French artist Marie-Denise Villers (1774–1821), the sitter wears an unadorned chemise in lightweight muslin cotton, featuring a typical cross-over bodice of the period.

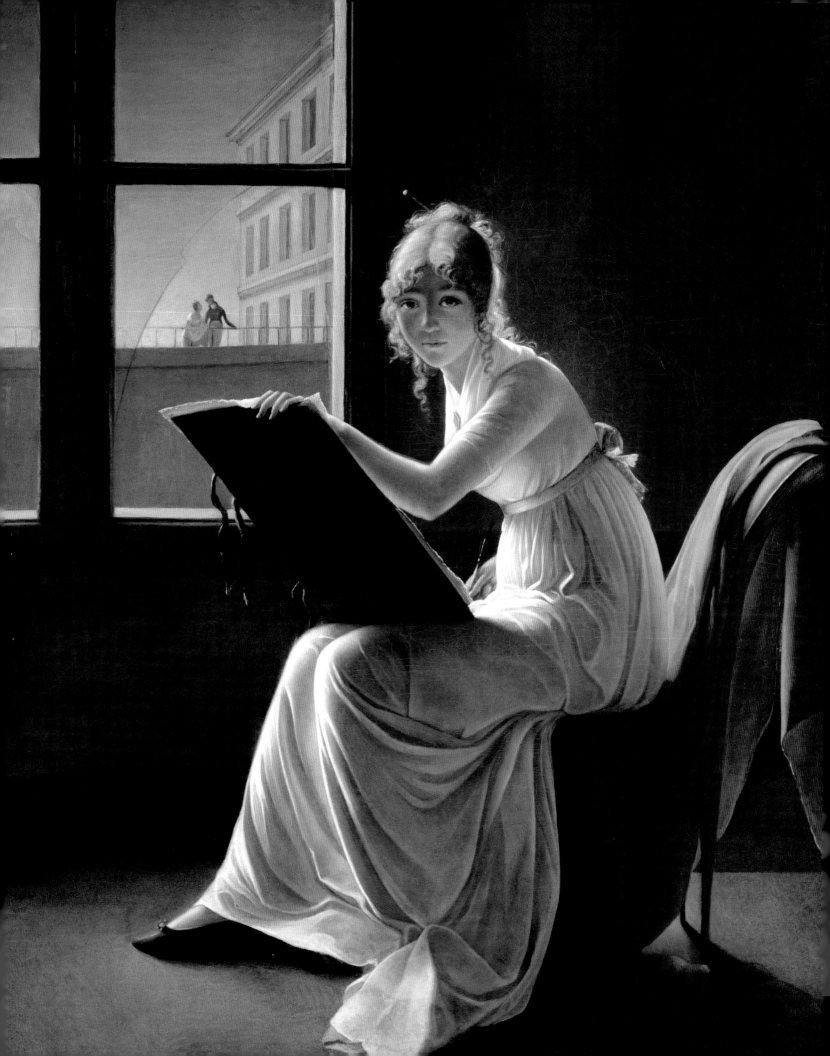

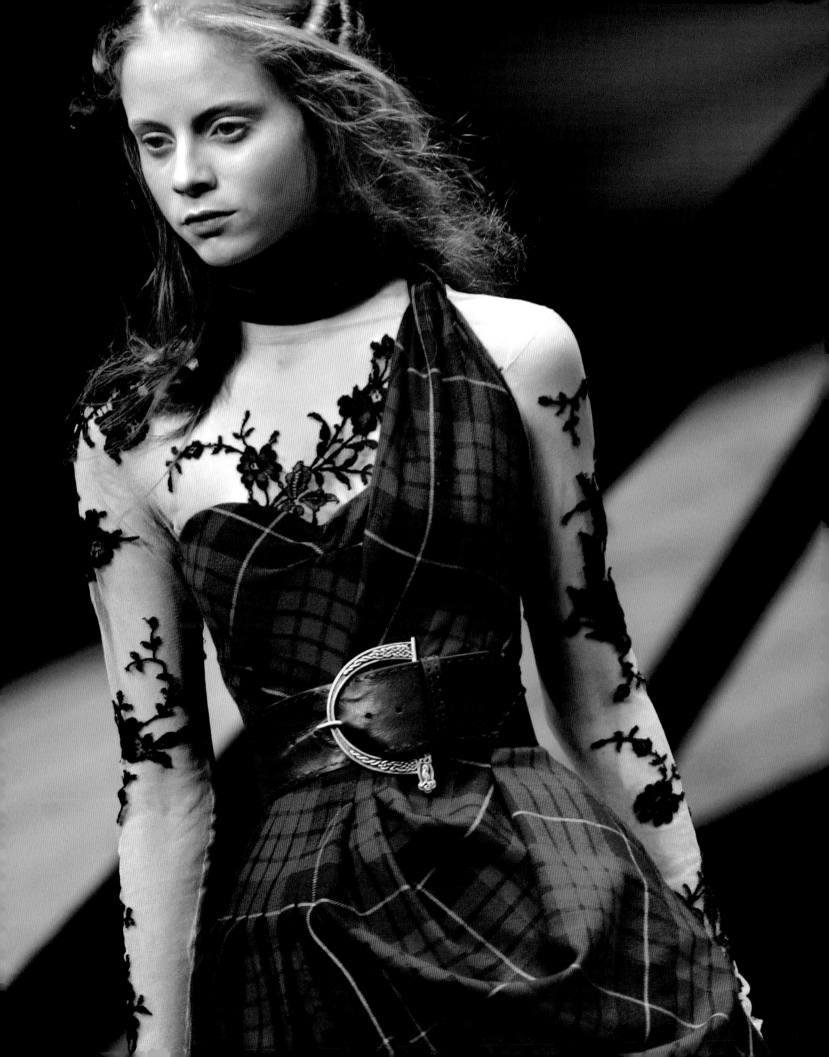

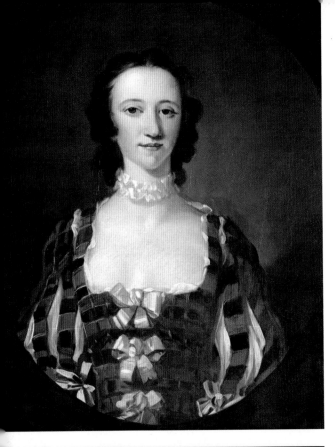

# Tartan Pattern

The distinctive checked pattern of tartan cloth has been a symbol of the Scottish Highland's identity for many centuries, and a visual signifier of clanship throughout Scottish history – one of the traditions of the Highlands was the provision by the chiefs of clothing for their retainers in the clan tartan.

Tartan refers to patterns or "setts" of interlocking stripes, running in both the warp and weft directions of the cloth – horizontal and vertical – and are created by using two colours of thread, resulting in three colour combinations. Originally, the tartan cloth was left uncut and worn as a "plaid" in the form of a mantle for men and as a shawl for women. The wearing of tartan was banned with the Disclothing Act of 1746, but was rescinded in 1781, when the threat of a Jacobite rebellion had ceased to exist. The following decades witnessed a subsequent revival in tartan prompted by Sir Walter Scott, who offered a romantic view of the Highlander with his novels such as *Waverley* (1814) and *Rob Roy* (1817). This was further consolidated by a young Queen Victoria who began to take her holidays in the Highlands and bought the Balmoral estate in 1848.

Early tartans were relatively muted in colour and created from natural dyes, but the trend for more colourful patterns emerged as aniline dyes became available, resulting in the garish tartans popular in the Victorian era. Tartan continued to be an option for traditional rural dress, but the textile only entered the fashion arena in the late twentieth century when previous punk protagonist and fashion maverick Vivienne Westwood began using long-established manufacturing processes and appropriating indigenous materials such as Harris tweed and tartan. For her "Anglomania" collection (*see also page* 40), Westwood created her own clan and tartan, MacAndreas, named after her third husband and creative collaborator, Andreas Kronthaler. Alexander McQueen also created his own sett in black, red and yellow, which he used for his "Highland Rape" collection of Autumn/Winter 1995–96. This referenced the eighteenth-century Jacobite rebellion and acknowledged his outrage at the genocide perpetrated by the English during the nineteenth-century Highland Clearances.

Tartan now consistently provides inspiration to a number of designers, including the Henry Holland's label House of Holland, which was awarded the "Best Use of Tartan" award at the Scottish Fashion Awards in 2008 for a purple and yellow tartan.

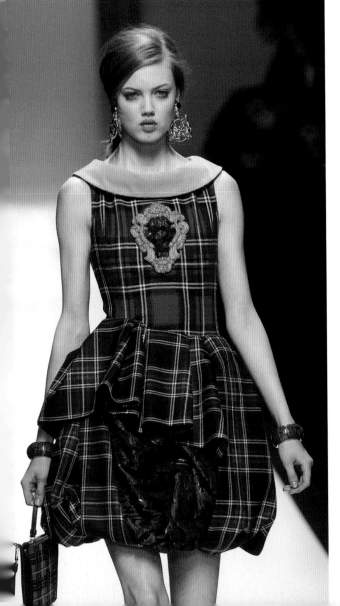

**OPPOSITE:** The emblematic power of Scottish tartan was revisited by Alexander McQueen (1969–2010) for "Widows of Culloden" A/W 2006–7, following "Highland Rape" in 1995–6. The full pleated skirt of the traditional male Scottish kilt is refreshed by the incorporation of a tartan bustier.

**ABOVE LEFT:** Flora Macdonald was imprisoned in the Tower of London for enabling Prince Charles Edward Stuart (Bonnie Prince Charlie) to escape the British after the Battle of Culloden in 1746. After her release in 1747, she commissioned this portrait, in which she wears the Stuart tartan.

**LEFT:** Rossella Jardini continues the legacy of the label founded by the provocative "bad boy" of fashion, Franco Moschino (1950–94). For A/W 2003–4, she created a pastiche of Scottish baronial style with a puffball kilt in the signature red and black of the label, with gold insignia on the bodice.

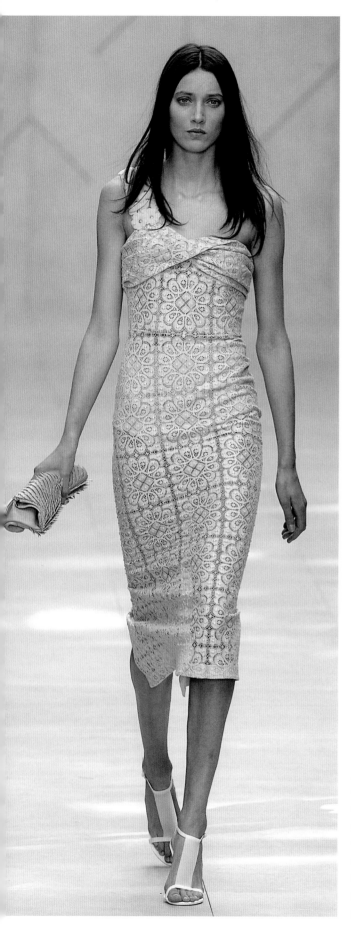

# The Lace Dress

Few fabrics are capable of sustaining such polarized interpretation as lace; its power often transposed from the pristine and pure to the decadent and sensual by the simple addition of colour to its perforated structure. Residual connotations of innocence and piety endure within rites of passage such as christenings and matrimony. In the secular sphere, lace remains an integral component of contemporary fashion yet it is also a heritage fabric that has long held a unique place in the pantheon of luxury fabrics. Its precise origins are obscure, but lace as an openwork fabric, created with a needle and single thread (needle lace) or with multiple threads (bobbin lace), was developed during the second half of the sixteenth century. The prerogative of persons of a high social status such as the aristocracy and royalty, handmade laces were used for the accoutrements and trimmings of garments, from the sixteenth-century ruffs of geometric needle lace to the delicate French needle laces adorning the bodices and sleeves of the *robes volantes* and the *robes à la française* of the eighteenth century.

By 1870 virtually every type of handmade lace had its machine-made equivalent but, although machine-made lace became more readily available, it remained a precious commodity, adorning the aristocratic Edwardian beauty, from the insertion lace of her high-boned collar to her ground-sweeping train. With the introduction of synthetic yarns in the 1950s, lace became ubiquitous but remained primarily in the boudoir. The exceptions were the specialist laces such as guipure, a heavy lace in which the patterns are connected by fine threads with overlapping motifs, forming a many-layered texture, a favourite of couturiers such as Christian Dior and Balmain, who usually confined its use to eveningwear.

In the twenty-first century, lace has undergone a reappraisal, and guipure lace was most recently used by Italian label Prada for their Autumn/Winter 2008–9 collection. Leavers lace, dyed hot pink and orange in the collections of Italian designers Dolce & Gabbana for Spring/Summer 2010, and an all-over Cluny lace fashioned into romantic cream dresses for British designer Vivienne Westwood's Gold label (Spring/Summer 2012), were all sourced at the heritage company Cluny Lace, the single remaining manufacturer of Leavers lace in the UK – it began manufacturing lace in the 1760s at the start of Britain's Industrial Revolution. Tapping into the "Made in Britain" ethos, British designer Christopher Bailey of Burberry Prorsum also used lace from the Midlands-based company, once the centre of the global lace-making industry.

**LEFT:** Christopher Bailey (1971–), for Burberry Prorsum, sources Cluny lace for S/S 2014, marking one of the periods in the twenty-first century when lace resides as a high fashion statement for daywear, rather than being marginalized as wedding finery or confined to lingerie.

**OPPOSITE:** The three Callot sisters opened their couture salon – initially, a lingerie and lace business – in 1895, with Madame Marie Callot Gerber acting as head designer. The technical expertise of the sisters working with lace is evident in this gown dating from 1915.

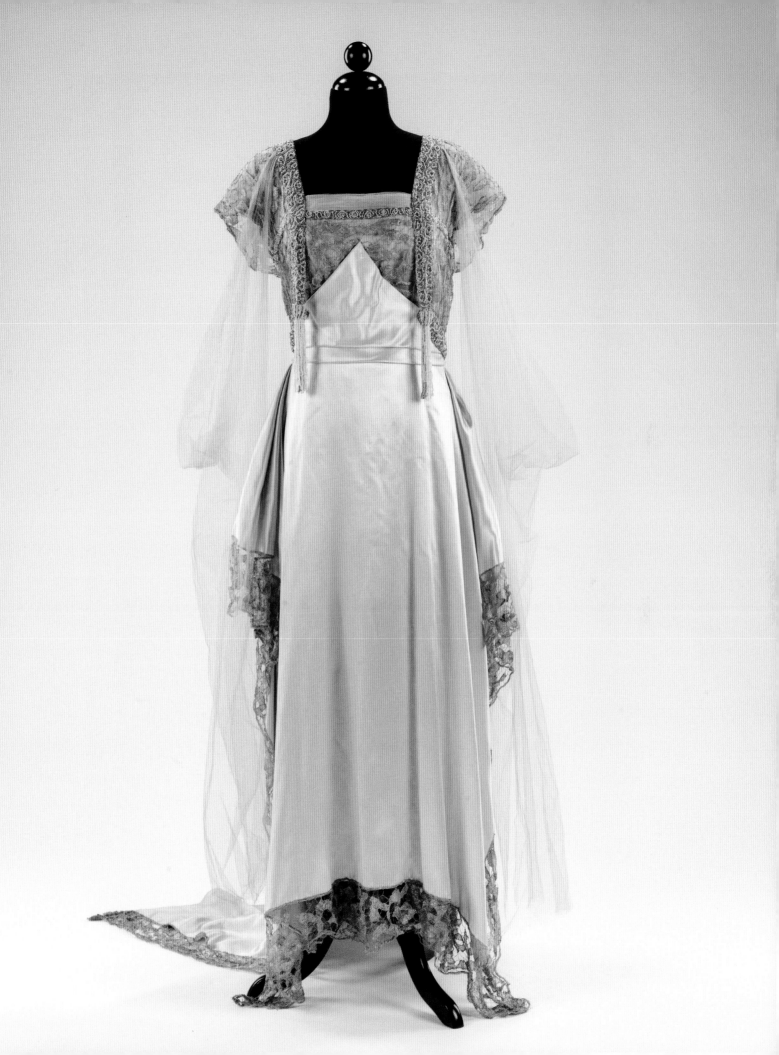

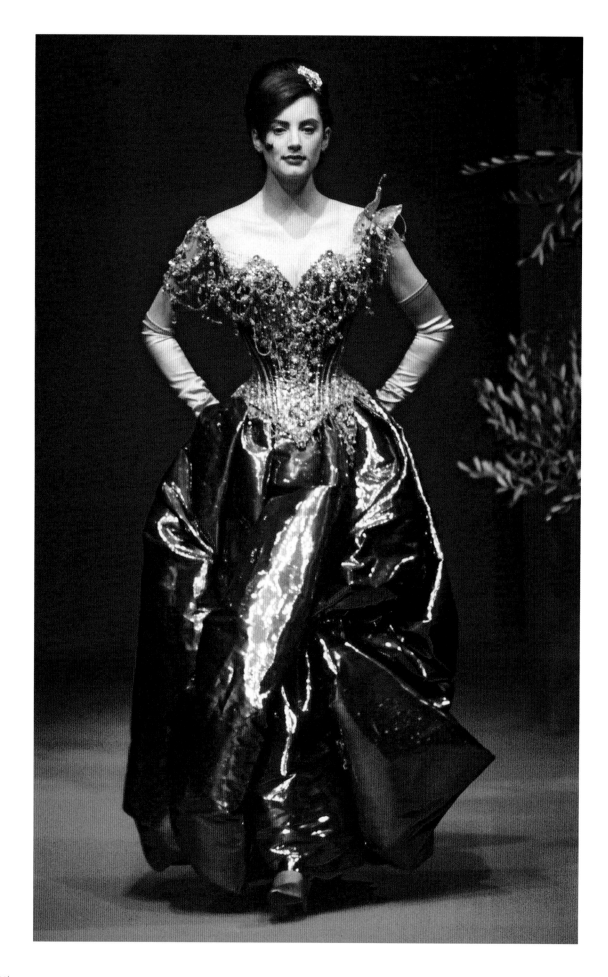

Worn by women throughout the Western world, the corset has been an essential element of fashionable dress since the Renaissance, an unseen component of a woman's wardrobe visible only through the shaping of the body. Once considered by the medical profession and various dress reform movements as the cause of ill-health, and by feminists as an instrument of female oppression, in contemporary fashion the corset has been reinvented as an item of fashionable outerwear and a symbol of female sexual empowerment.

No longer the hidden aid to an hourglass figure, the corset has become a visible and socially acceptable form of erotic display. Vivienne Westwood appropriated the corset's titillating identity for her "Portrait" collection of Autumn/Winter 1990–1, with both shape and printed image borrowed directly from the eighteenth century. The corset features flexible internal boning, wide shoulder straps and a V-shaped panel at the front featuring a photographic printed detail of the 1743 painting *Daphnis and Chloe* by François Boucher. The lacing is replaced with a zip at the centre back.

OPPOSITE: Evoking the fashionable beauties of the society portrait painter Giovanni Boldini (1842–1931), with the jewelled corset, bare shoulders and voluminous skirts of heavy lamé satin, Christian Lacroix summons up the era of the Belle Èpoque in 1996.

BELOW: In her A/W 1992–93 collection "Always on Camera", Vivienne Westwood took inspiration from the corsets of the eighteenth century that constrained the billowing volumes of opulent fabrics. Westwood's crumb-catcher bodice is fabricated in darker shades, drawing the eye from the delicate tones and nebulous form of the skirt to the embonpoint focus.

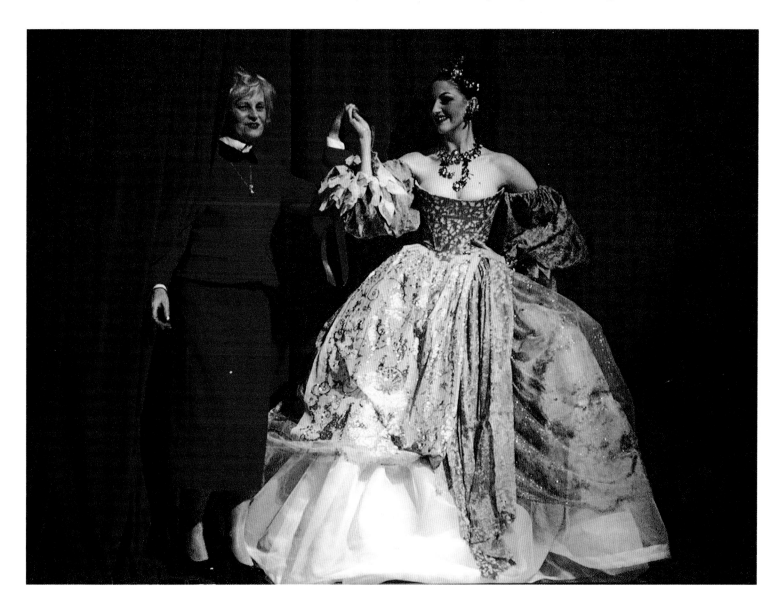

For French designer and aesthetic provocateur Jean Paul Gaultier, the corset offers a reminder of his grandmother's salmon-coloured lace-up corset, his first fetish and the inspiration for many of his boudoir-inspired clothes, most notably those for Madonna and her *Blonde Ambition* world tour of 1990, for which he designed a nude satin corset with free-floating suspenders. The designer's "Barbès" collection of 1994 integrates the bra and corset in one for his famous "corset" dress in orange rayon velvet. The dramatically exaggerated conical breasts, pointing aggressively upwards and outwards, are attached to a reinforced torso, resonant of the controlling panels of the corset.

During the 1990s, the corset became ubiquitous, appearing in the collections of most major designers including John Galliano, Versace and Italian design duo Dolce & Gabbana, who created black satin corset dresses of decadent sensuality. The nineteenth-century historical romanticism of Christian Lacroix resulted in an idealized and romantic view of the 1880s corset combined with a bustle, where the laced fastening was on display rather than concealed. Introducing the corset as fetish into mainstream fashion is designer Thierry Mugler, who created corsets as body armour, with women encased in rigid materials such as Plexiglas, metal, and sculpted and embossed black leather. Iconoclastic designer Alexander McQueen included tanned crocodile-skin corsets, strapped and buckled at the back for his "Natural Dis-Tinction, Un-Natural Selection" collection for Spring/Summer 2009.

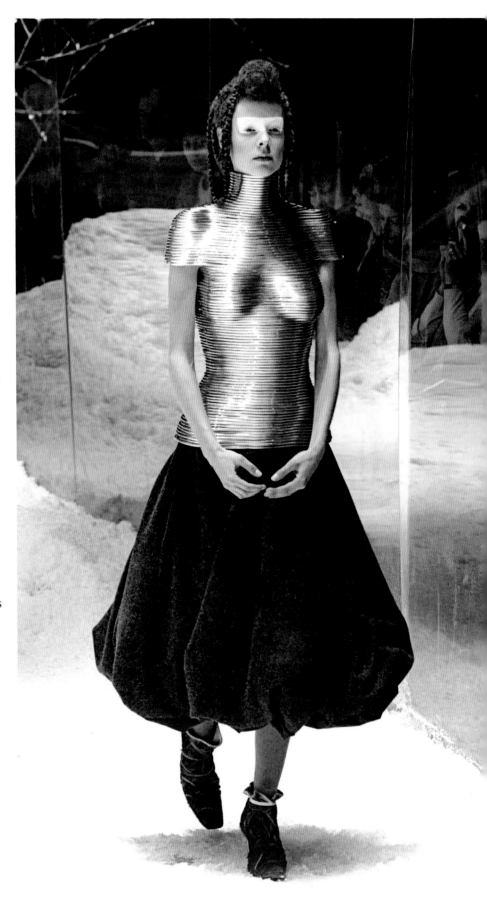

**LEFT:** Alexander McQueen's A/W 1999–2000 collection "The Overlook" featured an oppressive coiling aluminium corset designed by jeweller Shaun Leane. The piece draws on disparate connotations: Dalí's Surrealist take on the *Venus de Milo*, the abstract human forms of Giorgio de Chirico and Burma's Kayan Lahwi, and South Africa's Ndebele neck-ring traditions.

**RIGHT:** Jean Paul Gaultier made an ironic comment on the traditional corset for his 1984 "Barbès" collection. Featuring a contour-stitched bra and a torso of ruched panels, resonant of 1950s controlling stays, the orange velvet fishtail dress was also modelled by men.

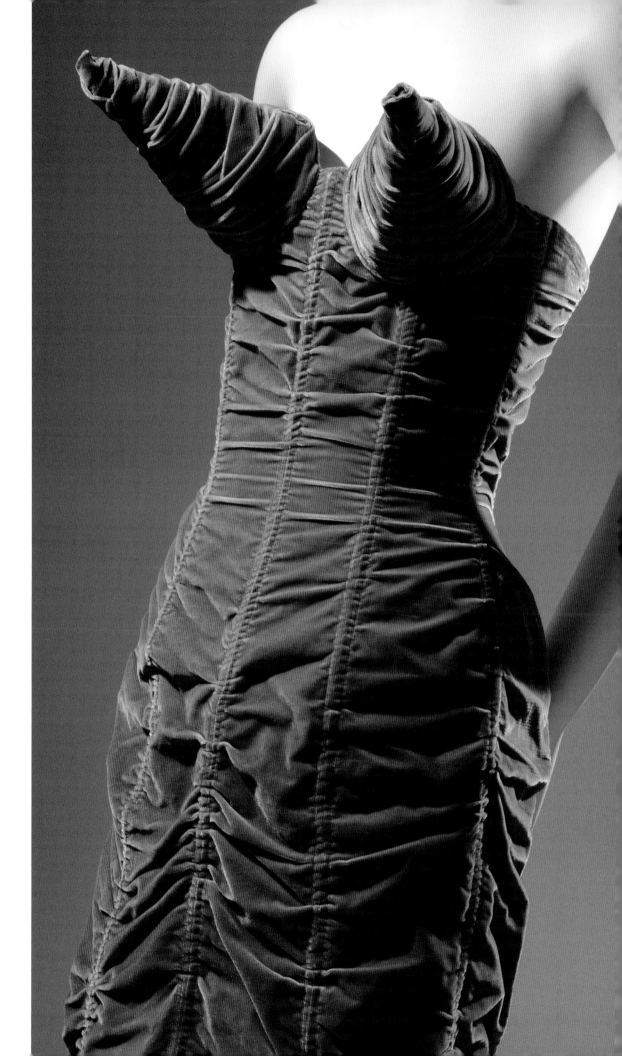

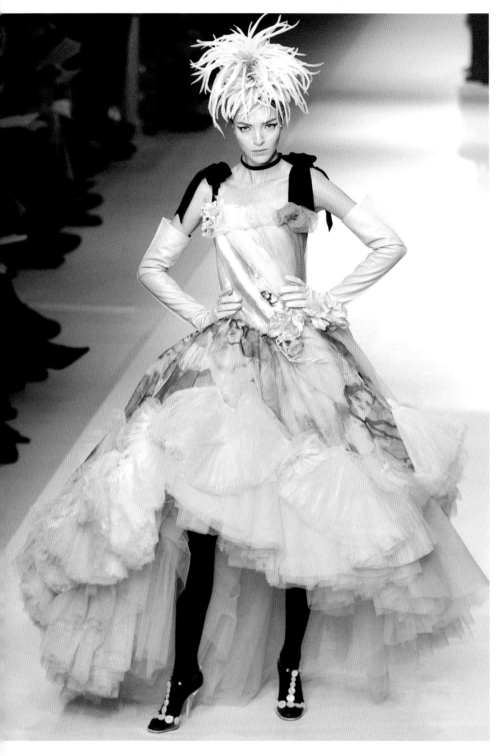

# The Tutu

The tutu in tulle – very fine netting in silk – has long had connotations of fairy princesses, fulfilling many a young girl's dream of being a ballerina. Usually in pink, this was epitomized by style icon Sarah Jessica Parker, who wore a pink tutu to twirl on the streets of New York in the opening credits of the original series of cult TV sit-com *Sex and the City*. The ballerina's tutu – layers of airy tulle attached at the waist to a close-fitting basque and worn with a shaped bodice – first appeared on the stage in 1730, when the *danse basse* (moving from pose to pose) was replaced by the *danse haute*, where dancers took to the air. This required women to discard their heavy costumes for garments that emphasized their other-worldliness.

The first tutu was ankle-length and created from several layers of soft tulle, worn by Marie Taglioni in a performance of *La Sylphide* in 1832. Over time, the skirt became increasingly shorter and formed into a pancake or platform tutu, allowing the female dancers to show off the point work and multiple turns that form the focus of dance practice. The circumference and horizontal rigidity of the platform tutu does not lend itself so easily to fashionable dress as the classical or romantic tutu, however Vivienne Westwood created a tulle tutu worn with a red jersey top for her Gold label in 1990, worn by Kate Moss and photographed by Mario Testino. The ultra-femininity of the tutu is frequently subverted by designers such as Jean Paul Gaultier, who emphasized the fragility of the garment by partnering the ethereal skirts with a studded black leather basque and coat, and Converse trainers for Spring/Summer 2007.

Nineteenth-century French artist Edgar Degas depicted evocative images of dancers backstage or in rehearsal in complex layers and textures of paint or pastels. His models wear the bell-shaped classical tutu, and provided inspiration for the Mulleavy sisters and their label, Rodarte, in 2008. Pleated lengths of silk chiffon in various shades of pale tan, apricot and cream are whip-stitched into place and decorated with tiny glittering iridescent beads to create a form-fitting bodice. Layers of fibrous textured fabric with unfinished edges are gathered into the waistband to create the knee-length, bell-shaped skirt.

**ABOVE:** For S/S 2003 Jean Paul Gaultier used the volume of a crinolined tutu to animate figurative trompe l'oeil images of ballet dancers – taken directly from the work of French artist Edgar Degas – with flounces of tulle escaping the surface of the dress.

**OPPOSITE LEFT:** A contemporary version of the bell-shaped classical tutu is deconstructed by the use of unexpected materials, a nude colourway and rough-hewn techniques in 2003 by Kate (1979–) and Laura (1980–) Mulleavy, of the American couture label Rodarte.

**OPPOSITE RIGHT:** Ever fashion's leading demagogue, Vivienne Westwood includes a billowing cloud-like white satin and pink tulle tutu in a collection dubbed "+5°" – as in the five degrees the earth's average temperatures are calculated to rise as $CO_2$ levels rise.

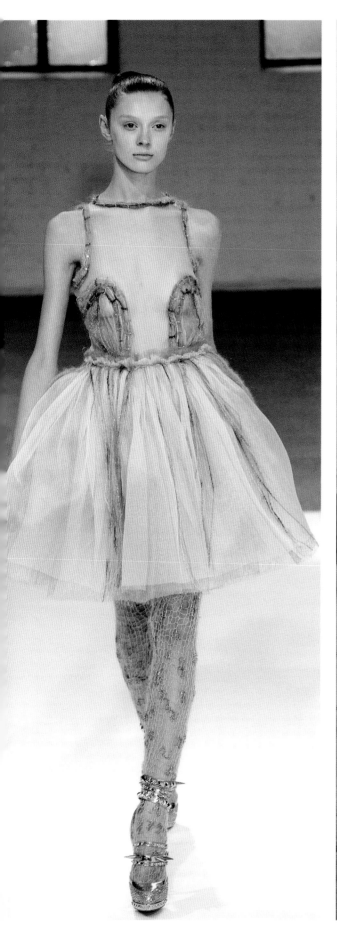
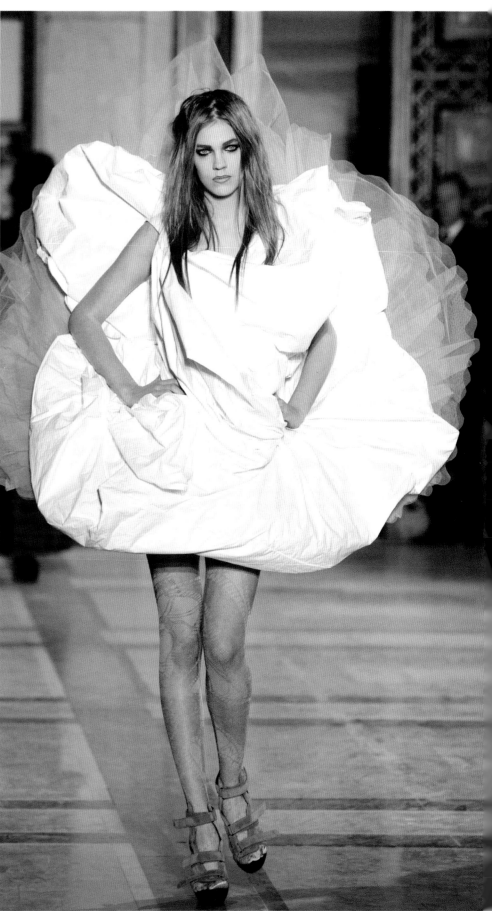

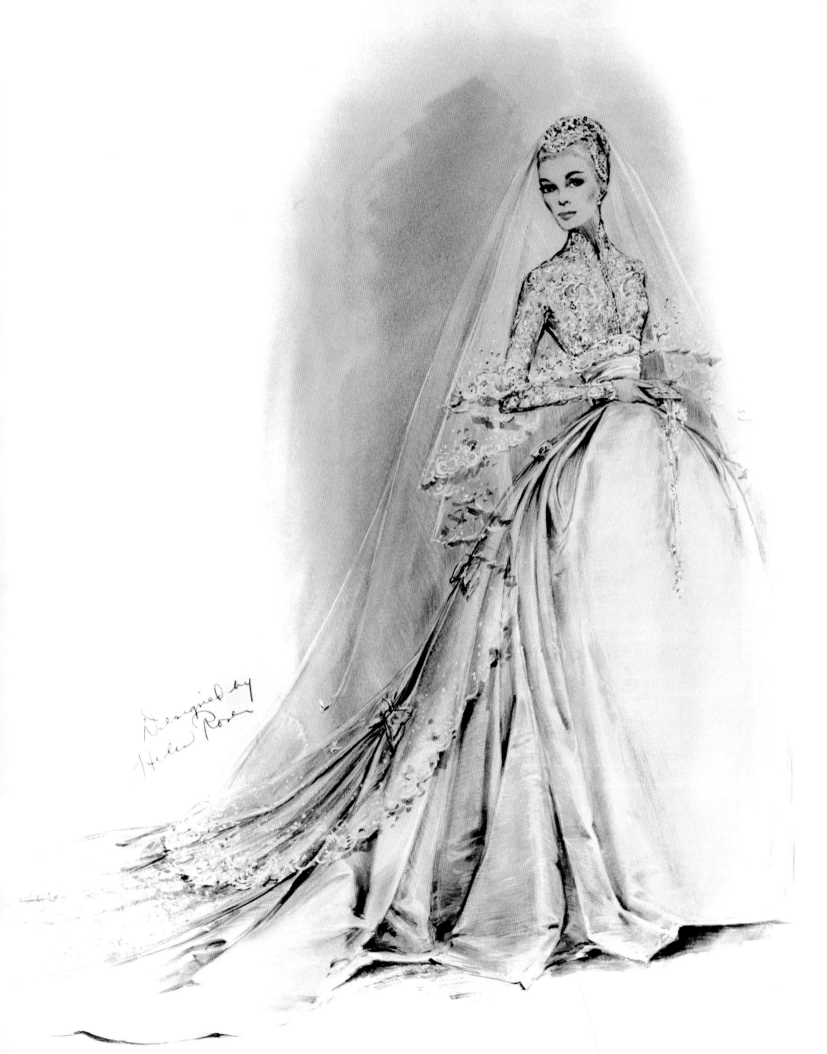

Designed by
Helen Rose

# The Wedding Dress

The style of the wedding dress has evolved alongside changes in fashion, although the Victorian crinoline remains a perpetual favourite. The all-white wedding dress was popularized by Queen Victoria on her marriage to Prince Albert of Saxe-Coburg-Gotha in 1840, and the full-skirted ivory silk and Honiton lace gown worn by the monarch – together with the veil and train – established the paradigm for wedding gown design for future generations of brides. Brides have not always worn white; previously they wore their "Sunday best", whatever the colour.

At the beginning of the 1920s, the S-shaped silhouette of the Edwardian period was replaced by a vogue for a romantic version of medieval style, which evoked notions of chivalric ideal made popular by court dressmaker Lucile and her competitor Ada Wolf. Increasingly, this low-waisted style became tubular and heavily embellished with crystal beadwork and appliqué embroidery, with the hemline rising to mid-calf. With the popularity of the cinema in the 1930s, Hollywood brides influenced wedding dress style, from the screen sirens of the 1930s costumed by Adrian in slithers of body-skimming bias-cut satin to the nuptials of Elizabeth Taylor to Conrad "Nicki" Hilton and the royal wedding of Grace Kelly to Prince Rainier of Monaco in 1955. Both dresses were designed by Oscar-winning Hollywood costumier to the stars, Helen Rose, who introduced the Sweetheart line, a dress with a heart-shaped bodice with a nipped-in waist and billowing skirt.

The scaffolding that underpinned the 1950s bride was discarded in the decade of the miniskirt and youth-led fashion when the bride wore a simple sheath dress that skimmed the thigh. Formality in wedding fashion re-emerged in the 1980s, an era of conspicuous consumption in which the wedding ceremony became an aspirational, theatrical spectacle. The marriage of Lady Diana Spencer to Charles, Prince of Wales, in 1981 heralded a return to the crinoline. Designed by David and Elizabeth Emanuel, the cloud of paper taffeta and corseted waist influenced the style of wedding gowns for the decade to come. The 1990s provided a backlash against the "meringue"-style dress, and US designers such as Vera Wang and Narciso Rodriguez set the trend for understated simplicity, with classical columnar shapes structured in architectural heavy duchesse satin. With the wedding ceremony now more usually undertaken in secular venues rather a place of worship, it has become increasingly acceptable to display more flesh. Where once the wedding dress represented virginity and purity, the fashionable wedding dress is now often strapless and cut to display the undulating curves of the bride.

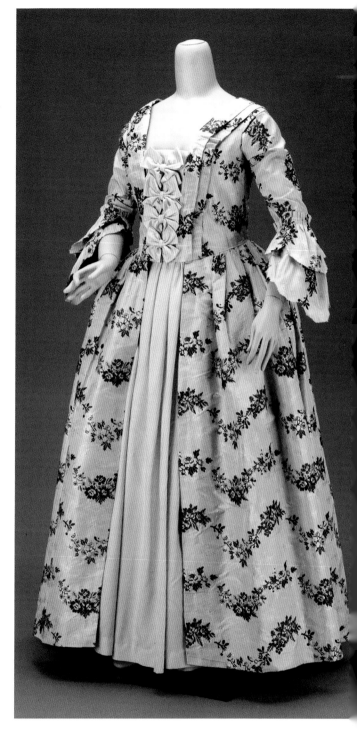

**OPPOSITE:** Representing demure and regal simplicity, the gown worn by Grace Kelly on her marriage to Prince Rainier of Monaco in 1955 was designed by Hollywood costumier Helen Rose. It followed the prevailing hourglass shape, with a tightly fitting bodice and bell-shaped taffeta skirt.

**ABOVE:** Dating from 1763, the wedding dress once worn by Sarah Tyng Smith was based on the *robe à la française*, a silhouette that remained consistent from 1720 to 1780. Flowers are a dominant motif of the bodice and overskirt, which is worn over a silk plain-weave underskirt.

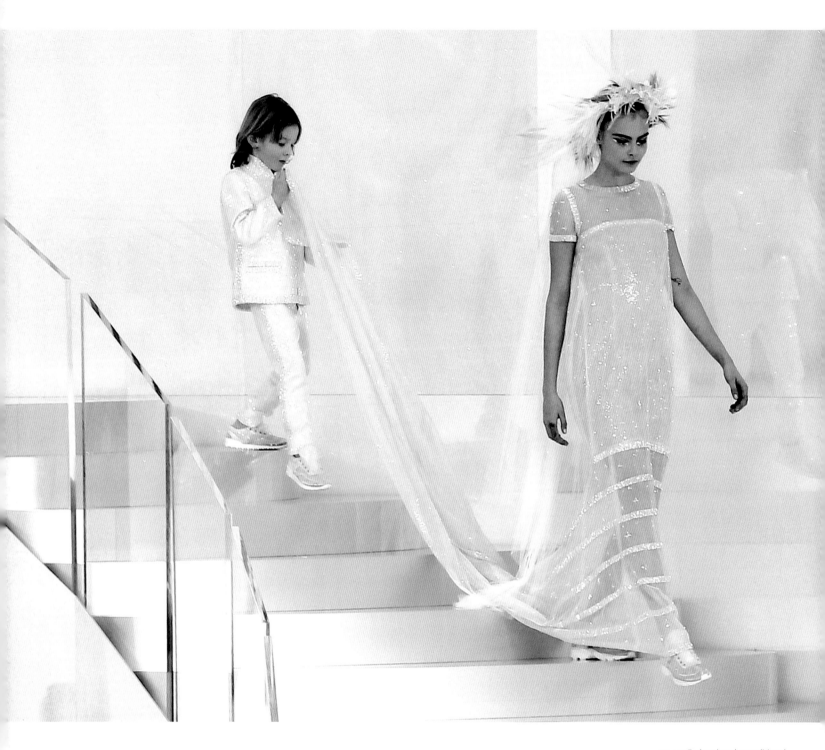

ABOVE: Eschewing the traditional wedding-gown silhouette – more usually either crinolined or sheath-like – Karl Lagerfeld for Chanel Haute Couture in 2014 introduced a 1960s-inspired space-age futuristic chemise in metallic semi-transparent fabric, modelled by Cara Delevingne and accessorized with trainers.

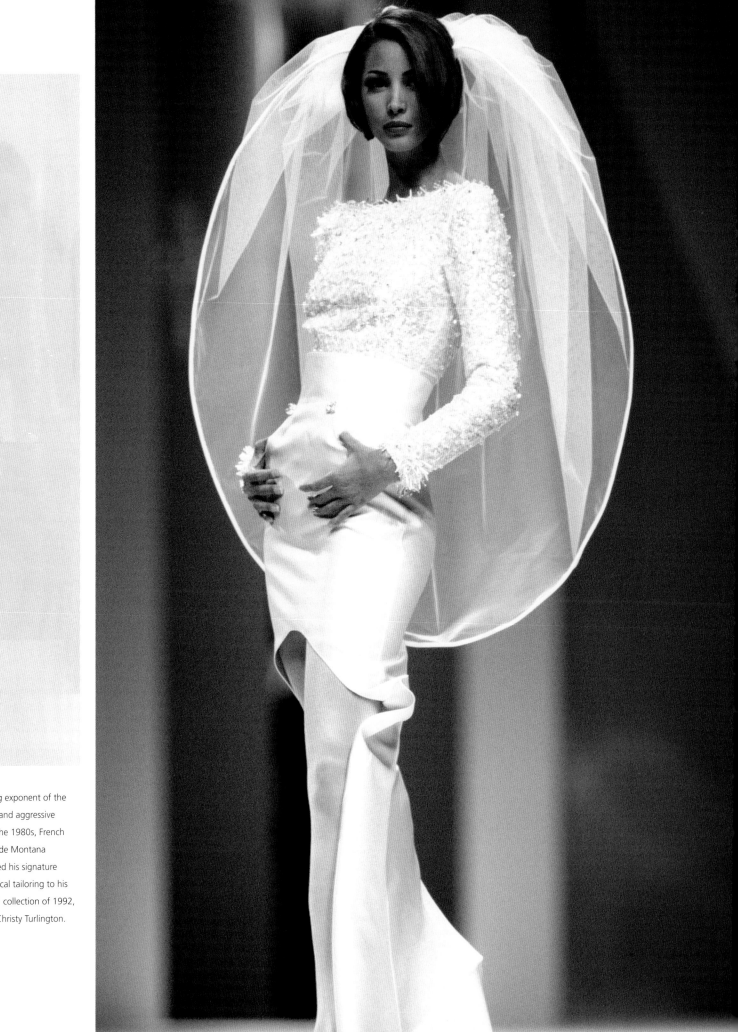

RIGHT: Leading exponent of the shoulder pad and aggressive silhouette in the 1980s, French designer Claude Montana (1949–) applied his signature style of technical tailoring to his "Bridal Wear" collection of 1992, modelled by Christy Turlington.

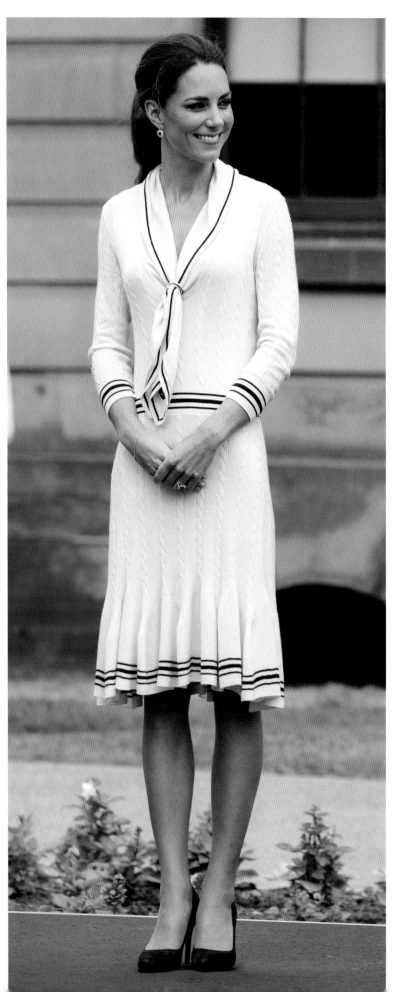

# Nautical Dress

The perennial appeal of sailor chic lies mainly in the fail-safe colour combination of navy blue and white and its association with the romance and freedom of life on the sea. The birth of the official Navy uniform in England in the mid-nineteenth century was marked by Queen Victoria in 1846, who dressed her four-year-old son, the Prince of Wales, Albert Edward, in a sailor suit to wear aboard the Royal Yacht, a scene captured by the artist Franz Xaver Winterhalter. Prompted in part by patriotism – a desire to show support for the British Empire – and also by regular excursions to the coast with the development of rail travel, the sailor suit became a classic children's style. Early examples of maritime-inspired fashion for adults were intended to be worn for appropriately nautical pursuits, with yachting outfits featuring braided collar and cuffs and brass buttons.

It was only in the later Edwardian period that nautical styles were incorporated into fashionable garb, particularly the middy blouse – from the term "midshipman", an officer in the Royal Navy – a loose-fitting blouse featuring a square shawl collar and braiding. Sailor collars proliferated in the 1920s atop loose, low-waisted summer dresses, and were mostly worn as part of the *la garçonne* look for sporting activities such as tennis. Coco Chanel made an enduring fashion statement in the same decade with her appropriation of the striped top worn by Breton fishermen, which she partnered with wide-legged bell-bottomed trousers – cut to provide ease of movement around the deck of a boat.

In the golden years of Hollywood, silver-screen goddesses such as Jean Harlow and Bette Davis sported glamorous versions of the middy dress, and the appearance of Ginger Rogers in a silk satin sailor suit partnering Fred Astaire in the 1936 box-office success *Follow the Fleet* consolidated its popularity. The middy dress reappeared in the youth-led fashions of the 1960s with drop-waist dresses and pleating on the hip, similar in style to the versions seen in the 1920s. Generally confined to the Spring/Summer collections, contemporary sailor style is a favourite of American designer Ralph Lauren. The designer retells the preppy myth with navy-and-white striped sailor's maillots, British naval heritage double-breasted blazers with soutache braiding and gilt buttons, and loose linen dresses with middy collars.

**OPPOSITE:** Incorporating a middy collar and striped borders into a fine cable-knit sweater dress, Sarah Burton for Alexander McQueen provided the Duchess of Cambridge with a patriotic acknowledgement of Britain's seafaring heritage, combined with demure, fail-safe sailor style, for her appearance on the royal tour of Canada in 2012.

**RIGHT:** The striped Breton jersey T-shirt is a perennial staple of quintessentially French designer Jean Paul Gaultier, and a favourite garment in his personal wardrobe. Reworked for the Haute Couture line in 2000, the designer extends the stripes into the mermaid tail of an angel fish.

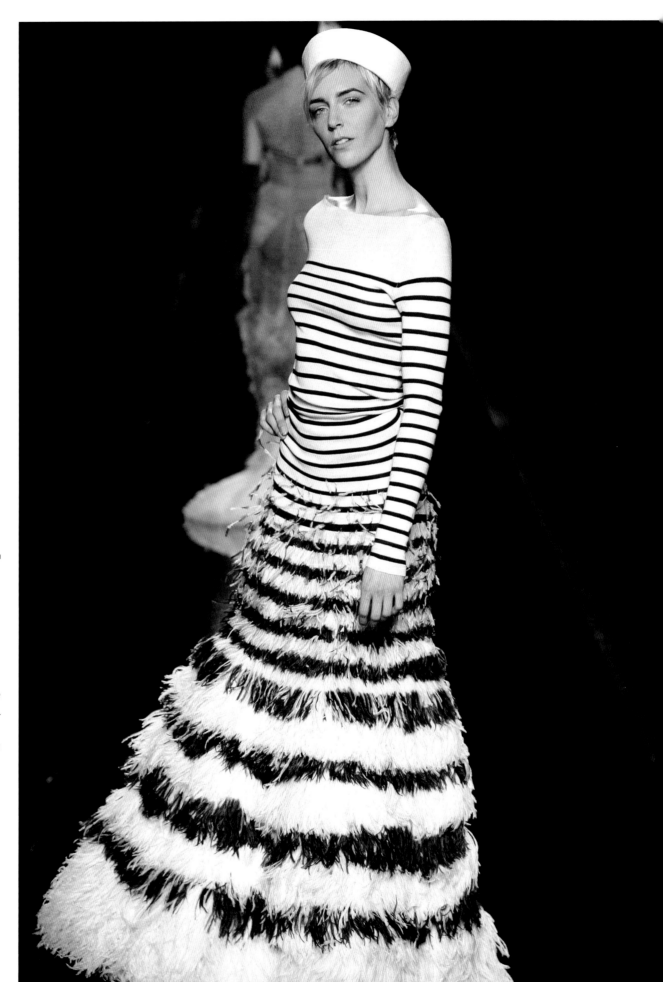

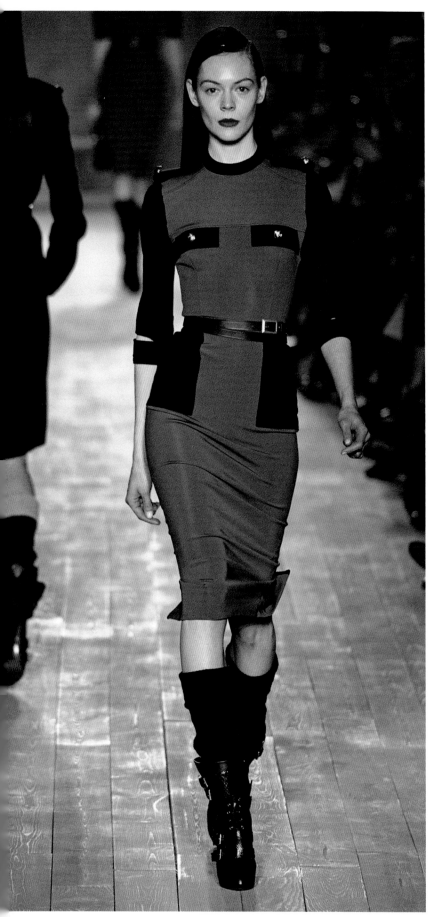
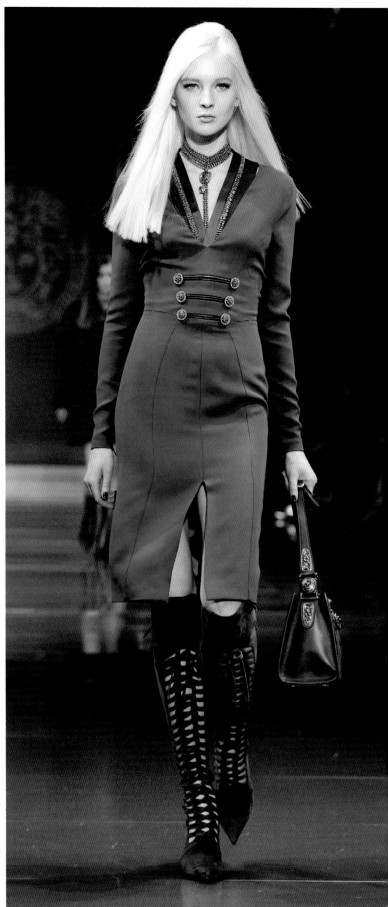

# Military Dress

The crisp tailoring, hussar braid and piping, epaulettes, coats of arms and the "bellows" pockets of military uniforms have continuously been incorporated into civilian dress, including haute couture, particularly at times of conflict. During the Napoleonic Wars between France and England, the pelisse – originally worn by hussar mercenaries of Hungary in the seventeenth century – was in use throughout most armies in Europe in the nineteenth century. A short and extremely tight-fitting jacket, the pelisse was decorated with patterns sewn in bullion lace, with several rows of parallel frogging and loops, and rows of either three or five lines of buttons. Features such as the tight fit across the upper body, cropped waistline, frog closures and braid trim were then applied to women's fashions, with fur trimmings becoming particularly popular following Napoleon's defeat in Prussia of 1806. Frogging, loops and lanyards also supplied the trimmings for Donna Versace's Autumn/Winter collection of 2014–15, a series of bias-cut dresses in the typical military colours of blue, red and gold.

Military-inspired fashion not only incorporates the decorative details of military uniform, but also its functionality. The Autumn/Winter 2010–11 collection of Burberry Prorsum included a range of aviator-inspired shearlings, military-drab overcoats and leather strap and buckle details on a series of khaki-coloured zipped and draped dresses. Khaki – from the Persian word *khak*, meaning dust, earth or mud – was first used officially for uniforms by British troops during the nineteenth century, and consists of a subtle mix of green and brown.

Camouflage, the pattern used by military defence to disguise personnel and equipment and derived from the French word *camoufler*, meaning to "blind or veil" (the term was first used in the *London Daily News*, May 25, 1917), was a technique borrowed from the patterned skins of animals which rendered them inconspicuous to their predators. The colouring of many animals varies in depth, being darker on the back and lighter underneath; this variation breaks up the surface of the creature and obscures its position. Pop artist Andy Warhol is often credited with the introduction of camouflage print into high fashion. His colourful prints paved the way for designers such as New York-based Stephen Sprouse, who was given permission to use one of Warhol's "Camouflage" screen prints for his Autumn/Winter 1987–8 and Spring 1988 collections. Later in 2000, Jean Paul Gaultier made a couture collection of ballgowns from camo-printed silk tulle.

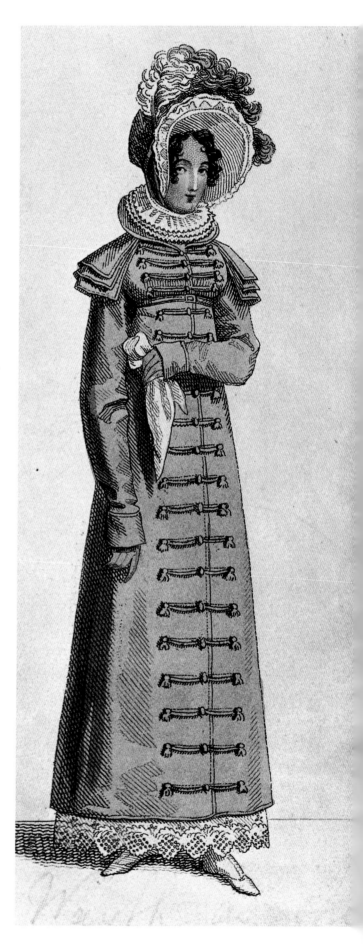

**OPPOSITE LEFT:** Constructed from a figure-forming dense rib jersey in black and olive drab, the long, lean lines of the military-inspired dress by Victoria Beckham (1974–) for A/W 2012–13 feature epaulettes, flapped pockets with brass buttons and a double leather belt.

**OPPOSITE RIGHT:** Capturing a mid-1960s mood, when the youth of "Swinging London" appropriated vintage military uniforms, Donatella Versace (1955–) incorporates petrol blue and scarlet with outsize trimmings in a tailored pastiche of toy-town soldiers.

**RIGHT:** Featured in a fashion plate dating from 1818, the coat adheres to the tight-fitting lines of the military uniform of the hussars, together with the parallel rows of frogging and loops. It also adopts the multi-caped sleeves of men's riding dress.

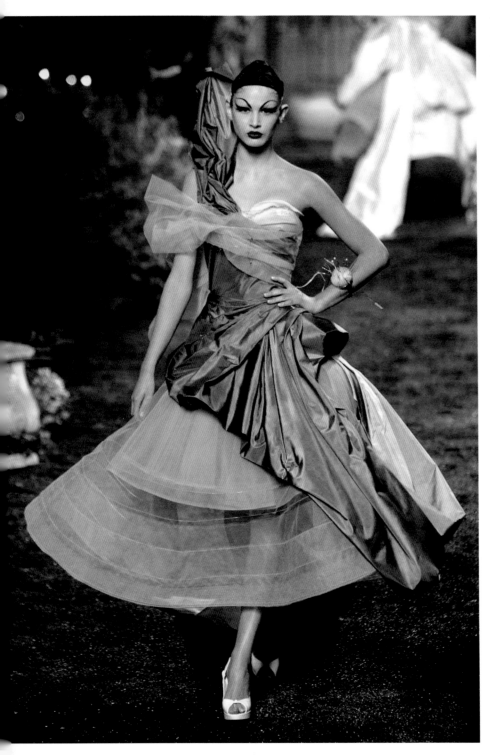

# The Colour Mauve

When Queen Victoria wore a mauve velvet dress to the wedding of her eldest daughter Vicky in 1858, she was marking the introduction of a radical change in the development of textile dyes. Her appearance in the colour created a universal desire for "Queen's lilac", as it became known, stimulating a widespread interest in the various shades of purple. By 1859, mauve was one of the most fashionable colours to be worn both sides of the Atlantic. The influential leader of fashion, Empress Eugénie, wife of Napoleon III, wore the new *couleur mauve* because she thought it matched her eyes. The popularity of the colour was such that in 1859 the satirical magazine *Punch* described its effect as "the mauve measles".

The glandular mucus of molluscs had previously been used to create the colour known as Tyrian purple, an arduous process that restricted its use to robes of royalty. With the development of aniline dyes, man-made from coal, and an accidental discovery by chemist William Perkin in 1856, mauveine became available for mass consumption. Named after the French word for the brightly coloured mallow flower, playwright and aesthete Oscar Wilde described the colour as "pink pretending to be purple". Mauve was followed by magenta, developed by Frenchman François-Emmanuel Verguin. Other synthetic dyes included Lyons blue, methyl green in 1872 and, in 1878, a new strong red appeared that was to rival cochineal. The vividness of the colours produced by the new synthetic dyes was criticized as crude by the cultural critics of the day, believing that the democratization of colour resulted in deteriorating public taste. The 1890s became known as the "Mauve Decade" or the "Gilded Age", characterized by its social prosperity, and aniline purple became the perfect signifier for both radical and artistically inclined dressers. The shade became associated with the flaunting of social norms, specifically with decadent art and homosexuality – which was symbolized by lavender in the 1950s.

Various depths of the colour, from palest lilac to deepest purple, have intermittently appeared in contemporary fashion, although during the twentieth century the deeper tones of mauve were considered matronly, with connotations of blue-rinsed hair and twinsets. Much fresher and more youthful, lilac is usually partnered with turquoise, lemon, pale blue and pink in a summer palette of pastels, as seen in John Galliano's Resort collection for Christian Dior Haute Couture 2011.

**ABOVE:** John Galliano for Christian Dior's Haute Couture A/W 2005–6 collection references the decadent luxury of the *fin de siècle* and the "Mauve Decade", with sculptural swags of mauve silk taffeta threaded through a corseted bodice of pale gold tulle.

**OPPOSITE:** Before 1856, purple and lilac ribbons were deemed appropriate for mourning, but mauve soon became fashionable, as shown in the 1859 portrait of Countess Alexander Nikolaevitch Lamsdorff by Franz Xaver Winterhalter, just three years after the invention of the chemical dye.

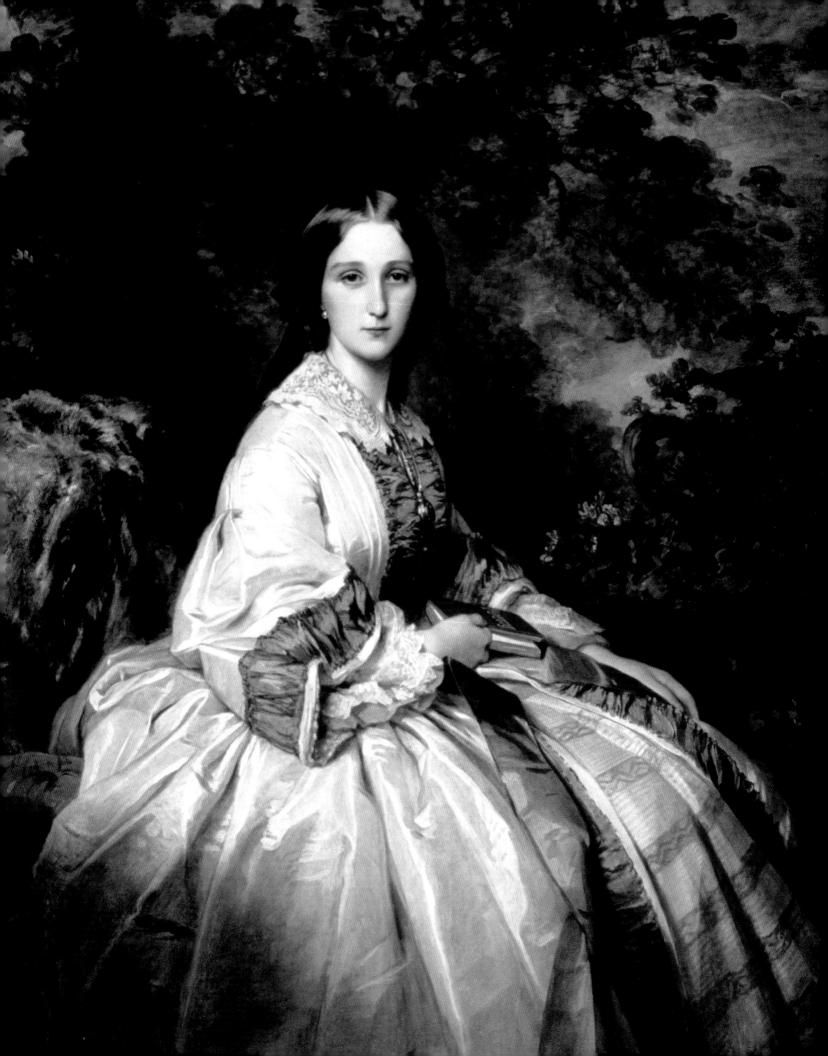

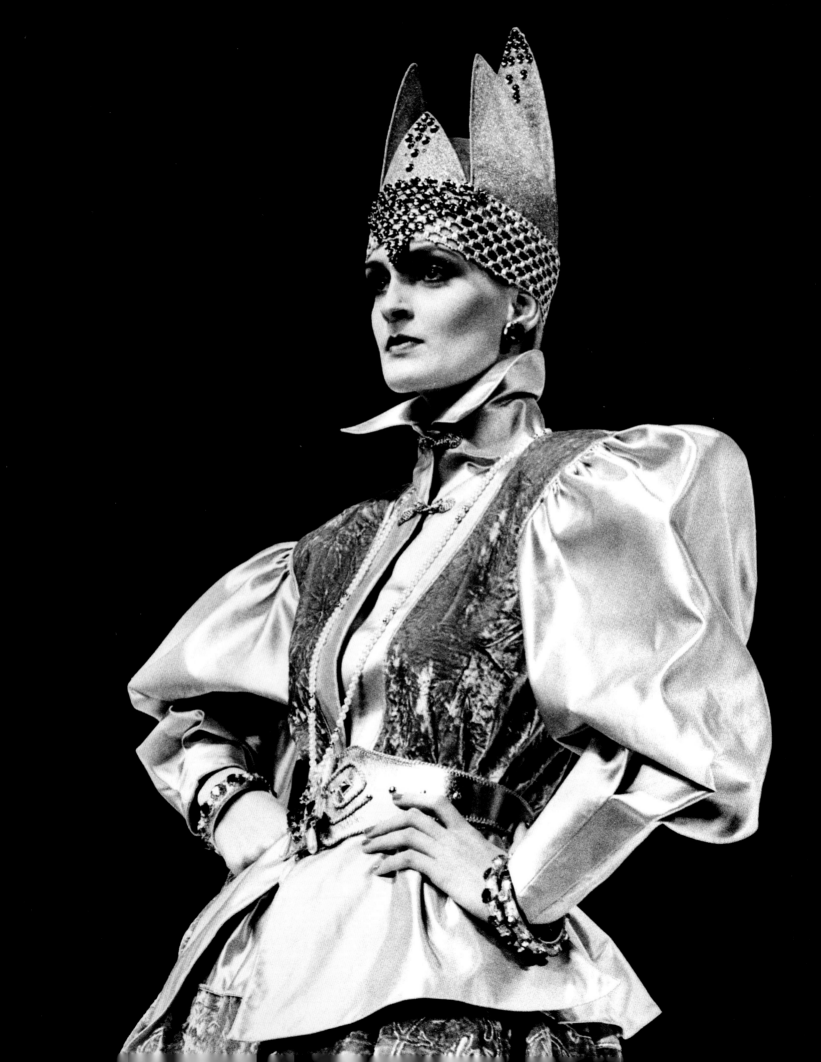

# The Peplum

Whenever the fashion silhouette marks the indentation of the waist, the peplum makes an appearance. With its origins in the Greek word *peplos* (meaning shawl), the peplum is a flared piece of fabric attached to the waist of a jacket, bodice or the waistband of a skirt, creating the illusion of a hand-span waist by adding volume to the hips. During the 1930s, the peplum consisted of draped swathes of horizontal or asymmetrical fabric, or featured handkerchief points in keeping with the influence of Art Deco and the era's streamlined yet feminine silhouette. By 1947 and the return of the hourglass figure, following the masculine-inspired narrow-hipped line of World War II, the peplum became more pronounced. Christian Dior's New Look featured a stiffened peplum on the skirt of the Le Bar jacket, a directional detail that was taken up by others, including British-born couturier Edward Molyneux, who introduced it into the newly fashionable cocktail dress. During the 1980s, the width of the peplum was balanced by the extreme width of the shoulders, as seen in the hard-edged Parisian power dressing initially introduced by Paris-based designer Claude Montana. Fellow Parisian Thierry Mugler also created fiercely aggressive silhouettes for his powerfully sexual images of Amazonian women, where the peplum is formed by extending the corset outwards from the waist.

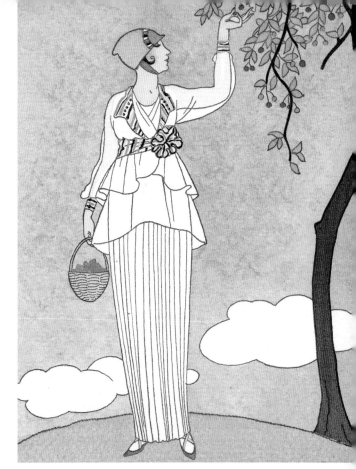

The structured outline in unyielding fabrics such as duchesse satin and leather promulgated by both designers formed a reverse triangle, with the exaggerated shoulders further emphasized by outsize collars, tapering down to a narrow, figure-hugging pencil skirt, interrupted only by the waist-defining peplum. This aggressive tailoring was disseminated by the American TV cult series *Dallas* and *Dynasty*, which featured British-born actress Joan Collins as über-bitch Alexis Colby in a succession of show-stopping outfits designed by American designer Nolan Miller.

Discarded during the minimalism of the 1990s, in the twenty-first century the peplum has undergone a reappraisal by contemporary designers. Flared, ruffled, gathered, pleated or fashioned into a fishtail, the peplum has appeared on the runway of a number of designers, including London-based designer David Koma. He presented a variety of peplum dresses in a collection for Spring/Summer 2012, some created in classically inspired pleated white leather, others fringed like a gladiatorial skirt. A collaboration with jewellery designer Sarah Angold included a peplum highlighted with shards of three-dimensional beading in iridescent Perspex discs.

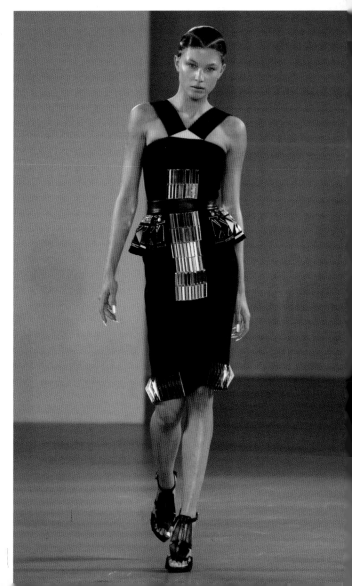

**OPPOSITE:** Epitomizing the exaggerated silhouette of the early 1980s, an extreme peplum by French designer Claude Montana (1949–) was matched to an excessive shoulder width, creating a small waist, further emphasized by a broad metallic leather belt.

**ABOVE RIGHT:** The forerunner of the fashion magazine, the influential *La Gazette du Bon Ton*, first launched in 1912, features a *pochoir* plate – a hand-stencilled print – of a dress by British designer John Redfern, similar in silhouette to Paul Poiret's "lampshade" dress (*see page* 94).

**RIGHT:** Shards of transparent plastic interrupt the silhouette of a second-skin dress designed by David Koma (David Komakhidze), born in Georgia but now based in London. The beading in iridescent Perspex discs is the result of a collaboration with jewellery designer Sarah Angold.

# The Empire Line

A perennial favourite of designers, the elongated line, high waist and columnar silhouette of the Empire line has long represented an informal simplicity, from the daring version that dominated fashion from 1780 to the 1820s to its implication of ingénue charm in the 1960s. The whalebone and hoops of "armoured" dress for women were discarded, along with rich materials, for the relative freedom afforded by the high-waisted chemise, which was inspired by the civilian dress of antiquity. It first gained widespread appeal from the fashions of Empress Joséphine and the Napoleonic court with its connotations of republicanism and democracy, embodied in copies of Greek and Roman draped costume. Named after the First Empire, when Napoleon Bonaparte crowned himself Emperor in 1804, the gown was known as *à la greque* in court. In England the style was termed "Regency", coinciding with the Regency of the Prince of Wales from 1811 to 1820. In women's dress, attention gradually rose from the waist towards the breasts, with a shortened bodice overlaid with a broad sash. Without gathers in front, fullness was confined to the back of the dress, with gathers attaching the back of the skirt to the bodice, which at its most extreme stopped short at the armpits. A small pad was attached to the waist, with tapes beneath the dress at the back to sustain the vertical line. Fluid materials, such as imported Indian white muslin, were used in several layers to give substance to the silhouette. Attention was drawn to the upper arms with the use of frilled scarves, tied crossways across the bust. As England and France were at war during this period, the English Empire style

**RIGHT:** An engraving of Empress Joséphine in her robes for the Coronation festivities on December 2, 1804. The Empire line was first seen at the Coronation, when the Empress and her ladies wore dresses designed by the court painter Jean-Baptiste Isabey but made by the dressmaker Leroy, previously the hairdresser to Marie Antoinette.

**OPPOSITE:** An illustration of Empress Joséphine at the Château de Fontainebleau, Seine-et-Marne, France, in 1808 by Baron François Pascal Simon Gérard (1770–1837). The tight-fitting sleeves topped with a short puffed shoulder were a common feature of the "classical" line.

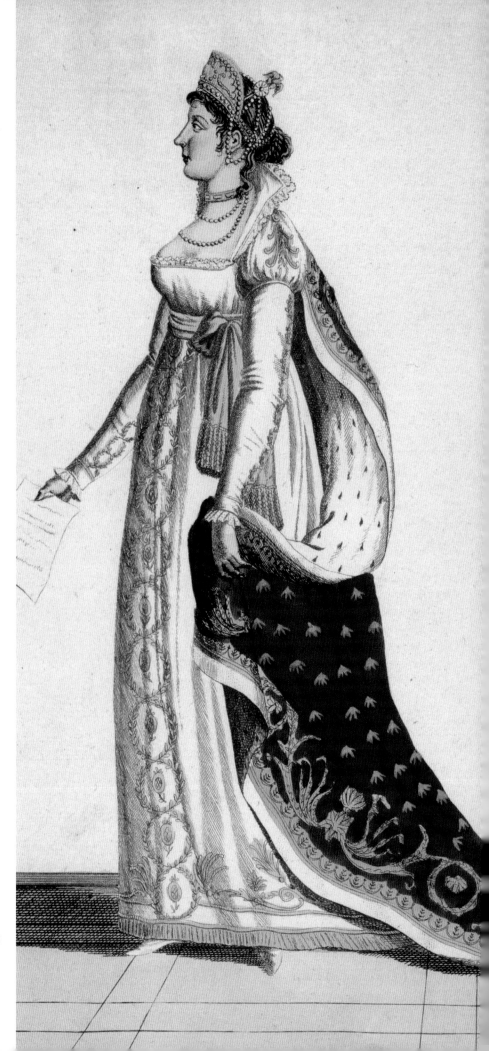

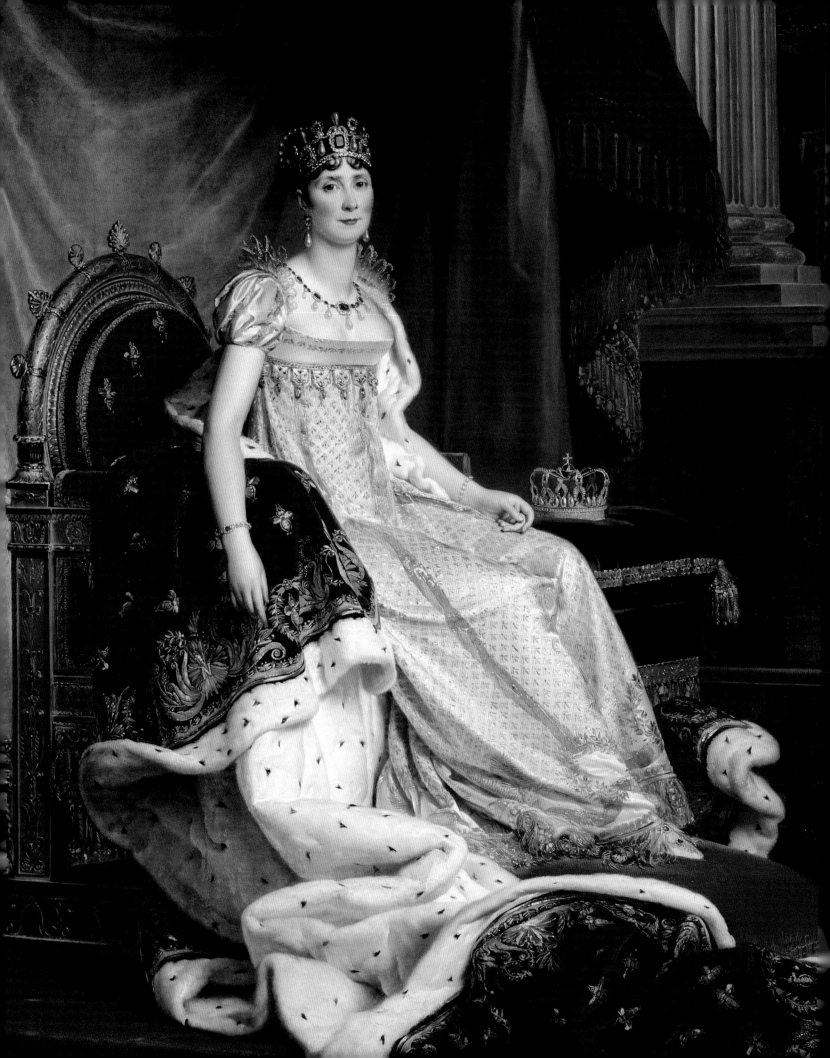

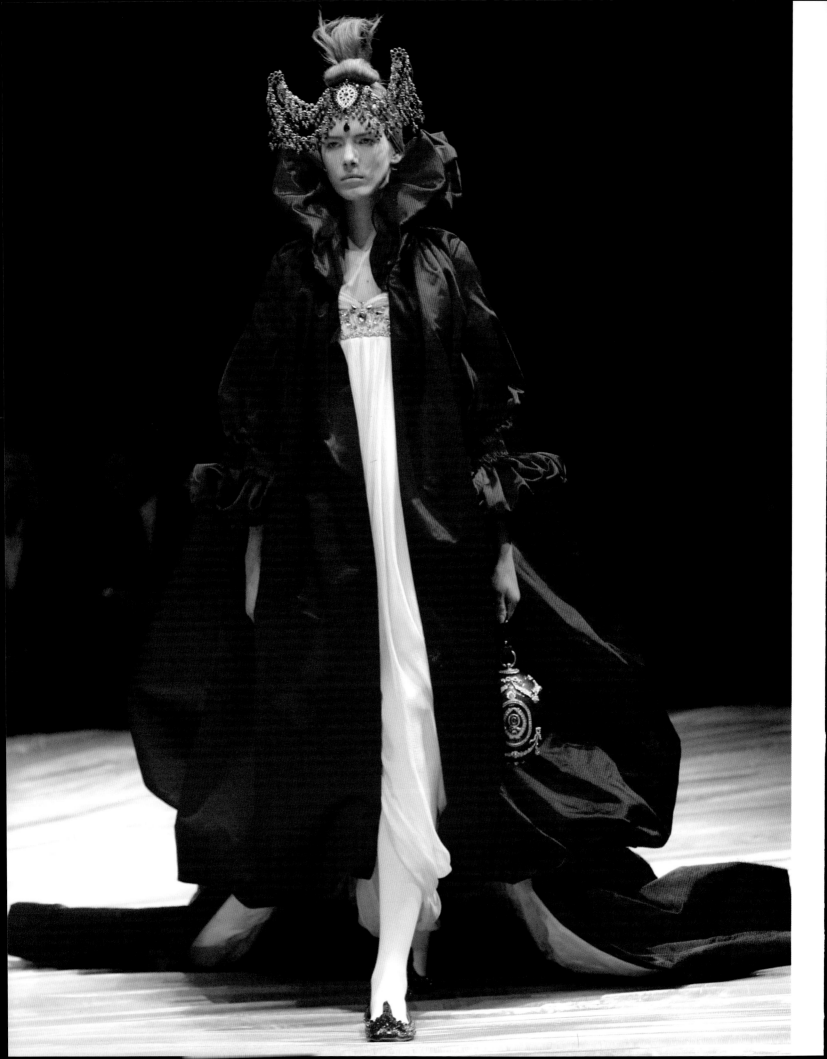

was overlaid with elements of Romanticism and the picaresque, such as puffed and slashed Elizabethan-style sleeves.

Unsupported columns of fabric falling from a high waist reappeared in the 1960s, seen in opulent eveningwear, wedding gowns and daywear. Chief exponent of the Empire line, British designer John Bates, elevated the waistline in a series of softly constructed dresses that featured a bra-top bodice with a floating chiffon skirt attached, also a signature of the designer. These were often embellished with minute faux flowers, and the high waist decorated with a loose, chiffon bow. A slight raising of the waist gives the appearance of longer legs, a device adopted by Catherine, Duchess of Cambridge, for many of her bespoke tailored outfits and eveningwear.

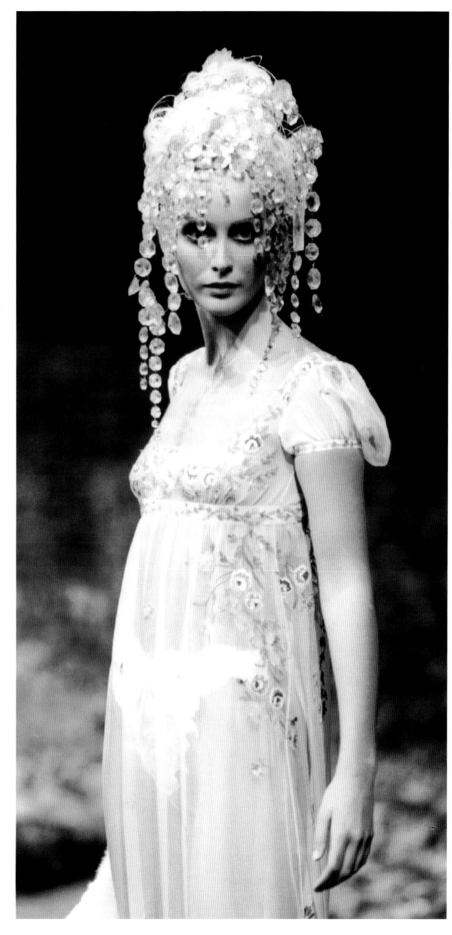

**OPPOSITE:** Based on the fantasy of a young girl emerging from a tree to meet and marry a prince, Alexander McQueen's "The Girl Who Lived in a Tree" collection from A/W 2008–9 incorporates an ingénue Empire-line dress worn beneath an imperial scarlet cloak in duchesse satin, accessorized with a lantern and pagoda hat.

**RIGHT:** Long inspired by the fashions of the eighteenth century since his post-graduate collection "Les Incroyables", John Galliano referenced the Napoleonic and Regency periods for his 1996 collection, while creative director of couture house Givenchy, with this transparent gown worn over a *cache-sexe* in lace.

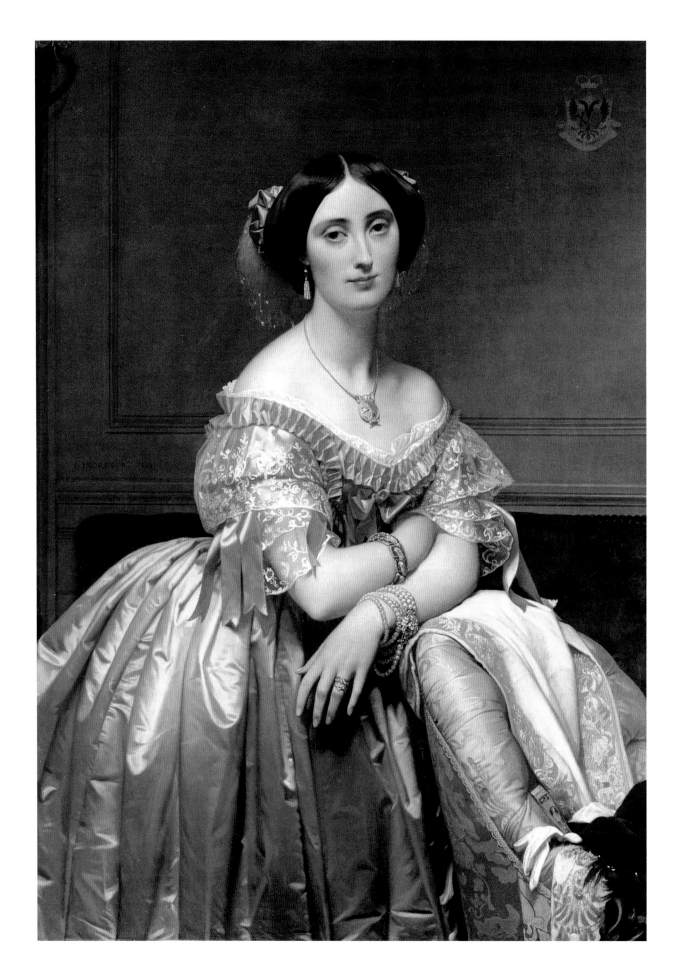

# The Second Empire

In England, the crinoline became associated with the confined lives of the housebound woman and notions of propriety in her role as the "Angel in the House", the protagonist of Coventry Patmore's poem idealizing Victorian womanhood. In contrast, the expansionist tendencies of the crinoline in France, and the period in which it reached its greatest circumference, were directly related to the extravagance of the Second Empire, the regime of Napoleon III, which lasted from 1852 to 1870, a time of material prosperity and licentiousness also known as the "Golden Age".

The lavish and luxurious confections of couturier Charles Frederick Worth came to represent the opulence of the era. He first came to the attention of the French court through the patronage of Princess Metternich, the wife of the Austrian ambassador to Paris, and by 1860 the couturier was responsible for dressing Empress Eugénie, wife of Napoleon III, and her court for the many formal state occasions, as well as designing her evening gowns for the frequent social gatherings. In a reciprocal arrangement, Worth's opulent gowns, featuring swathes of fabrics and trimmings, tied in with the Empress's remit from Napoleon to promote the then-ailing French textile industry, particularly the silk mills of Lyon. Worth's international reputation for clothing the fashionable elite was disseminated by the artist Franz Xaver Winterhalter, the chief portraitist of the Imperial family and the French court. His portrait of Elisabeth of Austria (1837–98), the wife of Franz Joseph I, describes the deep décolleté and extreme tight lacing typical of an era in which the *Grandes Horizontales*, or courtesans, such as Cora Pearl, lover of Napoleon, represented the decadent demi-monde of the Second Empire.

Extreme silhouettes, opulent fabrics and lavish trimmings are the prerogative of those contemporary designers who deploy artisanal virtuosity with the theatricality of historical revivalism, a combination exemplified by British designer John Galliano. For his acclaimed Spring/Summer collection of 1994, Galliano created the fictional Princess Lucretia, fleeing from Russia to Paris at the time of the Second Empire. The designer interprets the loucheness of the period with the *déshabillé* bodice and deconstructed outsize crinoline, which he juxtaposes with exemplary tailoring, as the heroine of his story pursues her life among the demi-monde.

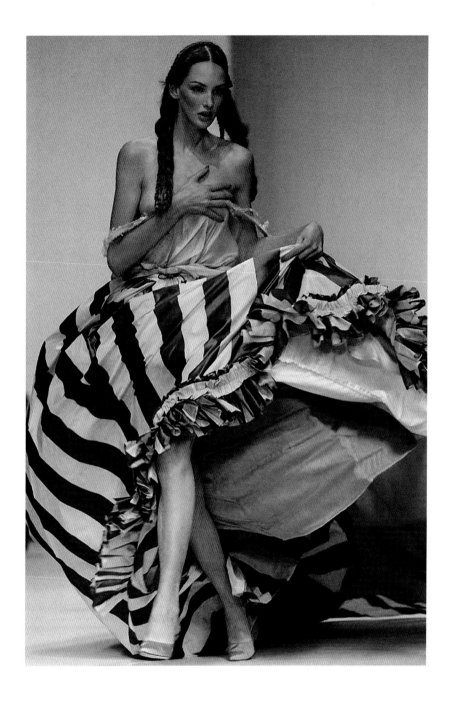

**OPPOSITE:** A member of the upper echelons of the Second Empire, Joséphine-Eléonore-Marie-Pauline de Galard de Brassac de Béarn, Princesse de Broglie, was renowned for her great beauty. French painter Ingres (1780–1867) renders in exquisite detail the fine lace and rich satin of her gown and her elaborate jewellery.

**ABOVE:** Using the catwalk as theatre, John Galliano, consummate conveyer of a dramatic narrative, described the flight of a fictional Princess Lucretia for his S/S 1994 collection, shown in Paris. The extravagantly engineered crinolines were supported by collapsible telephone cables.

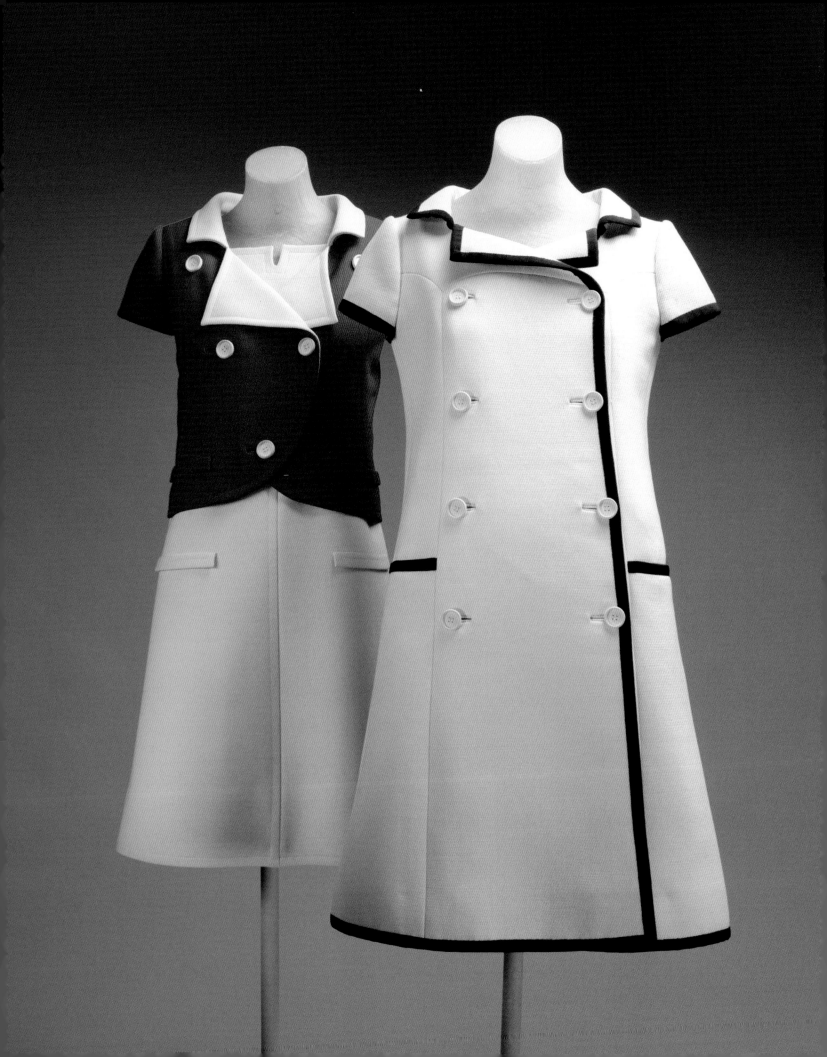

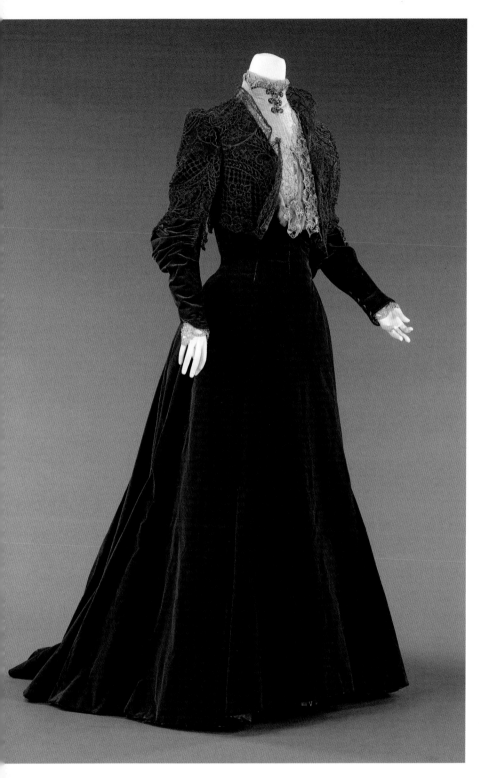

# The Princess Line

The crinoline was rendered obsolete when Charles Frederick Worth, founder of the first *maison de la couture*, introduced his renowned Princess line. In his commanding role he was largely influential in determining the changing nineteenth-century silhouettes, and the Princess line was a significant departure from the prevailing garment construction, where the bodice of the dress was sewn to the skirt by the means of a seam at the waist. Reputedly named for Alexandra, Princess of Wales, the fashion-conscious queen consort of King Edward VII of England and one of his most influential clients, the innovative silhouette was introduced by Worth in the early 1870s. Skirts were initially cut into gores, triangular pieces of cloth sewn together vertically to provide volume at the hem while retaining smoothness over the hips. It was a simple step for the gores to be extended to the shoulders in shaped panels, incorporating the bust darts and skimming past the waist. This resulted in an elongated line and a moulded, close-fitting bodice, creating a similar silhouette to that of the tight-fitting *cuirasse* bodice, a garment that had gradually been increasing in length, and which by 1878 reached the thighs. The two ideas subsequently merged and, with the dispensing of the horizontal waist seam, shaping was provided by shoulder-to-hem panels. The Princess line came in a variety of styles, including the polonaise (a looped overskirt, *see page* 39), a nostalgic reference to the fashions of the seventeenth century.

The Princess line has evolved into a versatile method of shaping the garment to the body, with the potential for either fluidity or stiffness and structure, depending on the fabric used. As all shaping darts at bust and waist are dispensed with, the result is a modern, streamlined silhouette. Pauline Trigère, pioneer of high-end ready-to-wear in mid-century America, manipulated the vertical shoulder-to-hem seams to create a form-fitting sculpted coat. During the 1960s, the Princess line became less curvilinear and evolved into a looser-fitting, narrow high-waisted style, with flare added to the seams at the hem to create an easy-to-wear A-line. This is seen in the architectonic and strict tailoring of Parisian futurist André Courrèges, who also incorporated vertical pockets into the seams.

**OPPOSITE:** In contrast to the fluid lines of Worth's innovative princess line, the futuristic coat dress designed by André Courrèges (1923–) is sculpted into shape with the use of densely woven fabrics that emphasize the vertical seaming of the garment.

**ABOVE:** Charles Frederick Worth frequently experimented with two-dimensional pattern cutting rather than draping on a mannequin, and one of his most lasting contributions was the vertical-seamed Princess line, as seen in this 1889 grey silk velvet afternoon dress.

# Maternity Dress

Maternity-wear as a commercially viable niche in the fashion market was prompted by the late twentieth-century interest in celebrity pregnancy and the introduction of stretch into fabrics, when women no longer tried to hide or disguise their pregnancy but celebrated their burgeoning curves. Long associated by default with female sexuality, pregnant mothers in the past attempted to conceal their pregnancy or even disappeared from public view for a period of "confinement". Unlike the poor, who made do with their everyday clothes, the fashionable elite has always accommodated its expanding silhouette with adjustments to the prevailing style of the era, ever since the French-inspired emphasis on contour and cut in the fourteenth century, which replaced the loose T-shaped *cotte* (tunic). Although cut to accommodate a late pregnancy, the voluminous Adrienne dress, the first recorded maternity gown, evidenced all the opulence and heavy ornamentation of the sixteenth-century Renaissance period, and maternity-wear over the following centuries was simply a matter of loosening the stays or corsets.

One of the most characteristic garments worn by pregnant women was a long apron tied over the clothing under the breasts and covering the abdomen, a custom that continued into the eighteenth century. The high-waisted, uncorseted styles of the early nineteenth century were usually fitted to the upper body with drawstrings, and the absence of a natural waistline made it easy to adapt the dress to accommodate the changing circumference of the female body. The late nineteenth-century propensity for disguising bodily functions – in spite of Queen Victoria's prolific fecundity – resulted in maternity clothing that was tailored to hide a pregnancy. The same diffidence continued throughout the early twentieth century, until Lucille Ball made television history in 1952 by being the first woman to show off a pregnancy onscreen despite the word "pregnant" being banned on air. The actress assumed the popular tent-like smocks on screen in *I Love Lucy*, cropped at mid-thigh and with neck details such as outsize bows to distract the eye from the "bump".

Presidential First Lady Jackie Kennedy set the paradigm for discreet *enceinte* style in 1960 with her customary predilection for simple, structured shift dresses and boxy suit jackets that bypassed her burgeoning silhouette without additional volume. In the 1990s, a number of labels tapped into the specialist market by offering body-conscious dresses that wrapped, draped and exposed the pregnancy silhouette. However, the fashion-led contemporary mother-to-be no longer buys solely maternity-wear, but adapts her existing wardrobe and wears dresses bought from non-maternity shops.

**BELOW LEFT:** Described by Marylin Bender in her book *The Beautiful People* (1968) as "the first pop fashion goddess", America's First Lady Jacqueline Kennedy continued to purvey her pared-down, discreet style of a columnar silhouette in textured fabrics throughout her burgeoning pregnancy.

**OPPOSITE:** One of the "pregnancy" portraits popular during this era, *Portrait of an Unknown Lady*, attributed to the Flemish-born Marcus Gheeraerts and painted in 1595, features a heavily pregnant woman adorned in pearls – an attribute of the virgin martyr Saint Margaret of Antioch, the patron saint of childbirth.

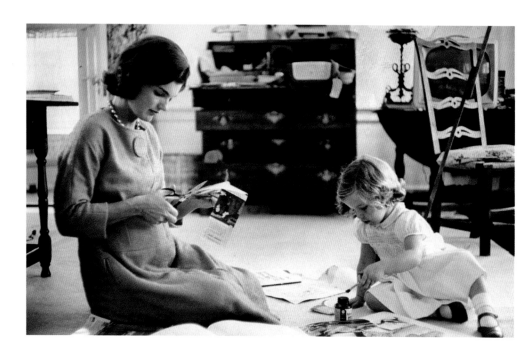

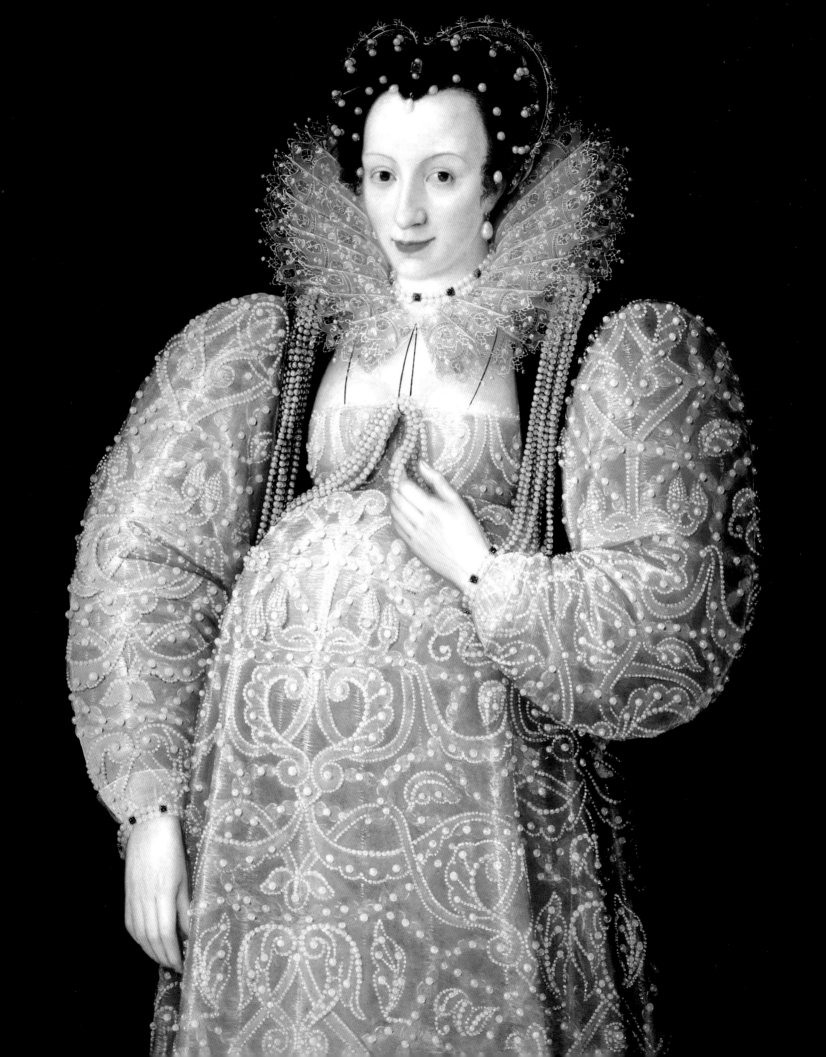

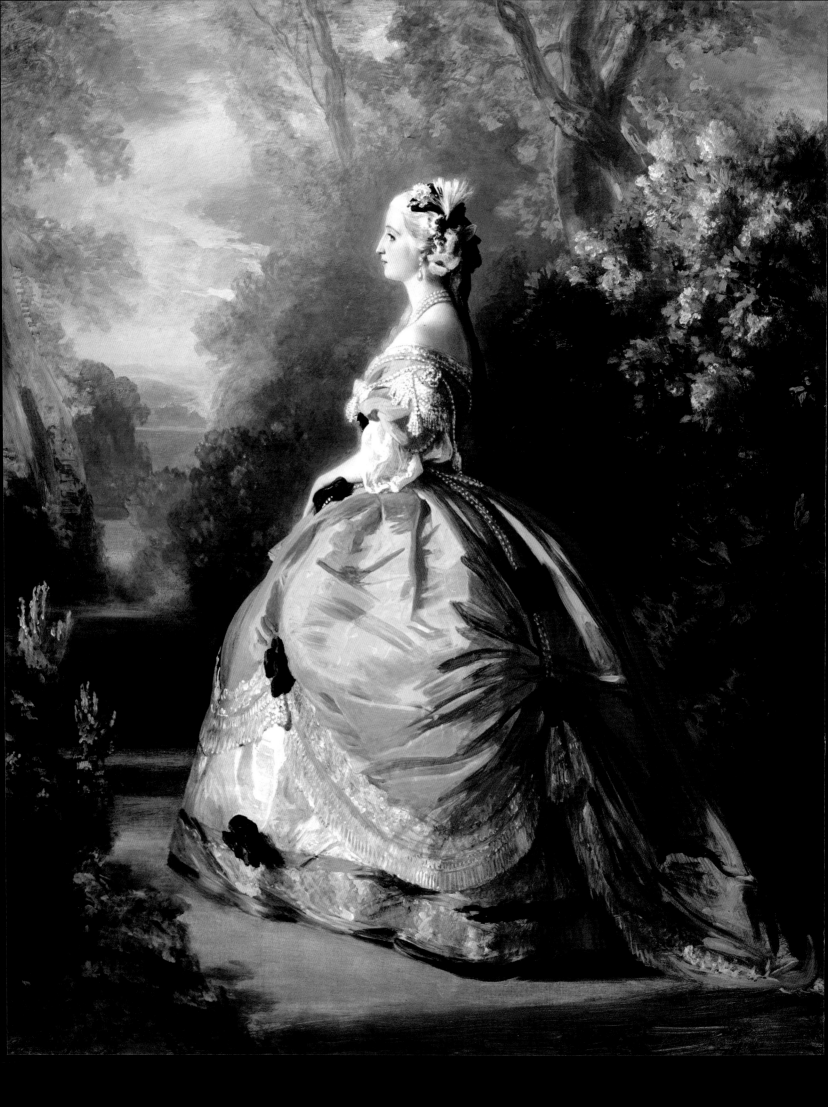

# The Crinoline

Numerous ways have been used throughout fashion history to extend the circumference of the female skirt, including the farthingale in the sixteenth century, hoops in the eighteenth century and, in the nineteenth century, the crinoline. The fullness of the skirt in the Victorian period was first supported by stuffed pads and numerous petticoats stiffened with horsehair (*crin* in French) until in 1856 the first cage crinoline appeared, dispensing with the need for heavy, unhygienic and cumbersome layers of petticoats. The steel crinoline was patented by C. Amet in Britain in 1856, consisting of concentric flexible fabric-covered steel hoops that allowed the crinoline its characteristic dip, sway and tip with movement. The circumference of the skirt – up to six feet – distanced the wearer from personal contact and rendered the woman almost immobilized by its lavish layers and heavy trimmings. As respectable femininity increasingly came to be associated with pliancy, dependency and the narrowly defined world of home, the crinoline became ever larger, reaching its apotheosis in 1859. The silhouette now formed two triangles, with an indented, tightly corseted waist in the centre, with fullness at the bosom and hips. This set the paradigm for the hourglass feminine ideal and represented the embodiment of the fairytale princess – the crinoline remains the favoured silhouette of the white wedding dress. The late Queen Elizabeth The Queen Mother secured her place in the nation's heart when she embarked on a state visit to France with a wardrobe of "Winterhalter" crinolines in 1938 designed by court dressmaker Norman Hartnell, a style from which she never deviated.

The attempt to reprise the crinoline in the late 1930s was interrupted by the exigencies of wartime clothing and only remerged with Christian Dior's New Look in 1947 and with New York-based couturier Charles James. The American couturier achieved cult status with his engineered gowns based on the cage crinoline, which he produced between the years 1947 and 1954, particularly the Four-leaf Clover ballgown, which featured an asymmetrical bodice designed to support the voluminous and undulating overskirt and thereby distribute its great weight. Contemporary avant-garde designers continue to play with the proportions and structure of the crinoline, as seen in Vivienne Westwood's "Mini Crini" collections of 1985 and 1987, and Japanese designer Rei Kawakubo for her label Comme des Garçons, where the crinoline is constructed outside the garment as a form of exoskeleton.

**ABOVE:** In opposition to the power dressing of the time, and supported by meticulous historical research, Vivienne Westwood first introduced the "Mini Crini" collection in 1985. It featured abbreviated nineteenth-century-style hooped crinolines with a structured boned bodice, which were worn with rocking-horse platform shoes.

**OPPOSITE:** *The Empress Eugénie*, painted by Franz Xaver Winterhalter in 1854, shows the wife of Napoleon III walking in the Tuileries. Her skirt is in the style of Queen Marie Antoinette, shaped by a crinoline petticoat and stiffened with a combination of horsehair and flax. Her elegance and style were an inspiration to the French fashion industry, but it was not until 1860 that she became a patron of the newly established couturier Charles Frederick Worth. The cage crinoline removed the necessity for layers of petticoat and provided a frame that gave lightness and movement to the costume, and the Empress was one of its great advocates. By 1865 Worth, who disliked the overblown silhouette of the crinoline – sometimes as wide in circumference as the woman was tall – introduced the flat-fronted style.

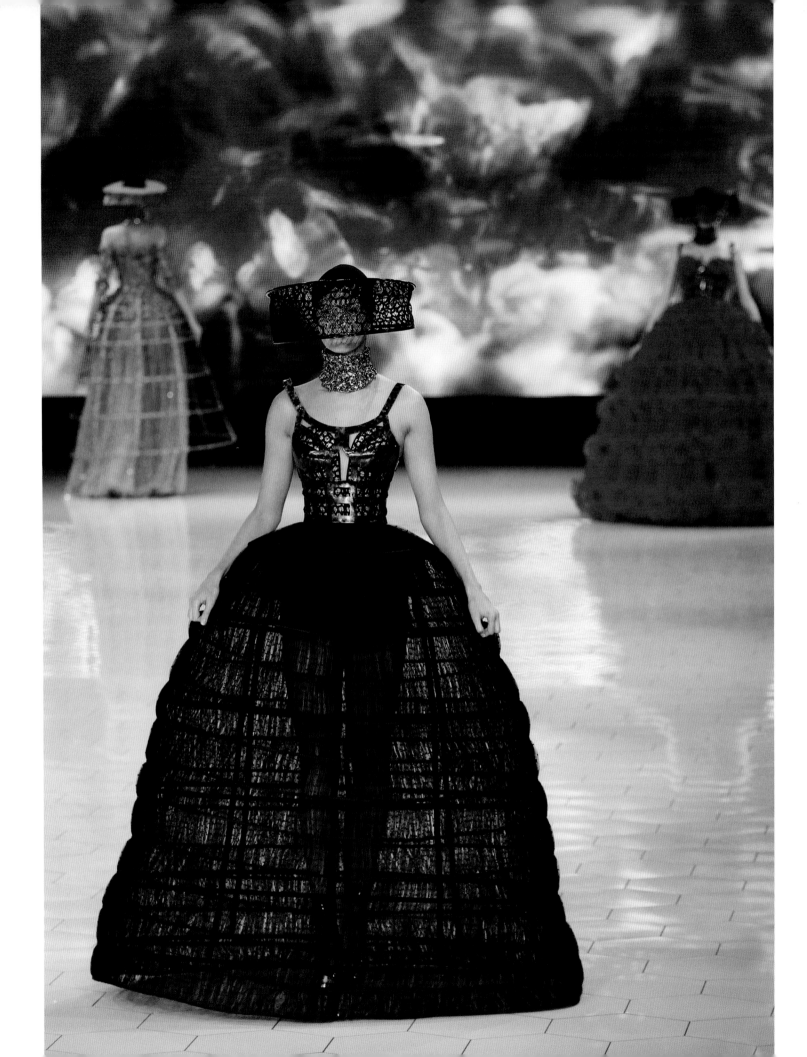

**OPPOSITE:** Sarah Burton, creative director of Alexander McQueen, presented a collection for S/S 2013 based on the theme of bees. The final section featured cage-crinoline-style overlayers and this black silk, hooped, dome-shape skirt and imitation tortoiseshell harness.

**RIGHT:** Rather than supporting the weight of a skirt, the cage crinoline is left bereft of its outer layers to form an exoskeleton. Designed by Hiroshima-born Yohji Yamamoto (1943–) for A/W 2010–11, it is juxtaposed with an eighteenth- century-inspired scarlet redingote.

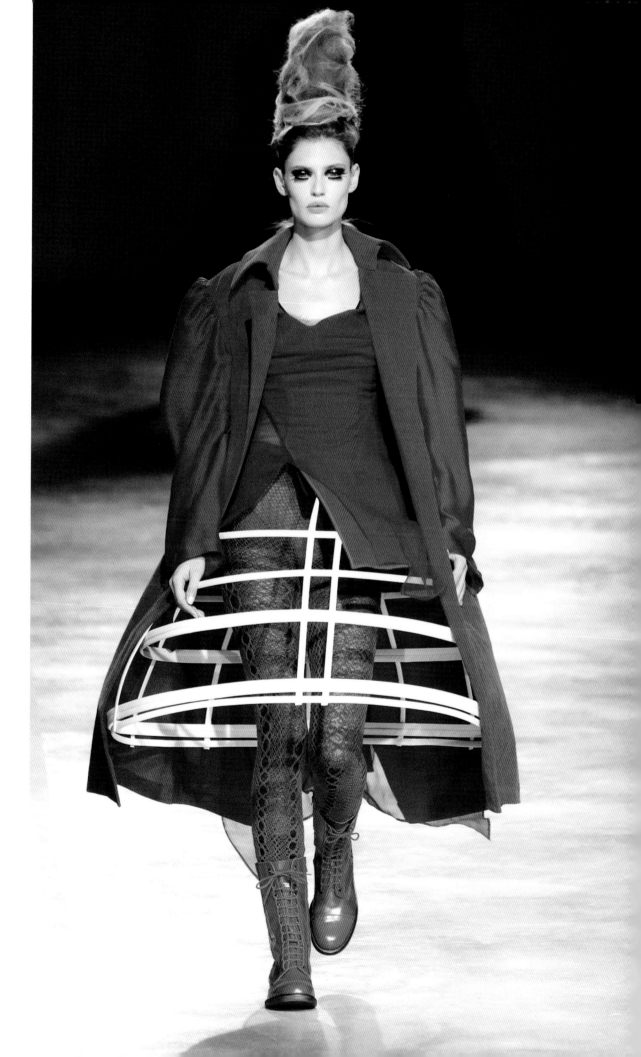

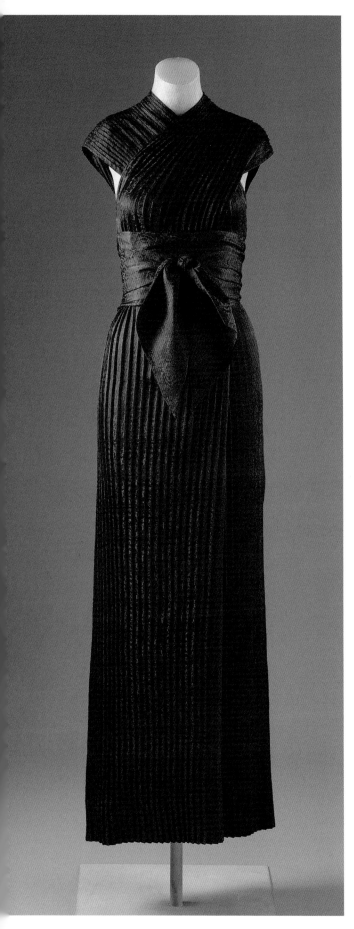

# The Pleated Dress

Pleats – a type of fold formed by doubling fabric back upon itself – alongside tucks and gathers, are just some of the many ways of manipulating fabric to add movement, structure and controlled volume to a garment. Working out of his workshop in Venice, the Spanish-born theatre designer, painter and couturier, Mariano Fortuny, created sculptural pleated fabrics from which he derived his Delphos dress, first introduced in 1909. Looking to classic Hellenic dress – the *chiton* and the *himation* (*see also pages* 12–13) – the gown was a ground-grazing column of finely pleated shimmering fabric created from rich vegetable dyes with lustrous gold pigments. Fortuny's early experimentations in classically influenced dress were originally designed to be worn as tea gowns, a style of at-home dress popular in the late nineteenth and early twentieth centuries, worn as an alternative to the silhouette accorded by the prevailing S-shaped corset. By the 1920s, Fortuny's Delphos and its variations were becoming acceptable for wear outside the home. Although Fortuny was unwilling to disclose his methods, it is probable that he created the pleated silk by loosely stitching the panels of fabric by hand across the width of the fabric, subsequently gathering up the thread to create a hank of fabric, which would then be set by passing it through heated ceramic rollers. The pleats had to be reset if they were flattened or dampened. It was not until the 1960s and the invention of the permanent press that pleats remained resistant to water and wear, a process patented by dress manufacturer Koret of California.

The use of pleated fabric dictates a pared-down, simple silhouette, seen in American designer Claire McCardell's evening gown, which evokes the Japanese kimono and features a crossover wrap bodice, cut high on the back of the neck and fastened with an obi-like sash. Subsequent textile experimentation by Japanese designer Issey Miyake led to the Pleats Please line, a combination of pliable architectural exoskeletons and innovative garment forms first launched in 1993. Made from single pieces of 100 per cent polyester fabric, the garments were first cut and sewn together two-and-a-half to three times larger than the finished piece. Individual pieces were then hand-fed into a heat press, sandwiched between two sheets of paper, to create permanent pleats. Vertical, horizontal and zigzag pleating was used to create varying effects that transcend the conventional parameters of fashion, allowing the behaviour of the patented fabrics to determine the forms of his garment collection.

**LEFT:** Finely pleated silk in Chinese red is simply wrapped around the body, creating a columnar silhouette, typical of the minimalist, practical approach to the manipulation of fabric by American designer Claire McCardell (1905–58). The pleated structure adds weight to the base fabric.

**OPPOSITE LEFT:** Issey Miyake has maintained his inventive Pleats Please range in the marketplace for an extraordinary three decades. In 1995 his Minaret variation, seen here, made the most of the innate architectural potential of his heat-treated polyester pleating, to form deceptively soft, spatial geometry.

**OPPOSITE RIGHT:** The languid drapery in marble seen in classical caryatid temple figures is readily recalled by the fluid heft of Mariano Fortuny's pleated silk Delphos series of dresses. When at rest, these dresses generate the columnar architectural impact of the ancient Greek precedent.

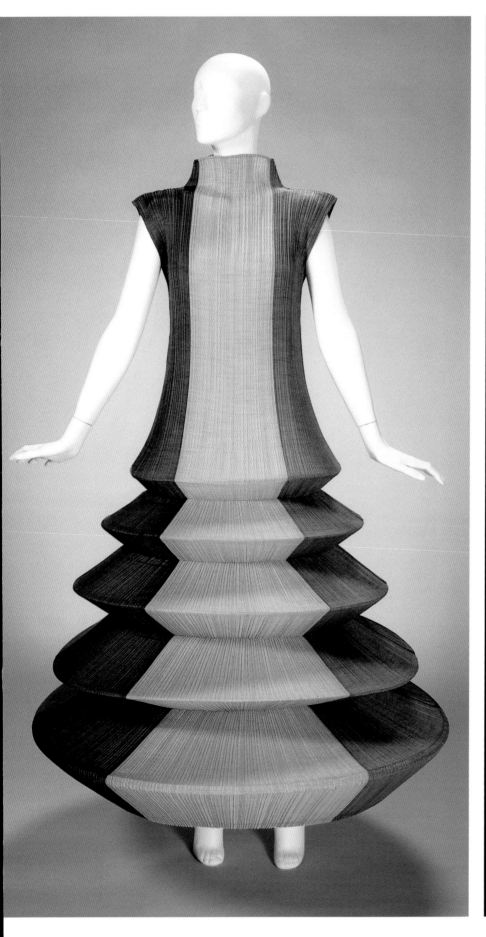

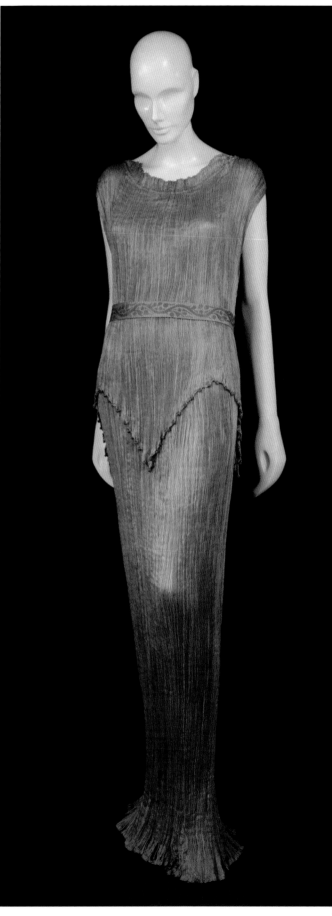

# Artistic Dress

The voluminous skirts and tight-laced corsets of the Victorian feminine ideal were challenged by the dress reformers in 1881 with the creation of the Rational Dress Society. Their edicts not only emphasized the deleterious effects on health of the corset but they also fulminated against the over-embellishment and perceived opulent vulgarity of the prevailing fashion. At the same time, a revolution was underway in the applied arts as a reaction to the ugliness of the Machine Age and mass-industrialization seen in the Great Exhibition of 1851, prompted in part by the Pre-Raphaelite Brotherhood, an artistic movement founded in 1848 by Dante Gabriel Rossetti, William Holman Hunt and John Everett Millais. Both movements contributed to an alternative way of dressing that was perceived as "artistic" – manifested in fashion by the wearing of loosely draped robes inspired by the medieval *bliaut*, an ankle-length gown of unpressed pleats caught low on the waist with a sash. The sleeves were also loosely fitting, often gathered into the sleeve head and embellished with smocking and attached from a deep arm scye to provide freedom of movement. Disseminating an alternative ideal of feminine beauty, this style of dress was adopted by those in literary and artistic circles, including the models and mistresses of the Pre-Raphaelite painters, among them Jane Morris and Lizzie Siddal, brooding and languid of pose, pale of complexion with undressed coils of lustrous hair massed in tones of deep red, conveying a sexually charged message in an era of Victorian prudery. The artistic dress of the 1860s became less popular in the 1870s, and evolved into the fashions of the Aesthetic Movement, which emphasized the importance of beauty in every aspect of life. Eschewing the newly developed aniline dyes of viridian green and mauve, colours were vegetable dyes of terracotta, cream, reds and blues, and a soft sage green known as "greenery yallery", a description thought to epitomize the pretentiousness of the style, which was much satirized by a series of cartoons by George du Maurier in *Punch* magazine. Any embellishment to the garments was craft-based, with a popular motif being the sunflower, the emblem of the aesthetes, along with the lily and peacock feathers. The influence of the Orient was also evident, prompted by a display of Japanese applied arts at the International Exhibition in London of 1862. This inspired a young Arthur Lasenby Liberty to open his own Oriental Emporium in 1875, importing fabrics popular with the artistic set, including James Whistler, George Frederick Watts and Lord Frederick Leighton.

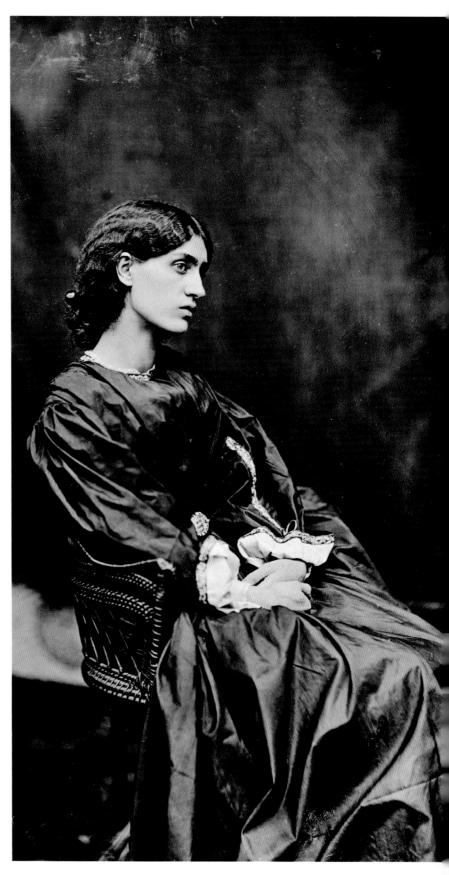

**OPPOSITE:** Jane Burden, the wife of William Morris and mistress and muse of Pre-Raphaelite painter Dante Gabriel Rossetti (1828–82), is captured in typically languid mood by the photographer John Robert Parsons in 1865, wearing an uncorseted dress – in sharp contrast to the constricted form of her Victorian peers.

**RIGHT:** Epitomizing fashionable ennui in the painting *Day Dream* (1880) by Dante Gabriel Rossetti, Jane Burden poses against a woodland background in a voluminous forest green robe, with a loosely draped bodice, representative of "artistic" dress.

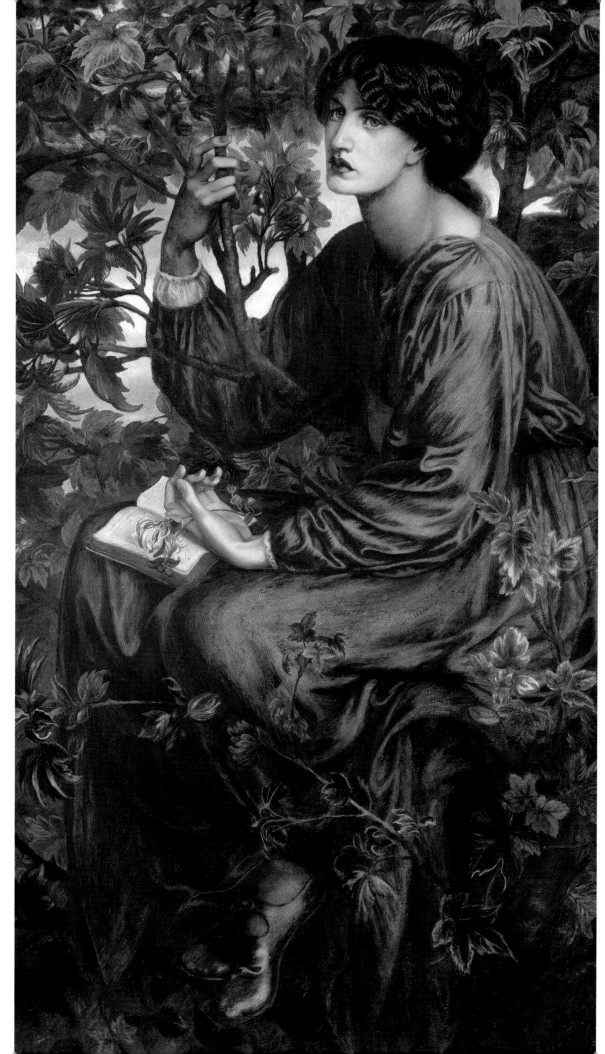

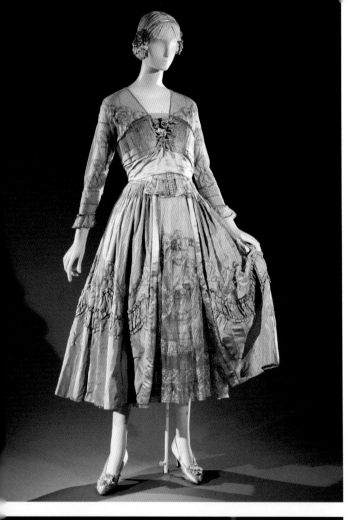

# The Tea Gown

In the 1870s, during the High Victorian period and the era of the tightly cinched waist, women abandoned the constraints of boned corsets and adopted *déshabillé* – the freedom of a semi-fitted or loose tea gown – to take part in the rising middle-class ritual of afternoon tea. Early tea gowns were a European development influenced by Asian clothing, and these were often made by combining "exotic" fabrics with elements of historical dress. By 1900 this more relaxed style of dressing evolved into daywear and was also worn for informal evening occasions outside the home with close friends. The emergence of the neo-Directoire line at the beginning of the twentieth century – a silhouette inspired by the columnar lines of the French Revolutionary period – consolidated the desire for a more free-flowing and fluid silhouette, epitomized by British court dressmaker Lucy, Lady Duff-Gordon (1863–1935). One of the first designers to abolish corsets and introduce the tea gown as acceptable daywear outside the home, she was a shrewd businesswoman and entrepreneur, opening Maison Lucile in 1894 in London's Old Burlington Street, before moving to Hanover Square in 1896. Here she instigated a version of the first catwalk show and held intimate "tea-time" salons. Although her clients included royalty and the British aristocracy, she also influenced the mass market with her diffusion lines, which were published in America's Sears-Roebuck catalogue. Her fashion columns in *Harper's Bazaar* and *Good Housekeeping* continued until the 1920s.

In the US, the tea gown was popularized by the American designer Jessie Franklin Turner (1881–*c*.1956), one of the first couturières of the twentieth century, who went on to play a prominent role in the development of the American high-fashion industry. Her signature tea gowns were based on non-Western garment construction, such as the rectangle, and featured rich embroidery and antique textiles. These were an early forerunner of late-twentieth-century kaftans adopted by the hippie counter-culture of the late 1960s, being fundamentally T-shaped garments incorporating non-Western fabrics and embellishments. The tea gown has also entered the fashion lexicon as the tea dress, an informal garment usually of soft, floating lines, which has consistently reappeared throughout the decades with slight mutations in hem length and fullness of skirt. Usually in a floral printed silk, the tea dress has appeared in the contemporary collections of Ralph Lauren and Bottega Veneta.

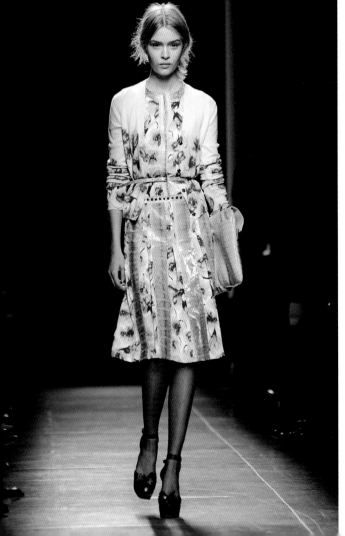

**ABOVE LEFT:** Designed by British court dressmaker Lucile – Lady Duff-Gordon – in 1915, the silk taffeta, tulle and chiffon tea gown represented a softer, uncorseted silhouette, a shorter, more practical hemline and a more relaxed approach to formal evening dressing.

**LEFT:** Inspired by the 1940s, the tea dress by German-born designer Tomas Maier (1957–) for Italian luxury label Bottega Veneta in S/S 2013 owes its retro styling to collaged flower prints on a fluid silk ground, partnered with a matching printed, edge-to-edge cardigan.

**RIGHT:** For relief from corsets, women in the 1870s began to adopt versions of *déshabillés*, or tea gowns. "Negligées", as the style came to be called, continued to be worn informally throughout the early twentieth century. Designed by Jessie Franklin Turner in 1940, this alternative form of formal dress has intimations of the boudoir.

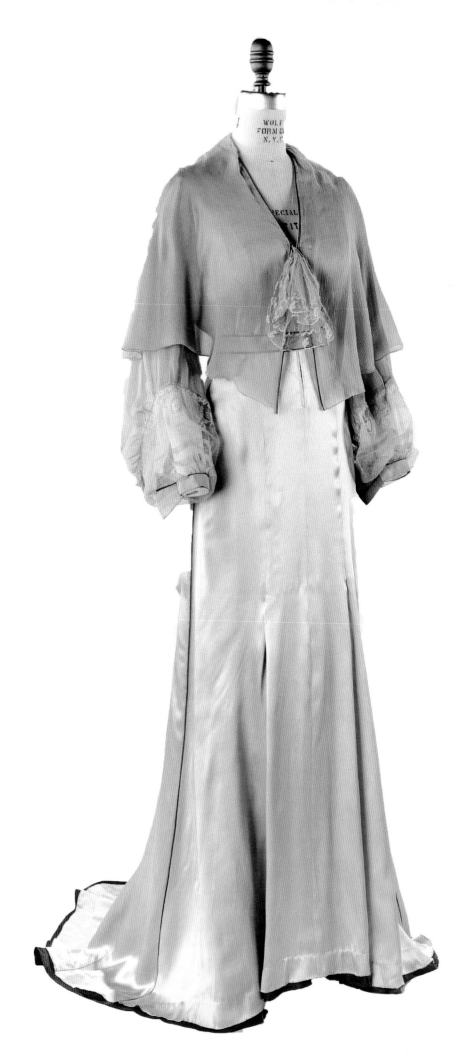

# The Hobble

Although Parisian couturier Paul Poiret claimed to release women from the rigidity of the prevailing S-shaped corset with the introduction of his tubular Directoire line in 1906, he also tethered their ankles with the incorporation of the hobble skirt into his evocations of an imagined "Orient" and the fashions of the Near, Middle and Far East.

These were prompted in part by the wave of enthusiasm that heralded the 1909 Ballets Russes production in Paris of *Scheherazade* – a rewriting of *One Thousand and One Nights*. Poiret was one of the first European couturiers to disseminate to a wider audience the dazzling colour combinations and patterned profusion seen in Léon Bakst's costume and set designs. Expert in the art of self-promotion, in 1911 Poiret held the One Thousand and Second Night Party, a lavish extravaganza to which the Parisian elite were invited to attend in Ottoman-inspired costumes. Wearing a "lampshade" tunic over Persian-inspired *jupe-culottes* (bejewelled harem pants) and an *aigrette* (a feather-topped turban), Denise Poiret appeared at the ball to launch her husband's new designs. The lampshade dress featured a kimono-style tunic, wired at the hem to stand away from the body, and worn over the daring jupe-culottes or the hobble skirt. The top-heavy silhouette created the effect of a table lamp. It was later known as the "minaret", after costumes designed by Poiret for Richepin's 1913 play of the same name.

The ever-decreasing skirt width limited a woman's stride to a few inches, which necessitated the incorporation of a fetter of braid worn around the skirt under the knees to prevent the skirt tearing when walking. There were also "hobble garters" worn beneath the skirt, made up of two connected loops, one to be worn on each leg just below the knee. Ironically, these were popular at the same time as suffragists were demonstrating in the streets, many wearing the hobble skirt. Due to its impracticability and the impossibility of getting in and out of the newly introduced motor car, the hobble skirt proved a short-lived trend.

The implication of clothing that suppresses movement and tethers limbs is one in the remit of bondage and fetish fashion. Vivienne Westwood introduced her bondage trousers in 1976 in what became known as the punk revolution, by utilizing a very similar device to that worn beneath the hobble skirt at the beginning of the century.

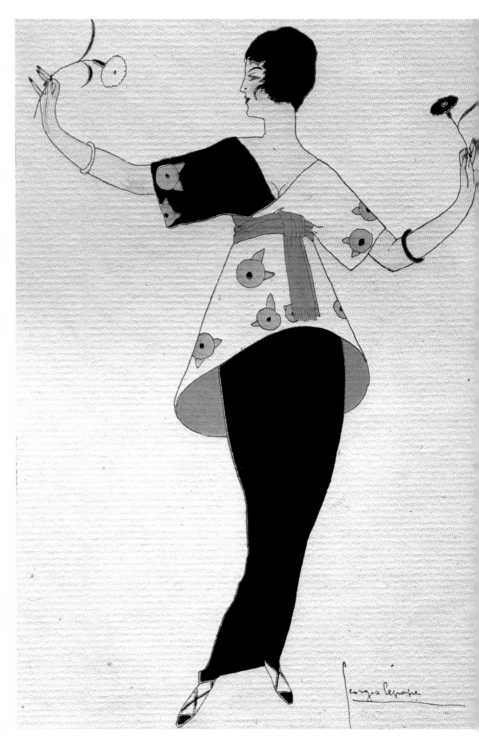

**ABOVE:** Paul Poiret commissioned fashion illustrator Georges Lepape (1887–1971) in 1911 to illustrate his second album of designs, *Les Choses de Paul Poiret*. Rendered in a flat, graphic style, Lepape perfectly disseminated the prevailing archetype of female beauty.

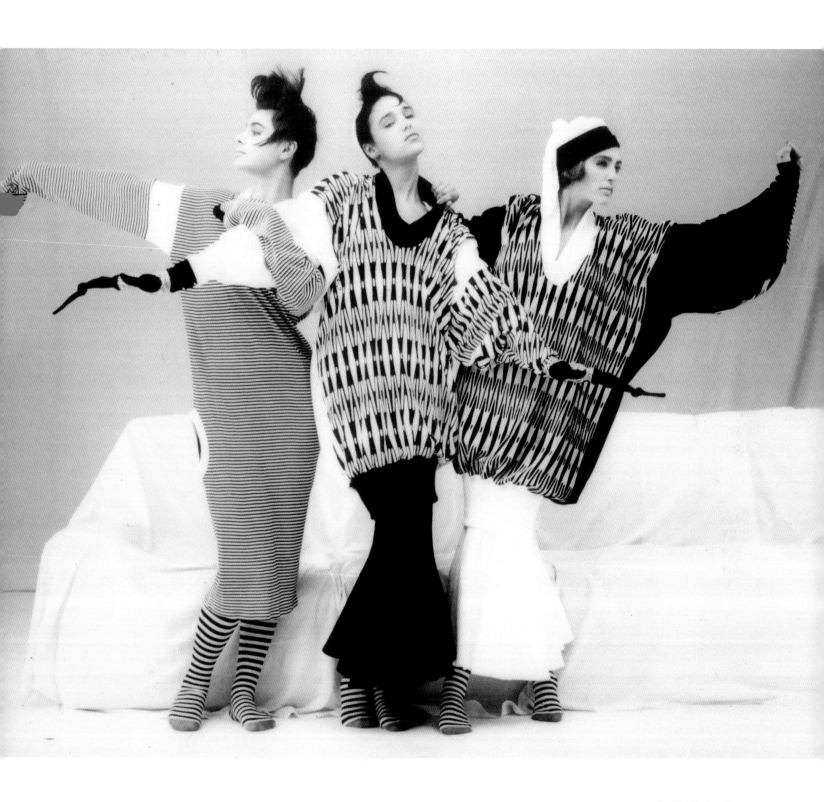

ABOVE: Double-sided waffle viscose and cotton – developed by Swedish textile manufacturers Fixtriksfabrika – was used by British design label Bodymap to create a contemporary hobble skirt for their 1984 collection, "The Cat in a Hat Takes a Rumble with a Techno Fish".

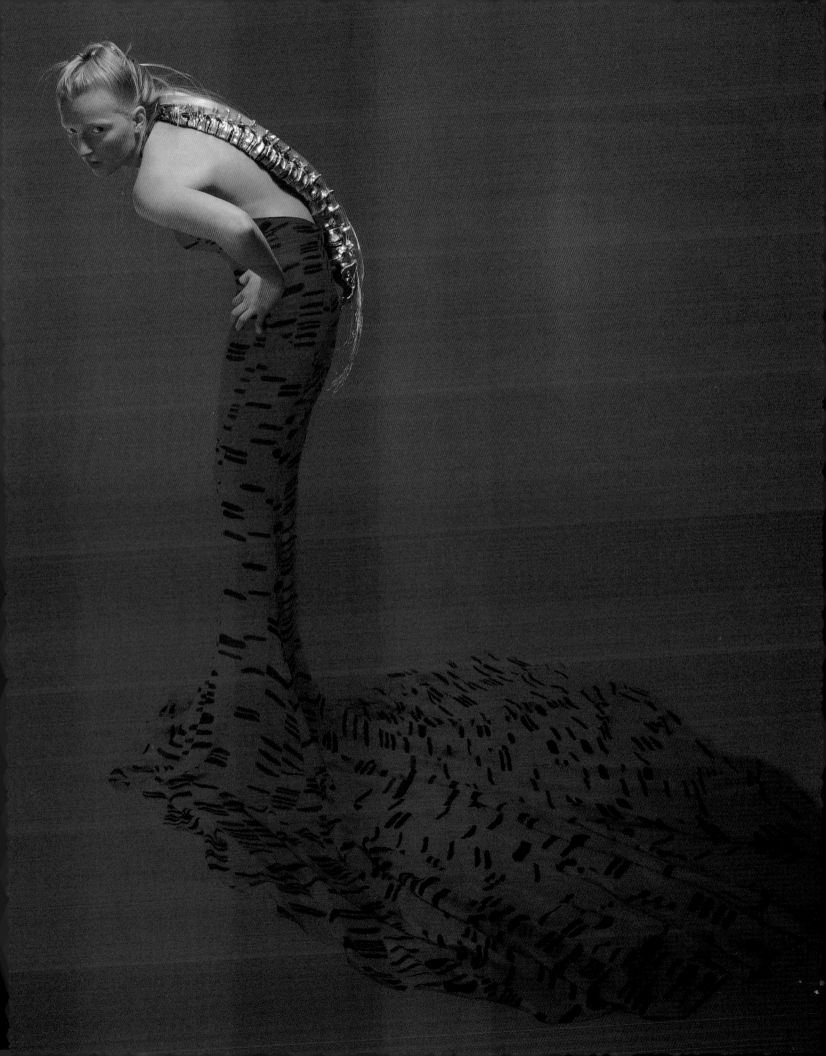

# The Skeleton Dress

The notion of the fashion designer as anatomist has its origins in Elsa Schiaparelli's incorporation of the spine as a decorative detail into a full-length evening gown in 1938. Whimsical and witty rather than a memento mori, the skeleton imagery is described by the technique of trapunto quilting on a fine matt black silk surface, with the "bones" outlined in stitching through two layers of padded fabric. The dress was from the designer's "Circus" collection, created in collaboration with leading Spanish Surrealist artist Salvador Dalí. More sinister in intent was the gothic imagination of British designer Alexander McQueen, whose use of materials that more usually evoke feelings of shock or disgust, such as blood, bone and skin, are represented in a realistic manner. The label has continued to use the skull as a signature print, a decorative motif that is nevertheless a constant reminder of the brevity of life and bodily disintegration. In 1998, jeweller Shaun Leane collaborated with McQueen on an aluminium ribcage cast from a real skeleton to augment a black dress, an image that has also appeared on a range of printed T-shirts. McQueen further responded to the ambivalent fascination with the corporeal by placing worms in a transparent plastic bustier, evocative of intestines – an act of transgression of the natural constraint of maintaining the perceptual separation of the internal and external structures of the body. As a light invocation of sentiment, the human heart is commonly represented as a red "heart-shaped" stylized motif, however Belgian designer Olivier Theyskens appliqués a fully forensic representation of the organ amidst a tracery of red veins and arteries, transposed onto the surface of a transparent body stocking for his Autumn/Winter 1998 collection.

The construction of an exo-skeleton is now rendered more effectively by contemporary hi-tech processes such as laser cutting and three-dimensional printing techniques. Amsterdam-based designer Iris van Herpen's technically accomplished and complex skeleton dress was created by a pulsed laser that consolidates powdered polymers or metals into a layered form, controlled by computer, creating an incandescent lightweight structure that appeared not only on the Paris catwalk but was styled up by Carine Roitfeld for the pages of Chanel's book *The Little Black Jacket*. The skeleton as an ongoing pop culture motif was confirmed with the appearance of Lady Gaga wearing a pleather version designed for her 2009–11 "Monster Ball" tour, created for her by British set designer and illustrator Gary Card.

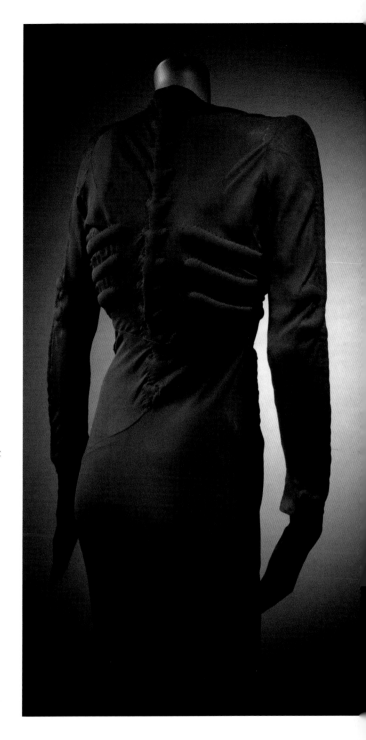

**OPPOSITE:** Helen Storey created her Spinal Column dress as a component of a conceptual series in collaboration with her sister, a developmental biologist. Asserting a profound relationship between science and art, the collection claims to denote the development of the human embryo in the form of dresses – here patterned with DNA scans.

**RIGHT:** The loose approximation of anatomical detailing in Schiaparelli's 1938 skeleton dress has the same easy draughtsmanship of the 1929 cartoon *The Silly Symphony*, where skeleton figures perform a surreal *danse macabre*. This genre was revisited in 1937 in the film *Skeleton Frolic*, giving topicality to Schiaparelli's comedic/couture interpretation.

**OVERLEAF LEFT:** The exoskeleton fabricated into a corset for Alexander McQueen by jeweller Shaun Leane is part of the neo-gothic inheritance of sci-fi Surrealism. This is coherent with the fantastical hyper-realism of H.R.Giger's painting *Necronom IV*, the basis of his Oscar-winning designs for Ridley Scott's *Alien*.

**OVERLEAF RIGHT:** Iris van Herpen has become the leading protagonist of technological futurism in fashion. She has adopted the additive manufacturing principles of 3D printing in her production of externalized skeletal structures, evocative of unknown life forms and incomprehensible fetishism.

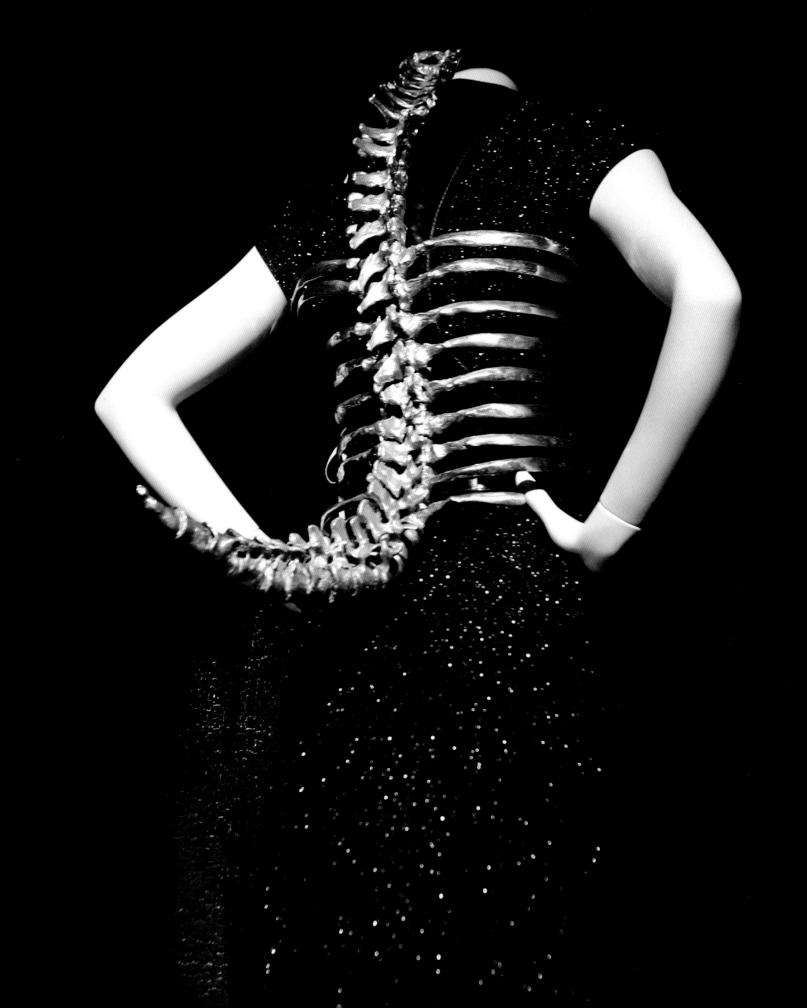

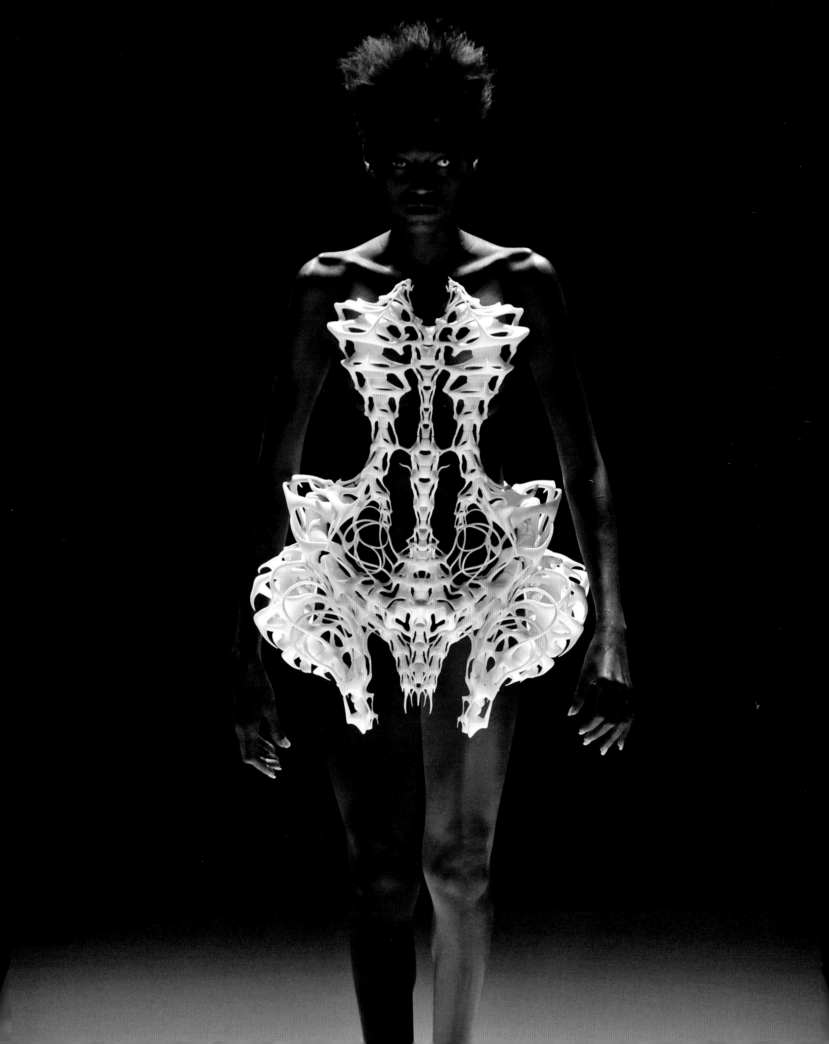

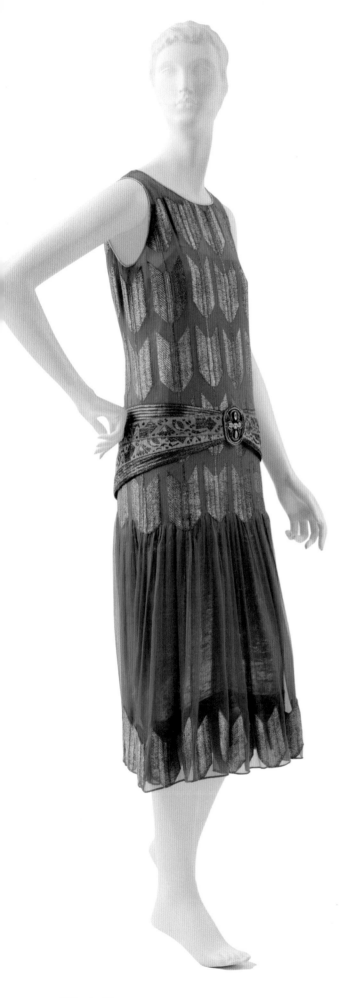

# Art Deco

Celebrated in the *Exposition Internationale des Arts Décoratifs et Industriels Modernes* (International Exhibition of Modern Industrial and Decorative Art) in 1925, the Art Deco movement originated in Paris, where it was called the *Moderne*. The exhibition was largely conceived as a propaganda exercise to establish Paris as the global capital of luxury and style, although other countries were also represented, including Britain, Denmark, Greece, Japan and the Soviet Union. The exhibition further provided a platform for radical architects such as Le Corbusier and avant-garde artists including Sonia Delaunay. Additionally, it exerted a subsequent influence on architecture, interior design, textiles and fashion. Art Deco marked the culmination of a number of cultural and artistic tendencies, some of which had been growing in significance since 1910, including Cubist and Futurist abstraction, Surrealism, African art and an interest in Japanese woodcuts. In particular, with the opening of Tutankhamun's tomb in 1922, there was a wide engagement with all the aspects of Egyptian artefacts, from scarabs, palm trees and pyramids to hieroglyphs and sphinxes. These various influences provided the most recognizable motifs of Art Deco: angular and abstracted form, ziggurats, sun-ray, stylized shell and fan motifs, and chevron patterns. Streamlining also swept through design as a result of the influence of Italian Futurism and the dawning of the age of speed, reflected in the silhouette of the fashionable body honed in the pursuit of sport and outdoor activities, while clothed in the simple lines of the chemise (*see also page 50*). This was a loose-fitting, tubular-shaped dress that bypassed the natural waist to fall straight to the hem, which from 1925 to 1928 was just above the knee. The chemise dress relied for impact on decoration, and as the silhouette grew simpler, the forms of decoration grew more ornate; for evening, the chemise was heavily embellished with fringing, beading, appliqué and light-reflecting silver and gold thread embroidery. By day, the jacquard-knitted cardigan suits and tricot dresses, popularized by Coco Chanel and Jean Patou, featured the chevrons and geometric forms typical of Art Deco, as the very nature of knitted fabric – its innate structure of horizontals and verticals – allowed for the easy translation of the pattern into garments.

Art Deco underwent a revival in the 1960s, spearheaded by Bernard Nevill, professor of textiles at the Royal College of Art, and head of print at London store Liberty. This coincided with a nostalgic view of the 1920s and 1930s and the interest in "Odeon" style, when the restraint of Bauhaus modernism gave way to Hollywood glamour, epitomized by Barbara Hulanicki's retail emporium Biba in the Art Deco department store in Kensington High Street, London.

**OPPOSITE:** Barbara Hulanicki, of influential retail emporium Biba, combined an all-over multi-directional print featuring Art Deco stylized motifs with a silhouette resonant of the 1940s. This is evident in the gathered shoulder head and the A-line skirt of the simple jersey dress.

**LEFT:** Designed by Paul Poiret in 1924, the green silk chiffon of the chemise dress is embroidered with a broken chevron pattern in the form of an arrow in metallic gold thread. An embellished belt loosely marks the line of the hips.

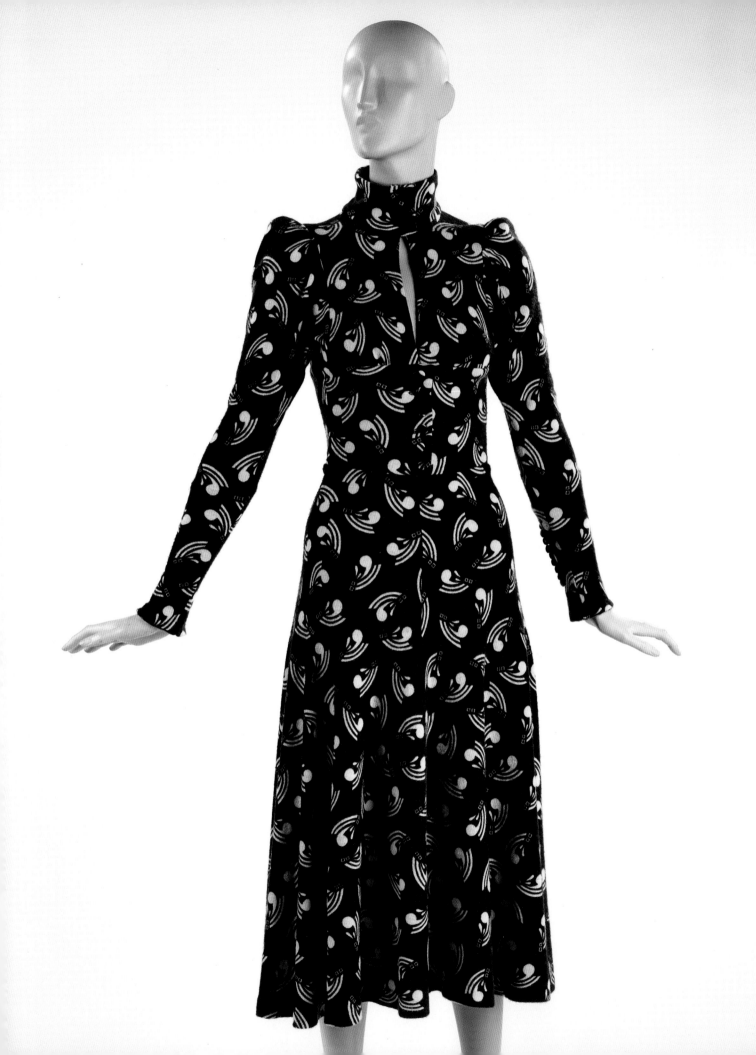

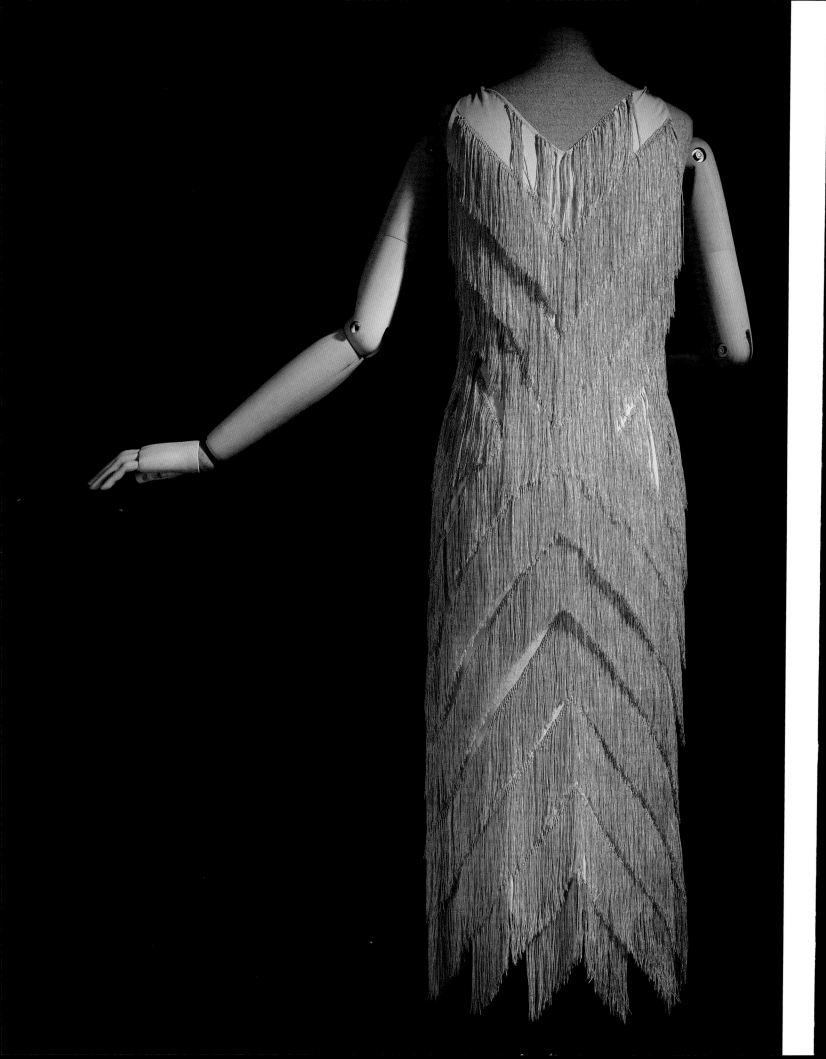

# The Fringed Dress

Crafted tassel fringes were a decorative detail lavishly deployed by the couturier Charles Frederick Worth in his role as promoter of the French textile industry. His experiments with flat-fronted crinolines and gored skirts in the mid-1860s included the use of *passimenterie* – tassels, braids and fringing – which became a favourite with the fashionable Victorians who included it in their vast vocabulary of trimmings.

Far removed from the cumbersome constructions of Worth were the flying fringes of the 1920s. Jazz-obsessed, febrile and fast – in movement as well as morals – the 1920s flapper embodied the spirit of modernism as she moved to the syncopated rhythmic dance music originating in black American culture. Symbols of the new modernity – from the streamlined silhouette of the new motorcars to the flying fringes of the Charleston dress – signified a break from the past. The brief tubular-shaped chemise dress allowed the flapper freedom of movement to embrace her partner for the Turkey Trot or to enjoy the uninhibited Charleston, a show dance first performed by the Ziegfeld Follies in 1923.

Fringing added fluid movement to the strict lines of the chemise and worked in confluence with the geometric staggered forms of Art Deco, providing asymmetry or stepped seams for added interest. It was usually attached at the hipline and reached to the hem of the dress for maximum shimmering impact. Later in the decade, as hemlines hovered between the knee and mid-calf, fringing and triangular inserts of godets were a way of attuning the eye to a change in length. As backless styles became fashionable, fringing was also hung from the shoulder seams in long, sweeping tassels, or attached to ends of shawls to provide cover for the arms. However, fringing fell out of favour throughout the 1940s and 1950s, and when fashion hit the global trail during the late 1960s and early 1970s, it was associated with hippies and their appropriation of America's First Nation, rather than with eveningwear.

Fringing continues to be shorthand for exotic embellishments, seen in the Pucci collection for Spring/Summer 2014 by Peter Dundas, who combines it with Maasai embroideries. More usually, in contemporary fashion, fringing tends to be limited to the short ends left with the vogue for deconstructing textiles to leave a raw edge – a popular device deployed by Karl Lagerfeld at Chanel.

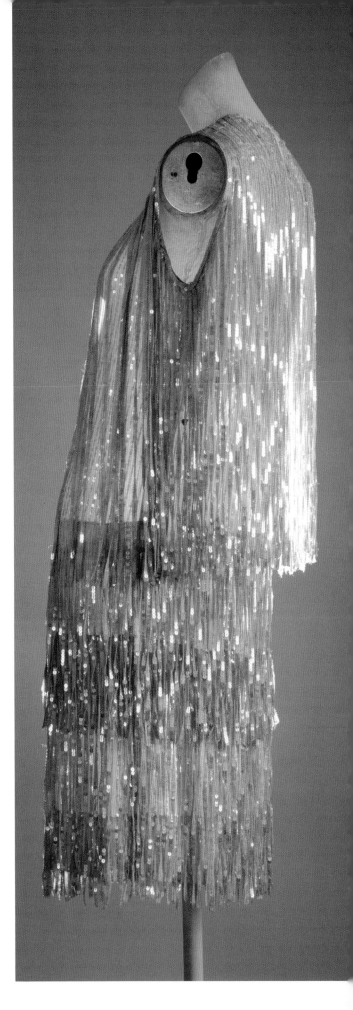

**OPPOSITE:** Articulating the lines of a tubular chemise, the chevron pattern of the fringing – a favoured motif of Art Deco – creates a focal point at the small of the back and an irregular hem. Designed by Vionnet in the 1920s, the fringed dress was created for movement – sitting would displace the line of the fringing.

**RIGHT:** Evidence of the couture provenance of this chemise by Edward Molyneux from 1926 is in the detailing of the fringing. It is constructed from narrow lengths of silk georgette, each embellished with a line of sequins, adhered to the dress in three tiers, to create a shimmering light-reflecting surface.

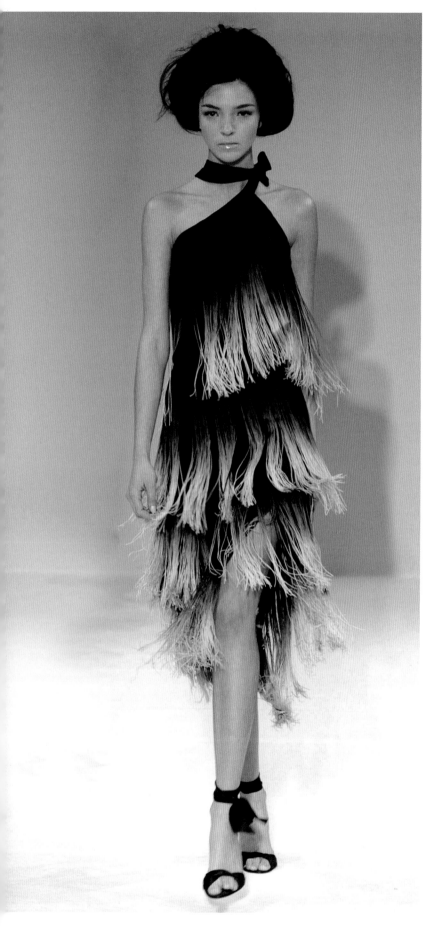
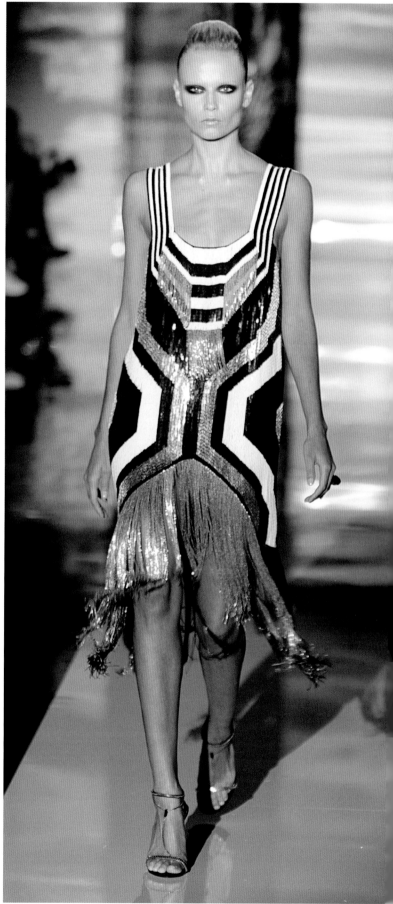

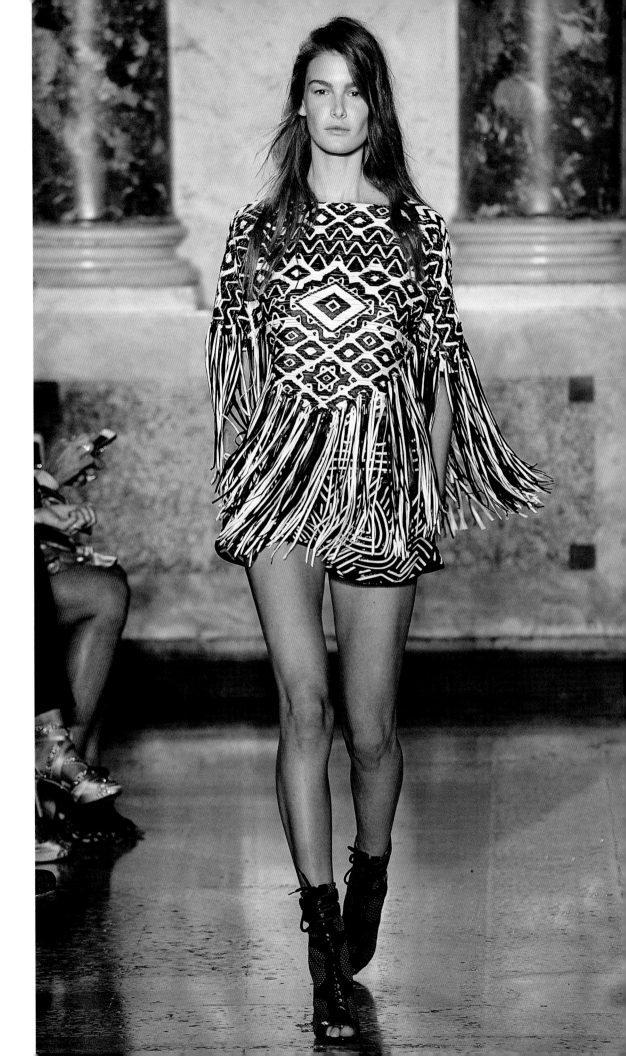

**FAR LEFT:** An extra dimension is added to the the flourish of asymmetrical fringing on this Julien Macdonald (1972–) dress, for Givenchy Haute Couture S/S 2004, with the technique of ombre dyeing. The strands graduate from orange through grey to the black base of the dress.

**LEFT:** Frida Giannini for Gucci provides a contemporary version of the embellished 1920s chemise dress for A/W 2011–12, incorporating gold with black beading. This intense surface decoration enhances the Art Deco sensibility and Cubist-inspired patterns of the design.

**OPPOSITE:** Once the prerogative of the 1960s jet-set and "beautiful people" such as Jackie Kennedy, the Italian luxury label Emilio Pucci, renowned for its polychromatic prints and now headed by Peter Dundas, adds beaded fringing to the mix with Maasai-inspired decoration for S/S 2014.

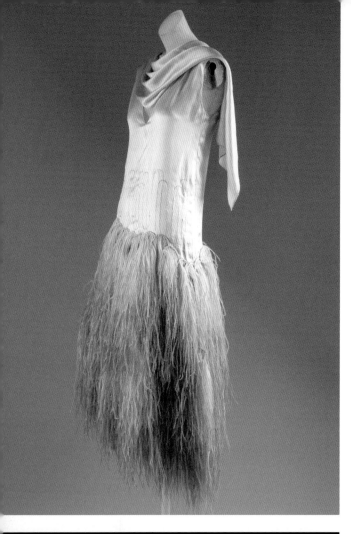

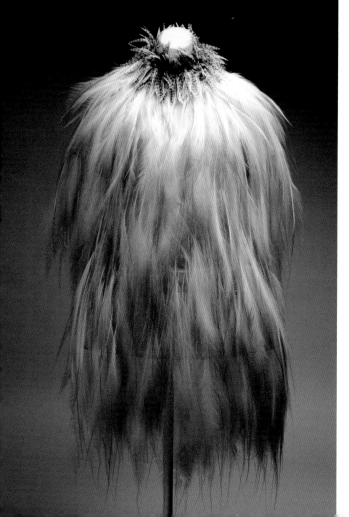

# The Feathered Dress

Fashion's fascination with feathers as ornamentation dates back to the sixteenth century, when explorers such as Ferdinand Magellan brought back exotic specimens from their global expeditions. Over the centuries feathers have more often been used as trimmings, rather than for whole garments, to provide face-framing interest around the head and neck. Feathers denote an airy excess, from the egret, ostrich and birds-of-paradise feathers adorning the piled-up hair of Marie Antoinette, the Queen of France, to the plumed accoutrements adding show-stopping height to the be-feathered twentieth-century showgirl. Symbol of feminine flightiness, ostrich plumes were used to decorate the skirts of 1920s and 1930s eveningwear, and proved popular once again in the 1960s, when couturiers exploited their *tremblant* qualities at neck and hem to animate a dress. In 1969, Yves Saint Laurent created a series of evening dresses made entirely of birds-of-paradise feathers, fragile pom-poms in pastel colours. A triumph of the *plumassier*'s art the feathered showpieces were constructed in the workshops of the House of Lemarié, the feather specialists, an atelier of highly skilled and specialized craftspeople. Each individual feather had to be split, dyed and twisted, then individually attached to the base fabric to create Laurent's flight of fancy.

The graphic markings described in the exotic plumage of the peacock feather proved particularly appealing to the print designers of the 1960s, when the fashionable flamboyance of both men and women demanded vibrant colour and pattern. In 1970, fashion and textile designer Zandra Rhodes was inspired by a visit to the National Museum of the American Indian to subsequently design the "Indian Feather" collection. This combined engineered prints of feathers fashioned into free-floating silk-chiffon dresses, with strips of silk chiffon crafted into fringes of faux feathers at the hem.

Birds are powerful symbols: Alexander McQueen made them a recurring motif in his collections, whether as whole birds, as in his "Horn of Plenty" collection when he constructed a dress from thousands of black-dyed duck feathers, or birds depicted in embroidery and printed fabrics. As well as printed versions of feathers, fake feathers are often used to replicate their effect. Designer Sarah Burton's "Ice Queen and Her Court" collection for Alexander McQueen, Autumn/Winter 2011–12, combined a raw-edged tulle skirt with a bodice embellished with three-dimensional silk organza feathers, the faux feathers replicating the neck plumage of a bird.

**ABOVE LEFT:** In 1927 Louise Boulanger founded her own salon in Paris, where she originated her *pouf* line, which launched a bouffant rear-slung full skirt from a straight-line bodice. Her stranded feather-fringed dress achieves this signature profile as the columnar bias-cut body explodes with loose fronds of plumage at the dropped waist.

**LEFT:** In 1969 Yves Saint Laurent created a flimsy, knee-length tunic of bird-of-paradise tail feathers, mounted on silk organza. At the throat, a choker of patterned wing feathers is used as a delicate restraint of the floating motion of the dress in flight.

**OPPOSITE:** In 2010 Sarah Burton presented her first collection for Alexander McQueen after his untimely demise. While making her own statement, Burton was able to recall the elegant animist inclinations of McQueen with an owl-like combination of corn dolly bustier and oriental pheasant feather skirt.

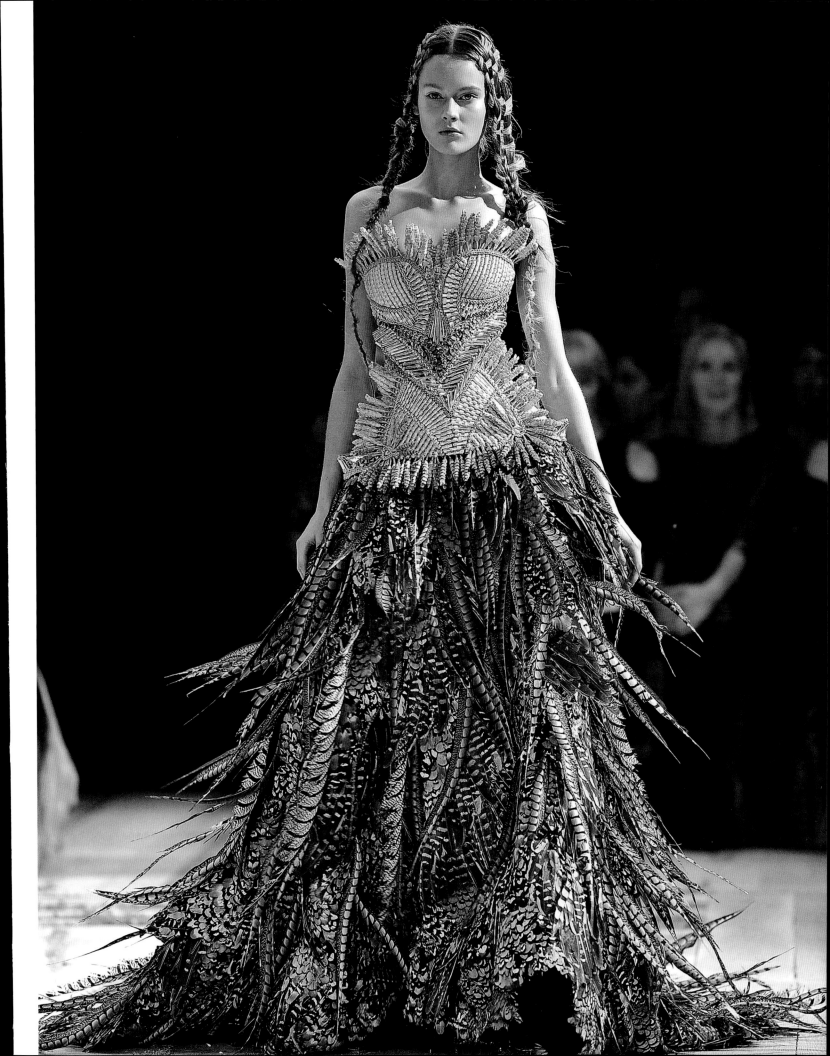

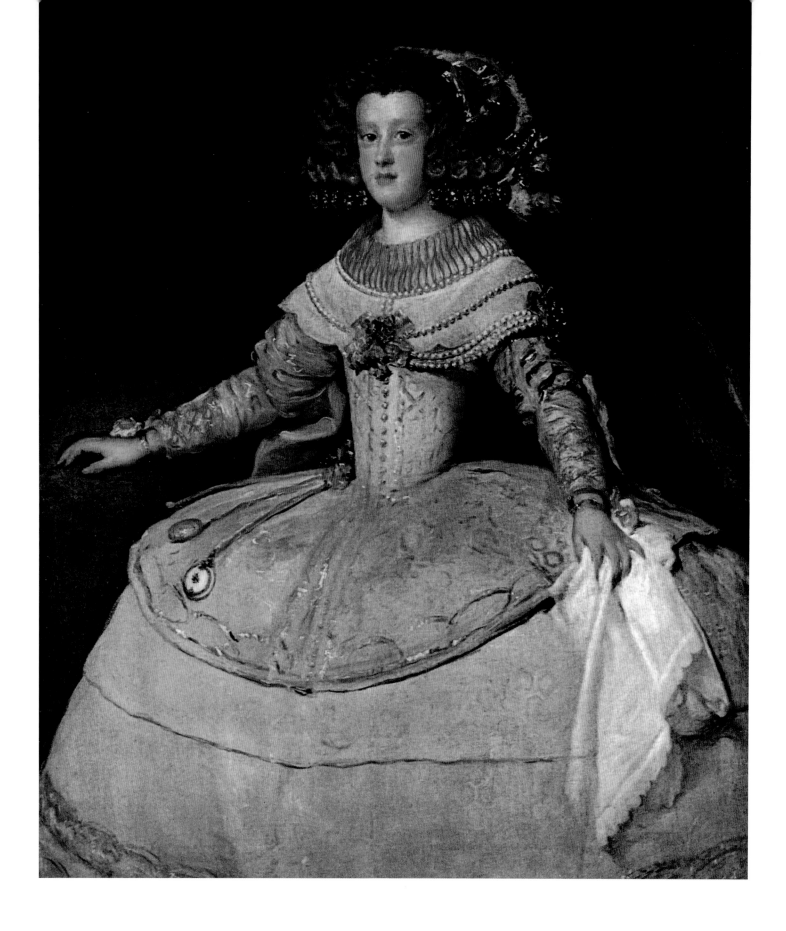

# Robe de Style

Developed as a romantic alternative to the tubular chemise dress adopted by *la garçonne* (*see page 50*), the low-waisted, wide-hipped silhouette known as the *robe de style* was created by Parisian couturière Jeanne Lanvin in the 1920s to showcase her exquisite embroideries and to promulgate a level of couture artisanship that had little place in the simple lines of the chemise. The semi-formal ensemble obscured the figure, making it attractive for those clients of any age and shape who were not slender enough to wear the tubular lines of Chanel or Patou. Although the *robe de style* is usually associated with Lanvin – and she designed many variations up to the early 1930s – other couturiers added the dress to their repertoire, including the Callot Soeurs, Lucile and the French house of Boué Soeurs.

The silhouette of the dress owes its width to a lightweight adaptation of the *pannier* (French for basket), a wood or whalebone contrivance worn in the eighteenth century, with its origins in the infanta dresses of seventeenth-century Spain. These skeleton forms were used to extend the width of the skirt at the side, while leaving the front and back relatively flat. This extension provided a panel to display the elaborate decorations and rich embroidery of the *ancien régime* – the device was similarly exploited in the *robes de style* designed by Sylvie and Jeanne Boué. The sisters rendered the cumbersome silhouette and sumptuous decoration of the eighteenth century into modern, wearable yet formal garments for court appearances and formal balls. The ruching and appliquéd work typical of Rococo dress decoration, which was often confined to the bodice area in the eighteenth century, grew in cascading bouquets over an entire Boué Soeurs dress, always with the inclusion of the signature Boué rose, folded and curled into high relief. Exquisite couched embellishment, entailing the manipulation of silk or lamé ribbons to create a flower-basket motif as an elaborate lace ground, became part of the recognized Boué handwriting on both sides of the Atlantic.

Following a decade dominated by the bias-cut gown, Madeleine Vionnet created a *robe de style* in black silk tulle. Less fluid and more severe in structure than those from the 1920s, and with less opulent decoration, Vionnet used horsehair stiffening and a detached basket-shaped understructure to create the width at the hips. Finally, in 1938 and 1939, full-skirted romantic fashions appeared in a nostalgic look at the past, only to be eclipsed by the onset of World War II.

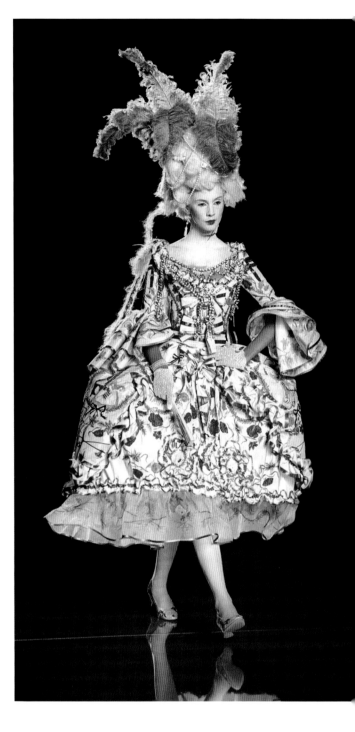

OPPOSITE: Worn initially at the Spanish court during the early sixteenth century, the farthingale was the first device that was used to extend the width of the female skirt, as seen in the portrait of the Infanta Maria Theresa of Spain (1653) by Diego Velázquez (1599–1660).

ABOVE: Reinterpreting the historical dress of France's *ancien régime* and the court of Marie Antoinette, John Galliano for Dior Haute Couture appropriates the panniered excess, lavish use of fabric and the whalebone corset of the *robe à la française* for A/W 2001–2.

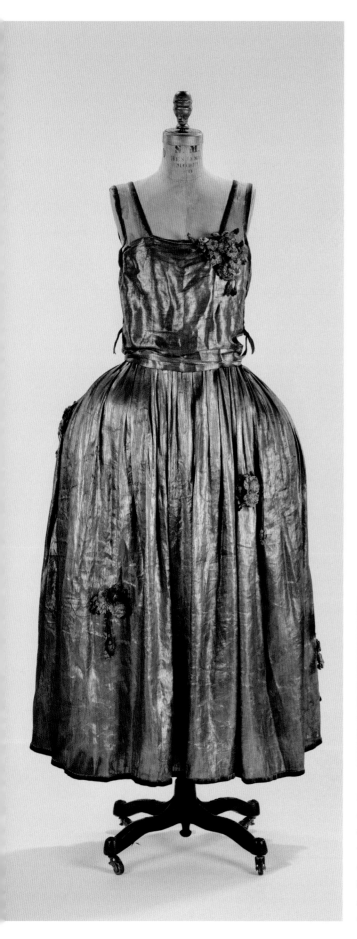

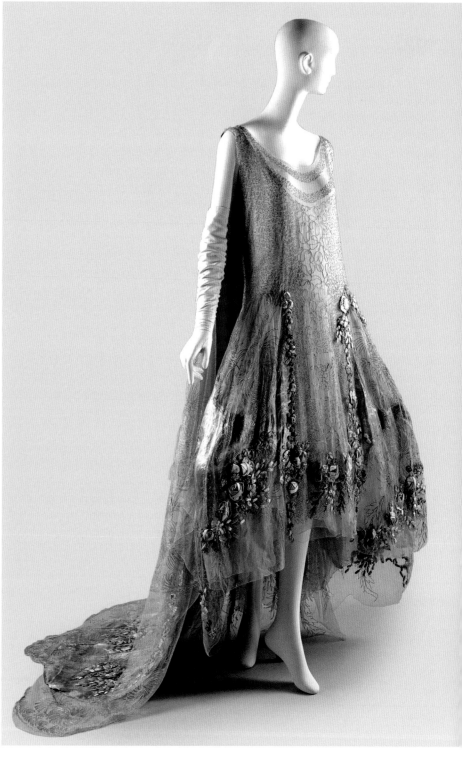

**LEFT:** Jeanne Lanvin (1867–1946) established France's oldest couture house in 1889. Known for her exquisite *robes de style*, characterized by their panniered skirts and delicate embroidery, appliqué and beadwork, this dress dates from 1922.

**ABOVE:** Providing a contrast to the spare and narrowly cut clothes of the era, the ebullient decoration of the *robe de style* of this court presentation ensemble from 1932 by Boué Soeurs represents the unparalleled craftsmanship of early French couture.

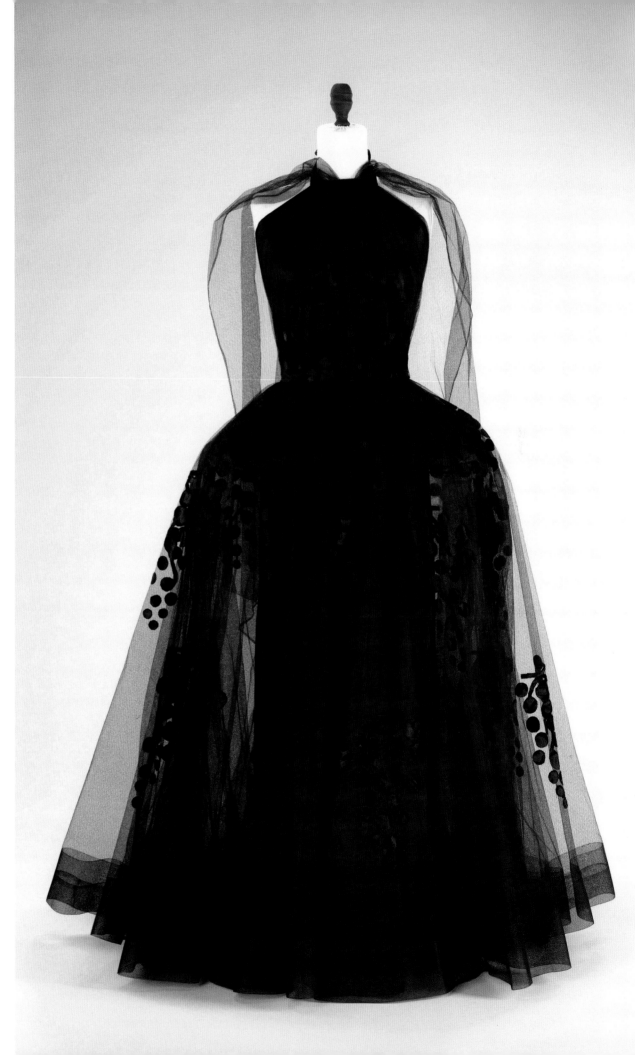

**RIGHT:** Dating from the later years of her career in 1939, this *robe de style* marked a change of direction for Madame Vionnet, renowned for the classicism of her columnar bias-cut gowns. Simply decorated with an overlay of spotted tulle, the emphasis continues to reside with the silhouette.

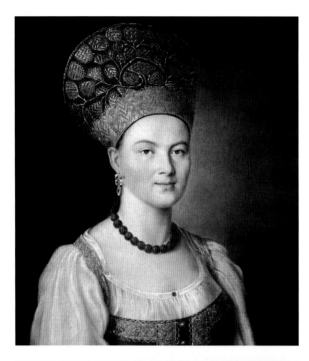

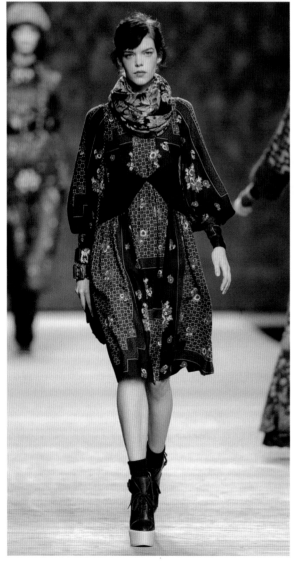

# Russian Dress

Traditional Russian dress, Byzantine in origin, was abandoned in Moscow in favour of European fashions in the seventeenth century by the command of the reigning tsar Peter the Great, part of his drive to transform Russia into a major European power. Although European fashions remained the standard for public life throughout Russia, certain basic articles survived as central to Russian dress, which by the eighteenth century were already associated with the national costume. The *rubakha*, a type of blouse, was worn during the Kievan era, which ended in the thirteenth century. It featured delicate, pictorial embroidery around the hem, sleeves and collar, and was worn by both sexes, but the female *rubakha* was ankle-length and featured a slightly gathered neckline. It was worn beneath a *dalmatic*, a tunic from the Byzantine era made from silk or fine linen, dyed bright colours.

During the Muscovite period that followed, the *rubakha* was worn beneath the *sarafan*, a long, trapeze-shaped pinafore dress with thin shoulder straps over which a *dushegreya* – a sleeveless waistcoat/ vest, gathered on the back into tubular folds – was sometimes worn. Ceremonial *sarafans* were embroidered with lavish floral bouquets and garlands, and were ornamented with golden galloons and metallic lace with silver or gilt buttons forming a decorative pattern along the seams. *Sarafans* were girdled at the waist with narrow plaited belts, the ends left loose. In Russia's northern provinces, the silk sarafan was usually worn with a headdress, the *kokoshnik*, decorated with needlework, pearls, golden and silver threads, and mother-of-pearl plaques, although a headscarf tied under the chin or at the back of the head was accessorized with the less ornate sarafan, worn for everyday.

Both the folkloric nature of the *sarafan* and the singular embellishment of Byzantine-inspired textiles have continually provided inspiration to designers. Yves Saint Laurent introduced a plethora of "Oriental" influences for his 1976 collection, which included references to the costume designs by Léon Bakst for the Ballets Russes of the early twentieth century, as well as richly embellished versions of the *dushegreya* and the *rubakha*. Characterized by the use of luxurious fabrics such as gold brocade, duchesse satin and iridescent silks, the collection was heralded as one of the designer's most beautiful, consolidating the trend for luxe hippie style and giving birth to many trends that resurfaced over the following decades, including fur Cossack hats, dirndl skirts and "peasant" blouses.

**ABOVE LEFT:** A portrait of an unknown girl in Russian costume (1784) by Ivan Petrovich Argunov (1727–1802) displays the *kokoshnik*, a traditional Russian headdress worn by women and girls to accompany the *sarafan*. Married women wore a version which covered their hair.

**LEFT:** Sardinian-born designer Antonio Marras (1961–), creative head of Japanese label Kenzo, is faithful to the label's heritage of combining complex patterns in a single garment. The geometric blocks of floral print create a trompe l'oeil version of the *sarafan* for A/W 2009–10.

**OPPOSITE:** In homage to the Ballets Russes, Yves Saint Laurent (1936– 2008) presented a collection in 1976 that confirmed the designer as the most significant exponent of haute couture of the era. The juxtaposition of Russian folkloric detail with lavish materials set the paradigm for luxe hippie style.

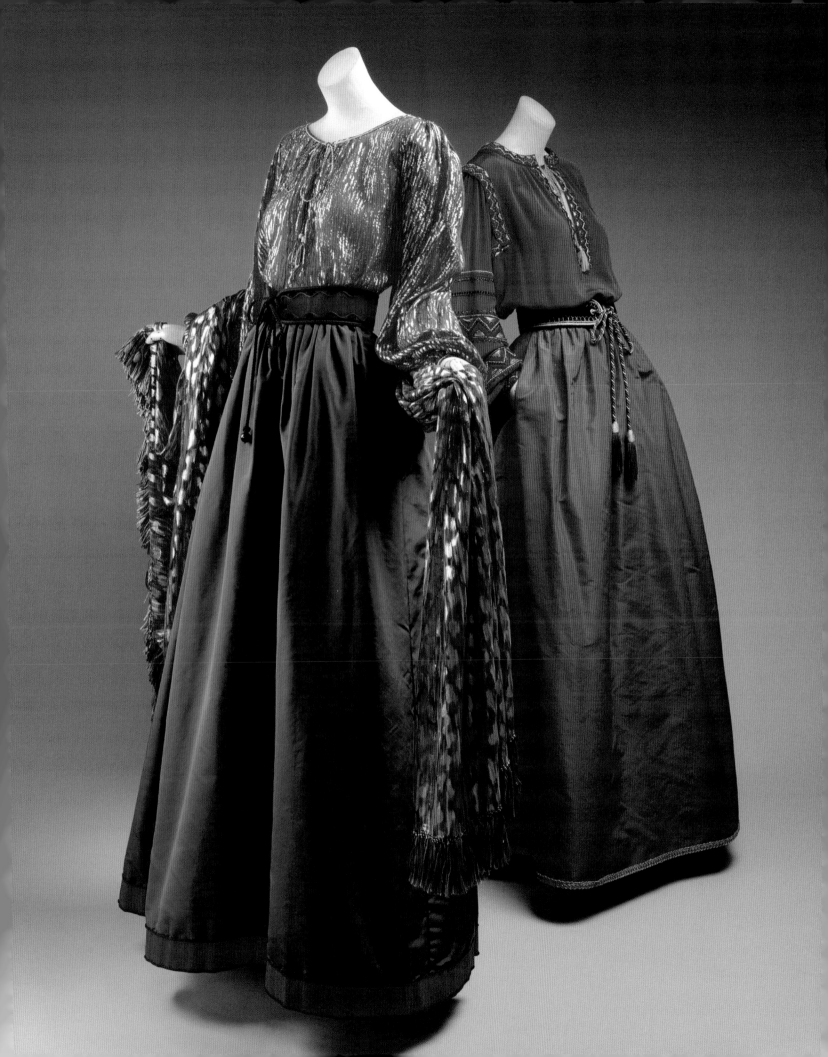

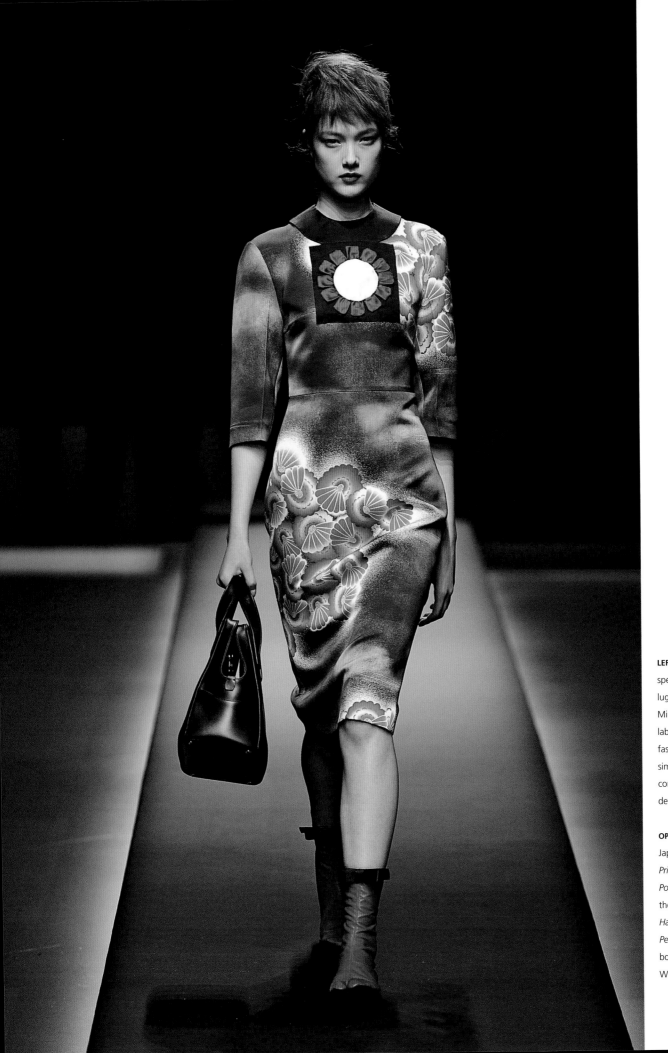

**LEFT:** Originally a small store specializing in luxury leather luggage, under the aegis of Miuccia Prada (1949–), the Prada label became an influential leading fashion brand in 1988. Here the simplicity of cut of the kimono is combined with Samurai-inspired detailing for S/S 2013.

**OPPOSITE:** Exemplifying Anglo-Japanese style, the painting *Princess from the Land of Porcelain* (1864), featured as the centrepiece of the interior *Harmony in Blue and Gold: The Peacock Room* by American-born artist James Abbott McNeill Whistler (1834–1903).

# Japonaiserie

The influence of Japan on Western clothing was established with the display of Japanese applied arts at the International Exhibition London in 1862. This was curated by Rutherford Alcock – the then British General Consul in Japan – and was prompted by the opening up of Japan to the West in 1853. The exhibition stimulated an interest in oriental and exotic products, and a young Arthur Lasenby Liberty, the son of a Buckinghamshire draper and then an employee of Farmer and Rogers' Great Shawl Emporium in Regent Street, persuaded his employers to open an Oriental department. Liberty subsequently opened his own Oriental Emporium in 1875, initially called East India House, and from the late 1870s it was known as Liberty & Co.

In addition to the importation of original textiles and garments, in 1884 Liberty opened a dressmaking department overseen by progressive designer and leading member of the aesthetic movement E.W. Godwin, then secretary of the Costume Society. The store became a depository of Japanese style, and instrumental in disseminating the aesthetic to a wider audience; garments such as the ornate kimono had previously been the privilege of an artistic minority. Generally recognized as the national dress of Japan, the kimono – meaning "the thing worn" – is a simple T-shaped garment constructed from a rectangular length of cloth folded to form a square-shaped sleeve, with a stitched seam allowing for a small slit for the hand. A versatile garment, at the end of the nineteenth century and the beginning of the twentieth, the kimono provided the basis for a form of "undress", worn without corsets by women in the boudoir and by men as a form of dressing gown.

The fusion of East and West continues to provide a source of inspiration for designers. Kimonos, obis, origami tailoring and geisha make-up were appropriated by John Galliano for Dior's Haute Couture Spring/Summer 2007 collection. In 2013, Italian designer Miuccia Prada combined the armour and artefacts worn by the Samurai – the military nobility of pre-industrial Japan – with a dress cut with the ease of a kimono and decorated with sprays of chrysanthemums, known as *kiku* in Japanese – historically the flower that represented the Imperial House of Japan and long associated with notions of rejuvenation and longevity. Tabi, the traditional Japanese socks with a separation between the big toe and the other toes, provided inspiration for the shoes.

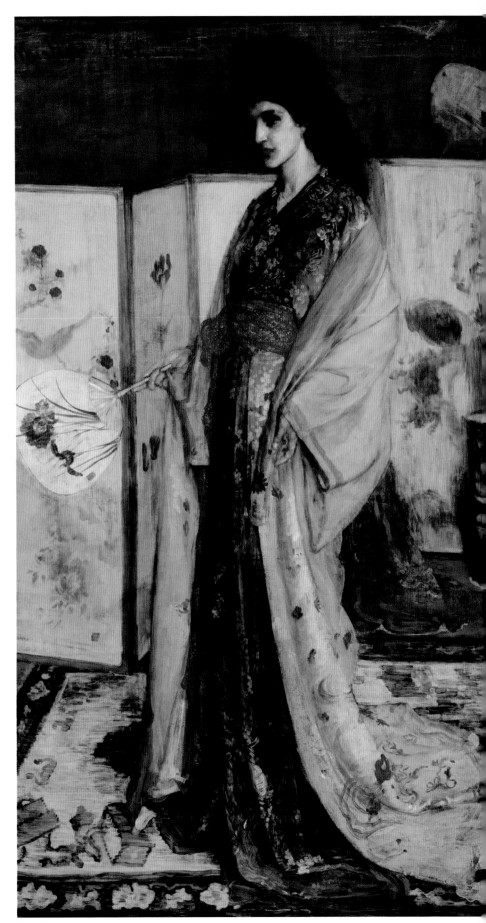

# Chinoiserie

As European trading companies expanded during the eighteenth century, Near, Middle and Far Eastern styles of dress were increasingly introduced into European fashion. The borrowing and reanimation of foreign dress and textiles included the eighteenth-century propensity for chinoiserie – a style held in particular favour during the Rococo period and the court of Louis XV, noted for its use of woven, printed and embroidered silks. Imported goods were initially the privilege of the artistic minority, but as the style became increasingly popular, British silk weavers imitated the original designs, and a bastardized generic style developed, featuring an anglicized version of dragons, pagodas, phoenixes, stylized landscapes and floral designs in colours such as a pale yellow and a light "Chinese green". These textiles were used for the brocaded silk *mantua*, a formal gown worn over wide-hooped petticoats that displayed the expensive fabric and the rich detailing of the design to full advantage. A major resurgence in chinoiserie style took place in the 1930s with modernist designers embracing the dramatic lacquered interiors, resulting in an exotic shorthand of an imagined China.

The trend in Hollywood for films set in China and using Chinese culture as both a style and narrative inspiration disseminated the popularity of the *qipao* – known as the cheongsam in the Cantonese-speaking British colony of Hong Kong. It was formerly a loose-fitting dress with an upright collar worn in China after 1850, and evolved into a tight-fitting version with splits in the side seams giving rise in the West to the notion of "Oriental decadence" following the release of films such as Josef von Sternberg's 1932 *Shanghai Express*. Chinese actress Anna May Wong, who appeared in the movie with Marlene Dietrich, went on to star in *Limehouse Blues*, set in London's Chinatown. Wong's Dragon dress, a lustrous silk gown displaying all the key features of chinoiserie, includes the cheongsam neckline and a gold dragon motif that sensuously slithers along the length of the bias-cut dress.

Chinoiserie is a frequently recurring trend in fashion, but few designers have taken the aesthetics of a blue-and-white Ming vase and applied them quite so directly to the shape and surface decoration of a garment as Italian designer Roberto Cavalli for his Autumn/Winter 2005–6 collection.

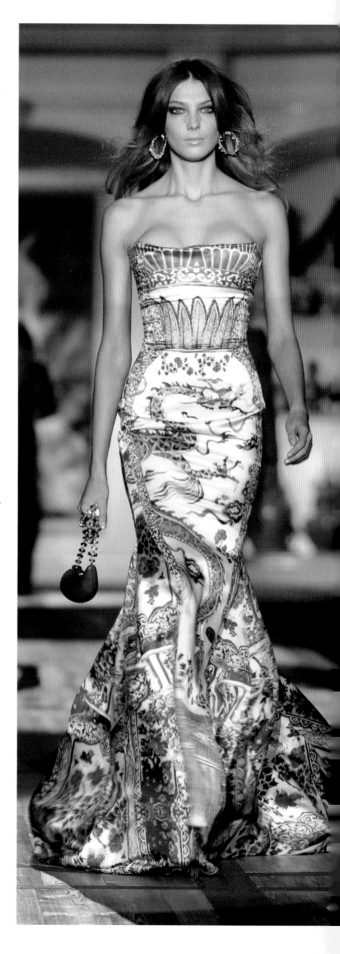

**RIGHT:** Italian designer Roberto Cavalli (1940–) translates the cobalt blue underglaze – a colour exported from Persia in the fourteenth century and called "Islamic blue" – found in hand-painted Chinese porcelain of "blue and white wares" (in Chinese, literally "blue flowers") for a show-stopping evening gown for A/W 2005–6.

**OPPOSITE:** Wearing a form-fitting version of the *qipao*, or the cheongsam, embroidered with a golden dragon, Chinese-American film star Anna May Wong (1905–61) in Alexander Hall's film noir *Limehouse Blues* (1934) epitomizes the early twentieth-century archetype of the mysterious "exotic" femme fatale.

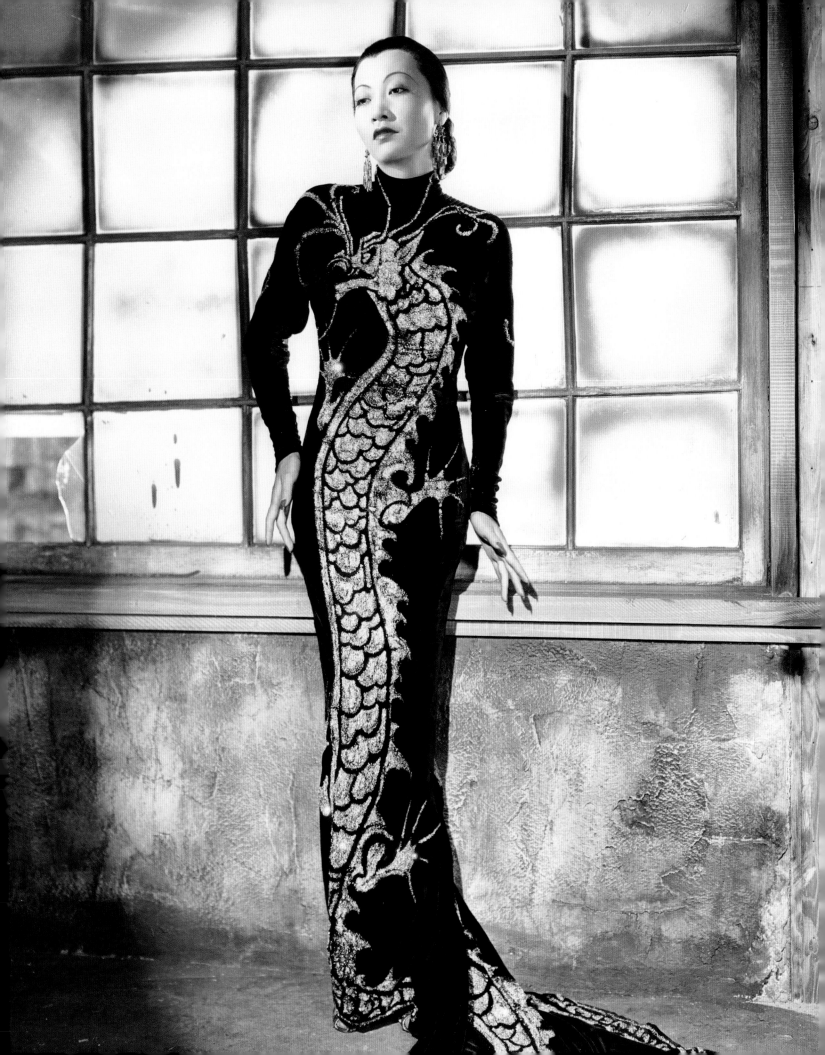

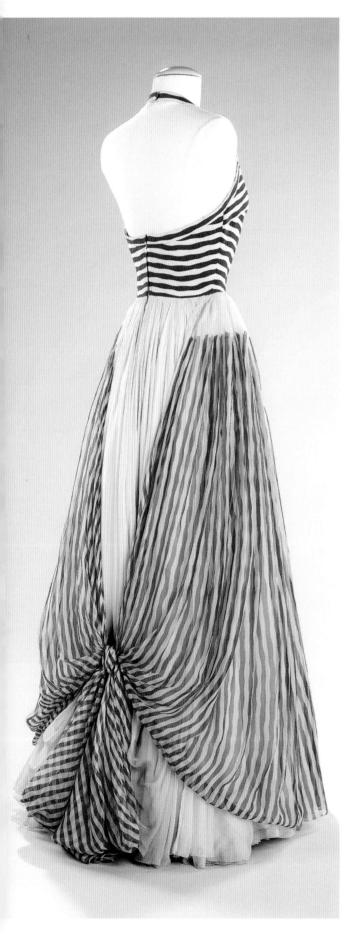

# The Striped Dress

A dynamic surface structure, the stripe animates all it touches. The human eye is programmed to seek out straight lines, and an innate preference for order makes stripes one of the most convincing of print motifs, where variation is reliant on proportion and colour. In medieval times, stripes were traditionally perceived as transgressive – the striped cloth represented disorder and was relegated to outcasts or reprobates such as jugglers and prostitutes – and horizontally striped garments continue to be a visual shorthand for comic-strip burglars, schoolboys and convicts. Stripes are not only useful environmentally, as warning devices for such things as pedestrian crossings, but they also result in the wearer of striped clothing standing out from the crowd, or being easily identified as part of a group, evident in the striped hooped shirt of the rugby team or the regimental tie. Stripes are the simplest of all patterns, consisting of a series of parallel lines going in one direction, but they can also be used to create more complex surfaces.

In fashion, the potential effects of manipulating stripe-printed and woven cloth have been explored by many designers, particularly the effect created by mitring – cutting the end of two pieces of cloth at 45 degrees before joining them together – a design trend that emerged in both Paris and New York around the 1930s. This process was deployed by American designers of luxurious ready-to-wear Elizabeth Hawes and later Gilbert Adrian, who used mitred striped fabric for his signature skirt suits worn by Hollywood stars such as Joan Crawford. Renowned for his dextrous use of silk chiffon, American couturier James Galanos designed a nautically inspired red-and-white-striped evening gown in 1955. The irregularity of the wavy stripes, the bare-backed halterneck redolent of the bathing costume, and the tie at the hem all lend the dress an air of nautical informality. The transparency of the silk chiffon reveals the stripes beneath, causing a diffused chequered effect.

Polychromatic warp-knitted stripes have been the unmistakable signature of Italian company Missoni since the inception of the label. During the 1970s, the company's multicoloured stripes and zigzags in effervescent space-dyed yarns distanced knitwear from its homespun image and placed it at the forefront of fashionable glamour. The signature polychromatic stripes of British designer Paul Smith feature on a plethora of products, from a discreet silk lining to a jacket to a slip dress, where digitally printed vertical stripes combined with vibrant florals for his Spring/Summer 2005 collection.

**LEFT:** Designing high-end ready-to-wear, such as this red-and-white striped silk chiffon dress, of couture-quality workmanship in luxurious fabrics, James Galanos (1924–) was one of a new generation of US-based designers who challenged the dominance of French couture in the mid-twentieth century.

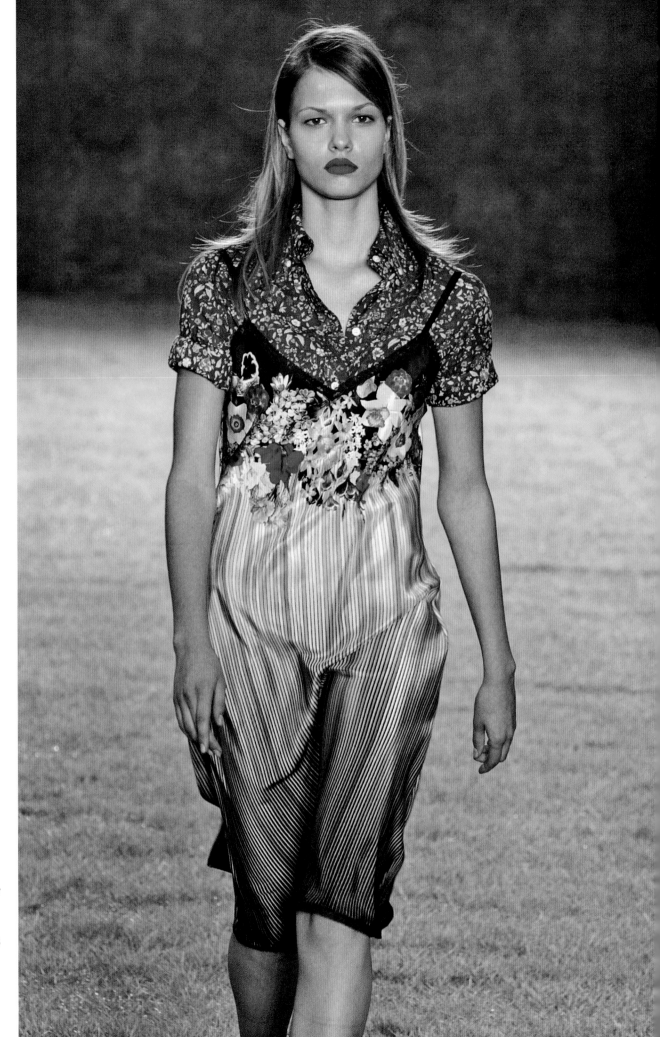

**RIGHT:** Quintessentially British designer Paul Smith (1946–) combines a photo-realist digital print of various flowers created by the use of high-resolution digital photography with his signature polychromatic stripes for S/S 2005 – in a pinafore dress worn over a seed-packet print blouse.

# Africana

The tropes and aesthetics of African indigenous art and textiles have long held a fascination for European designers who are intrigued and inspired by the directness of expression such art practices allow, compared to the perceived restraint and over-intellectualized refinement inherent in the Western European tradition. Hitherto treated with derision as something primitive and savage, African-American and African art and music were embraced by Western culture in the Roaring Twenties, epitomized by Josephine Baker and *La Revue Nègre*. Nancy Cunard, obsessed with primitive art, wore rows of African ivory bracelets stacked up each arm from wrist to elbow. A published poet, founder of the Hour Press, and author of *Negro*, published in 1934, Cunard was immortalized by sculptor Brancusi in *Jeune Fille Sophistiquée*, the archetypal "bright young thing" of the era.

US designer Mary McFadden sparked an interest in African textiles when she worked as merchandising editor for *Vogue* South Africa in 1965. Intense colours, animal jewellery and safari jackets all appeared in the New York and Paris collections of 1966 and 1967, including that of Parisian designer Yves Saint Laurent. He incorporated a number of shift dresses decorated with wood, shells and glass beads inspired by African art in 1967, which US *Harper's Bazaar* described as "a fantasy of primitive genius", a look revisited by both Italian luxury label Dolce & Gabbana (Spring/Summer 2005) and Gucci (Spring/Summer 2011). In 1968, Saint Laurent introduced the safari jacket, a multi-pocketed soft-tailored jacket in neutral linens, which subsequently became a seasonable staple, being particularly popular with the release of such films as *Out of Africa* (1985).

John Galliano's debut collection for the couture house Dior in 1997 combined the corseted Belle Èpoque silhouette with the intricate beadwork of the Maasai women of Africa. The transposition of the decorative elements of the Maasai, a Nilotic ethnic group of semi-nomadic people located in Kenya and northern Tanzania, to the catwalks of European couture may be perceived as cultural degradation, particularly as beading has been an art form of Maasai women for centuries and has prescribed social and hierarchical implications. In addition to utilizing distinctive batik wax prints in deep, earthy colours, Christopher Bailey of Burberry Prorsum also featured Maasai-inspired wide beaded collars on simple linen shifts for Spring/Summer 2012. The draped and knotted dresses were teamed with wooden, bead and raffia embellishments and accessories.

**RIGHT:** Replicating the traditional colours of indigo and dark brown found in the original Javanese batik technique – a hand-crafted method of wax-resist dyeing – Christopher Bailey for Burberry S/S 2010 twists and knots the length of printed fabric around the body, to create a deceptively simple dress.

**OPPOSITE:** John Galliano's debut collection of 50 dresses for Christian Dior Haute Couture in 1997 featured his customary eclectic sourcing of historical and global detail. Here the designer combines the glamour of 1930s bias-cut satin with a Belle Èpoque corset constructed from Maasai-inspired beading.

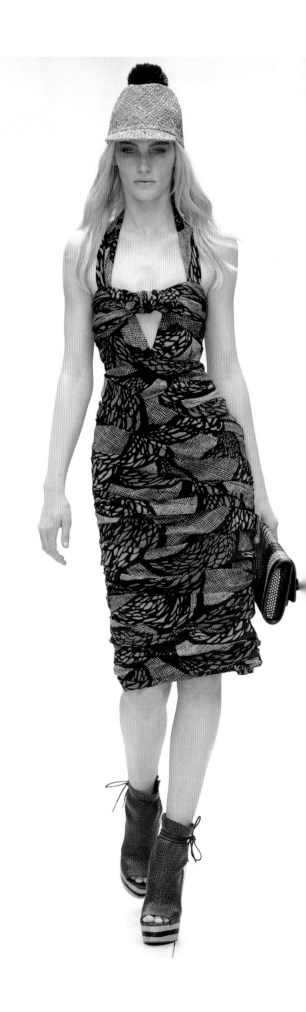

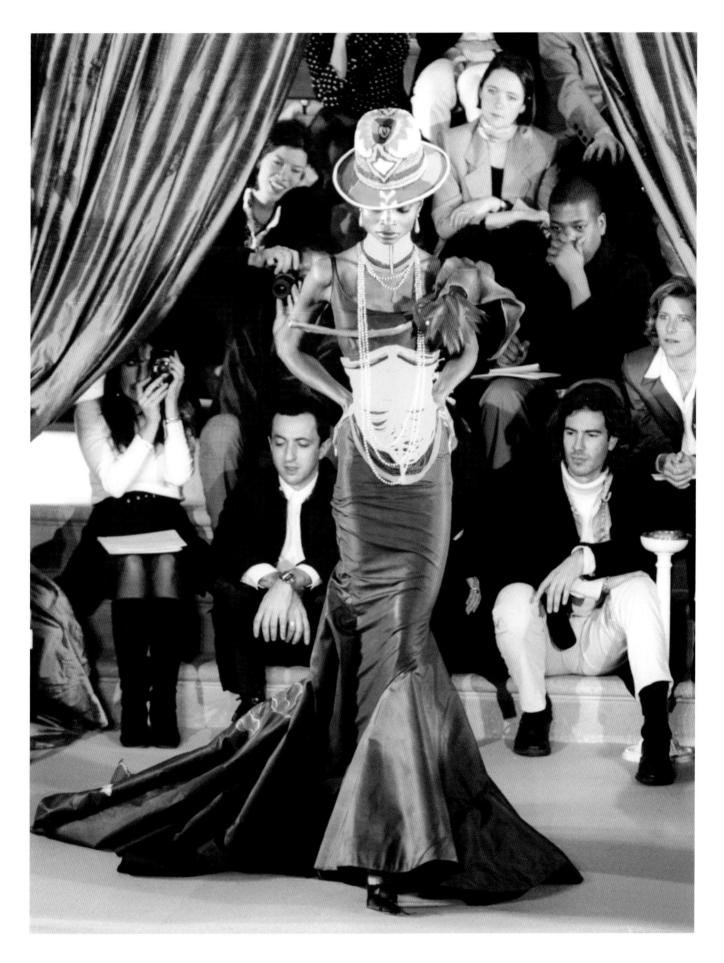

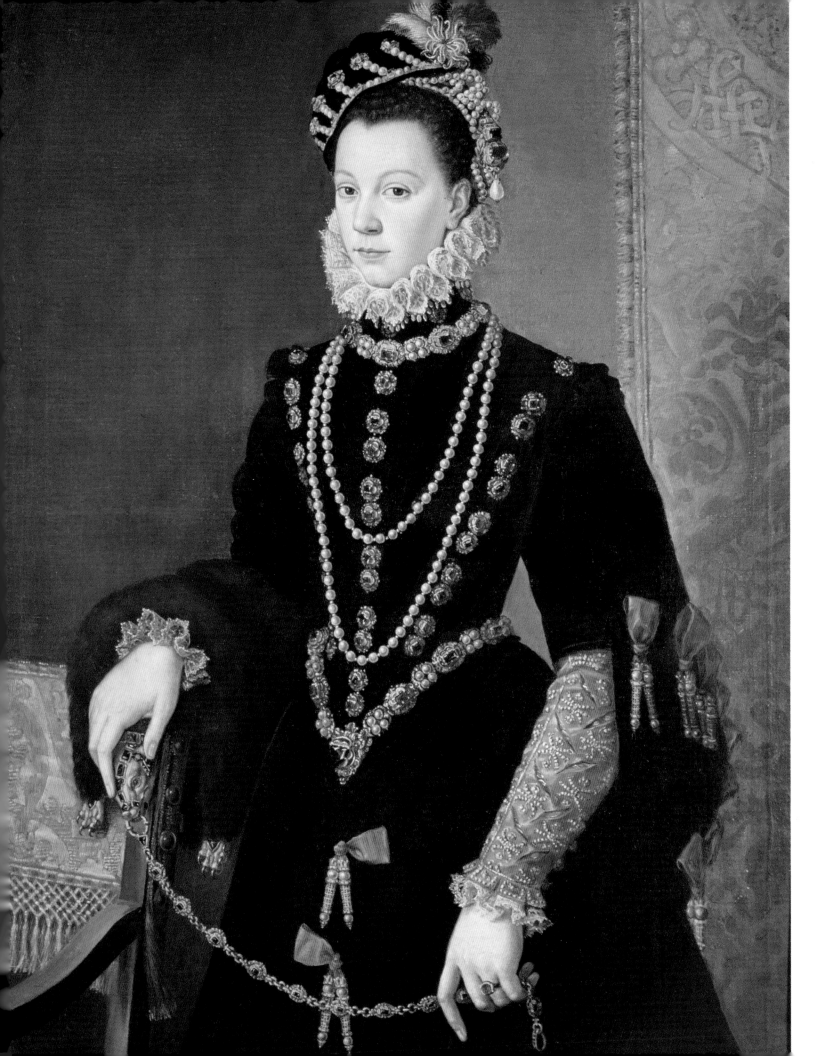

# The Little Black Dress

The ubiquity of the Little Black Dress (referred to commonly as the LBD) is evidence of its success as a wardrobe staple and the go-to garment for instant chic. Universally considered to be a timeless classic, Chanel's black Ford dress was described by US *Vogue* magazine in October 1926, as "*The Chanel 'Ford', the frock that all the world will wear*" owing to its ubiquitousness and the fact that, like the Model-T motor car, it came only in black. The dress was the brainchild of French couturière Coco Chanel, one of the most influential designers of the twentieth century, who offered functional, easy-to-wear clothes that resonated with the modern woman of the 1920s and her new-found athleticism. With an ever-diminishing skirt length – 1926 was the year that the skirt was at its shortest, two inches above the knee – the dress was cut to bypass the contours of the body and fall straight to the hem from the shoulder seam, resulting in the fashionable *la garçonne* look made popular by the flappers of the era. Previously relegated for wear only by the older woman or at funerals and in mourning, Chanel made black a sophisticated choice for the youthful, worn during the day and for the newly popular early-evening cocktail party that required something less formal than a ballgown.

Inextricably linked to the understated glamour of the Little Black Dress is film actress Audrey Hepburn. During the 1950s, couturier Hubert de Givenchy designed the costumes for Hepburn in Billy Wilder's 1954 film *Sabrina*. The actress, reputedly reluctant to rely on Hollywood costumier Edith Head for the film's wardrobe, consulted Givenchy on her costumes, which record her character's metamorphosis from awkward chauffeur's daughter to a sophisticated woman of the world. The film was an extended catwalk production for a predominantly female audience and rendered Hepburn a style icon, further consolidated by her role in Blake Edwards' *Breakfast at Tiffany's* (1961) when the actress appeared in Givenchy's archetypal Little Black Dress, partnered with pearls, sunglasses and a highlighted up-do.

In contemporary fashion, the LBD has evolved from a streamlined architectural sheath dress of perfect simplicity into one that encompasses infinite permutations in length, fabric and texture. The elaborate ornamentation of the final collection of Marc Jacobs for Louis Vuitton, Spring/Summer 2014, incorporated layers of devoré, lace, latticework, jet fringing, crystals and feathers in a cornucopia of showgirl excess.

**OPPOSITE:** Painted by Juan Pantoja de la Cruz (1553–1608), the portrait of Isabel of Valois (c.1605), the third wife of Philip II of Spain, exemplifies the extreme formality and discreet elegance of the Spanish court of the period, as evidenced by the unembellished black material of her gown.

**RIGHT:** The 1920s heralded the arrival of modern fashion; unstructured clothes that allowed free movement in fabrics such as knitted jersey. In 1926 Coco Chanel (1883–1971) introduced the archetypal Little Black Dress, which became an enduring wardrobe staple, acknowledging the new informality in eveningwear.

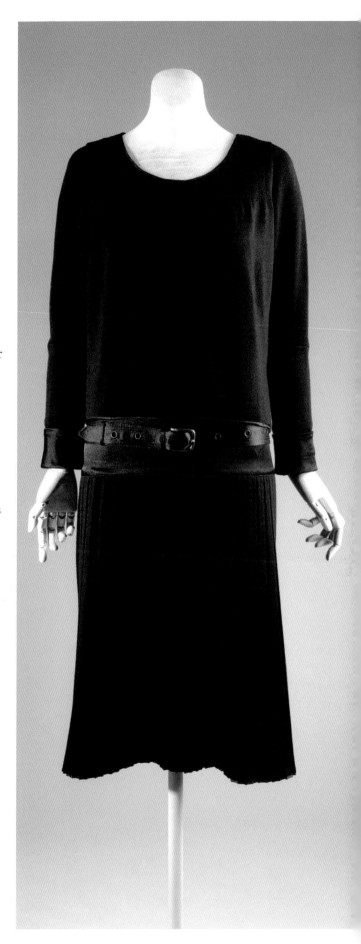

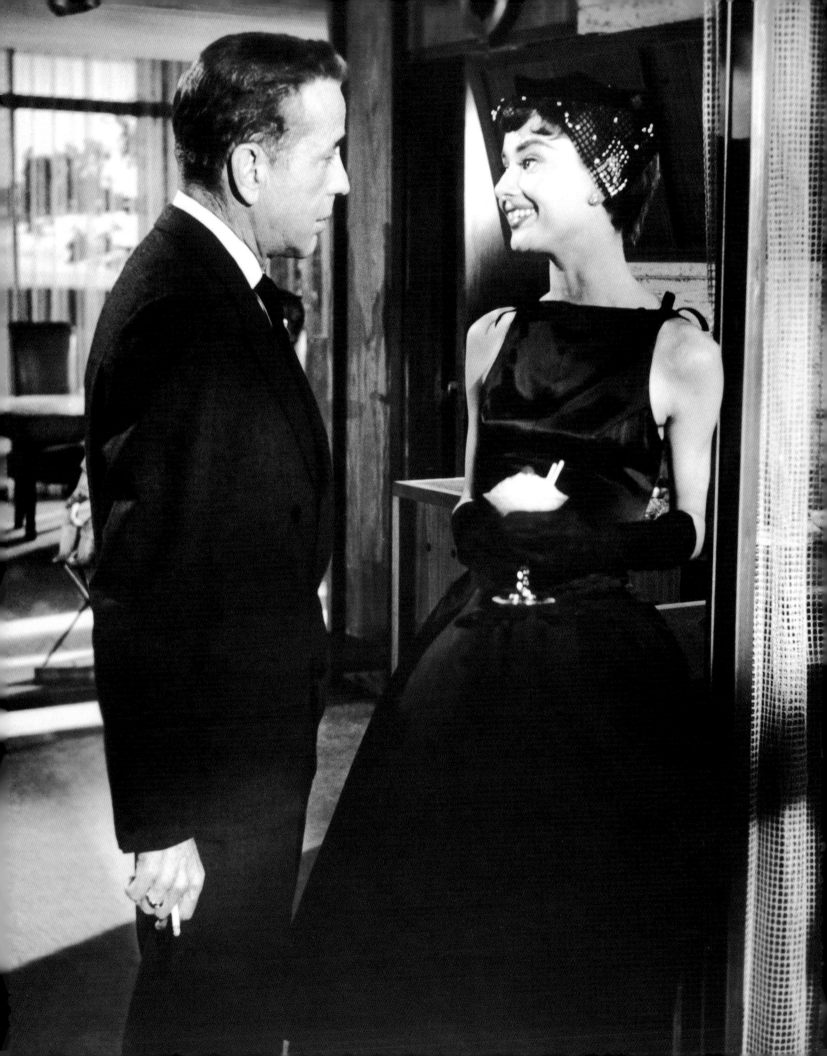

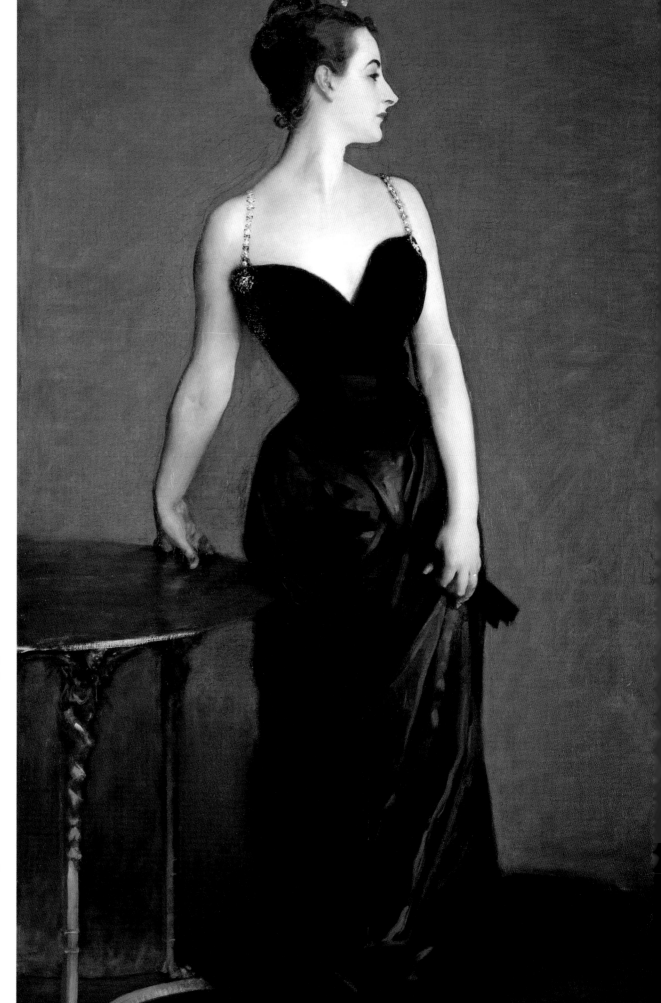

**LEFT:** Initially designed to disguise the prominent collarbones of film actress Audrey Hepburn, Givenchy devised a neckline cut horizontally from shoulder to shoulder and high on the neck. The Little Black Dress worn by the star for her appearance in Billy Wilder's film *Sabrina* (1954) incorporates this boat-necked style.

**RIGHT:** Painted by John Singer Sargent (1856–1925), the erotic charge of dense black satin against the unnatural pallor of the sitter's skin rendered the portrait of *Madame X* (Madame Pierre Gautreau) controversial when it was first presented at the Paris salon of 1884.

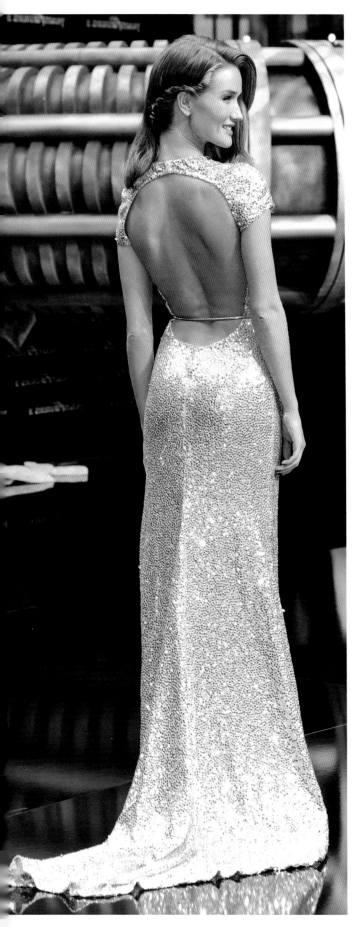

# The Backless Dress

The erotic power of the naked back was first displayed with the glamorous backless evening gowns of the 1920s. Bathing costume and leisurewear worn for sunbathing, swimming and water sports had already pushed the boundaries of propriety. This allowed the photographers of the day, such as George Hoyningen-Huene to legitimately disseminate images of near nudity in the press and magazines, paving the way for greater acceptance of relative nakedness elsewhere. As more women pursued diet and exercise regimes, they were able to adopt body-revealing styles, as a youthful, slender body that required no support for the breasts was a prerequisite for wearing a backless garment.

Madeleine Vionnet introduced the backless bias-cut gown which followed the contours of the body – often featuring intricate seaming that defined the small of the back – to couture customers in Europe around 1930. The slither of silk satin quickly proved irresistible to Hollywood screen sirens such as Jean Harlow and Carole Lombard, who represented the epitome of provocative Hollywood glamour. Denied the exposure of cleavage by Hollywood's Hays Code, which set rigid guidelines on what was permissible to reveal, actresses instead removed their bras and displayed this new erogenous zone. Influenced by the fragmented geometry of Art Deco, the bare back was often framed by loose drapery hanging each side from the point of the shoulders, in addition to the triangular handkerchief points at the hem or flounces at the hips. Evening gowns were highly decorated in lustrous fabrics such as crepe de Chine, lamé and taffeta, with both the matt and shiny side of satin used in contrast to each other. More than any other era, the styles of 1930s eveningwear continue to influence contemporary designers. The classic red-carpet stance adopted by female film stars for the paparazzi shot is one where, turning away from the camera, with hand on hip, the actress coyly looks over her shoulder, exposing her back to the lens. With the long walk up the red carpet, the back view is as important as the front. Wearing a gown by Naeem Khan, Rosie Huntington-Whiteley, who models for Victoria's Secret, and actress Hilary Swank in Elie Saab Couture, exploit the properties of the 1930s-inspired, elongated backless gown for their red-carpet appearances.

**LEFT:** Contemporary backless gowns are cut in an increasingly deeper line, revealing the naked back both above and below the waist. Striking the archetypal red carpet pose, and ensuring a dramatic exit, Rosie Huntington-Whiteley wears a form-fitting gown designed by Indian-born, US-based Naeem Khan.

**OPPOSITE:** The sensuous slide of bias-cut satin over the contours of the body epitomizes the theatricality of 1930s glamour. Creating a focal point at the small of the back, the front of the gown is draped at the waist over a darker bodice to form a bow, before extending into a flowing train.

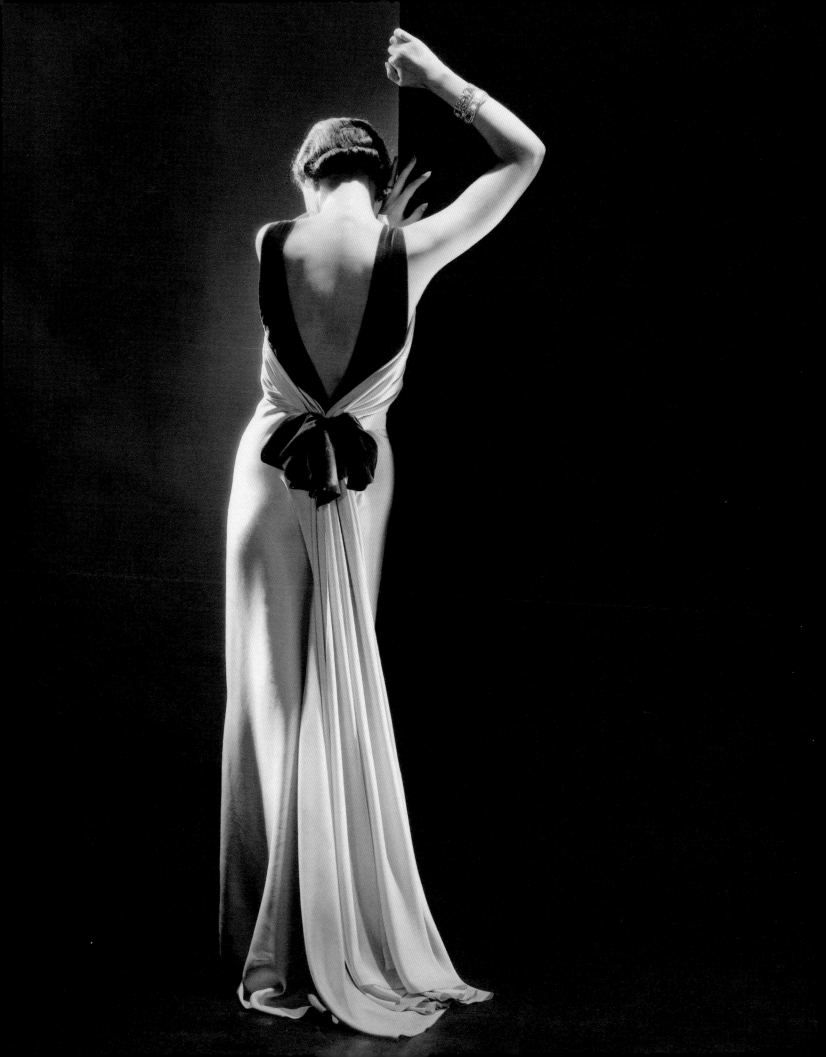

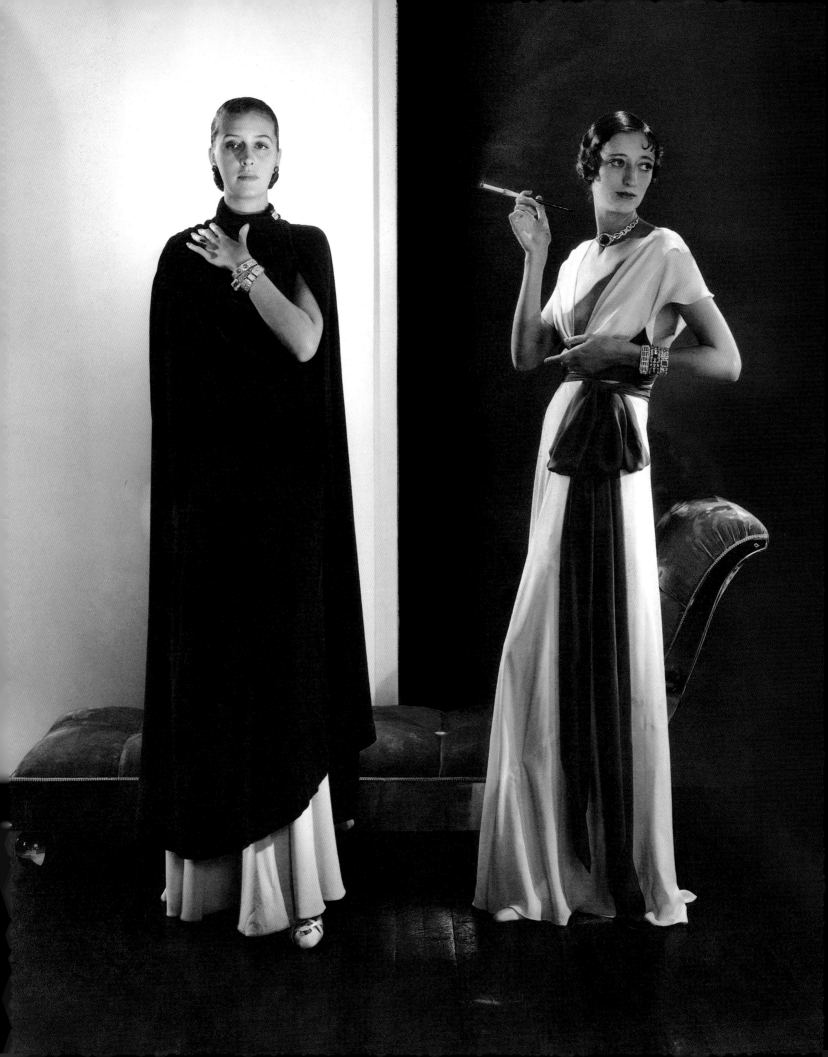

# The Bias Cut

With a sliver of bias-cut silk crepe, Parisian couturière Madeleine Vionnet created a new silhouette for the 1930s, one that celebrated the contours of the body and signified a move away from the tubular fringed and beaded chemise dresses of the 1920s. The austerity and restraint of the unadorned garments were representative of the inter-war move towards modernism, and were created by the manipulation of geometric forms such as squares and quadrants – four equally sized quarter circles – so that they draped around the body, the couturière working directly onto an articulated half-size mannequin, draping, pinning and cutting the cloth around the form.

Acknowledged as being the inventor of the "bias cut" – where fabric is cut across the grain rather than along it – Vionnet often cut the fabric on the straight of the grain (woven fabric has both a warp and a weft – horizontal and vertical threads that cross at right angles to form a straight grain), then turned the pieces of cloth 45 degrees so that they draped on the bias. The silk crepe fabric would then be weighted at the edges and hung in the atelier for several weeks before being sewn together to alleviate any unevenness of the hemline. Vionnet had previously experimented with cutting techniques as early as 1910, and honed the process while undergoing an apprenticeship with Callot Soeurs, and later Jacques Doucet, where Vionnet incorporated non-Western and classical techniques of garment construction based on the loom width of cloth involving minimal cutting.

The sensuous glamour of the bias cut was exploited by Hollywood screen sirens such as Carole Lombard and Jean Harlow, the original platinum blonde bombshell. She wore a satin bias-cut gown in the 1933 film *Dinner At Eight*, designed by head of costume Gilbert Adrian at Metro-Goldwyn-Mayer, who popularized Vionnet's figure-moulding gowns for an American audience.

The fluidity of the bias cut was exploited by self-confessed fashion fantasist John Galliano, progenitor of the archetypal bias-cut slip dress of the 1990s. The lingerie-inspired sensuous lines of the dress were cut narrowly to follow the contours of the body, and often featured thin "spaghetti" straps. Fashioned from clinging crepe or silk chiffon, the body-revealing dress was popularized by model Kate Moss, and created a furore when worn by Diana, the late Princess of Wales, at the Met Ball in 1996.

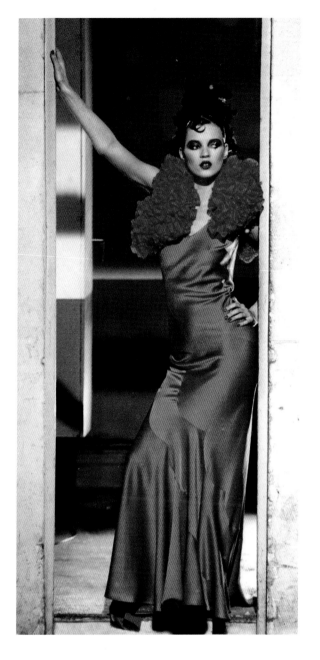

**OPPOSITE:** Rather than assembling pattern pieces, Madeleine Vionnet (1876–1975) draped and cut cloth by working directly on a half-sized articulated mannequin, creating deceptively simple eveningwear based on the classical aesthetic, with the emphasis on form rather than decoration.

**RIGHT:** John Galliano's mastery of piecing together fabric to effect a seductive silhouette is evident in the complex construction of this dress from A/W 1995–96. Working on the bias, the designer also incorporated two scalloped seams set diagonally across the skirt of the gown.

# The Peacock Motif

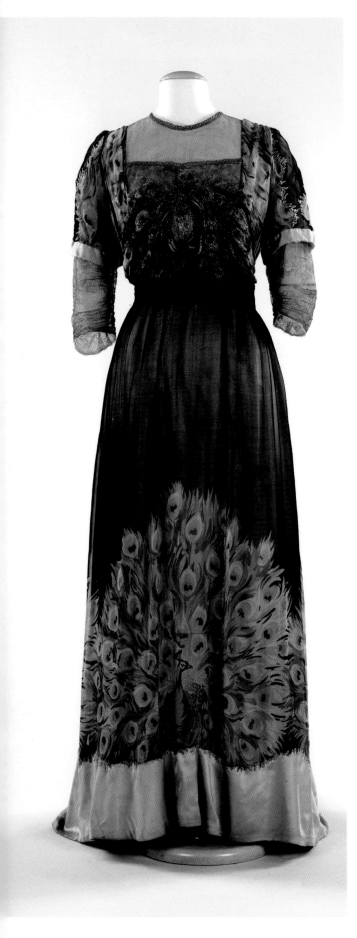

A bird of near-mythical status, the peacock is a potent signifier of excessive, narcissistic display, the lustrous surface, jewel-like colours and graphic patterning of the bird's feathers translating effectively into embellished and printed designs. Synonymous with the aesthete movement of the late nineteenth century, the plumage has proved to be particularly appealing at times of high decoration in fashion, and peacock feathers were used in their natural form for fans and dress accessories as well as for providing inspiration for the peacock-printed fabric designed by Arthur Silver, founder of the Silver Studio in 1880. This London-based commercial pattern studio established a fruitful relationship with London store Liberty, and the peacock feather design subsequently became inextricably linked with the store throughout the following century and beyond, updated on fabrics such as Tana lawn, Lantana wool, crepe de Chine, georgette, poplin, silk satin and jersey.

The peacock hails from Sri Lanka and India, where it was associated with royalty, hence the "peacock" throne, a symbol of Persian monarchy. Lady Curzon, wife of the Viceroy of India, wore a peacock gown to the state ball of Delhi in 1903, an occasion that proclaimed King Edward VII as Emperor of India. Designed by couturier Jean-Philippe Worth, the corseted silk dress featured a repeating pattern of peacock feathers hand-stitched in silver embroidery, with the peacock "eyes" highlighted with blue and green beetle wings.

A popular motif that captured the brilliance of the Belle Époque, the peacock feather featured in the collections of dressmakers and couturiers, including the little-known Parisian house of Weeks, which incorporated both printed and embroidered peacock motifs in a silk gown dating from 1910. The peacock became a fitting emblem of the free-thinking "rainbow decade" of the late 1960s, which heralded the arrival of historical revivalism, first invoked through the free-flowing forms of Art Nouveau, when designers incorporated the birds into their textiles. The heightened perception accrued from hallucinogenic drugs resulted in mesmerizing patterns and kaleidoscopic colours of which the peacock feather was a favoured motif, and one which represented the flamboyant fashions of the era. Confirming the association of the peacock feather with romantic bohemianism was the exuberant luxe-hippie aesthetic of UK designer and colour maestro Matthew Williamson, who introduced his signature peacock print into a collection for Spring/Summer 2004. Worn by friend and long-term muse Sienna Miller, the peacock print dress established contemporary "boho" style.

LEFT: The peacock-embroidered gown from the Parisian house of Weeks marks a shift in silhouette from the extreme hourglass figure of the Belle Époque to a more tubular outline in 1910, with the emphasis on two-dimensional embellishment rather than flounces and frills.

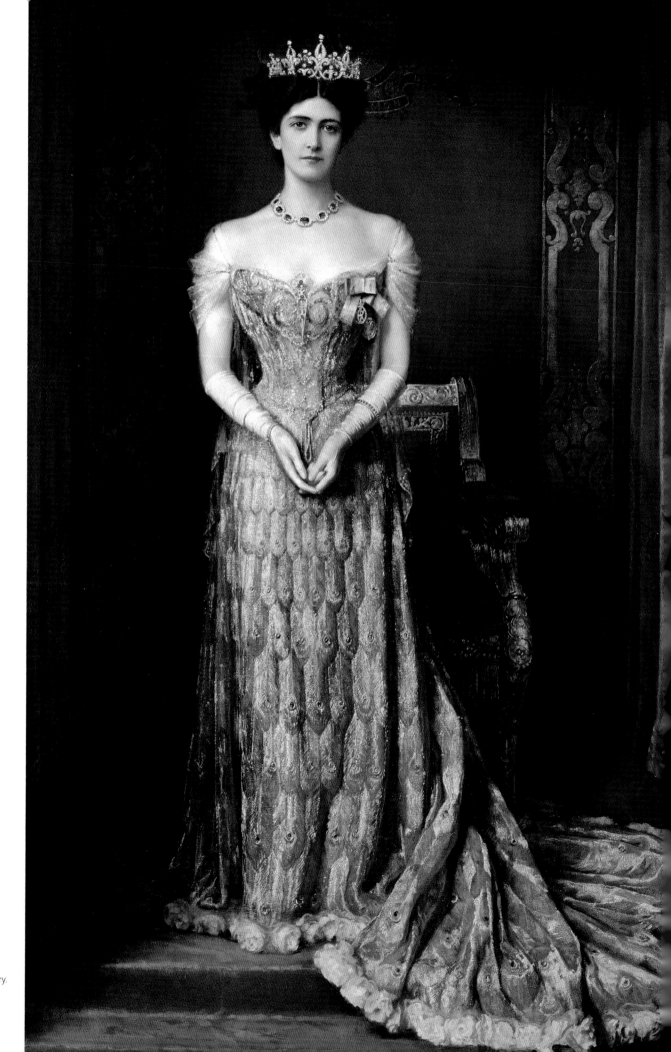

**RIGHT:** A full-length portrait of Lady Curzon, attributed to William Logsdail (1859–1944), encapsulates the full glory of the peacock feather plumage. The intense all-over pattern is fashioned into a corseted hourglass silhouette that was popular at the turn of the century.

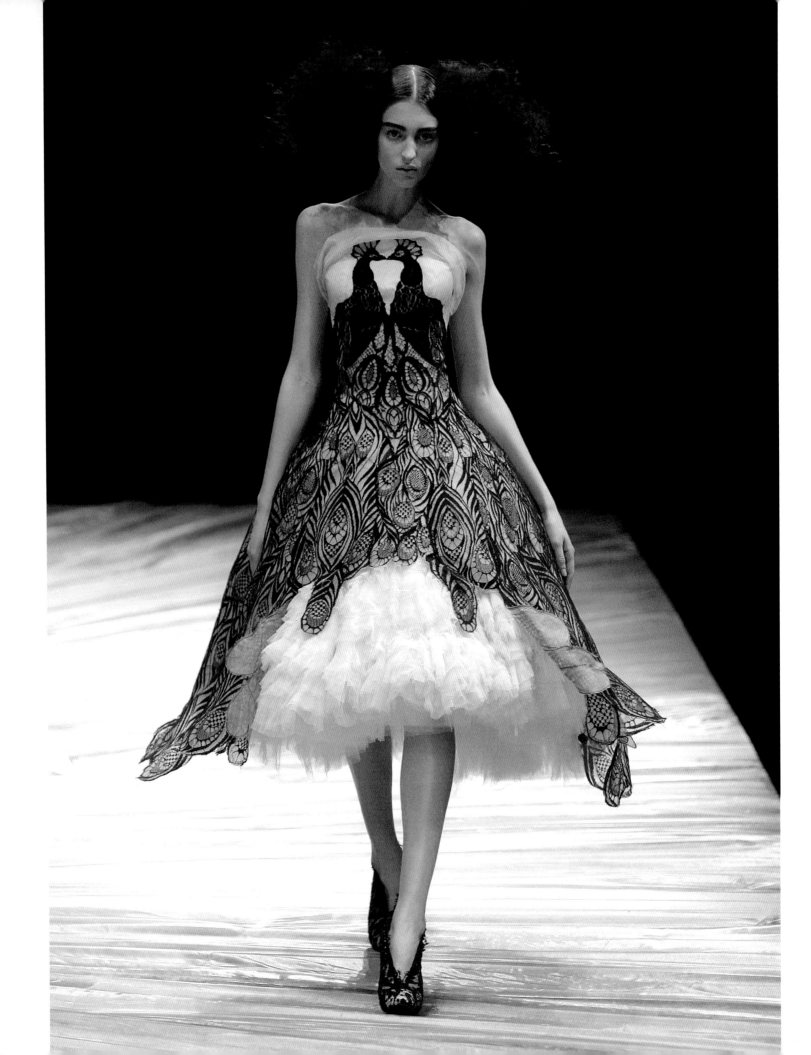

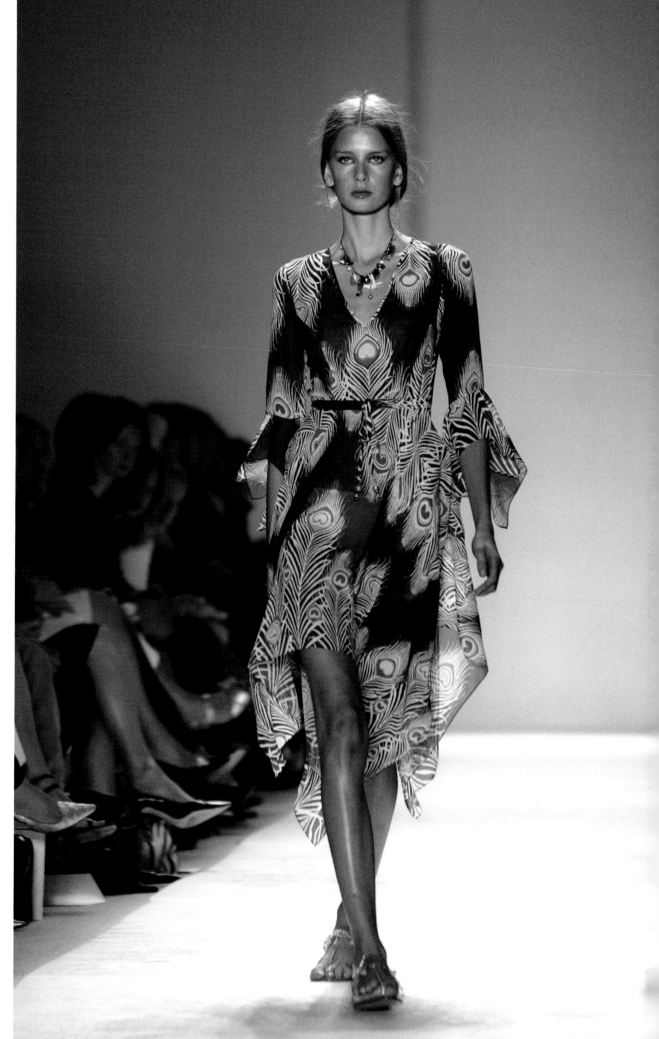

**OPPOSITE:** A mirror image of a pair of peacocks forms the strapless bodice of a ballerina-length dress by Alexander McQueen for A/W 2008–9. Fashioned from cut-out black lace engineered to fit the silhouette, the tail feathers fan out over ivory tulle petticoats.

**RIGHT:** London-based designer Matthew Williamson (1971–) exemplifies hippie luxe style, from his ebullient use of colour offset with black to the digital print of peacock feathers, cleverly engineered to emphasize the flowing lines of the handkerchief-hem dress from S/S 2014.

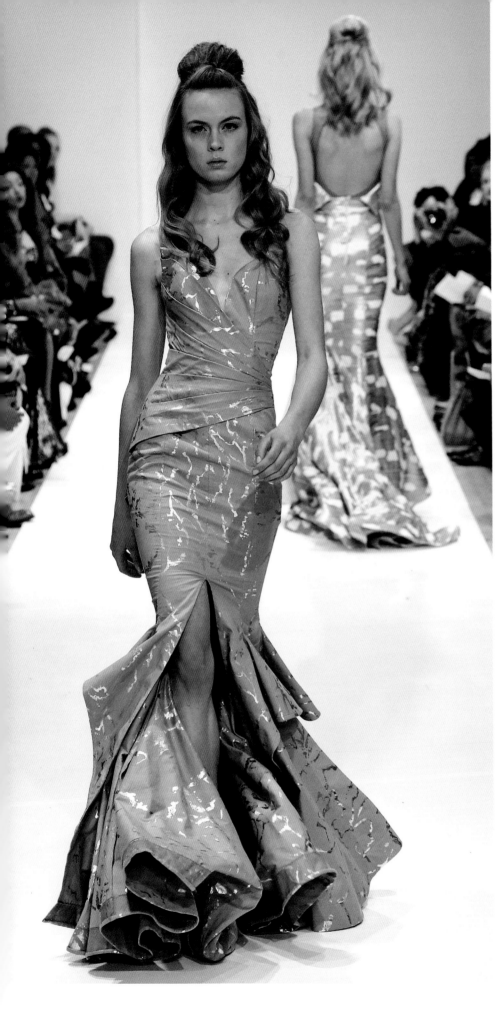

## The Fishtail

The undulating form of the fishtail silhouette is a modern fashion phenomenon that first appeared in the 1930s with the introduction of the bias-cut gown, although the effect was as much to do with the clinging satin or silk crepe used as an intentional fishtail hem. Characterized by a form-following skirt, narrowing at the knees, the fishtail hem splays out to varying degrees, depending on the fabric and the style of the gown. British court dressmakers Norman Hartnell and Victor Stiebel, among others, both introduced a gently fluted fishtail hem to mid-calf floral silk day dresses during the streamlined elegance of the 1930s, the wider hem offset by the era's structured shoulder, a look still prevalent in contemporary fashion with the popularity of the classic tea dress. For evening, a more pronounced fishtail was introduced, the result of the insertion of godets (triangular pieces of cloth), bias cutting or clever pleating, the resulting volume matched by neck, sleeve and shoulder detail or a frilled cape in the same material.

During the 1950s so extreme was the suppression of fabric around the knees in the construction of the fishtail that walking was restricted, an effect not unlike Poiret's hobble skirt from earlier in the twentieth century (*see also page 94*), the difference being a return to fullness around the ankles with the modern version. The strapless or halterneck version of the fishtail was a style much beloved of popular entertainers of the time such as chanteuse Peggy Lee and singer Della Reese, and it was frequently accessorized with a silver fox fur stole and over-the-elbow gloves. It was not a silhouette promulgated by the couturiers of the era; it was a show-stopper gown rather than one demanding couture construction techniques for an elite clientele.

A more exaggerated fishtail silhouette is most popular during periods when the hourglass shape is most prevalent, or most valued, such as on the red carpet. The indent at the knees adds an extra provocative curve to the classic hourglass outline, in addition to providing a flourish of fabric at the hem with movement. Pop icon Beyoncé favours the silhouette for her dramatic glamorous gowns, any question of slightly retro glamour dispelled with their emphasis on the deft manipulation of opulent fabrics and extensive ornamentation for the contemporary Hollywood moment.

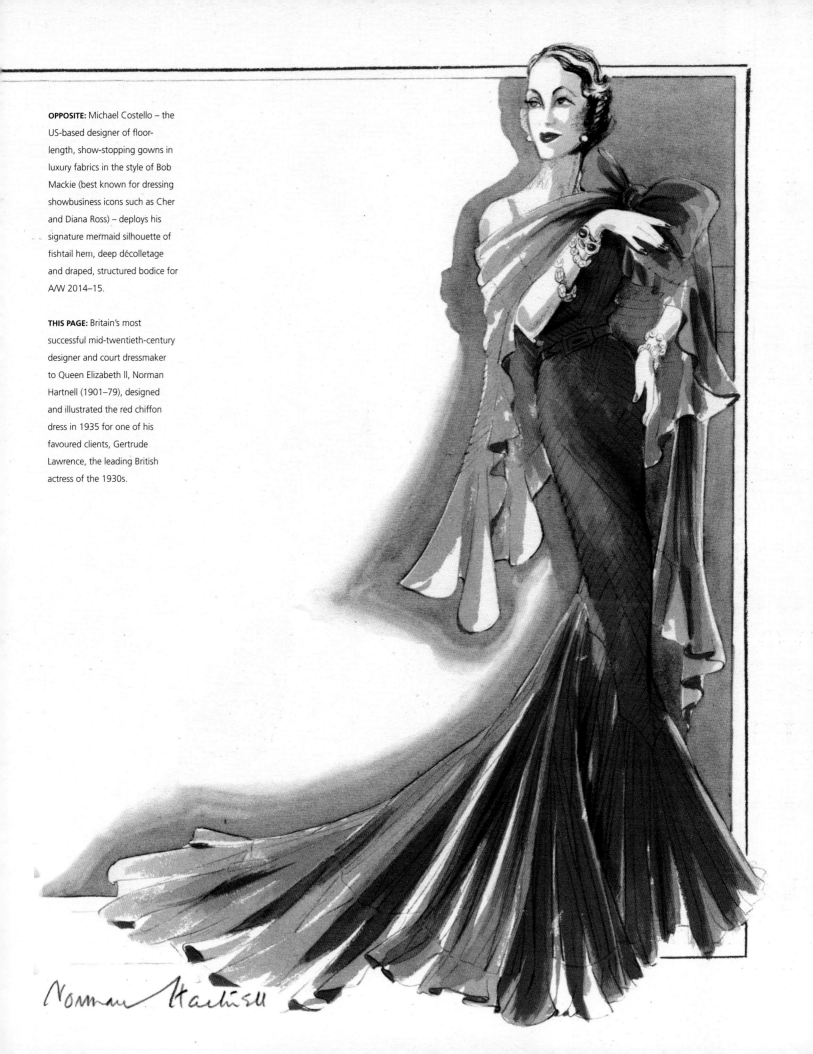

**OPPOSITE:** Michael Costello – the US-based designer of floor-length, show-stopping gowns in luxury fabrics in the style of Bob Mackie (best known for dressing showbusiness icons such as Cher and Diana Ross) – deploys his signature mermaid silhouette of fishtail hem, deep décolletage and draped, structured bodice for A/W 2014–15.

**THIS PAGE:** Britain's most successful mid-twentieth-century designer and court dressmaker to Queen Elizabeth II, Norman Hartnell (1901–79), designed and illustrated the red chiffon dress in 1935 for one of his favoured clients, Gertrude Lawrence, the leading British actress of the 1930s.

Norman Hartnell

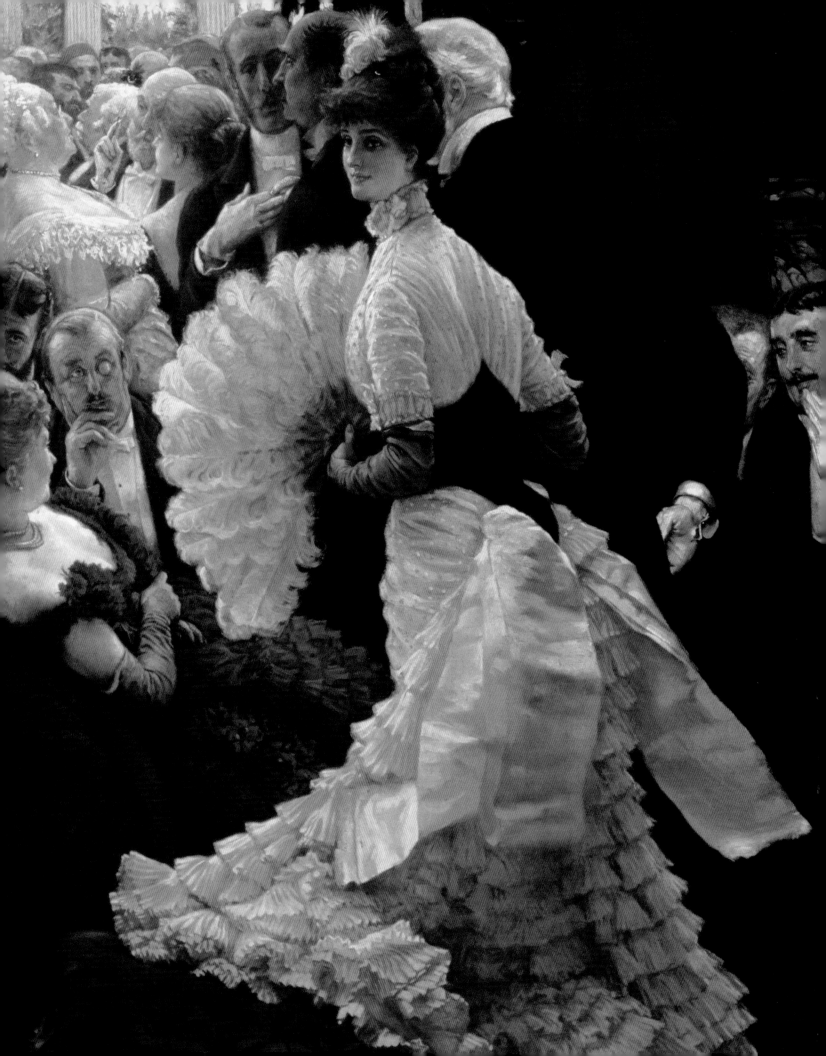

# The Frou-Frou Dress

The sound made by the rustling of silk, "frou frou" signifies the ultimate in frilled femininity. Captured with the unerring eye of French artist James Tissot – renowned for his detailed and accurate depiction of the fashions of the day – in his painting *The Reception*, or *L'Ambitieuse*, the cascading frills of the bustle represent the *fin de siècle* aesthetic of the late 1880s. The desire for the picturesque resurfaced towards the end of the 1930s, when the modern silhouette of the era was replaced by a romantic nostalgia for the fashions of the previous century. These were inspired in part by the images on the silver screen rather than the Parisian salon, as a Depression-hit United States sought escapism with a number of costume dramas.

Orry-Kelly designed the luxuriously befrilled skirts worn by Bette Davis in William Wyler's *Jezebel* (1938), and Walter Plunkett adorned screen rival and film actress Vivienne Leigh in her role as Scarlett O'Hara in a series of frilled crinolines in the big blockbuster movie *Gone with the Wind* (1939). The ascendancy of Hollywood over Paris as a generator of trends was further confirmed by the fashion phenomenon of the dress worn by Joan Crawford in the title role of Clarence Brown's feature film *Letty Lynton* (1932). The abundantly frilled long white evening dress in *mousseline de soi* with extravagantly frilled sleeves was designed by Hollywood costumier Adrian, and prompted numerous copies known as "butterfly-sleeve" dresses. Britain's Queen Elizabeth also bedecked herself in frilled layers of Valenciennes lace, silk, satin, velvet, taffeta, tulle and chiffon designed by British court dressmaker Norman Hartnell for her state visit to France in the early summer of 1938. Her "white wardrobe" – the death of the Queen's mother, three weeks before the visit, resulted in all the gowns being remade in white (a royal prerogative for mourning) – was inspired by the romantic images painted by Franz Xaver Winterhalter of Empress Elisabeth of Austria. This nostalgic pastiche of the crinoline form by couturiers prefigured the New Look by a decade and became the defining silhouette of the 1950s. The increasing relevance of couture in the twenty-first century and the commensurate attention to detail is evidenced by Alexander McQueen's Oyster dress, the skirt of which is composed of a millefeuille of frills, graduating layers of ivory silk organza.

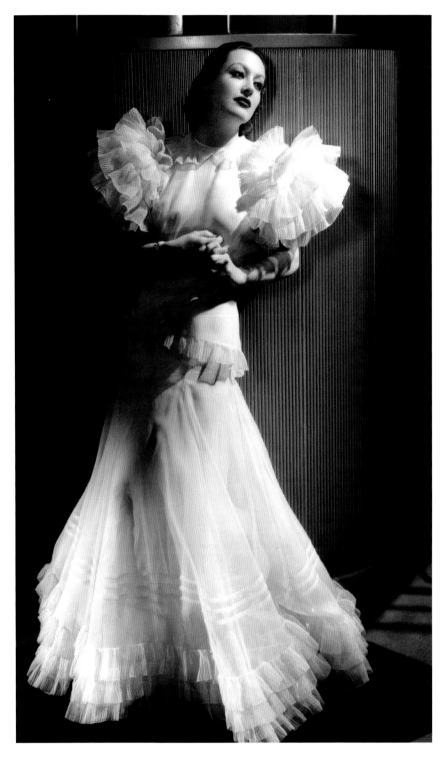

**OPPOSITE:** Capturing the elaborate complexity of fashionable dress, French painter James Tissot (1836–1902) renders in meticulous detail the all-concealing layers of ruffled fabric, from the high-boned collar to the sweeping bustled train, in *The Reception*, or *L'Ambitieuse* (1883–85).

**ABOVE:** A froth of ingénue femininity, the gown designed by Adrian (1903–59) for Joan Crawford in Clarence Brown's melodrama *Letty Lynton* (1932) provided a frivolous contrast to the austere tailored garments and masculine silhouette of 1930s daywear.

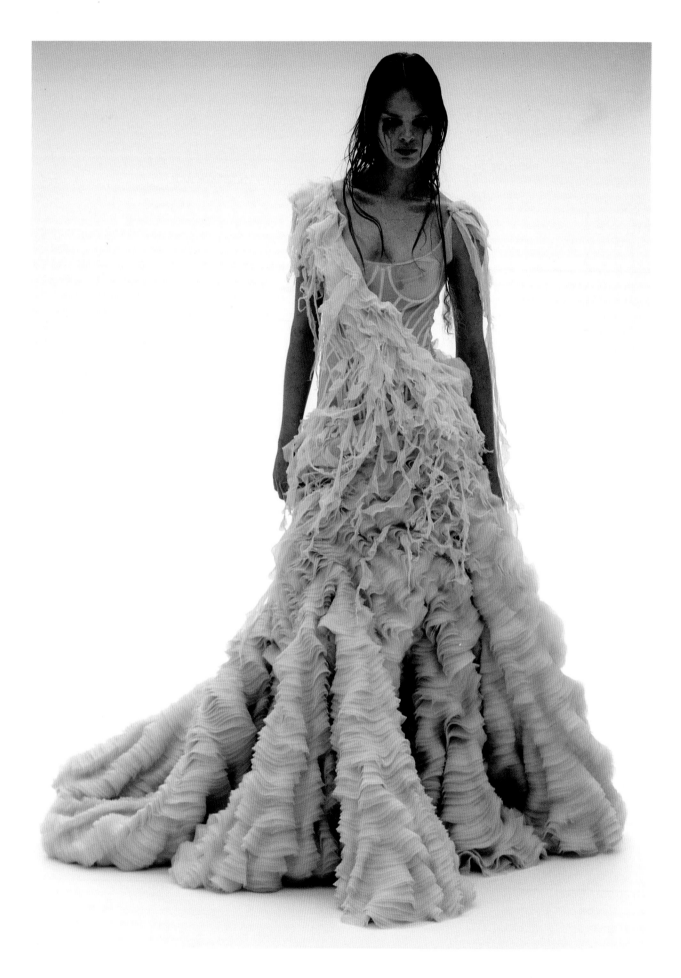

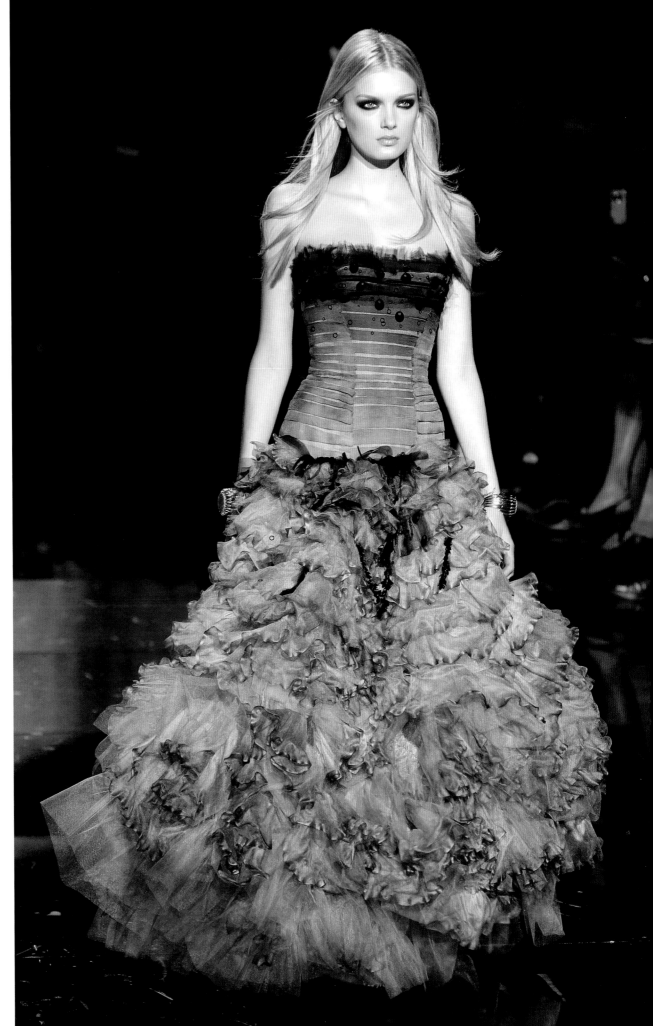

**OPPOSITE:** Presenting an epic narrative of a disaster at sea with Elizabethan pirates and drowned maidens, Alexander McQueen's Oyster dress from his "Irere" collection S/S 2003, included a gown of pale sea-washed sand with layers of frills redolent of the ridging on the surface of an oyster shell.

**RIGHT:** Inevitably associated with luxurious femininity, the flurries of multi-directional tremblant frills adorning the skirt of this red-carpet gown designed by Maria Grazia Chiuri and Pierpaolo Piccioli for luxury Italian label Valentino are in contrast to the strictly structured strapless bodice.

# The Halterneck

As with many designs that appear initially daring, the halterneck – named after the halter, placed around an animal's neck for restraining purposes – had previously been more commonly used in swimwear design, allowing for maximum sun exposure on the back, before being adopted as eveningwear in the 1930s. The prevailing silhouette was one of streamlined androgyny, and the halterneck – a single strap or piece of fabric running from the front of the garment around the back of the wearer's neck to hold up the bodice – placed emphasis on the shoulders rather than the breasts. Variations of the style included a drawstring tie used to gather up the fabric of the bodice, or the ends of the strap were brought forward to the front of the neck and tied with a decorative bow. All variations left the back exposed.

Adopting necklines that drew attention to exaggerated embonpoint, film stars of the 1950s, such as Elizabeth Taylor and Marilyn Monroe, frequently wore dresses that were strapless, off-the-shoulder or featured the halterneck, designed to both frame and support the breasts. Exemplifying undiluted sexuality, Marilyn Monroe wore a gold lamé dress by favoured film costumier William Travis for her role as husband-hunter Lorelei Lee in Howard Hawks' 1953 film *Gentlemen Prefer Blondes*. Although Ginger Rogers wore the same dress in the 1952 film *Dreamboat*, with Monroe's more lubricious appearance it was deemed too revealing, and featured only briefly. Fully aware of the impact of the design, Monroe once again wore a halterneck white pleated dress, one of the most iconic of film images, for her provocative pose over a subway grating in Billy Wilder's 1955 film *The Seven Year Itch*.

The contemporary halterneck dress is not designed to contain or emphasize the breasts, but seemingly to bypass them. Wearing a two-tone red halterneck dress from Valentino Couture, 2014, film actress Amy Adams represents the über-slender body of the era, requiring little support. Created from two triangular pieces of fabric without any apparent shaping, the bodice of the dress is attached to a high waist, exposing a new area of erotic interest and a new phenomenon to be seen on the red carpet, the so-called "side boob".

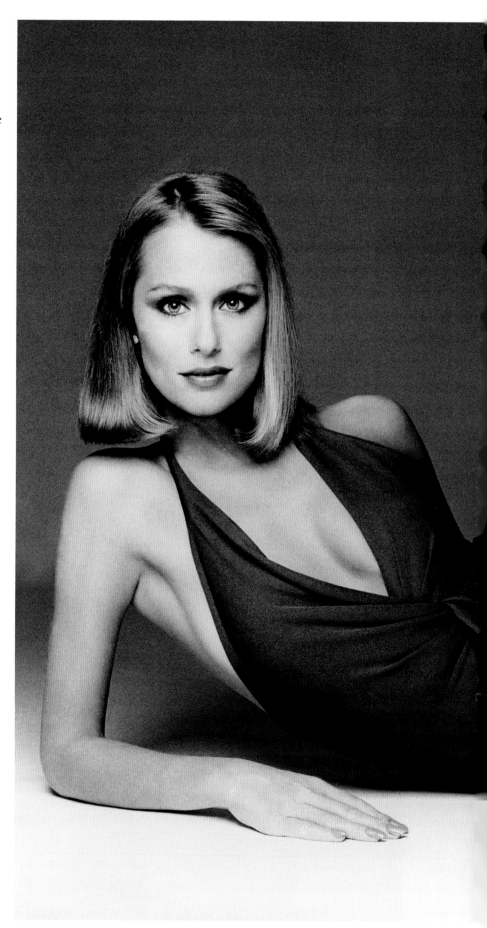

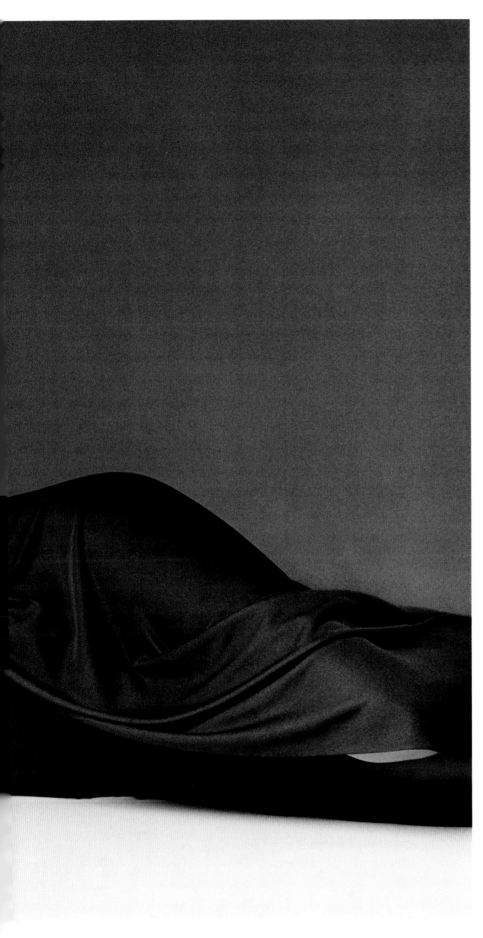

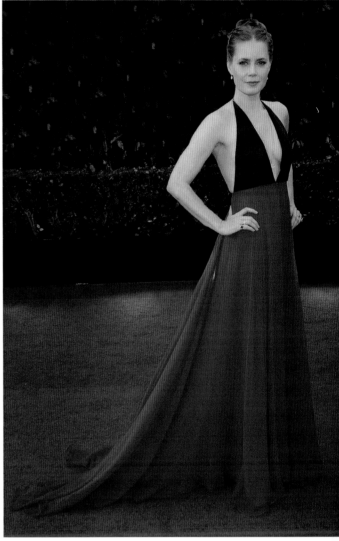

**ABOVE:** On the contemporary red carpet, a glimpse of the side of the breasts has replaced the décolletage as an area of erotic interest. Film actress Amy Adams wears a red halterneck gown designed by Maria Grazia Chiuri and Pierpaolo Piccioli for Valentino Couture from 2014.

**LEFT:** The fluid, sarong-inspired lines of the wrap-over dress became the dominant evening style in the 1970s in the USA. Halston (1932–90) promulgated this soft, pared-down, unconstructed look, which was exemplified by the matt jersey halterneck worn by 1970s leading model, Lauren Hutton.

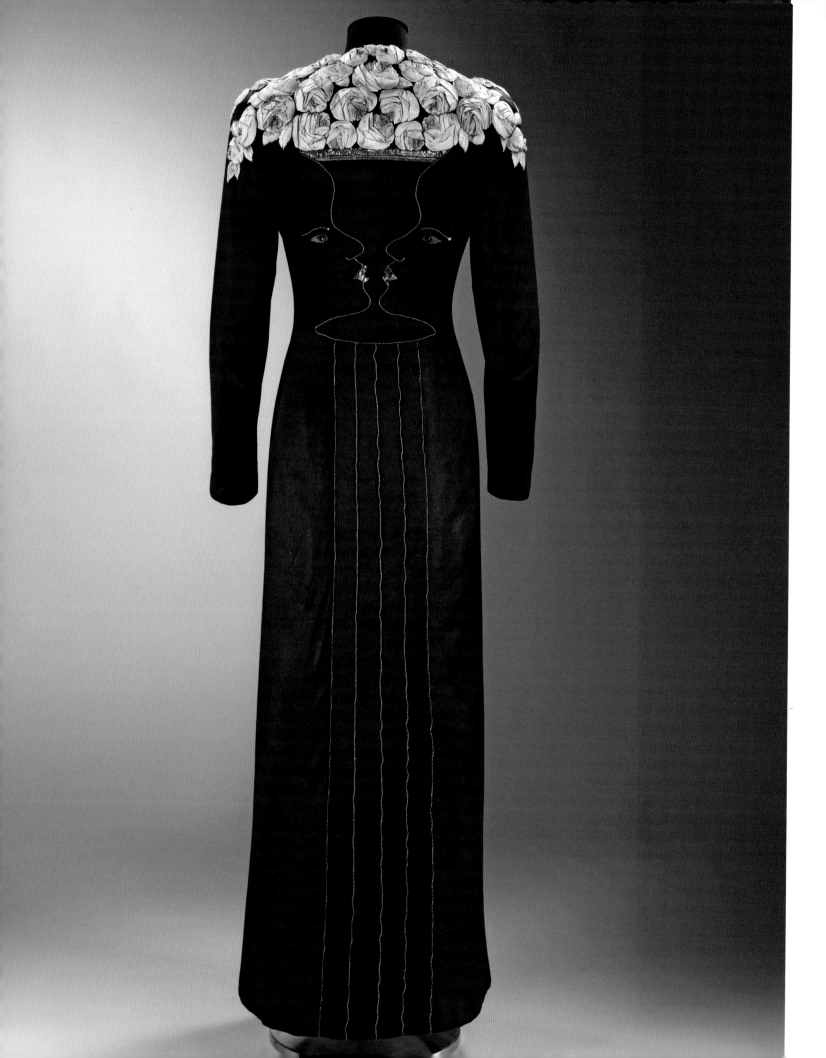

# Surrealism

The creative alliance between art and fashion reached its apotheosis with the collaboration between avant-garde designer Elsa Schiaparelli and the Surrealist movement of the 1920s and 1930s. Surrealism was founded by French writer and poet André Breton, who proclaimed, "Beauty will be convulsive or not at all," which explored the symbolic imagery released in dreams and hallucinations. It was an exercise in displacement that subverted the ordinary and placed it within a new, visually disturbing context.

While staying in New York after World War I, Italian-born Elsa Schiaparelli became involved with the Dada movement and their attempt to shake off artistic traditions. Once back in Paris she extended her friendships with Man Ray, Marcel Duchamp, Jean Cocteau, Alfred Stieglitz and Salvador Dalí, the self-appointed leader of the Surrealistic movement and as noted for his outrageous publicity stunts as for his paintings of theatrical dreamscapes of hypnagogic imagery and deliquescent watches in desert landscapes.

Schiaparelli's reputation as the "artist designer" was consolidated by the use of trompe l'oeil – literally "tricking the eye" – in her striking knitted garments, such as her bow sweaters of 1927. Her penchant for trompe l'oeil resulted in a natural collaboration with Dalí on a number of designs, including the Skeleton dress (*see page* 97) and the Tears dress; both featured in Schiaparelli's famous "Circus" collection of 1938. The painter designed the trompe l'oeil tears and rips in the cloth, which were cut out and lined in pink and magenta, suggestive of flayed flesh, a feature of Dalí's work.

Schiaparelli also collaborated with French artist, poet and filmmaker Jean Cocteau, who produced two drawings for Schiaparelli which were translated into designs for a jacket and an evening coat for her Autumn 1937 collection. The coat design exemplifies Cocteau's preoccupation with the double image, seen in the design which can either be read as two profiles facing each other, or a vase of roses standing on a fluted column. In a pun on the artist Man Ray, the pioneer Surrealist avant-garde photographer, French designer Jean-Charles de Castelbajac dubbed his Autumn/Winter 2011 collection "Woman/Ray". The designer was inspired by the Surrealist photographer's *Tears* and *The Violin of Ingres*, a photograph of the artist's companion and muse Kiki de Montparnasse, styled after *The Valpinçon Bather* by Ingres.

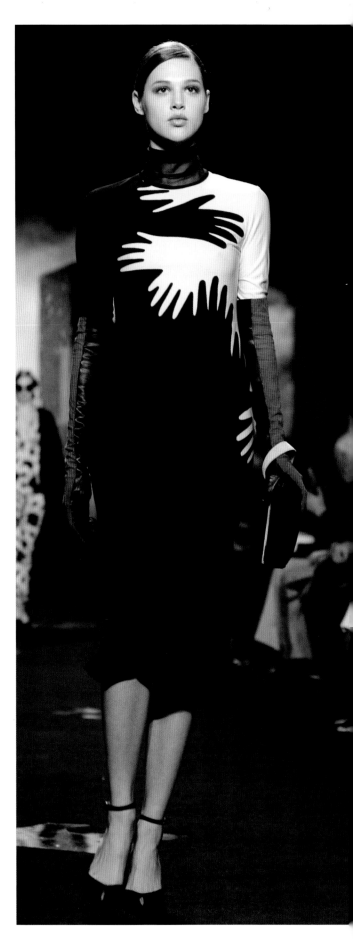

**OPPOSITE:** In 1937 Elsa Schiaparelli brought to fruition an elaborate optical illusion devised by Jean Cocteau, whereby embellishment on a dark ground was able to proffer disparate readings of positive and negative space. The conundrum of facial profiles vying with a classical vase for legibility was embroidered on silk jersey at the House of Lesage.

**RIGHT:** The stark graphic of interlocked black and white hands is used in Diane von Furstenberg's A/W 2012–13 dress to create a surreal illusion of the afterimage of an embrace. In combination with the form-fitting silhouette and the red and black opera gloves, the imagery has undertones of the sensual solitary caresses of the burlesque dancer.

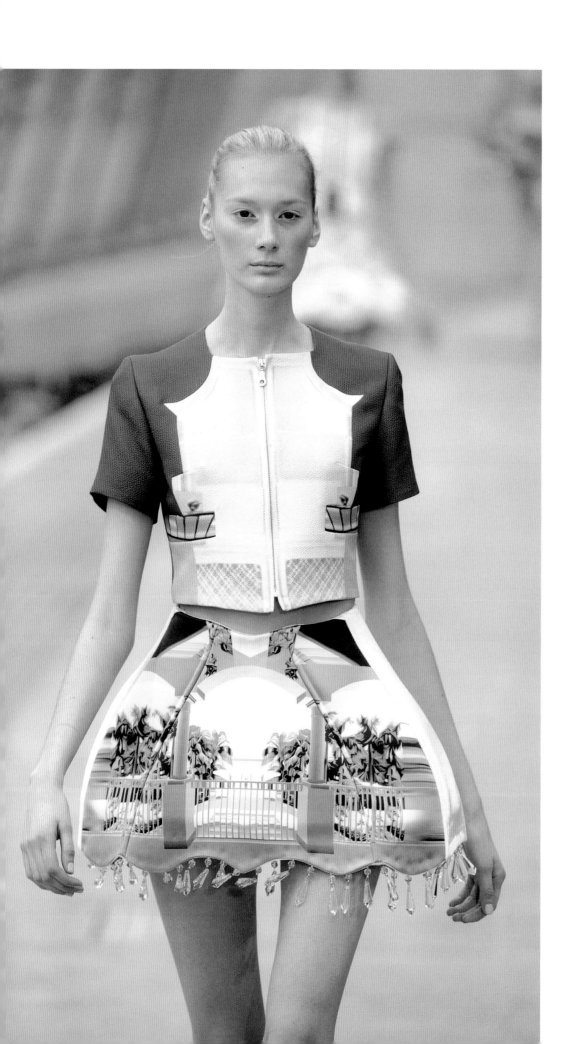

**LEFT:** Precisely visualizing perspective vistas that trickily recede into the taut panels of a mini-crini lampshade, replete with dangling Swarovski crystals, Mary Katrantzou extends her trompe l'oeil compulsion to surreal levels of digital complexity in her collection for S/S 2011.

**OPPOSITE LEFT:** Jean-Charles de Castelbajac continues the practice of historic revision that Man Ray indulged in when he created his Dadaist photograph *The Violin of Ingres* in 1924 – with the graphic addition of the sound-box openings of a cello. The famous back in the painting fronts a satin dress for A/W 2011–12.

**OPPOSITE RIGHT:** Moschino Cheap and Chic for A/W 2012–13 converts the simplest of printed tunic dresses into a spatially modulated form with a surreal montage of upscale facial anatomy, highlighted with lip detail, whimsically glossed with sequins. In homage to Dalí, a circus moustache in jet black sequins adds a comedic flourish.

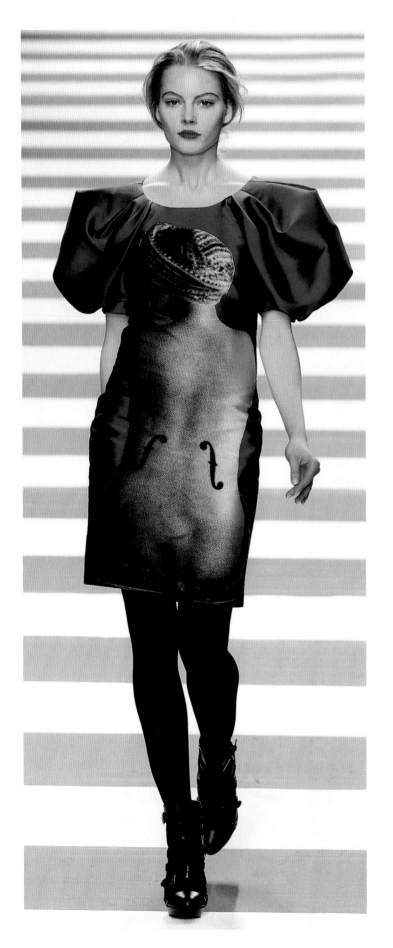

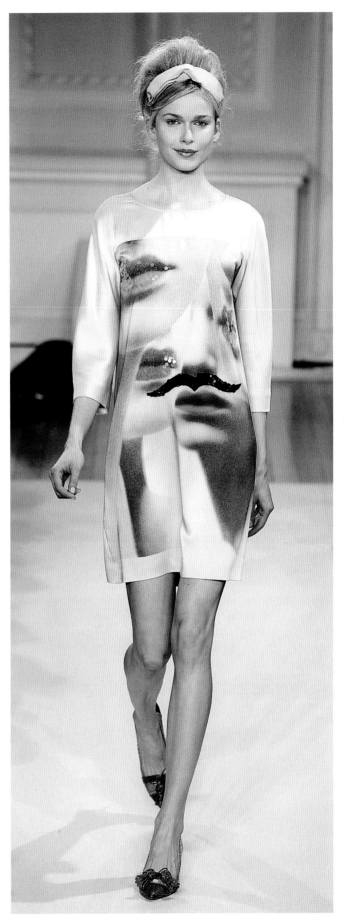

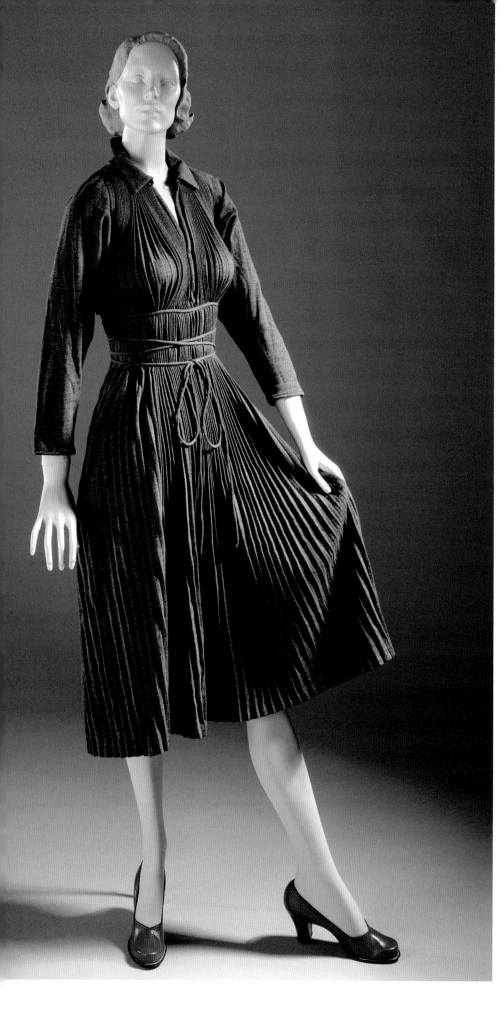
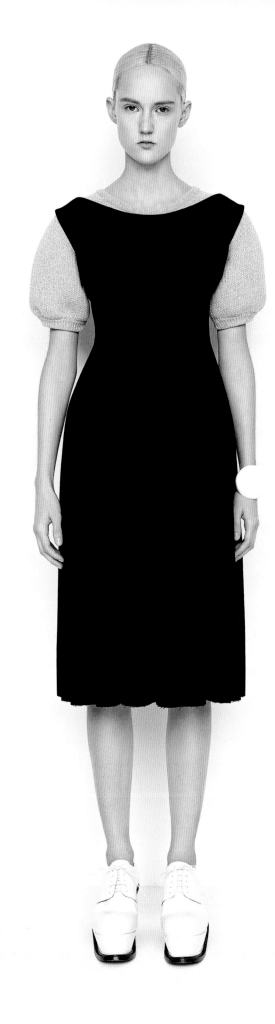

# The Monastic Dress

The Monastic dress was a breakthrough garment in establishing a modern dress code of easy-to-wear practical clothing for the mid-twentieth-century woman. From the 1930s onwards, American designers such as Clare Potter, Tina Lesser and, later, Bonnie Cashin exercised an independence from the authority of French couture by introducing active sportswear – known as leisurewear in the UK – that prized practicality and versatility above the dictates of Paris and upheld a democratic and casual approach to fashion.

Chief exponent of this new generation of influential women designers was Claire McCardell, who brought problem-solving ingenuity to the lives of the modern woman with various garment innovations: roomy pockets, dropped shoulder seams for ease of movement, wrap pinafore dresses, and simple, practical and accessible fastenings such as toggles and rope. These were all constructed in easy-to-launder fabrics such as gingham, jersey and denim, previously only used for men's workwear. McCardell first worked for retail entrepreneur Hattie Carnegie, before becoming head designer and eventually partner of mass-manufacturer Townley Frocks, producing garments under the label "Claire McCardell Clothes by Townley", making her one of the first American designers to have name recognition.

The designer's breakthrough came in 1938, when she created the Monastic dress, so called because it was cut like a tent-shaped monk's habit. The inspiration for the dress was an Algerian costume based on the *burnous*, a coarse woollen cloak with a hood, worn by Berbers and the Arabs throughout North Africa. The untailored dress with wide, loose sleeves was worn to hang loose from the shoulders or tied with a rope-like belt in a variety of positions by the wearer. The pull-on dress provided an alternative to the prevailing late 1930s structured and tailored silhouette, and was representative of the vogue for high-end ready-to-wear coming out of New York's Seventh Avenue. The timeless qualities of the Monastic dress, with its overtones of austere simplicity and a silhouette defined by soft, unpressed pleats, have been re-imagined over the decades. British designer John Bates introduced his Puritan look in 1971 – a full-length dress in grey wool jersey, named the Chorister dress – which became a much-copied bestseller. Into a collection of complex, abstract dresses for pre-Autumn 2014, UK-based designer J.W. Anderson – Jonathan William Anderson – featured a dress that was ecclesiastical in its simplicity and execution.

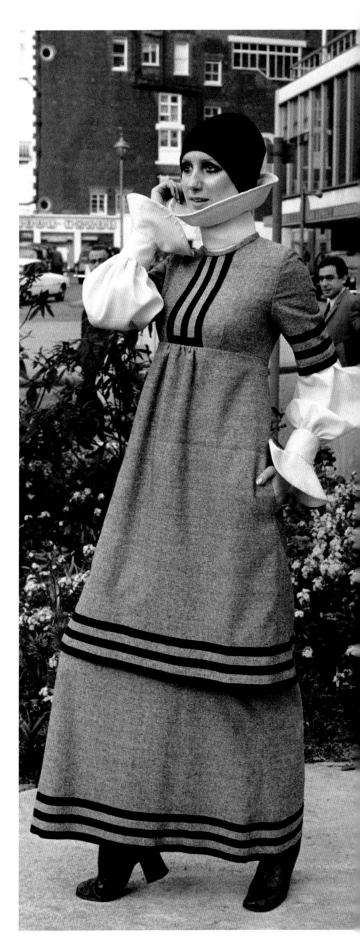

**OPPOSITE LEFT:** Originating in the 1930s, Claire McCardell's Monastic dress, a fashion staple, continued to be produced throughout the designer's career in various fabrics and widths. Ties, often made of bias piping, allowed her customers to decide where the waistline should fall.

**OPPOSITE RIGHT:** Pre-Autumn collections allow a designer to elaborate on ideas before committing them to seasonal collections. For pre-Autumn 2014, J.W. Anderson (1984–) offered austere simplicity in a dress where unpressed pleats were the only detail.

**RIGHT:** The two-tiered ankle-length dress in grey wool by iconoclastic designer John Bates from 1971 features dramatic horizontal bands. It is worn over a blouse with deep frilled cuffs and a raised collar, forming a pie-crust frill in the style of a young chorister.

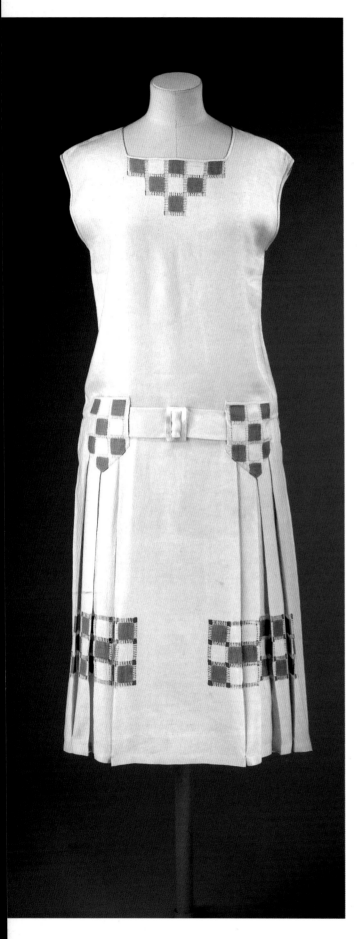

# The Tennis Dress

The popularity of all types of outdoor sports, such as golf, skiing and tennis, burgeoned in the 1920s as women left off their boned corsets and embraced a more active life. The tennis court became a site of upper-class social activity, whether attached to a private house or sited in one of the newly popular "country clubs". Women's increasing desire to actively participate in the game demanded liberating garments, simple and functional clothes that did not restrict movement. The lack of a specified uniform in tennis gave players a fashionable freedom, and Parisian designers were eager to create designs that focused on sportswear as a branch of fashion in its own right, a previously untapped market. Jean Patou, the leading exponent of sporting dress, freed women from the constraints of cumbersome heavily layered sportswear and introduced the notion of public "undress" in the form of sleeveless dresses and by shortening the skirt to mid-calf, a style closely associated with the tubular drop-waisted chemise of the prevailing *garçonne* look of the day.

The tennis dress was almost invariably in white, and rendered in lightweight fabrics such as crepe de Chine, French *toile de soie* and British wash silk. Patou was commissioned to design for sporting heroine, Suzanne Lenglen, known as "the Divine Lenglen", whom he dressed on and off the court and who was renowned for her athletic prowess and for the emancipation of her dress. Patou eventually went on to establish a specialized sportswear department, *le coin des sports*, within his couture house in 1924, as did Madeleine Vionnet, who added a sports-clothing department to her Paris boutique in 1926.

The stretch quality ideal for active sportswear was provided by knitted fabrics, including a loosely knit cotton piqué – a breathable fabric known as *jersey petit piqué* – first used by French, seven-time Grand Slam tennis champion René Lacoste for a white, short-sleeved shirt that he wore in 1926 for the US Open championship. The easy-to-wear textiles and informality of sportswear infiltrated everyday fashion, and tennis dresses with pleated skirts and tailored tops were even worn by the non-athlete, and were readily available with the emergence of mass production.

In 2004, Stella McCartney fused performance sportswear and fashion with her collaboration with Adidas, giving sports-inspired material such as Adidas Techfit/Powerweb technology and garment construction a high-fashion edge.

**LEFT:** Dating from 1926, the tennis dress followed the prevailing drop-waisted tubular silhouette of the chemise. Constructed from white linen, the dress features delicate drawn-thread work – more usually seen in lingerie – around the inset squares of appliquéd green linen.

**OPPOSITE:** In collaboration with Adidas, a leading manufacturer of sports clothing and accessories, London-based designer Stella McCartney (1971–) combined active sportswear with high-end fashion for a feminine version of the Lacoste tennis shirt attached to a wrap skirt, for S/S 2008.

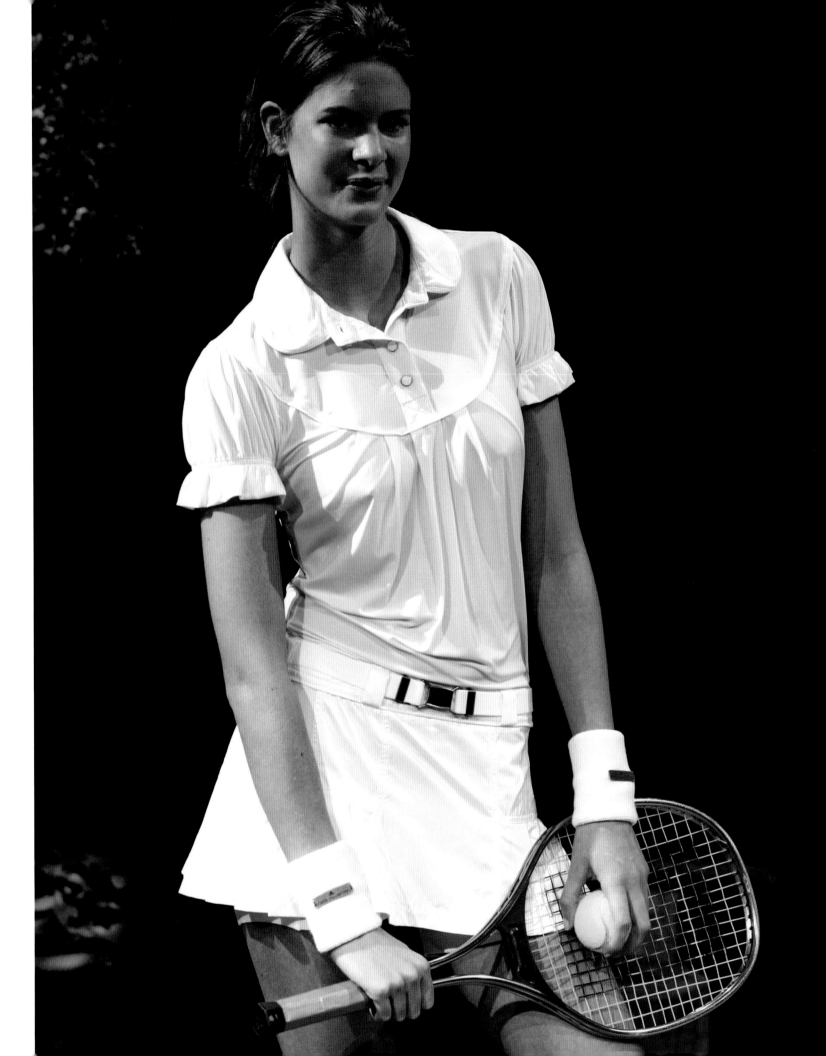

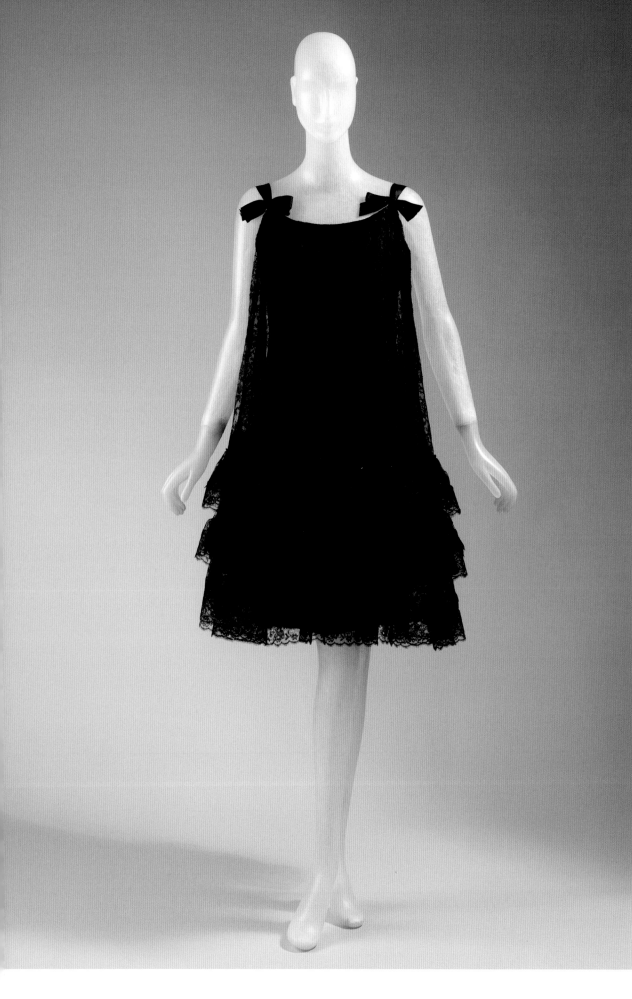

**LEFT:** With the ingénue appeal of the brief babydoll dress, secured with bows on the shoulders, Parisian couturier Balenciaga (1895–1972) also alluded to the tiered Flamenco skirts of the designer's Spanish heritage in this black lace dress dating from 1965–66.

**OPPOSITE:** London-based design partners Meadham Kirchhoff created the baby-doll dress for the modern era for S/S 2014, combining a sweetly pretty Peter Pan collar – named after the collar of Maude Adams' costume in her 1905 role as Peter Pan – and a high-yoked smock in semi-transparent silk chiffon.

# The Babydoll

Although the babydoll dress featured in the provocative pin-ups of the "Vargas Girls" created by illustrator Alberto Vargas in the 1940s for *Esquire* magazine, it was first described as such following Elia Kazan's 1956 film *Baby Doll*, starring Carroll Baker in the title role as a nineteen-year-old nymphet. A combination of ingénue innocence and a knowing sexuality, it was named after the short frilled dresses worn by infants and small children.

The ambivalence felt towards the Lolita-type figure was dispelled when the babydoll dress became closely aligned to lingerie, the boudoir effect enhanced by the use of diaphanous and lingerie-type materials such as chiffon, lace and silk in pastel tones of pink, blue, lilac and lemon. Trimmed with marabou, bows, ruffles and ribbons, the transparent dress fell to mid-thigh in a swaying A line. The overt sexuality of the garment was subsumed by designers and couturiers such as Balenciaga, who retained the ingénue femininity of the original but underpinned the silhouette of the dress with couture construction techniques to create substance beneath the frills.

These techniques were discarded in the 1960s when the babydoll dress was perfectly allied to the prevailing prepubescent figure of the era. Child-like, flower-strewn dresses with an *Alice in Wonderland* appeal in fabrics such as cheesecloth, broderie anglaise and spotted cotton were designed by Foale & Tuffin and Mary Quant. John Bates at Jean Varon placed lace over satin for a high-waisted dress with tiny fabric lily-of-the-valley decorating the bra-top bodice. Decorated with pin tucks and pleats, with puff sleeves, scooped necklines and cropped to the thigh, the babydoll dress represented a youthful simplicity and innocence, the impression of infantilism confirmed with the child-like poses assumed by models such as Twiggy.

The original tawdry sexiness of the babydoll was reclaimed by female grunge bands such as Kat Bjelland of Babes in Toyland and Courtney Love of Hole in the early-to-mid-1990s. Promulgating a "kinderwhore" look and worn with ripped tights, dishevelled hair and smudged maquillage, the babydoll dress became a highly eroticized form of apparel recognized by the UK label Meadham Kirchhoff. The components of the dress – silk and satin, puffed sleeves, lace inserts and edgings – have become the standby of the design duo Edward Meadham and Benjamin Kirchhoff. Sweetly pretty yet sexy in its *déshabillé*, in cream and off-white in their Spring/Summer 2014 collection, the babydoll is partnered with over-the-knee black socks in homage to Love.

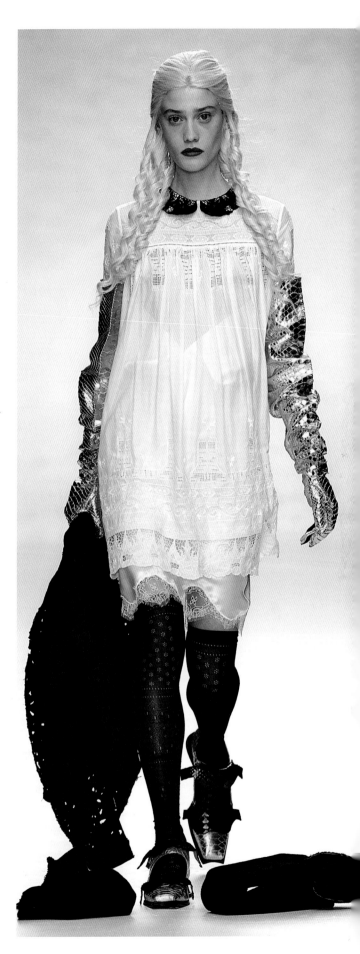

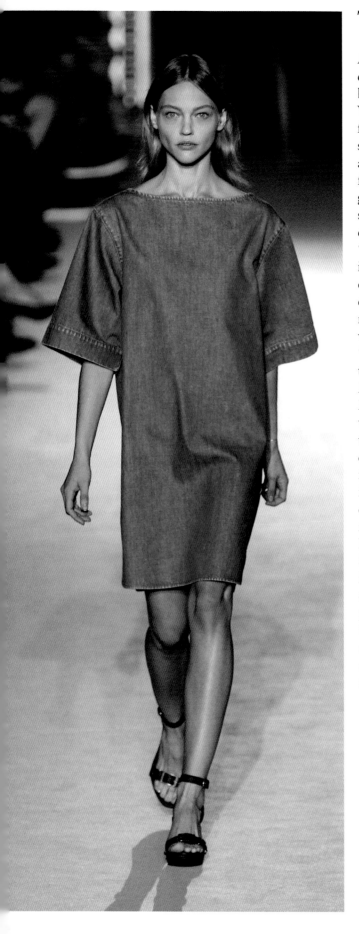

# The Denim Dress

An indigo-dyed cotton originating in the sixteenth century – the name derives from the cotton twill *serge de Nîmes* – denim has more usually been associated with blue jeans, the functional workwear of the American West, rather than high fashion. On the contemporary catwalk, denim has frequently become the favoured fabric of designers of influential labels such as Miu Miu and Stella McCartney, where its utilitarian properties are subsumed to high style. Denim was first introduced into mainstream fashion by Claire McCardell, considered the most influential of her generation of designers, and chief exponent of a uniquely American sportswear aesthetic. Eschewing any extraneous decoration, McCardell designed simply cut functional clothes and introduced the notion of "separates", a capsule wardrobe of easy-to-wear practical pieces that included American classics – the shirtwaist dress, tailored blouse, dirndl skirt, easy-wrap pinafores and high-waisted trousers. McCardell demonstrated ingenuity in surmounting the wartime rationing and restrictions imposed in 1942 by the American War Production Board, which placed limits on such luxury fabrics as silk and wool by utilizing "humble" fabrics such as jersey, cotton gingham, chambray and denim to high-fashion status. When American fashion magazine *Harper's Bazaar* requested a solution to running a household without staff, McCardell designed the "popover dress", a wraparound house dress with roomy pockets based on an easy-to-wear T-shape made from easy-to-launder denim. The designer continued to produce variations of this casual, practical garment, often manufactured in other fabrics for more formal occasions. American designer and big label brand Ralph Lauren frequently incorporates the great American staple into his collections, either in a romanticized perspective of the American Southwest with rodeo-wear and the Belle Époque bordello, or by offering an elegy to Dust Bowl America at the time of the Great Depression with his Spring/Summer 2010 collection. An homage to denim – faded, patched and frayed – was re-imagined by casting traditional shapes such as bib overalls and work shirts in luxe materials – a floor-grazing dress of pleated, frilled and beaded silk organza was distressed to look like denim. Cut with an easy fit, dropped shoulder and featuring a double row of stitching highlighting the minimal seaming, the simple, pull-on dresses and tunics by British designer Stella McCartney for Spring/Summer 2011 recall the same minimal tailoring of Claire McCardell.

**LEFT:** Stella McCartney used the traditional dark-dyed indigo denim – a sturdy cotton twill textile in which the weft passes under two or more warp threads producing a diagonal ribbing – tailored into a boxy tunic dress for S/S 2011.

**OPPOSITE:** During the period of austerity in World War II, Claire McCardell appropriated "humble" fabrics such as denim, gingham and jersey for her designs, in addition to chambray, a lighter denim, which she used for the pop-over dress for Townley Frocks, developed in 1942.

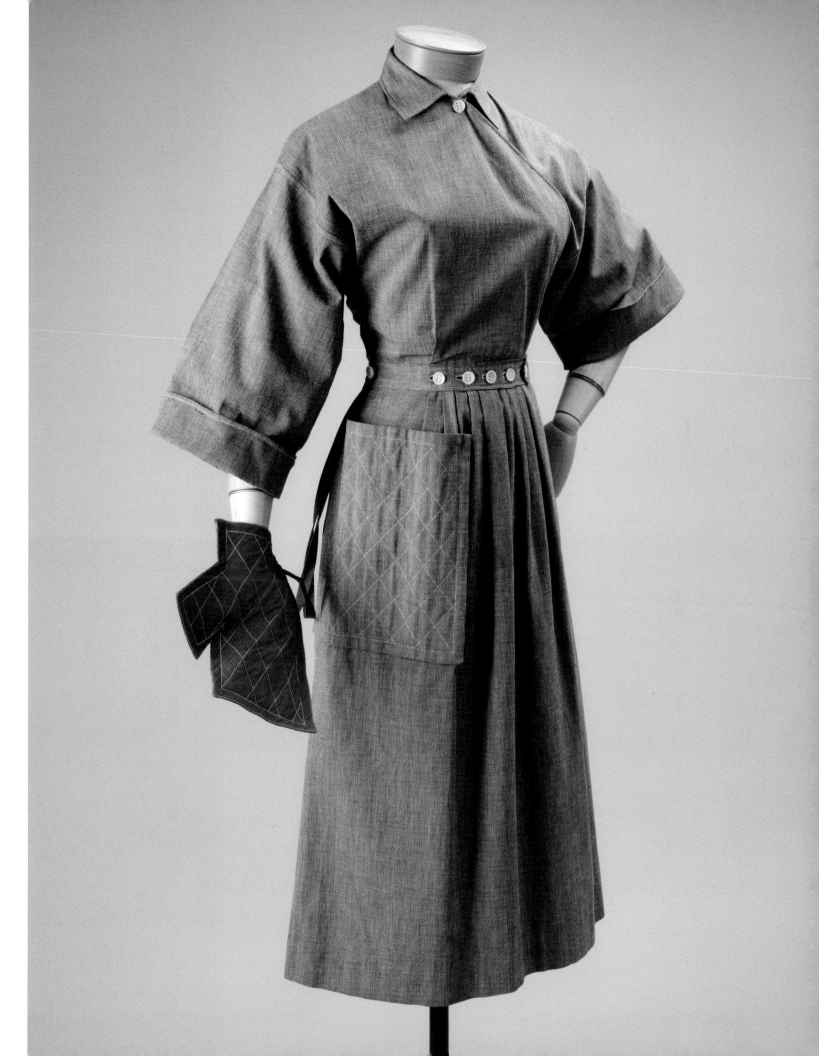

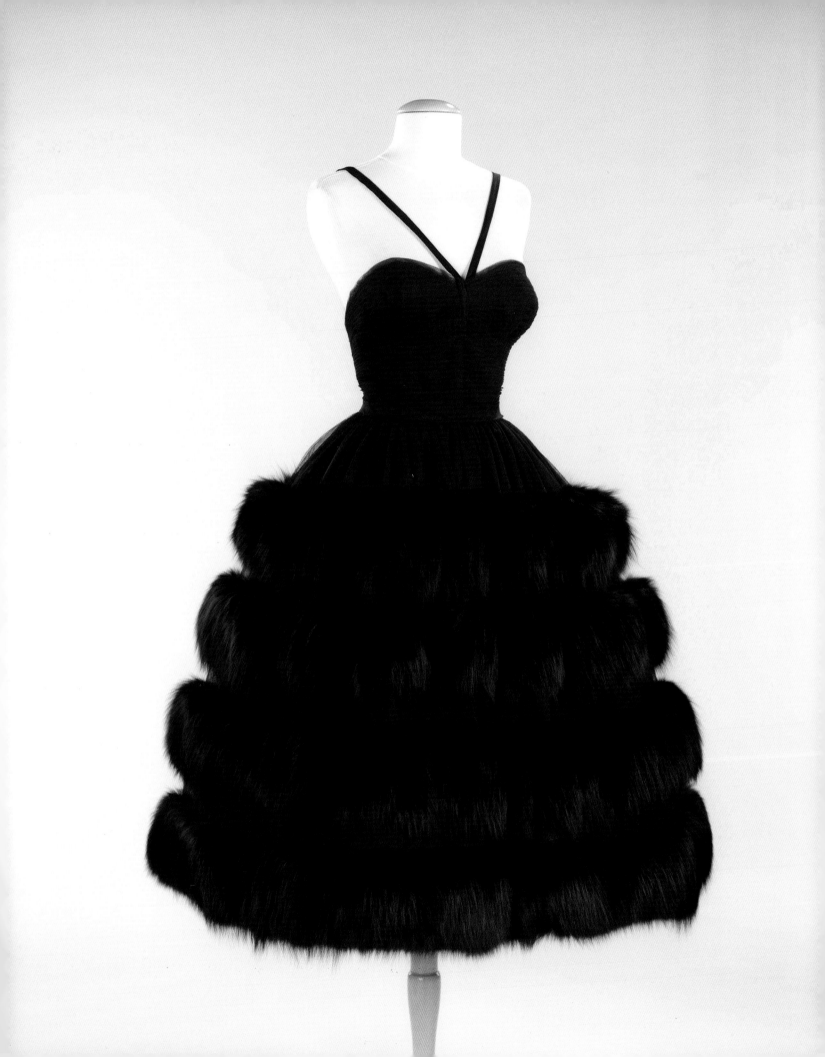

# The Fur Dress

Inextricably linked to notions of glamour, luxury and exclusivity, fur has always been subject to sumptuary legislation – clothing laws – since medieval times, restricting its use to the upper echelons of society, and reserving the rarest and finer pelts such as ermine and miniver for the nobility. From the seventh century until the late nineteenth century, fur was typically worn on the inside of garments or used as a trimming at cuffs and collar. It was only during the Victorian period that the fur side of the pelt was displayed on the outside, owing to the popularity of the fur coat. During the twentieth century, fur was linked to glamour and stardom, with the adoption of fur by old-style Hollywood, initially associated with the silver-fox screen sirens such as Mae West and Jean Harlow. Conversely, in the 1950s, the mink coat came to represent the apotheosis of bourgeois aspirations, a notion understandably discarded in the youth-led 1960s, when mink was replaced by novel furs such as pony skin and Mongolian lamb.

In 1965 Karl Lagerfeld was appointed as creative consultant to the Italian label Fendi – who originally specialized in fur and leather goods – to modernize the brand and to change the perception of fur as a conventional status symbol. The designer exploited innovative methods of processing fur in order to liberate the ways in which it was fabricated, resulting in pelts that handled as if they were woven fabrics. This disguised their origins and made the treated pelts virtually indistinguishable from their *faux* fur or "fun" fur counterparts.

World-wide politicization by the national and international legislation of the Endangered Species Act of 1973 in the United States, the Convention on International Trade in Endangered Species of Wild Fauna and Flora in 1975, and with the animal rights movement People for the Ethical Treatment of Animals (PETA) in the 1980s, the wearing of fur fell sharply due to hard-hitting anti-fur campaigns. These included David Bailey's notorious cinema advertisement of a model strutting the catwalk in a fur coat that first splatters blood across the stage, then over the spectators. Later came the advertisement showing supermodels without clothes, claiming they would rather go naked than wear fur. However, due in part to financial support from big-name furriers to support or subsidize their expensive catwalk shows, many designers increasingly incorporate fur into their collections.

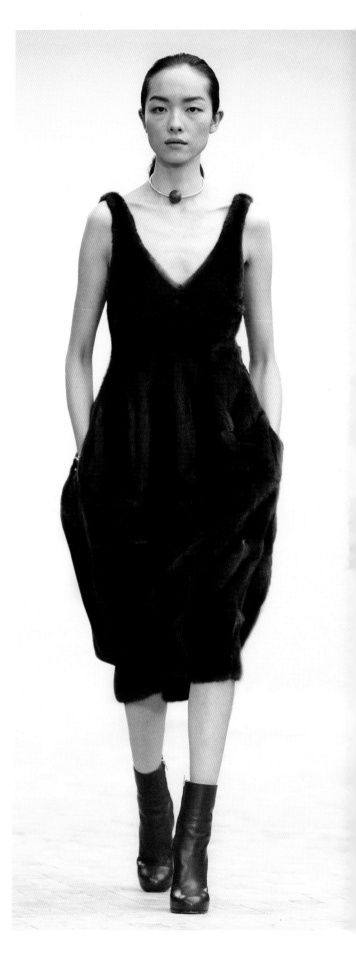

**OPPOSITE:** Representing post-war, high-style American fashion, the aesthetic of mid-twentieth-century American designer Norman Norell (1900–72) was characterized by discreet expressions of luxury, evident in his use of bands of black fox fur for an evening dress dating from 1958 for his own label, Norman Norell Ltd.

**RIGHT:** For A/W 2013–14, Phoebe Philo of French luxury house Céline adroitly utilizes pelts as if a simple woven fabric to invest them with a knowing perversity. Confecting the fur into a rounded ovoid skirt attached to a bra-shaped bodice, she assembles an unexpected cocktail dress with subtle fetishistic overtones.

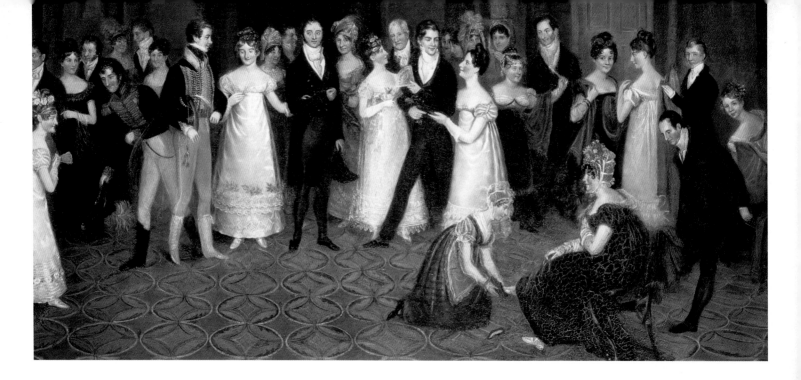

# Animal Print

The adoption of animal patterning by humans is rich with cultural and anthropological associations. Early cave paintings show human beings dressed in animal skins, not only as a form of camouflage to deceive the prey in hunting, but also, by clothing themselves in a second skin, the hunter hoped to take on some of the mythical qualities of the hunted beast. Whether as prey or predator, fashion's fascination with animal and reptile skins is predated by their use as the clothing of ancient goddesses, from the Egyptians, to whom the cat was sacred, to the legendary Amazons, predatory females who clothed themselves in the skin of the leopard. Perceived as "exotic", animal prints in textiles were popular at times of new discoveries revealed by explorations into the natural world in the Far East and Africa. Leopard prints were adopted at the end of the eighteenth century in France, when they were used as decorative trimmings, prompted by Napoleon's excursions into Egypt and a burgeoning interest in the classical world.

Animal prints came to be associated with animalistic traits in women, a metaphor for the uncontrollable forces of nature to be revered or feared. During the 1950s, animal prints, whether reduced to abstract form or as an exact replica, were used to signify the Hollywood screen siren, representing the powerful, untrammelled sexuality of the archetypal *femme fatale*, a modern-day huntress of fame, fortune and notoriety. Far removed from the "girl next door" of contemporary film stars such as Doris Day, animal prints were reserved for the bold attractions of sultry screen goddesses such as Ava Gardner and film actress and ballerina Belita, who starred alongside Gene Kelly as the *femme fatale* in the 1956 film *Invitation to the Dance*.

In the 1960s, radical US designer Rudi Gernreich explored the notion of second-skin clothes with three patterned ensembles that featured cheetah, tiger and giraffe prints, clothing the body from head to toe with matching hoods, tights and shoes, with only the model's eyes visible. Italian designer Roberto Cavalli is inextricably linked to a flamboyant use of animal and reptile prints. In his Spring/Summer 2000 collection, the designer clothed his women in scaled-down zebra markings, the models corralled in a zebra-printed room and tethered with diamanté collars and leashes.

**ABOVE:** English artist Rolinda Sharples (1794–1838) painted *The Cloakroom of the Clifton Assembly Rooms* in 1817, depicting a soigné group gathering in the cloakroom in preparation for an evening's entertainment. In an era when the commissioned hussar was invested with an aura of glamour, military dress codes and paraphernalia, such as the leopard-skin *shabraque* (saddle cover), could be adopted for fashionable purposes, as in the printed gown worn by the figure in the foreground.

**OPPOSITE:** Born Romain de Tirtoff (1892–1990), the designer and illustrator known as Erté – the leading exponent of extravagant theatricality and fashion fantasy – creates a woman equal in predatory intent as the matching leopard restrained by a ruby-encrusted leash at her side.

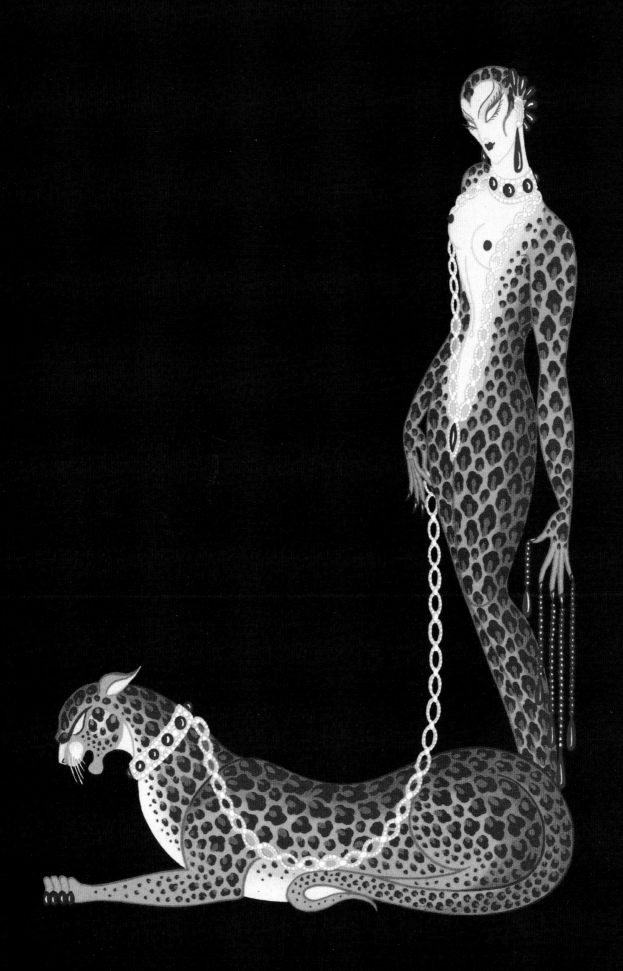

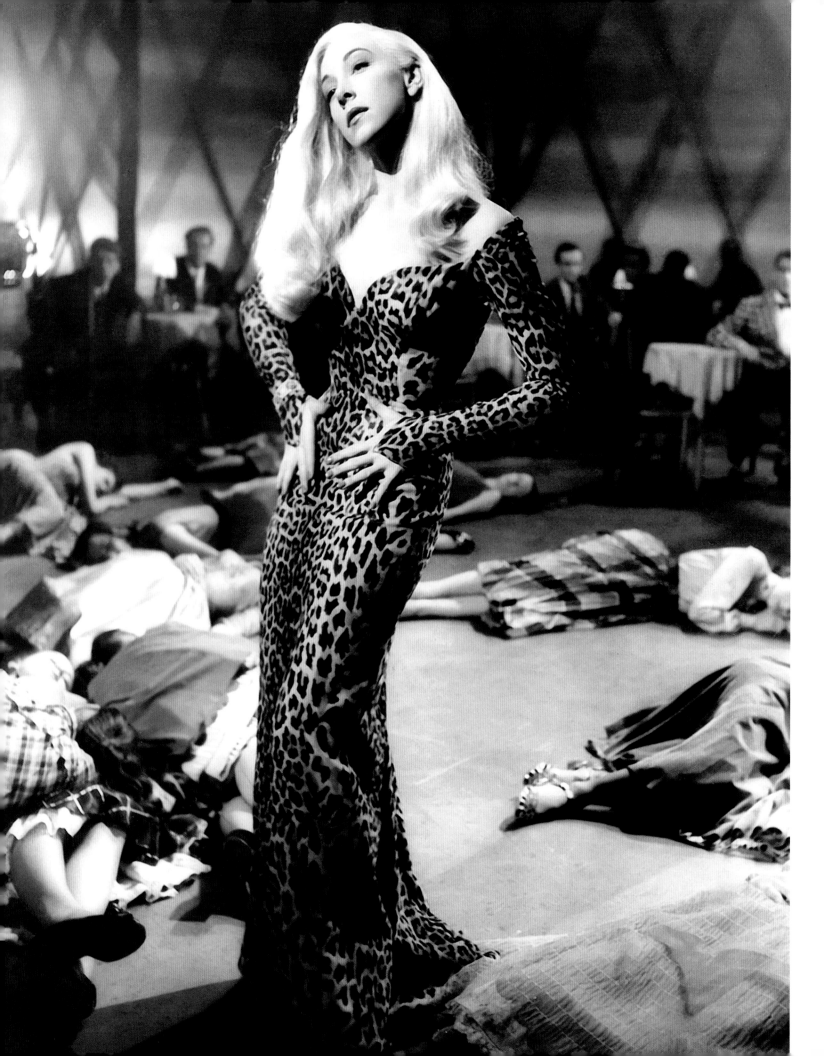

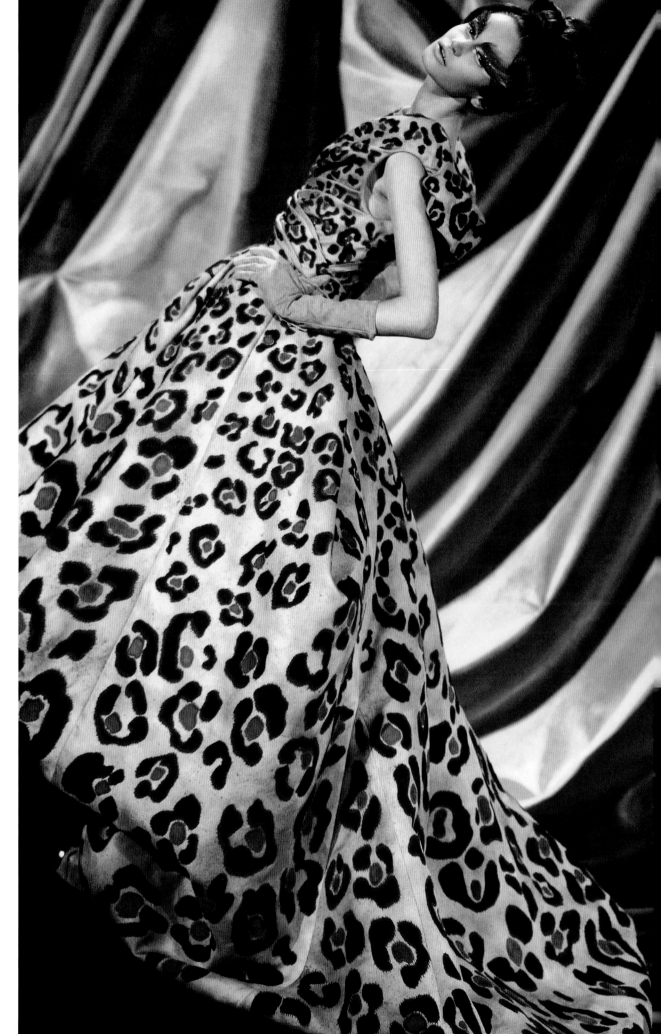

OPPOSITE: Olympic figure skater, dancer and film actress Belita (1923–2005) is captured in the seductive pose of the archetypal sultry man-eater in a costume designed by Rolf Gerard for her role in Gene Kelly's film *Invitation to the Dance* (1956).

RIGHT: With a silhouette inspired by John Singer Sargent's provocative portrait of the elusive *Madame X* (*see page* 125), John Galliano for Dior Haute Couture S/S 2008 adds a stylized leopard print on duchesse satin, which increases in size towards the hem for a full effect.

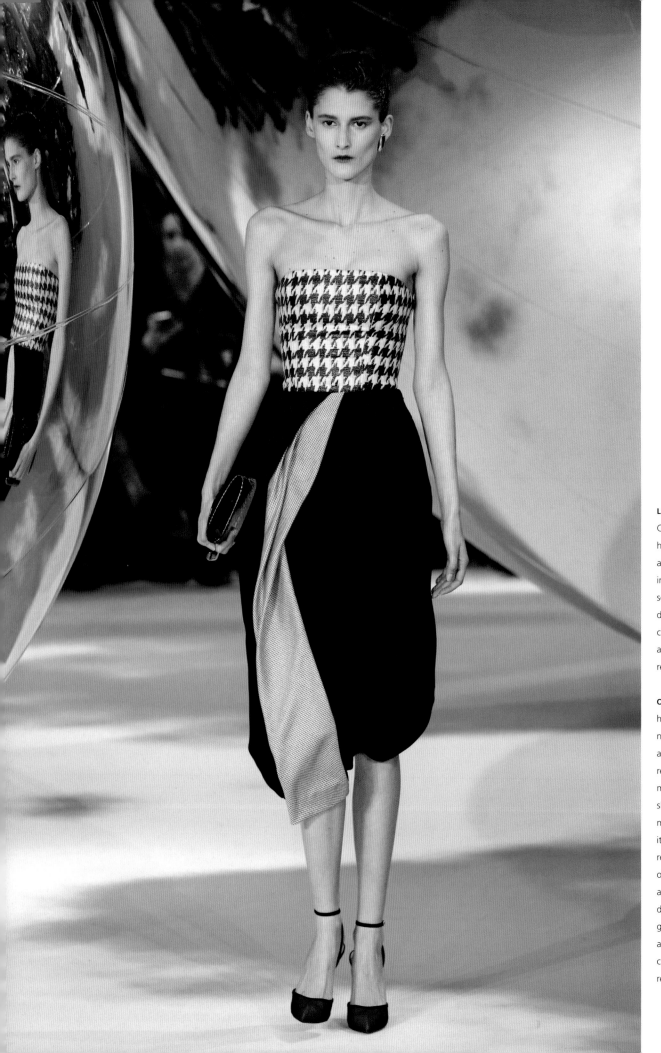

LEFT: The distinctive signature Christian Dior monochrome houndstooth check is briefly acknowledged by Raf Simons in a strapless bustier cleverly seamed to fit the body without disturbing the sequence of checks. It is incorporated into an asymmetrical wrap skirt for Dior ready-to-wear A/W 2013–14.

OPPOSITE: Coercing coarse houndstooth tweed to defy its natural inclination to remain rigid and boxy, Alexander McQueen reveals his mastery of the arcane mechanics of bias cut. His soft-shouldered and clinging dress moulds to the figure because it does not have to fight the rectilinear stability of the crossing of warp and weft. Rather, it adopts the line of least resistance, distorting the woven grid as gravity pulls across the diagonal axis. By contrast, the vast scrolling corsage of tweed is cut straight to retain its proactive form.

# Houndstooth Check

The high-impact drama of the black-and-white tilted tessellation of the houndstooth check is most closely associated with Christian Dior – the mid-century couturier was so enamoured of the pattern that he used it for the packaging of his first scent, Miss Dior. Thought to originate in nineteenth-century Scotland, the woven wool fabric was originally worn by shepherds – hence, "shepherd's check" – and the term "houndstooth" was only used for the first time in 1936.

The distinctive fabric, created by alternating groups of four black and four white threads woven together, first came to prominence when worked into a suit for HRH Edward, Duke of Windsor, when he was the Prince of Wales. It remained in the remit of aristocratic menswear, with brief forays into sporting dress for women during the 1930s, until Dior used variations of the pattern for his "*Ligne Envoi*" ("Line of Flight") collection of Summer 1948. The day dress in small-scale puppycheck was imbued with the drama of the bustle, created by the excess fabric caught up at the small of the back and featuring the moulded shoulder typical of the era.

The Japanese designer Yohji Yamamoto varied the bold checks in an entire collection devoted to the pattern, from voluminous pleated ballgowns to tailored tunics. Adhering to classic 1950s couture tailoring and playing with scale and texture, Alexander McQueen utilized the graphic quality of the houndstooth check for his Autumn/Winter ready-to-wear collection of 2009–10, in which he paid homage to the twentieth-century landmark fashion of Dior with razor-sharp tailoring. Exploiting the tessellated pattern, McQueen cut the cloth on the bias in a series of panels to create a structured day dress, with a flourish of textured frill at the neck. The designer even morphed the classic houndstooth into an M.C. Escher bird print.

Reinventing the houndstooth pattern for Spring/Summer 2001, Nicolas Ghesquière, as creative head of heritage house Balenciaga, introduced oversize houndstooth check in red and black on crackle-treated leather to form a futuristic exoskeleton coat with raglan sleeves and riveted Peter Pan collar. The pattern also travelled over various surfaces in the collection, degraded into soft tweed or used on the bias as an all-over print to form simple, sleeveless, sequinned dresses.

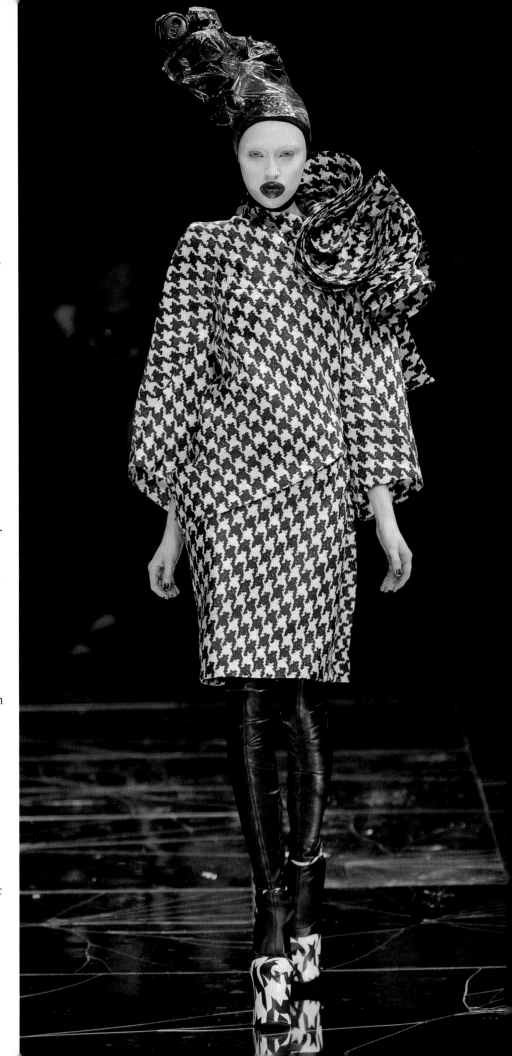

# The New Look

Regarded as one of the most influential collections of the twentieth century, the "Corolla", launched in 1947, dramatically changed the female silhouette and made a household name of the Parisian couturier Christian Dior. Named after the botanical term used to describe open petals, the line was instantly dubbed "The New Look" by fashion editor Carmel Snow of US *Harper's Bazaar*.

Although several Paris collections in the late 1930s had experimented with the extravagantly crinolined silhouette, the exigencies of World War II interrupted its development until a new era of luxurious feminity replaced the utilitarian and square-shouldered silhouette of uniform-inspired wartime clothes. In his biography *Dior by Dior*, the couturier records, "I designed clothes for flower-like women, with rounded shoulders, full feminine busts and hand-span waists above enormous spreading skirts." This was facilitated by a lavish use of textiles (Dior was financed by textile manufacturer Marcel Boussac), combined with a reactionary view of femininity in an era when women were being encouraged to leave their wartime occupations in favour of domestic ones. Although attracting opprobrium from the British government for the excessive amount of fabric used in the garments – fabric rationing was still strictly observed – the line was nevertheless adopted universally, even by the Princesses Elizabeth and Margaret.

**RIGHT:** Christian Dior's (1905–57) first collection for his eponymous couture house in Spring 1947 created a furore with its lavish use of fabric and hourglass silhouette, which subsequently dominated womenswear until the mid-1950s. The Bar jacket, with its rounded shoulders and padded hips, represented the new feminine ideal.

**OPPOSITE:** Deconstructing Christian Dior's signature ensemble from his New Look collection, creative head of the house Raf Simons transmutes Dior's classic hourglass silhouette for S/S 2013 by attaching the stiffened peplum of the Bar jacket onto a bustier bodice and a pencil skirt.

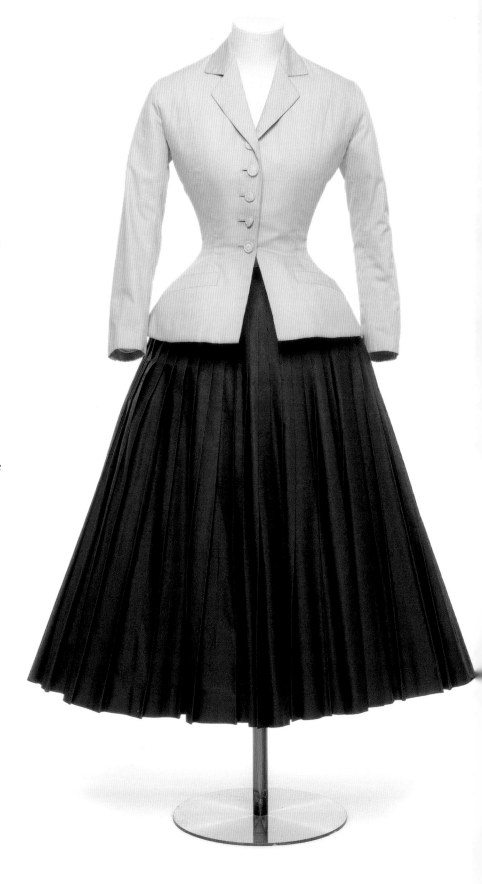

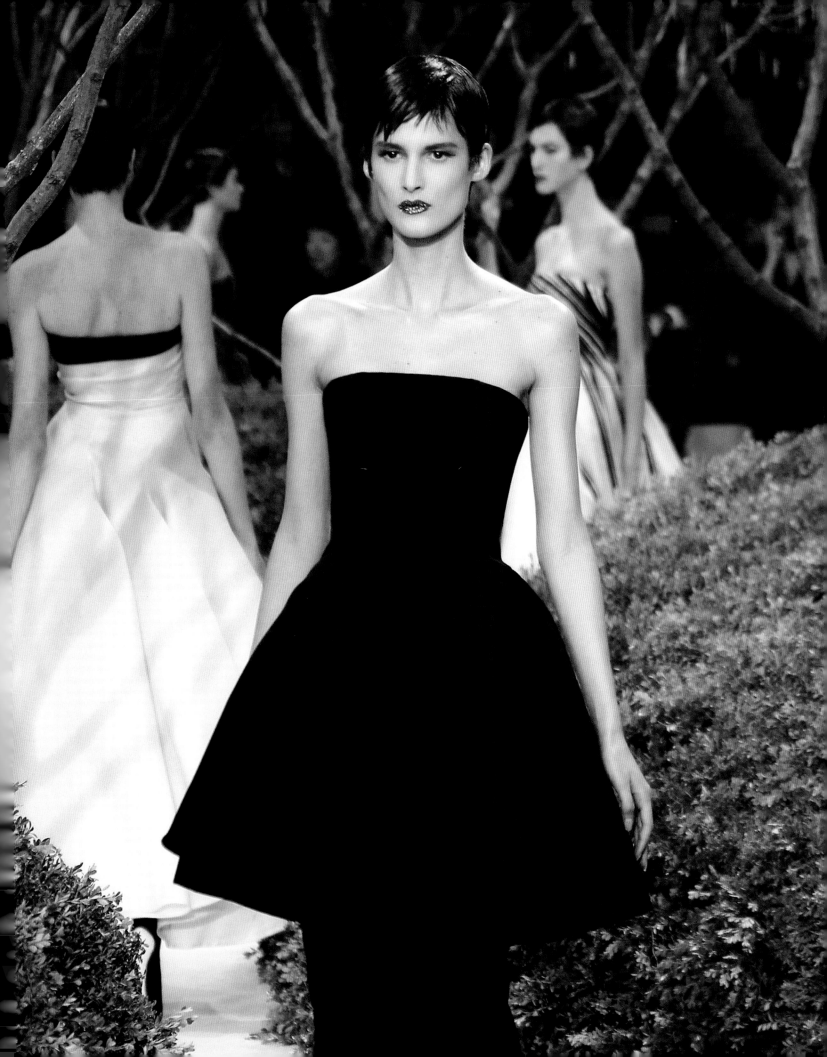

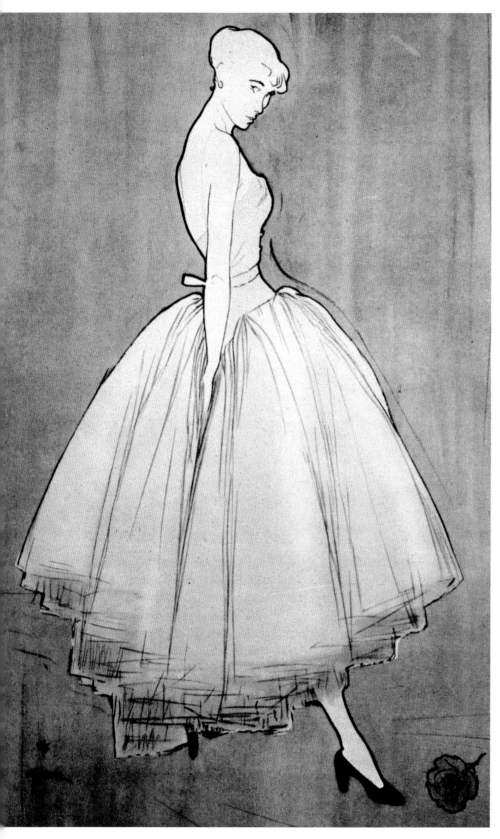

One of the bestselling items of Dior's New Look was the *Tailleur Bar* ensemble, or simply *Le Bar*, a two-piece suit that exemplified the exaggeratedly female silhouette by means of a rigid infrastructure of wire, whalebone and cambric that imposed an independent sculptural form over the natural lines of the body. The pale shantung jacket of the two-piece suit (*see page 162*) was heavily indented at the waist, before extending beyond the line of the hips to form a stiffened peplum over the knife-pleated, mid-calf black wool skirt, padded over the hips to emphasize the waist. The hourglass silhouette continued to dominate high fashion until the mid-1960s, when it was replaced by the pre-pubescent silhouette of youth-led fashion.

Subsequent designers at the house of Dior paid homage to the Corolla line of 1947. On taking over the helm as creative director, minimalist Raf Simons presented a subtle distillation of the archives and deconstructed *Le Bar* to present short tunics with structured torsos and stiffened extended peplums, worn over narrow, calf-length skirts. He also featured flower-strewn crinolines in the collection.

**LEFT:** One of the best-known artists of haute couture, and a personal favourite of Christian Dior, Italian-born René Gruau (1909–2004) dominated the high-fashion magazines of the 1950s. He interpreted the silhouettes of the era with a broad, flowing brushstroke, pen, Indian ink and gouache.

**OPPOSITE:** Legendary beauty Grace Kelly wears a Hollywood version of Dior's New Look in her role as the heroine in Hitchcock's *Rear Window* (1954). It was designed by costume designer Edith Head, who remarked on Kelly's faultless figure and carriage, which required none of the designer's customary disguises.

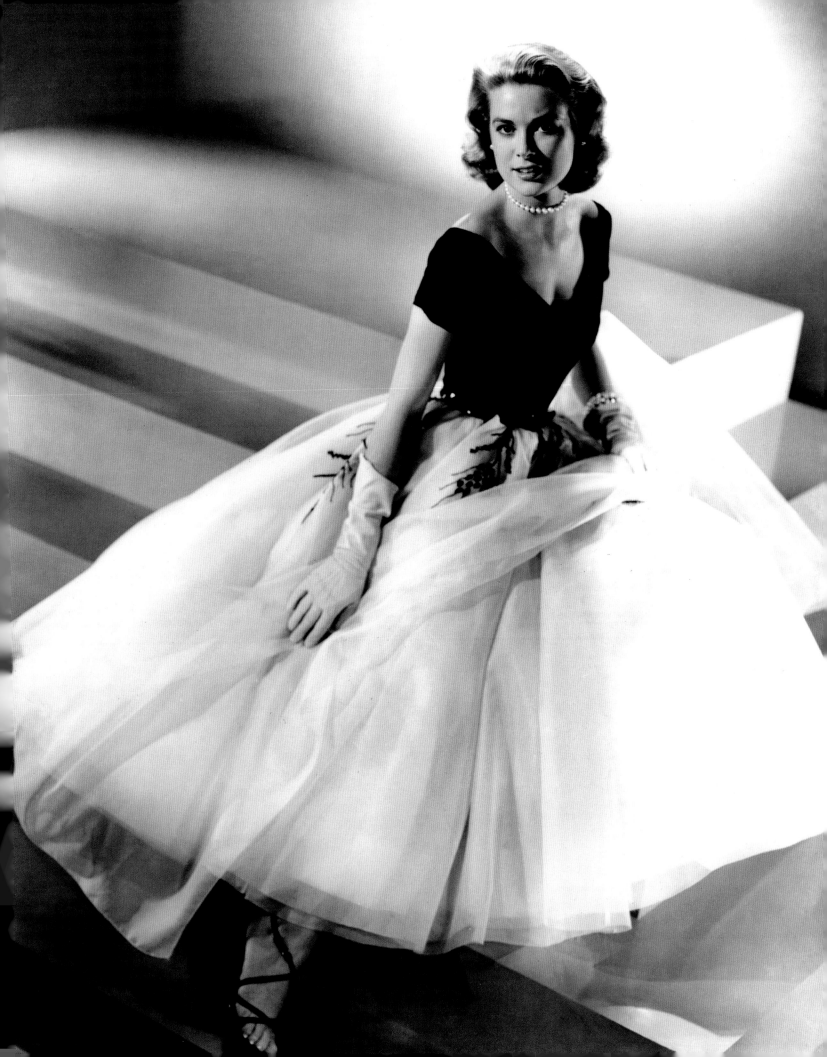

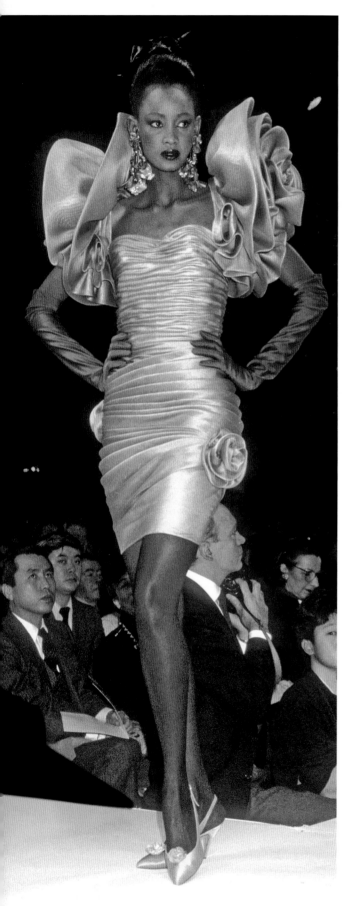

# The Cocktail Dress

The cocktail dress reached its apotheosis in the 1950s, when etiquette and formality decreed specific modes of dressing for every social occasion. Christian Dior described the cocktail dress in his *Little Dictionary of Fashion*, first published in 1954, as an "elaborate and dressy afternoon frock". He warns against making the mistake of dressing for a cocktail party as you would for a dinner party, recommending "a little strapless or very décolleté design".

The fashion for cocktails first arose in the 1920s, with the hours between 6 and 8 p.m. designated as the *heure de l'apéritif*. Private cocktail soirées and specifically designed cocktail lounges provided the venue, although in 1920 the eighteenth amendment to the US Constitution was ratified and America was plunged into Prohibition, which remained in place until 1933.

Coco Chanel's Little Black Dress, introduced in 1926 (*see also page* 122), provided the paradigm of cocktail wear, a short evening sheath dress in crepe de Chine or silk satin. The cocktail ensemble was always accessorized with a hat and short gloves. Day-into-evening versatility was introduced in the 1930s by the addition of a short jacket or bolero – a simple shape with a curved centre front and short sleeves, ending just above the midriff – over the sleeveless dress. Hemlines dropped to mid-calf and the tubular silhouette of the chemise dress was replaced by a greater emphasis on the natural lines of the female form provided by bias cutting and draping. An obsession with detail and outsized and exaggerated trimmings included an emphasis on costume jewellery. Gloves were still mandatory for early evening and a variety of hats reflected the importance placed on millinery in the decade.

With the emphasis on formality in the 1950s, Dior, along with other couturiers including Jacques Fath in Paris, Norman Hartnell in London and high-end ready-to-wear designers in the US Pauline Trigère and Norman Norell, promoted the concept of the cocktail dress as another market consumable through specific marketing strategies. Although cocktail dresses continued to be made until the early 1960s, the cocktail party was considered a quaint anachronism by a new generation of designers of the youth-led fashions. Women no longer changed their outfits several times a day, and the cocktail party was replaced by the hippie "happening". It was not until the 1980s and the return of formal dressing under the presidency of Ronald Reagan that the cocktail dress once more came into its own.

**LEFT:** Couturier of choice to the New York moneyed social set of the 1980s, the cocktail dress from the "New Baroque" collection by Emanuel Ungaro (1933–) featured the entire designer's tropes: an emphasis on the shoulders, a form-fitting, tightly swathed skirt and vibrant-toned silk jacquard fabric.

**OPPOSITE:** The mid-calf hemline and the ornamental neckline were a significant feature of the 1950s cocktail dress, emphasized with scallops, ruffles or bows. It was worn for informal occasions held during the early evening, where the men would be dressed in their business suits rather than evening attire.

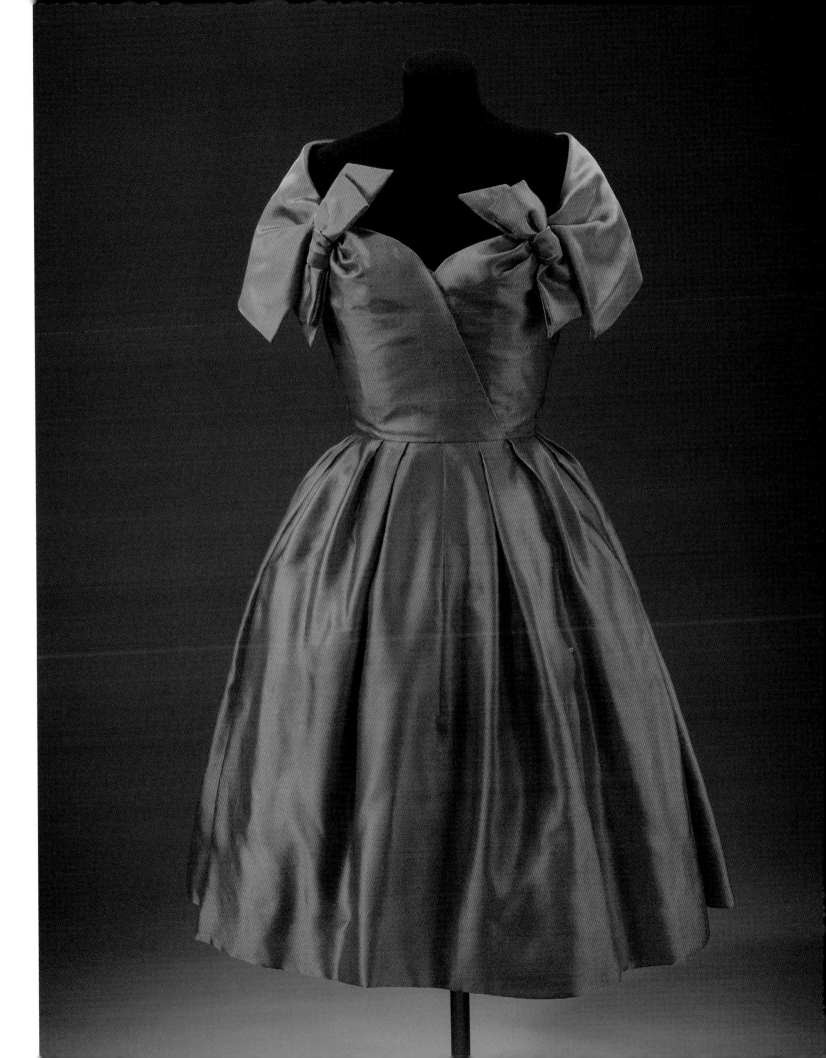

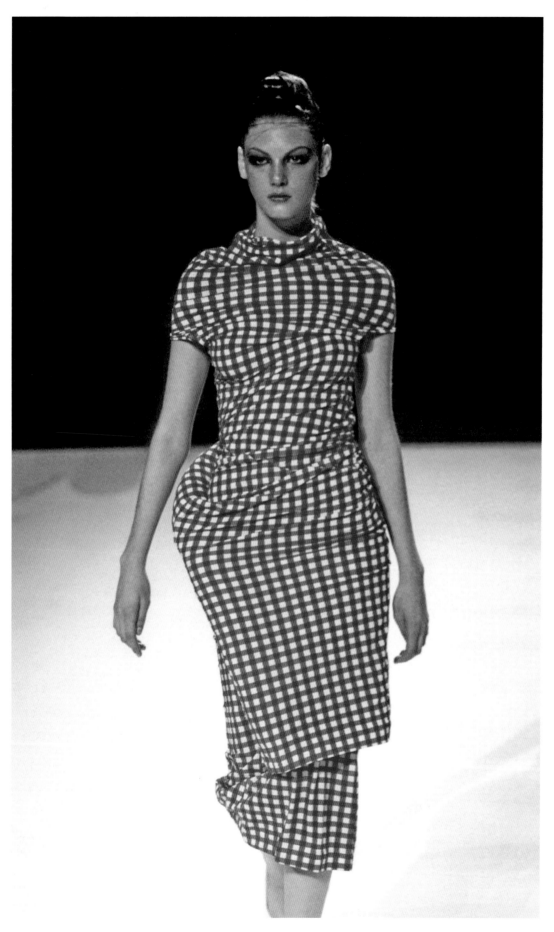

LEFT: With typical perversity, Kawakubo for Comme des Garçons appropriated homespun gingham to cover the misshapen padding and extraneous curvy growths featured in her collection "Dress Meets Body, Body Meets Dress and They Are One" of S/S 1997.

# The Gingham Dress

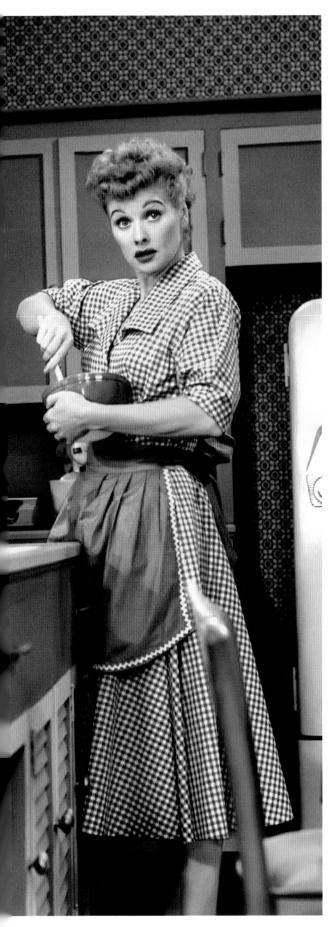

With connotations of the wholesome and the homespun, and as American as apple pie, much of mid-twentieth-century American fashion utilized the gingham in a romantic homage to the country's pioneering legacy at a time of excessive patriotism. Derived from the Malaysian word *genggang*, meaning "striped", the textile originated in the Dutch-colonized Malaysia, Indonesia and India, and was exported to Europe in the seventeenth century, and to the US in the eighteenth century. The humdrum fabric first reached fashion status when Adrian, renowned costume designer for Metro-Goldwyn-Mayer, created a gingham fabric dress for Katharine Hepburn in the movie *The Philadelphia Story* (1940). The Hollywood costumier also designed a series of cotton gingham hostess gowns in 1942 in the patriotic colours of the American flag in red, white and blue, rather than the more customary pastel pink and pale blue. Following the move towards domesticity after World War II, gingham was crafted into full-skirted shirtdresses in celebration of hearth and home – gingham is a check formed when two equal-sized stripes are woven together from pre-dyed yarn, producing no wrong or right side, therefore making it economical to use for the home dressmaker. Worn by Lucille Ball, playing an archetypal ditzy housewife in the perennially popular TV sit-com *I Love Lucy*, gingham represents her aspirations to be a perfect homemaker.

French sex symbol and film star Brigitte Bardot, celebrated for her role in *And God Created Woman* (1960), appropriated the tiny checked fabric for her wedding to Jacques Charrier in 1959. Designed by Jacques Esterel, the deceptively demure full-skirted dress with a *broderie anglaise* frill around the scooped bodice emphasized Bardot's curves and distanced the fabric from its utilitarian origins. Barbara Hulanicki of the iconic 1960s boutique Biba also brought a youthful emphasis to the textile with a sleeveless pink gingham dress sold with a Bardot-inspired kerchief via mail order. It received 17,000 orders and consolidated the appeal of the fabric as young and fresh.

Japanese designer Rei Kawakubo under the label Comme des Garçons (meaning "like boys") subverted the ingénue prettiness of gingham in her Spring/Summer 1997 collection "Dress Meets Body, Body Meets Dress and They Are One", more usually known as the "Lumps and Bumps" collection, a series of garments in which the human form is distorted by introducing padding in odd, unexpected places. This effect was emphasized by the use of outsize check gingham, creating further distortion to the unconventional forms.

**LEFT:** Darling of the 1950s TV comedy series *I Love Lucy*, actress Lucille Ball carefully calibrated her on-screen image – when off-screen she was a successful entrepreneur – to represent the archetypal scatty housewife by costuming herself in a red-and-white gingham check shirtdress.

# The Knit Dress

The unique quality of the knitted stitch provides a softer, more fluid alternative to garments constructed from tailored cloth. Chanel pioneered the use of knitted jersey for the three-piece cardigan suit, but until the 1930s, knitwear was generally confined to sweaters and skirts, when fit once again became of paramount importance following the body-skimming lines of the 1920s. Knitted garments filled the niche in the fashionable wardrobe of the 1930s between Hollywood-inspired glamour and the vogue for tailored daywear that increasing numbers of women wore to work. Manufacturers were quick to respond to the demand for the new leisurewear and moved their production from underwear to outerwear, and the term "knitwear" was coined to replace that of hosiery.

In the 1950s, an elongated version of the figure-hugging sweaters worn by Hollywood stars was the sweater dress, which, like its counterpart, delineated every curve. Manufactured by ready-to-wear designers such as New York-based Hattie Carnegie, sweater dresses became a mainstay of every woman's wardrobe, often with details that utilized the fluidity of the knitted fabric: boat-shaped necklines, off-the-shoulder and wide-rolled collars.

The fashionable tailored "sheath" dress inspired by couturiers Dior and Balenciaga also translated into a more relaxed version with the use of knitted fabrics, often caught at the waist with a belt. Textured yarns, particularly bouclé, were favoured for their dense texture and ability to hold their shape. Once the couture houses realized the commercial possibilities of ready-to-wear, knitted garments came into their own and were increasingly subject to the design process, with all the hallmarks of the signature detailing of the couturier.

During the 1960s, knitwear was no longer an adjunct to the fashionable wardrobe, but was now a mainstay as contemporary designers relished its versatility and used the knitted stitch to showcase patterns inspired by Op and Pop Art. British designer Jeff Banks, owner of 1960s boutique Clobber, produced see-through crocheted dresses for the "dolly birds" of the day, and the babydoll smocks of the era were interpreted by French label Dorothée Bis in lacy stitches and pastel colours. Sonia Rykiel was labelled "The Queen of Knitwear" in 1964 for her distinctive colour palette of stripes against a backdrop of black. The association between glamour and knitwear is exemplified by Welsh-born designer Julien Macdonald. The designer's near-naked web-like constructions reinvented the knitted dress, using a base of heavy nylon filament to construct his glamorous, barely-there, red carpet showstoppers.

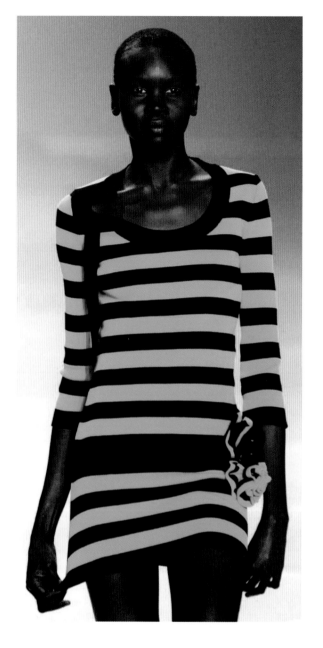

**ABOVE:** Sonia Rykiel (1953–) was responsible for designing knitwear that projected a more youthful and modern image in the 1960s. She structured a radical silhouette by cutting high in the armholes and close to the body with narrow sleeves, evidenced here in a sweater dress from 2000.

**OPPOSITE:** American designer and retail entrepreneur of high-end ready-to-wear, Hattie Carnegie (1880–1956) was quick to see the potential of the sweater dress as a new wardrobe staple for the working woman – who was also glamorous enough to dress up for the evening – during World War I.

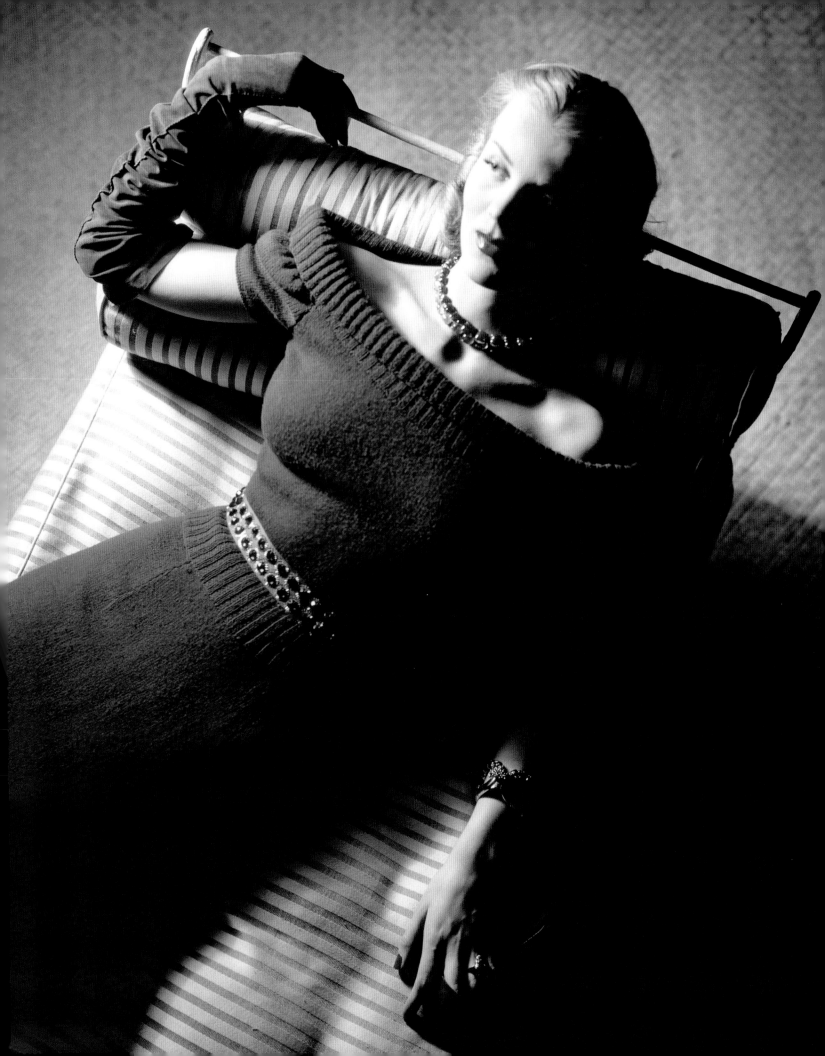

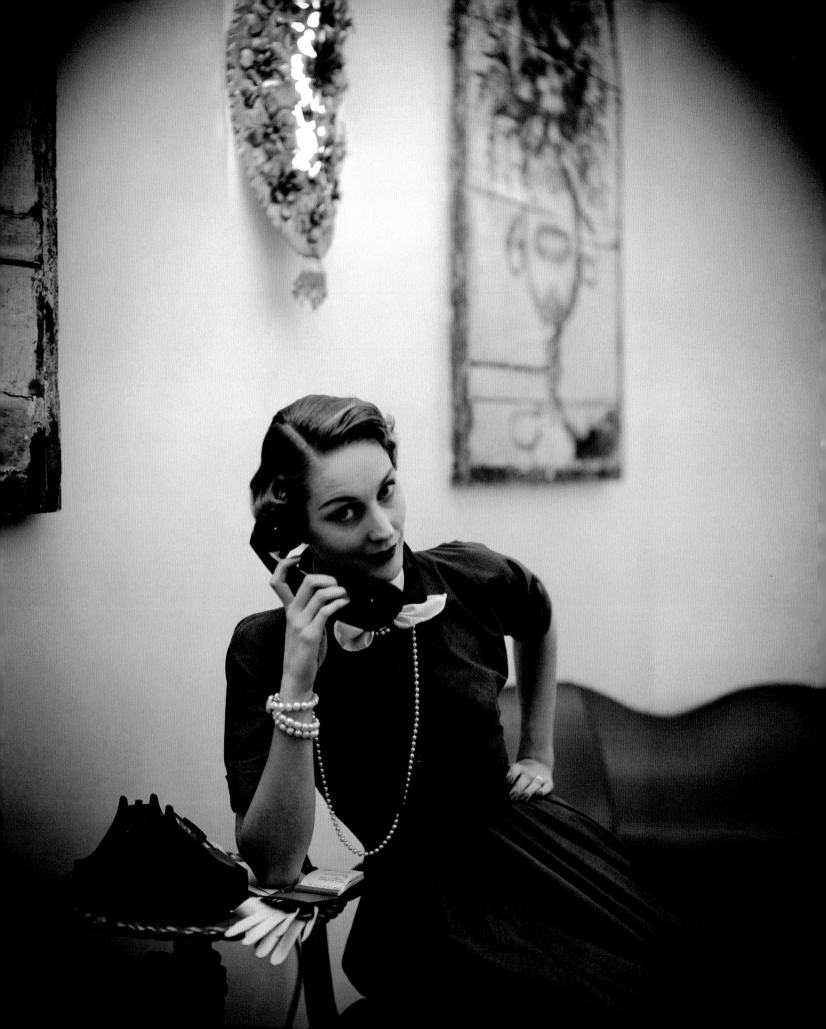

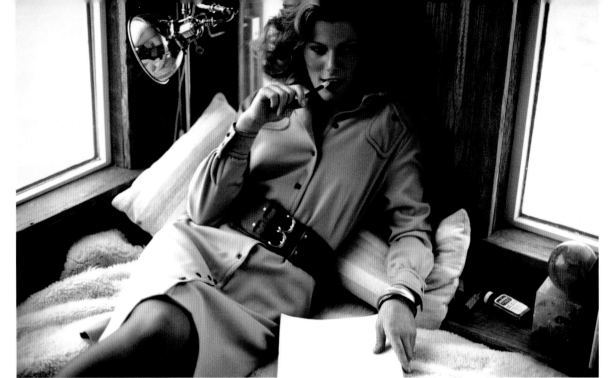

# The Shirtdress

Practical and versatile, the shirtdress evolved from its inception in the 1900s as a shirtwaist and skirt combination, "waist" being the term commonly used for the bodice of a dress or a blouse. Fashioned like a man's shirt, with a stand on the collar, a button-through centre-front fastening and cuffed sleeves, it was constructed from easily laundered white linen or cotton, and partnered with a flared, gored skirt, making the shirtwaist a practical option for the burgeoning number of women entering the workplace. It also allowed relative freedom of movement for women's increasing participation in the newly popular athletic pursuits such as tennis, horse riding and golf.

Conversely, during the 1950s, the shirtwaist dress came to embody the stay-at-home housewife, with the importance placed on hearth and home after the exigencies of World War II. The shirtwaist exemplified the feminine ideal, propounded by the emergence of Christian Dior's influential New Look, which appeared in 1947, a notion reinforced at the time by magazines such as *Good Housekeeping* and publications including *The Art of Being a Well-Dressed Wife* (1959) by American designer Anne Fogarty (1919–80). Advertisers also featured women wearing the shirtwaist to promote their domestic products, such as household appliances, shampoo and foodstuffs. Although the salient features of the masculine-styled shirtwaist remained the same – the collar and centre-front fastening – these were allied to a softly rounded shoulder line, a nipped-in waist and voluminous skirts, plus additional features such as pleats and pockets.

Re-contextualization of the classic shirtdress occurred in the 1970s, when once again it featured in the wardrobe of the working woman rather than of the housewife. American designer Diane von Furstenberg appeared on the cover of *Newsweek* in 1976 wearing a printed, loosely buttoned shirtdress, the forerunner of her iconic wrap dress. In keeping with the decade's elongated silhouette, the dress was streamlined by narrowing the skirt and sleeves, and lengthening the torso by raising the arm scye. American designer and fashion minimalist Halston also constructed his own bestselling version in Ultrasuede, a new washable, crease-resistant synthetic material.

# The Tied Dress

A dress that relies on ties for fit and function is a model of reductive form, where the attraction lies in the simplicity and ease of wear. Chief exponents of the tied dress were the American mid-twentieth century pioneers of high-end ready-to-wear, Claire McCardell and Bonnie Cashin. Both designers experimented with self-tied and wrapped closures in soft, flexible fabrics such as wool jersey, redefining the look of modern fashion and cutting-edge sportswear, and eliminating the need for bespoke fitting.

Ties ranged from narrow to broad, all of which could be passed around the neck or allowed to encircle the waist or hips to provide an individualized fit. The technique was exemplified by McCardell's renowned exercise in wrapping and tying, the "romper" bathing suit, based on a rectangle of printed cotton, and relying on ties for fit and construction. The bodice of McCardell's silk dress designed in 1944 is created from two triangles hooked behind the neck to create a simple halter, with the ends pulled round to the front and tied into a functional bow. Bonnie Cashin, meanwhile, looked beyond Western tailoring and appropriated the loose construction of the *nakajuban* and the *happi* for informal kimonos for functional one-size-fits-all daywear in luxurious organic materials such as leather, suede and mohair.

These early pioneers of a distinctive American style were succeeded by a new generation, including minimalist Halston, who utilized knots, ties and wraps in closing and fitting garments constructed from one pattern piece. These included kaftans and his strapless tube dresses of 1975, with a single length of silk shaped over the bust with a knotted closure.

Continuing the ideology of McCardell, Korean-born contemporary designer Jean Yu creates deceptively simple pieces, minimally cut before being deftly folded, tucked or gathered and then suspended from grosgrain ribbons, evocative of the art of Vionnet and Alix Grès. Ties and drawstrings may also be used as pulleys or cables to distort the fabric of the garment and create arbitrary volume throughout the silhouette. This technique was used by Cuban-born New York-based designer Isabel Toledo, who created her "suspension" dresses of irregular sculptural forms in jersey and taffeta in the late 1990s.

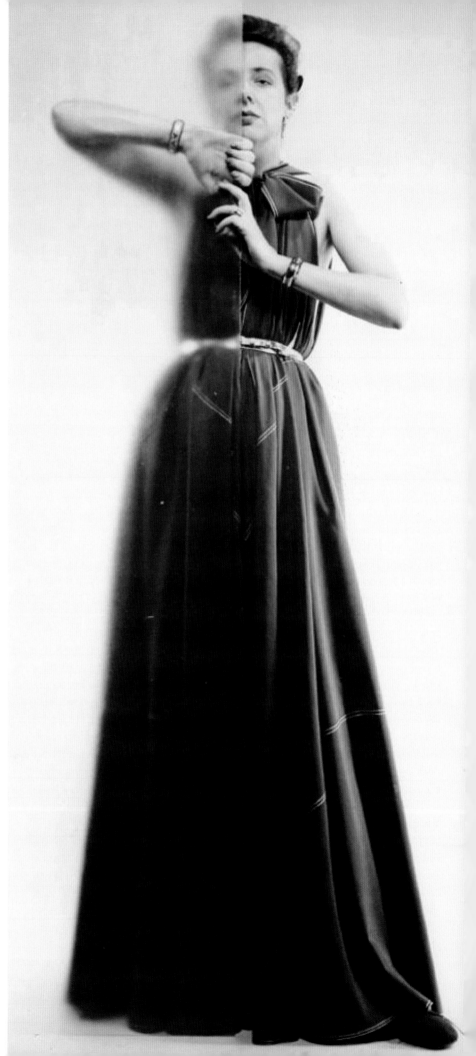

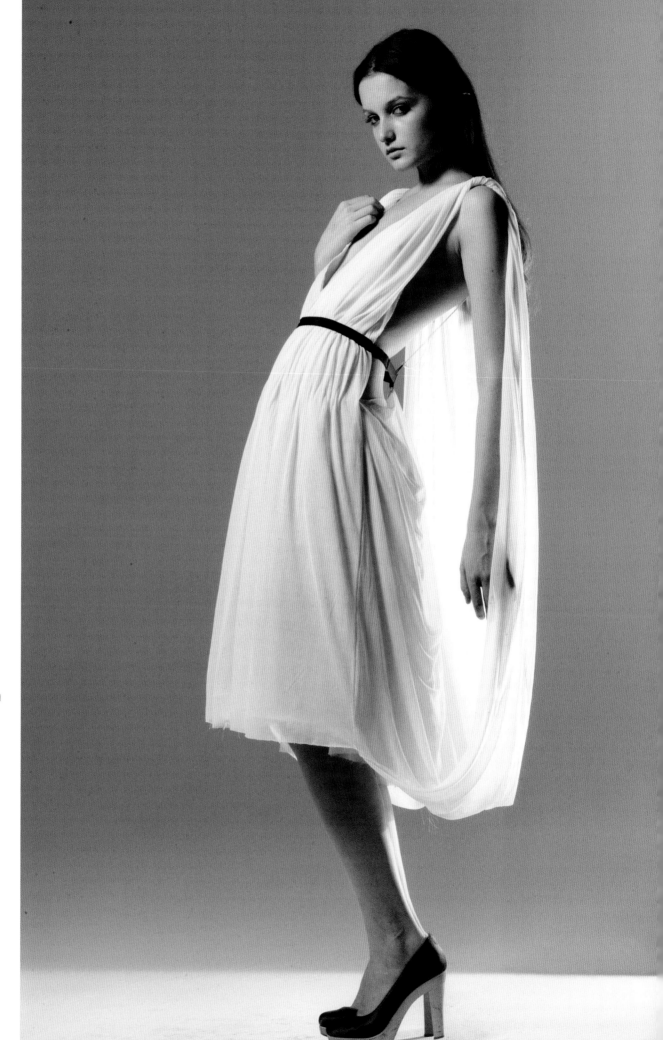

**OPPOSITE:** Remaining faithful to her own practical aesthetic, American designer Claire McCardell (1905–58), pictured here wearing her own design, believed that eveningwear should not only be flattering, but also as comfortable and durable as daywear. The halter ties gave the wearer the possibility of a high or low neckline.

**RIGHT:** Korean-born, New York-based designer Jean Yu floats weightless lengths of silk chiffon in complex layers around the body to form a bubble-shaped hem before being sewn together to form the two side seams. The front bodice is anchored with Yu's signature grosgrain ribbon at the waist.

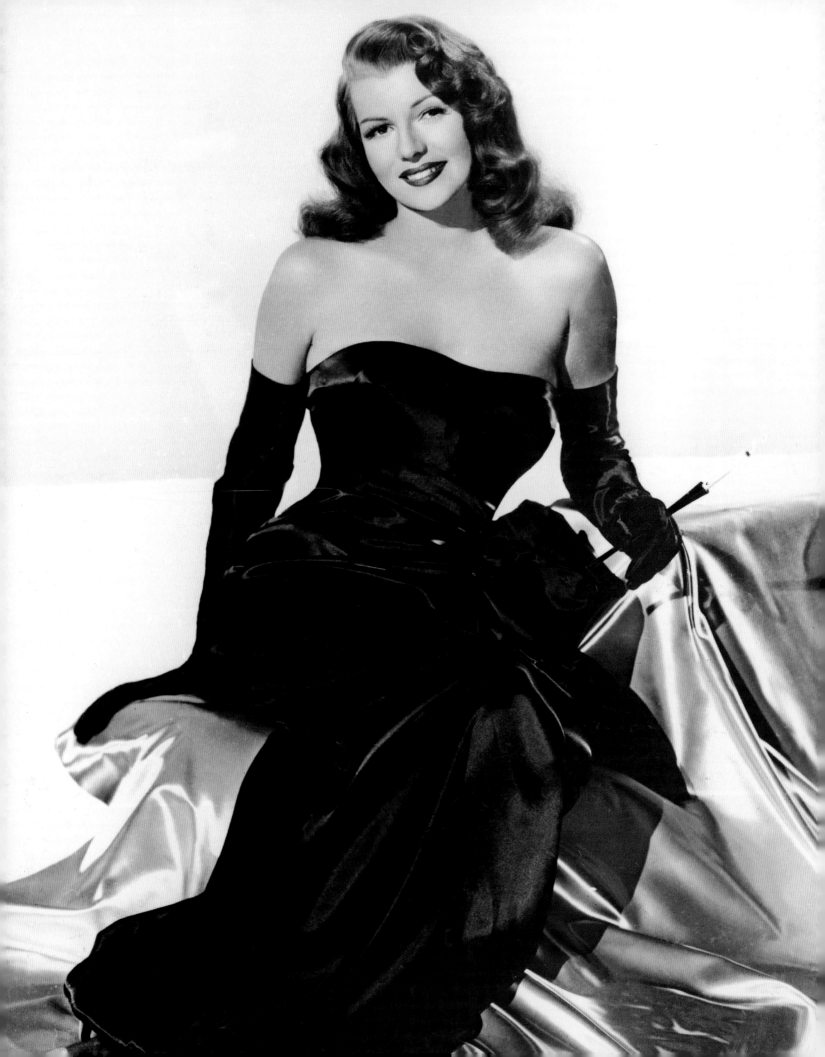

# The Strapless Dress

Daringly exposing the naked shoulders, and with no visible means of support, the strapless gown first appeared in the 1930s, where its use was strictly limited to late eveningwear by designers such as Mainbocher, who reputedly produced the first strapless gown in 1934. Relying on a rigid interior structure to hold the bodice in place, the strapless gown created an independent sculptural form over the natural lines of the body.

One of the best-known dresses in film history, the strapless black satin gown worn by Rita Hayworth in the 1945 film *Gilda*, epitomized sultry glamour. Contained within an inflexible bodice, the actress sashays her way through "Put the Blame on Mame", as the dress remains firmly fixed in place, a tantalizing exercise in concealment and disclosure. The over-the-elbow opera gloves are an important element of the burlesque performance; from the mid-seventeenth century, gloves increased in length to cover arms newly exposed, as sleeves were reduced.

The baring of the shoulders became increasingly popular in the 1950s, and was associated more with the elegance of couture and the post-war romantic idealization of femininity than the *chanteuse*. Parisian couturiers such as Christian Dior and Jacques Fath not only designed the strapless gown for formal evening occasions, but also introduced it into daywear with designs for the early-evening cocktail hour. With the breasts contained within a supporting infrastructure of whalebone, wire and cambric, the bodice either formed a sweetheart-shaped neckline as it followed the contours of the breasts, or was cut horizontally across the chest in a straight line. The structured ballgown underwent a reappraisal in the 1980s, when once again the fashionable elite invested in couture. Promulgated by Oscar de la Renta in the US and Emanuel Ungaro and Christian Lacroix in Europe, the big "occasion" dress featured the strapless bodice over a voluminous, puffed and flounced skirt. In contemporary fashion, the strapless gown remains a favoured style on the red carpet, but modern materials are now used to mould the bodice to the body, with couturiers often dispensing with the waist seam to provide an architectural streamlined Princess line from top to toe. The strapless gown also remains one of the most significant trends in wedding dress design.

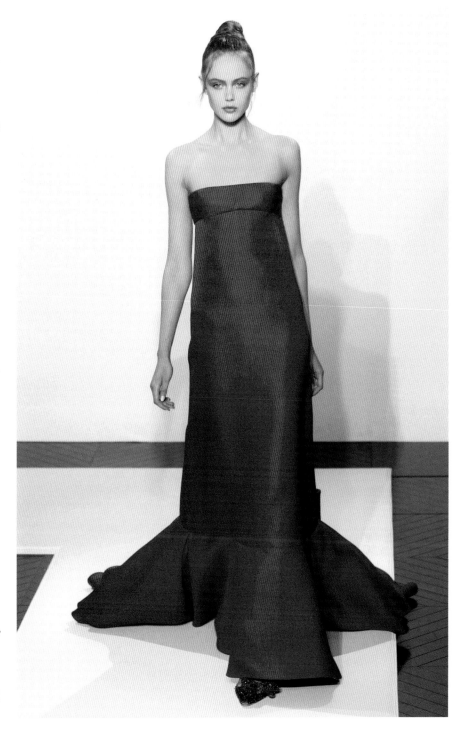

**OPPOSITE:** Exemplifying Hollywood glamour and the mid-century preoccupation with an exaggerated embonpoint – the first edition of men's magazine *Playboy* appeared in 1953 – Rita Hayworth provided a paradigm of sultry femininity as the eponymous heroine of Charles Vidor's film noir melodrama *Gilda*.

**ABOVE:** The enduring passion of Italian luxury label Valentino, launched in 1959, for a specific tone of red – known as "Rosso Valentino" – is exploited by designer Alessandra Facchinetti for an über-glamorous strapless gown created from a bandeau bodice, attached to a columnar silhouette, for A/W 2011–12.

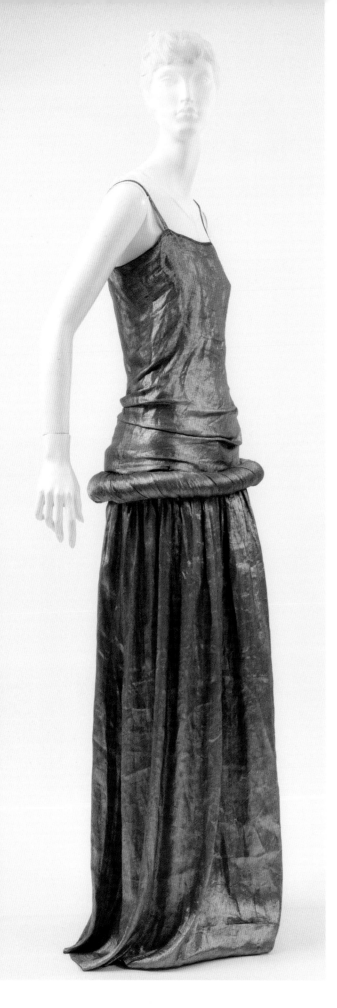

# The Gold Dress

Lustrous and impermeable, gold has been associated with wealth, status, ceremony, desirability and power since it was first discovered in the Middle East around 5500 BCE. Throughout fashion history gold has been linked with exclusivity and royalty, and gold thread incorporated into the weaving process has appeared in the robes of ancient Egypt, Greece and Byzantium, where gold textiles became an indication of imperial grandeur. Constructed from beaten gold worked into long strips and wound around a core such as silk – often in such a way as to reveal the colour of the fibre core to enhance the visual quality of the decoration – cloth of gold, imported from Italy to Europe from the fourteenth to the seventeenth centuries, continued to be worn only by royalty and the elite. When Henry VIII met his rival Francis I at Golden Vale in 1520, because of the highly textured and glittering surface of their dress and that of their courts, the meeting place was described as the Field of the Cloth of Gold.

With the introduction of gold-coloured metallic fibres, the use of gold in fashion became democratized. Lamé – a silk interwoven with metallic threads – was introduced in 1922, and in 1946 the Dobeckmun Company produced the first modern metallic fibre, trade-named Lurex. Metallic textiles, both silver and gold, were in vogue in the 1920s; Paul Poiret introduced his Irudrée evening gown in 1923, an icon of modernist design in its structural simplicity and metallic surface. Created out of a single circle of fabric, the gold lamé sunray-pleated dress worn by Marilyn Monroe in the 1953 film *Gentlemen Prefer Blondes* was designed by Hollywood costumier William Travilla. Worn for only a few seconds on screen and seen only from the back owing to its scandalous décolletage, the dress had no zip and the actress had to be sewn into the gown; she caused a furore when she insisted on wearing it for the 1953 Photoplay Awards.

The trend for gold in fashion is occasionally kickstarted by an event – such as the discovery of the tomb of the boy-pharaoh Tutankhamun in 1922 – or by an exhibition. In 2005, a blockbuster exhibition held at the Los Angeles County Museum of Art of the work of Viennese Secessionist artist Gustav Klimt, which showed a group of five of his early twentieth-century paintings, influenced a number of designers, including Christopher Bailey, who featured short metallic dresses for Burberry Prorsum, and shimmery shifts by Marc Jacobs and Gucci.

**LEFT:** Despite referencing the roll farthingale of the Renaissance – a padded cloth in the shape of a sausage, which widened the skirt at hip level – the tubular rouleau around the hips of the Irudrée evening gown from Paul Poiret in 1923 evinces modern simplicity.

**OPPOSITE:** Inspired by the pleated *kalasiris* of ancient Egypt, the gold lamé, sunray-pleated gown, designed by William Travilla, was worn only briefly by Marilyn Monroe in the film *Gentlemen Prefer Blondes* (1953) – it was judged to be far too revealing for the censors.

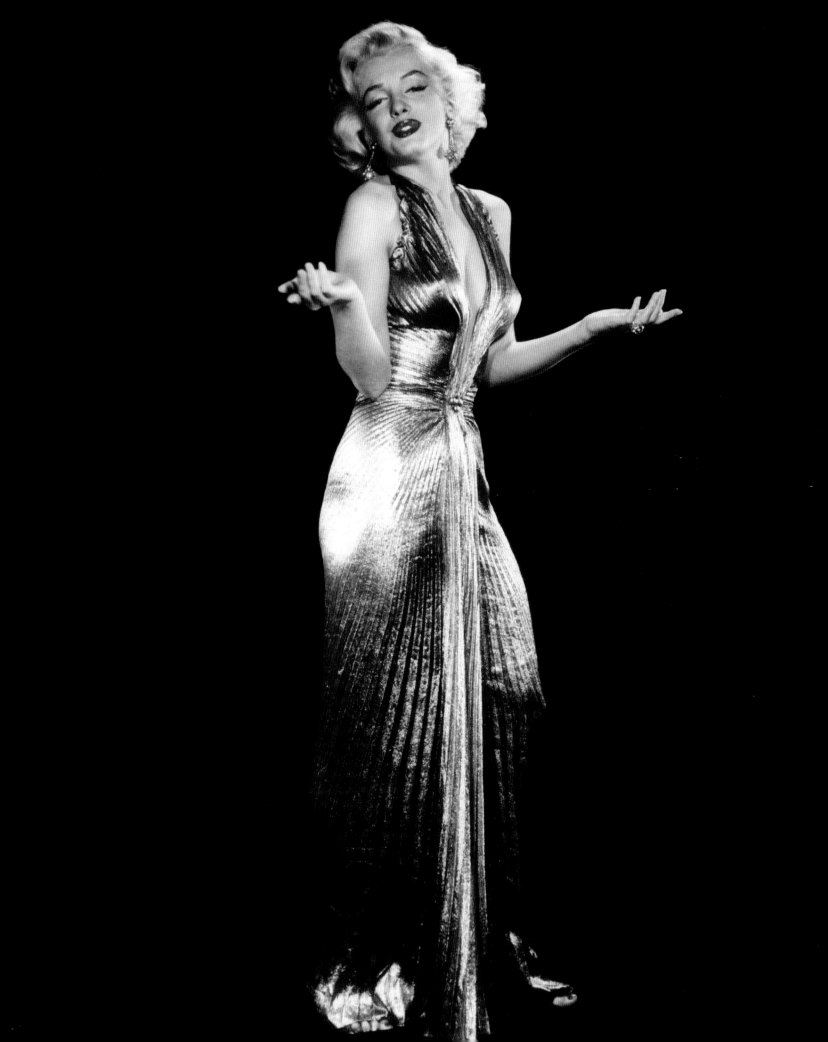

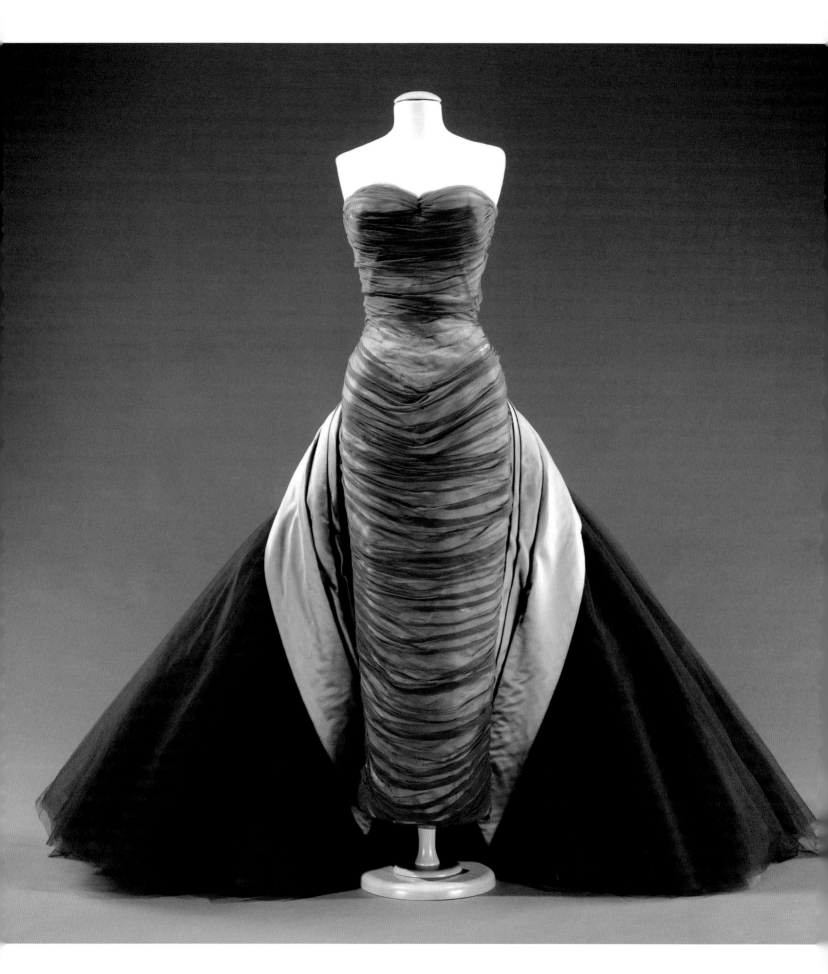

# The Butterfly

The ephemeral beauty of the butterfly symbolizes aspects of existential irony; the image not only evokes the extraordinary facility of nature to provide exquisite pattern and colour, it is also a symbol of transformation and metamorphosis, owing to its short lifespan and evolution from egg, to larvae (caterpillar), to pupa (chrysalis or cocoon), to winged butterfly. In many traditions, the butterfly is a symbol of the soul. In Chinese symbology, it represents immortality; to the Japanese, a white butterfly represents the soul of the departed. In Greek mythology, Psyche – which translates to mean "soul" – is represented in the form of a butterfly and its attribute of immortality.

By analogy, the meaning associated with the butterfly is the ability to move from one state or perspective to another, an ethos attractive to the Surrealists, who used it as a symbol of transformation or even death. Elsa Schiaparelli, an associate of the Surrealists, often used the butterfly decoratively to represent beauty emerging from the mundane, transforming the ordinary into the extraordinary. The hyperrealism of various insects used as adornment frequently inspires feelings of disquiet, but while there is a named phobia for moths – mottephobia – there is no word for fear of butterflies. The insects are seemingly universally appreciated for the beauty of their colour and the ordered patterning of their wings.

Embellishment of featherweight fabrics such as satin and gazar provide a floating background for butterflies embroidered, appliquéd or laser-cut and applied to the surface, creating the impression that the butterfly has only alighted for a moment. The image of the butterfly may be translated figuratively into a printed pattern, whether in an all-over multi-directional repeat pattern or one that is engineered to fit garments. Other designers diffuse and extend the pattern of the wings into a shimmering, abstract surface by the means of layered surfaces and embellishment.

Components of the insect are sometimes deconstructed to create various elements of the dress, the thorax becoming the bodice, and the wings contorted to provide a peplum or to emphasize the shoulders. American couturier Charles James created his Butterfly dress in 1955. The flourish of the side panels reference the forewing and a hindwing of the insect, while the tightly fitted torso resembles a chrysalis.

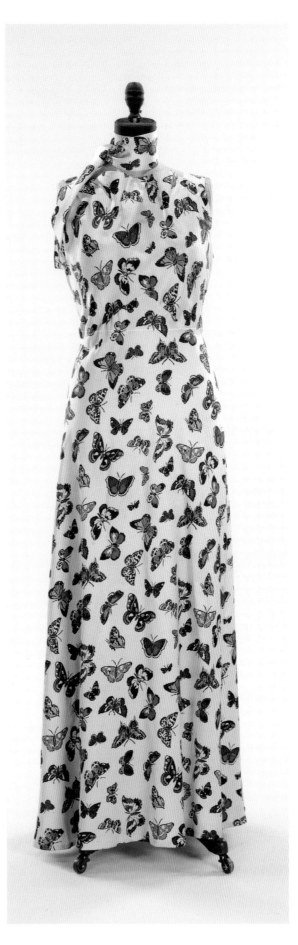

**OPPOSITE:** The figure-defining sheath in grey silk chiffon and satin of the Butterfly ballgown dating from 1955 by cult American couturier Charles James, (1906–78) represents a chrysalis, while the Victorian-inspired bustle, with its flourish of frothy tulle, its emerging wings.

**LEFT:** Renowned for her idiosyncratic aesthetic, Elsa Schiaparelli featured bold prints with unorthodox imagery throughout her career. In 1937 she created a full-length evening gown printed with butterflies – the Surrealist symbol for metamorphosis and death. It was worn with a matching parasol.

# The Tulip

The architectural silhouette of the inverted tulip-shaped dress is designed to emphasize the sensuous lines of the torso, replicating the undulating stem of the tulip by encasing the body from beneath the breast to the hips with a boned and seamed mid-section before exploding into a facsimile of closed tulip petals.

Reliant on fabrics with a stiff, dense texture for its structure, such as lustrous duchesse satin, silk faille or taffeta, when designed by New York-based couturier Charles James, the gown exemplifies the precision engineering for which he was renowned. A contemporary of Christian Dior, James deployed rigid under-structures to support complex seams that followed the curves of the body, which he combined with artful draping and supported volume to create sculptural silhouettes. At the height of his powers, between 1947 and 1954, the eveningwear designed by James perfectly matched the formal nature of mid-century social life and the desires of the fashionable elite.

The couturier's use of volume at knee level is supported with padding beneath the carefully controlled gathers of the inverted tulip-shaped skirt. The etiolated lines of the model – she is standing in what has been called "the Dior slouch", the fashionable C-curve posture that was adopted by models of the era, with hips forward, shoulders down and back concave – emphasizes the lines of the gown and the contrast between the rigidly controlled midriff and the deep V-shaped flounce at the hem, which reflects the angle of the supporting shoulder straps.

Hollywood costumiers frequently dressed the stars for the red carpet, and head of costume at Paramount Studios, Edith Head – with a career spanning nearly half a century – created an inverted tulip-shaped dress for film actress Shirley MacLaine for her appearance as an Academy Award nominee for her part in *Some Came Running* in 1959. The gown is similar in silhouette to the one designed by James but lacks the finesse or the perfect proportions seen in the couturier's craft. Constructed from a mid-brown duchesse satin, the moulded bodice ends in an inverted tulip-shaped skirt, which starts at the lower hips before billowing out in unpressed box pleats to the hem.

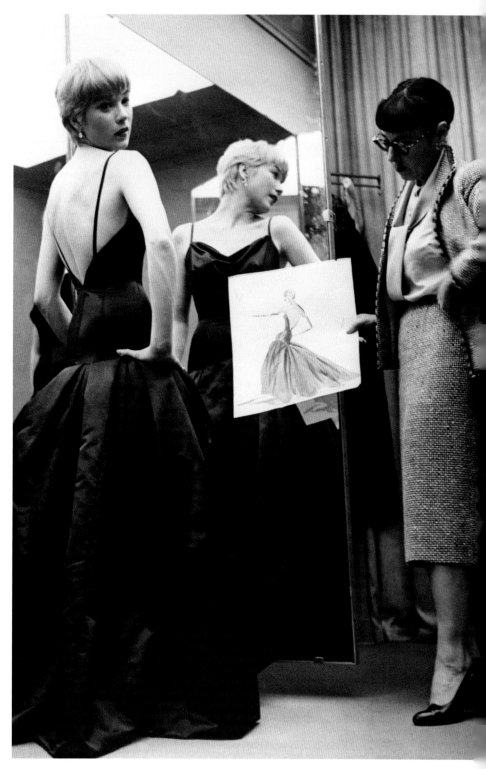

**ABOVE:** Ingénue actress Shirley MacLaine wears a gown designed by Hollywood costumier Edith Head, made in the workshops of the film studio rather than the couturier's atelier. The tulip-shaped gown from 1959 is a weak facsimile of James's Tulip line.

**OPPOSITE:** In an era when new and novel silhouettes preoccupied both designers and the fashion press, British-born, US-based couturier Charles James, a virtuoso of construction techniques and a master cutter, introduced the Tulip in 1950.

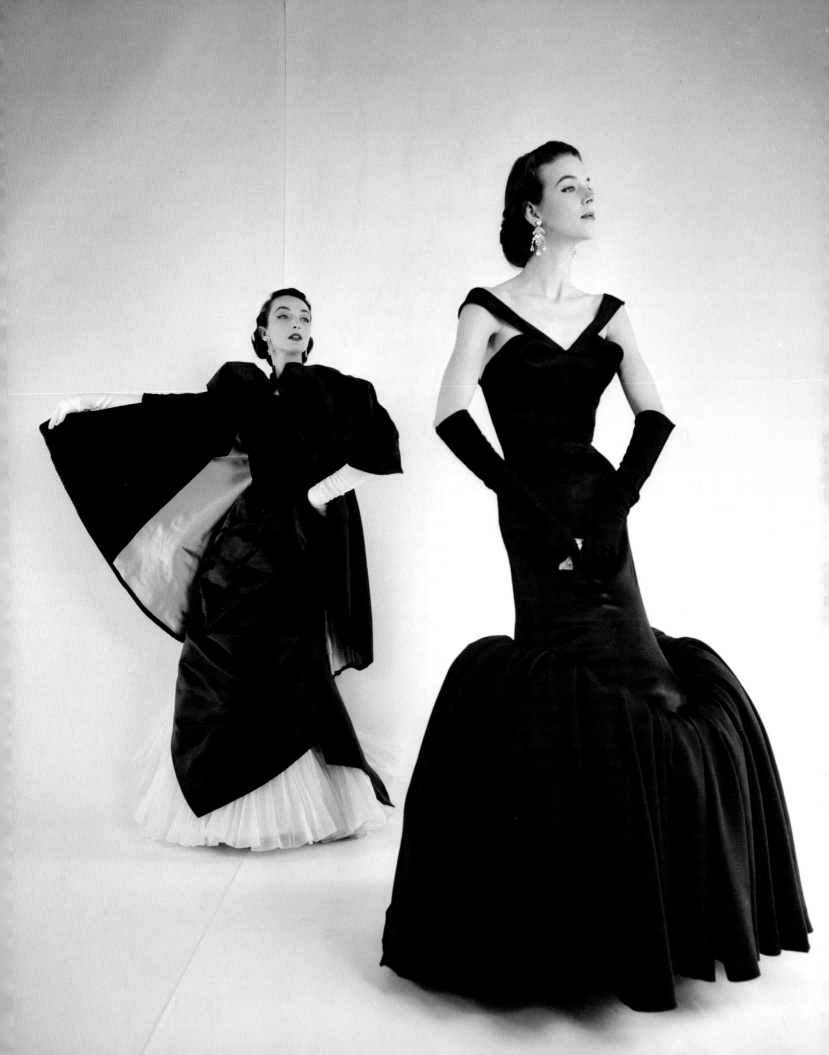

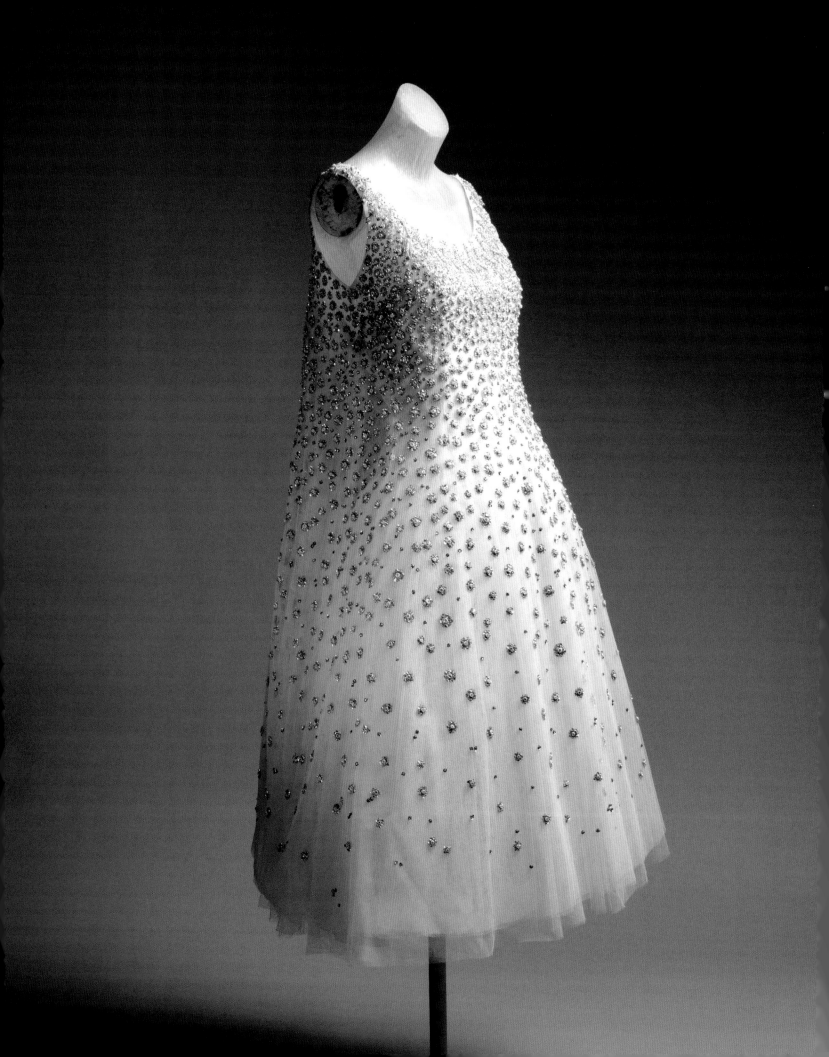

# The Trapeze Line

In 1958, for his first solo collection as creative head of couture house Christian Dior, Yves Saint Laurent introduced the Trapeze line, an exaggerated version of the A line propounded by his mentor in his 1955 Spring collection.

Following the success of his New Look, Dior organized his collections around specific themes, including those based on the letters H, A and Y, with the A line confined to a narrow-shouldered hip-length jacket using stiffened fabric to create the shape, worn over a full pleated skirt. The trapezoid dress designed by Saint Laurent also relied on narrow shoulders for the requisite silhouette, but the line extended out, unbroken, to the hem of the dress, which rested on the knee. All the details of the Trapeze dress were confined to the neckline, either by outsize collars or with a horizontal neckline cut straight across from shoulder to shoulder to balance the width at the hem. Day dresses featured outsize self-fabric or ribbon bows, the ends falling free to the hipline. The vertical shaping seams running from shoulder to hem incorporated pockets set at an angle, adding a relaxed swagger to the silhouette.

The formality of day dressing during the 1950s required the garment to be worn with gloves, as the dress was either sleeveless or with sleeves cropped above the elbow. Saint Laurent also incorporated the Trapeze line into a short evening dress, *L'Eléphant blanc*, in white silver-sequinned tulle, which provided a softer silhouette, although it was anchored by a boned corset. Parisian couturier Givenchy and American designer Oleg Cassini modified the Trapeze line to produce a gentler A line, popular with presidential First Lady Jackie Kennedy. She preferred an unadorned, sleeveless, body-skimming style with a single defining feature, such as a couple of outsize fabric-covered buttons or a flat bow. The dresses were partnered with cropped jackets, with three-quarter-length sleeves and low-heeled pumps.

The Trapeze line evolved into the tent dress in the 1960s as the result of a pattern-cutting technique known as "fit and flare", in which the bust dart is closed to create a circular flare starting at the shoulders, providing volume at the hem without fullness on the bodice. A free and easy style, the silhouette appealed to the younger market, and usually featured cutaway sleeves with a hemline positioned at mid-thigh.

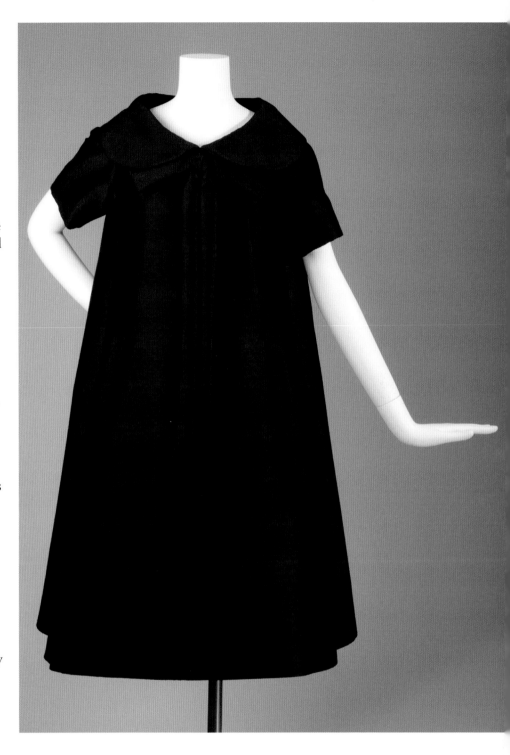

**OPPOSITE:** Yves Saint Laurent's innovatory Trapeze line for Christian Dior for S/S 1958 included *L'Eléphant Blanc*. This cone-shaped, wide-skirted silhouette was suspended on a rigid infrastructure, overlaid with layers of white net, embroidered with silver thread, rhinestones and sequins.

**ABOVE:** A mohair Trapeze-line afternoon dress from Saint Laurent's S/S 1958 debut collection for Dior. Confounding expectations that he would continue to promulgate the figure-following forms of Dior, the young designer introduced dresses devoid of the padding and structure associated with the house.

# The Petal

Christian Dior entitled his legendary 1947 collection "Corolla", the term for an assemblage of petals – the brightly coloured and highly scented outer leaves of a flower. The couturier continually made floral references in his designs, whether by acknowledging the silhouette of the bloom, as with the tulip shapes of the New Look (*see also page* 162), or with botanical embellishment.

Representing a post-war return to luxury, the sweeping skirt of Dior's Junon dress – named after the Roman goddess Juno, or Hera to the Greeks – is layered from forty-five petals of cotton tulle, sequinned in a tonal ombré from pale greens and blues to emerald green and navy blue. The skirt flows out from a mounted tulle waistband, the sequin-encrusted bodice forming the focal centre of the flower, designated in botany as the ovary. The stylized wing feather design taken from the peacock to represent overlapping petals is described in iridescent sequins, obliquely referencing the bird associated with the Queen of the Olympians.

John Galliano, for Christian Dior Haute Couture Autumn/Winter 2008–9, re-imagines the Junon gown by scattering feathery petals onto the surface of the undulating skirts of the dress, retaining the classic wasp-waisted silhouette of Dior's New Look and continuing the aesthetic of luxurious glamour established by the house over sixty years previously. On a grey silk background, each embellished petal is tonally shaded from lilac to blue, decreasing in size to meet the asymmetrical scalloped bodice.

Rome-based couturier Roberto Capucci approached design as a form of architecture, building structures around the body with line, colour, texture and volume. Capucci's major source of inspiration was drawn from natural forms, with curvilinear volumes replicating the undulating petals of flowers, and with crisp, pleated silks or voluptuous folds of taffeta forming the closed bud of a rose.

Valentino Garavani is master of über-glamour on the catwalk and a favourite of the fabulously wealthy, royalty and the Hollywood elite. In celebration of his 45 years as head of the Italian couture house Valentino, he utilized the expertise of the atelier for an effect called "pages", layered petals of organza that fluttered as they moved around the hem of a skirt or the shoulders of a cape. A similar effect was achieved by Christopher Kane in his Autumn/Winter 2014–15 collection, as 50 petals of organza, in palest pink edged with black, and in black edged with white, ruffled like pages of a book in a breeze, in homage to Roberto Capucci's experimentations with form and structure.

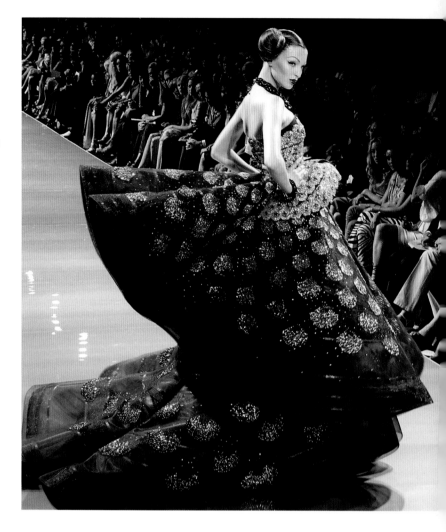

**ABOVE:** John Galliano's revision of key Christian Dior originals for the A/W 2008–9 couture collection includes a reappraisal of the Junon gown. Galliano creates a decadent interpretation by activating a dark ground of flaring stiffened organza, which carries encrusted embroidery of petal-like peacock feathers.

**OPPOSITE:** With sophisticated dexterity, Roberto Capucci crafts a finely pleated exotic bloom in rich hues. The strapless sweetheart bodice is employed for coherence with the petal-form peplums.

**OVERLEAF:** In profile and in suffused echoes of plumage shades, Christian Dior's Junon gown of 1949 (left) gently alludes to the mythical peacock with a train of exotic tail feathers, which default to a reading of oversize petals. The cascading bloom accumulates a ponderous quality from augmentation of beading at the hem of each subsequent layer. The skirts of the pale pink tulle dress (right), by John Galliano for Dior Couture from 2005, describes the heart of a many-petalled rose, with the edges left raw and organic, in a frothy homage to Edwardian opulence and femininity.

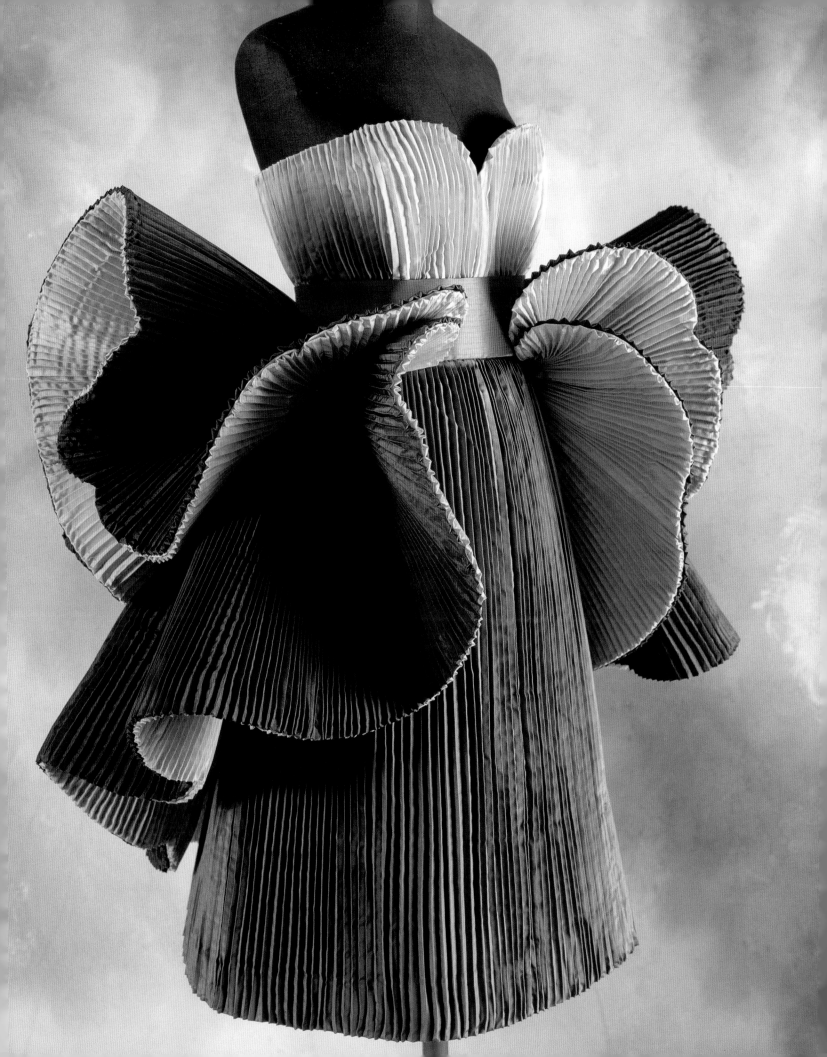

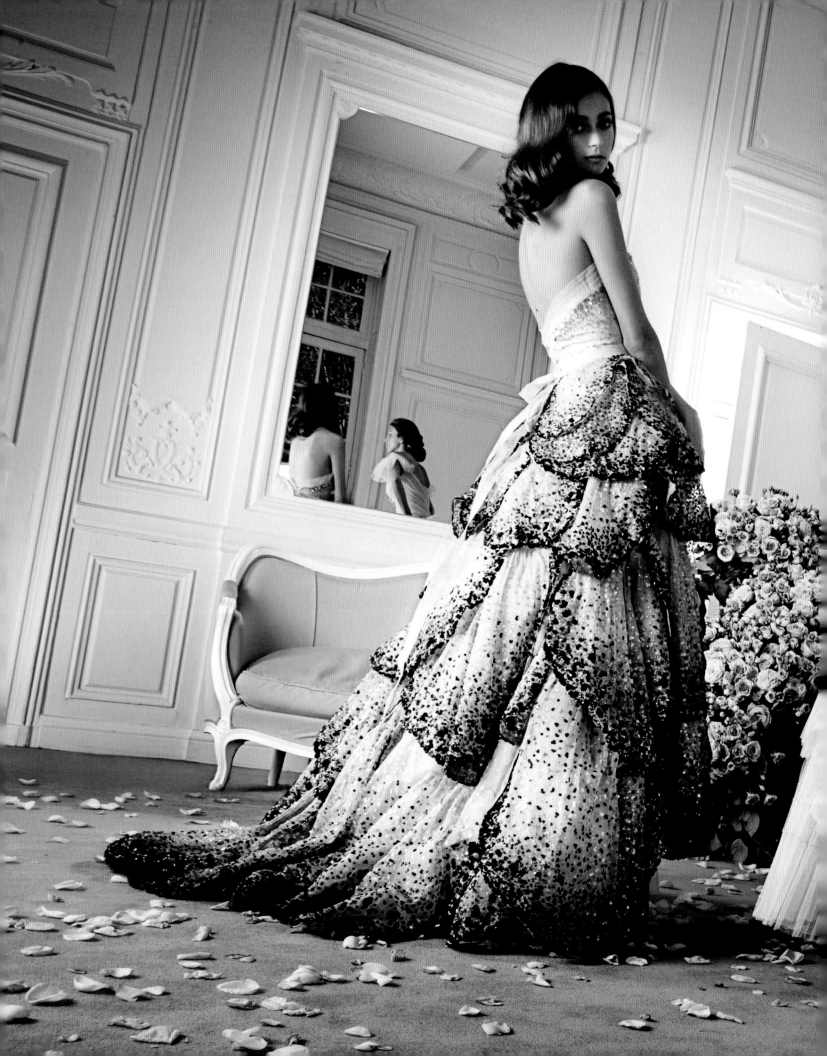

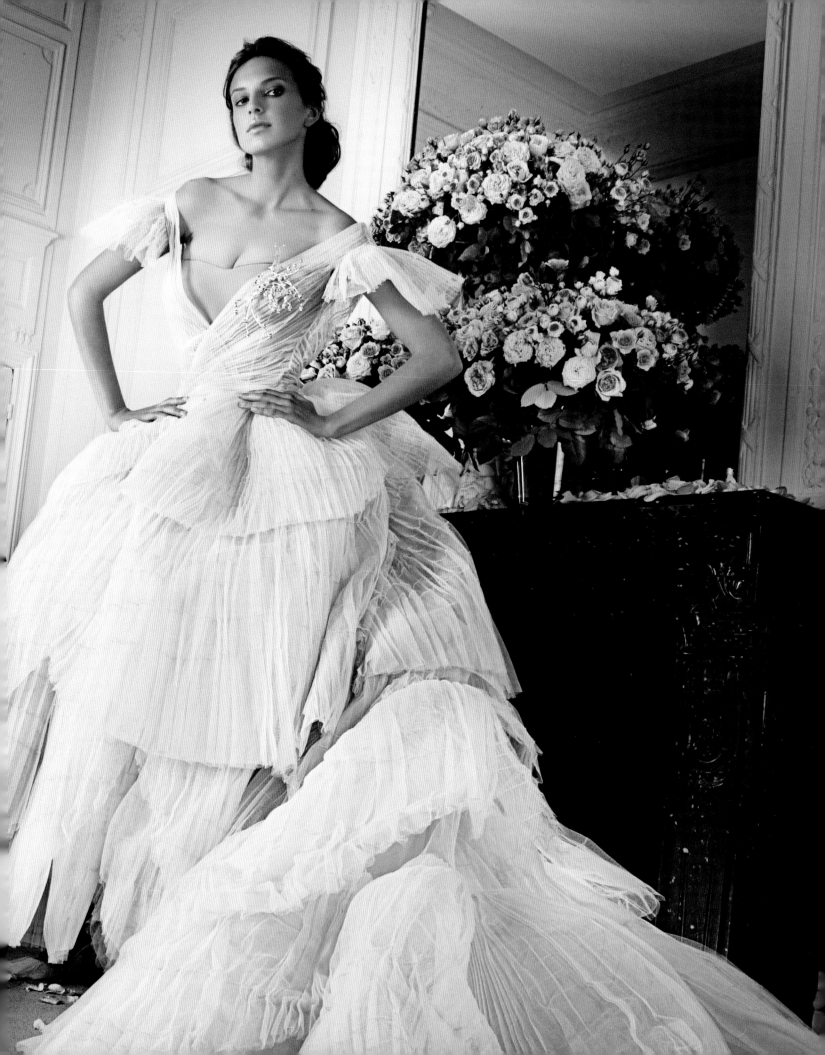

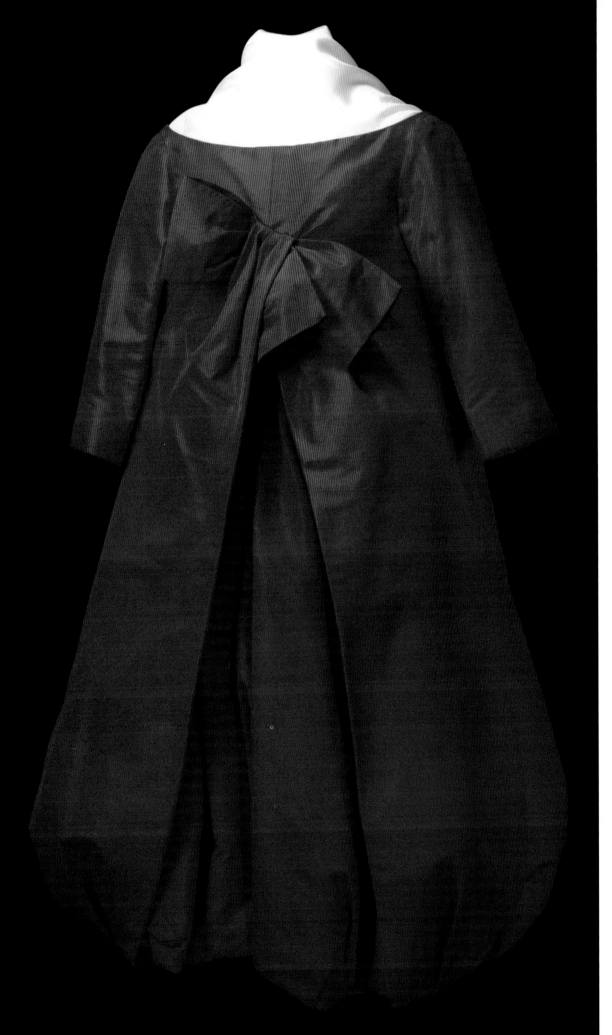

**LEFT:** The bulbous silhouette of a vast cellophane-wrapped and bow-tied Easter egg is attained by Dior's couture atelier in 1956 by employing an imperceptible internal textile scaffolding of tulle, faille, horsehair and canvas – hidden within a silk organdie lining. The red silk shell is bias-cut to afford the soft folds of the harem hemline.

**OPPOSITE:** Around 1987, French-born Christian Lacroix represented a capricious crosscurrent in the tide of fashion. By attaching a chef's hat skirt in pleated and quilted lemon satin to a piebald-hide bustier, the degree of whimsy is made evident.

# The Bubble

At a time when Paris lay claim to be the hub of haute couture and the epitome of fashionable glamour, a variety of silhouettes were introduced in quick succession, with Christian Dior as the leading protagonist. In the ten years between the inauguration of the New Look and his death in 1957, Dior never ceased to explore new directions as he repeatedly made changes to the fashionable silhouette, including the *Fuseau* line, the *Ailée* line, the Zig-Zag line, and, in 1956, the bubble dress.

This inflated silhouette had already been seen in the collections of Pierre Cardin and Hubert de Givenchy, and, by the end of the 1950s, it had become a popular choice for the cocktail party. The result of an engineered inner construction, the defining feature of the bubble dress was a bouffant skirt gathered in and under at the hem that ended just below the knee. This rigid, architectural shape was usually strapless, as an austere counterpoint to the volume below, and constructed in unyielding fabrics such as duchesse satin or silk moiré.

In the late 1960s and 1970s, Paris no longer held sway as couture lost its fashion relevance with the emergence of a youth-led *prêt-à-porter* and the influence of Milan. However, with the onset of the splash-your-cash 1980s and the demand for the big "occasion" dress, the fashionable elite once again invested in perfectly executed European couture, a revival owed in part to the emergence of Christian Lacroix. While at the couture house of Jean Patou, he introduced his version of the bubble, *le pouf*, or the puffball, in 1986, instigating a change to the decade's sharp-shouldered silhouette, disarming power dressing and promoting the notion of romantic revivalism. Such a structured and architectural silhouette as the bubble skirt and the commensurate infrastructure it required is no longer perceived as viable, and modern couture has deconstructed the bubble dress in both proportions and fabric.

The first collection in 2013 by Raf Simons as creative head of Christian Dior was shaped by the archive. Renowned for his minimalist approach, the designer presented the bubble dress as a cocoon of embroidered and appliquéd blooms that folded gently under at the hem. Miu Miu's approach is one of irony rather than homage: for her Resort collection of 2012, Miuccia Prada introduced the bubble skirt in a 1980s-themed collection, with Memphis-inspired prints and a witty irreverence.

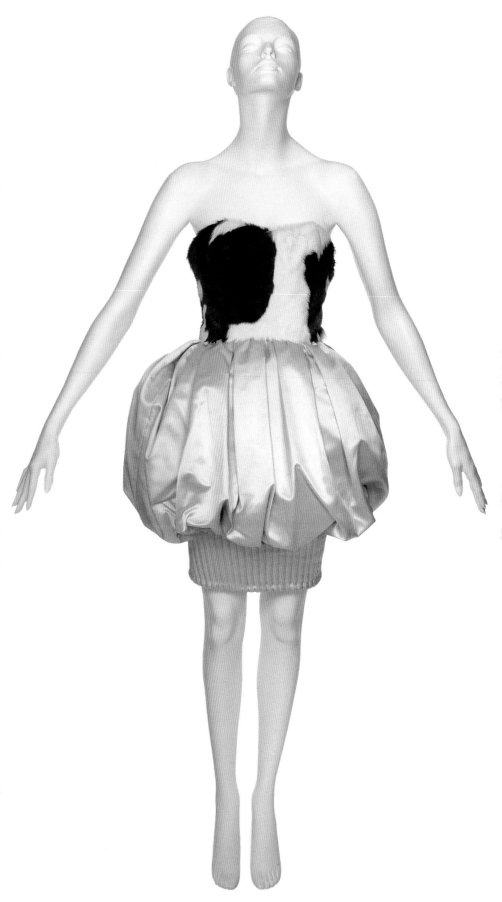

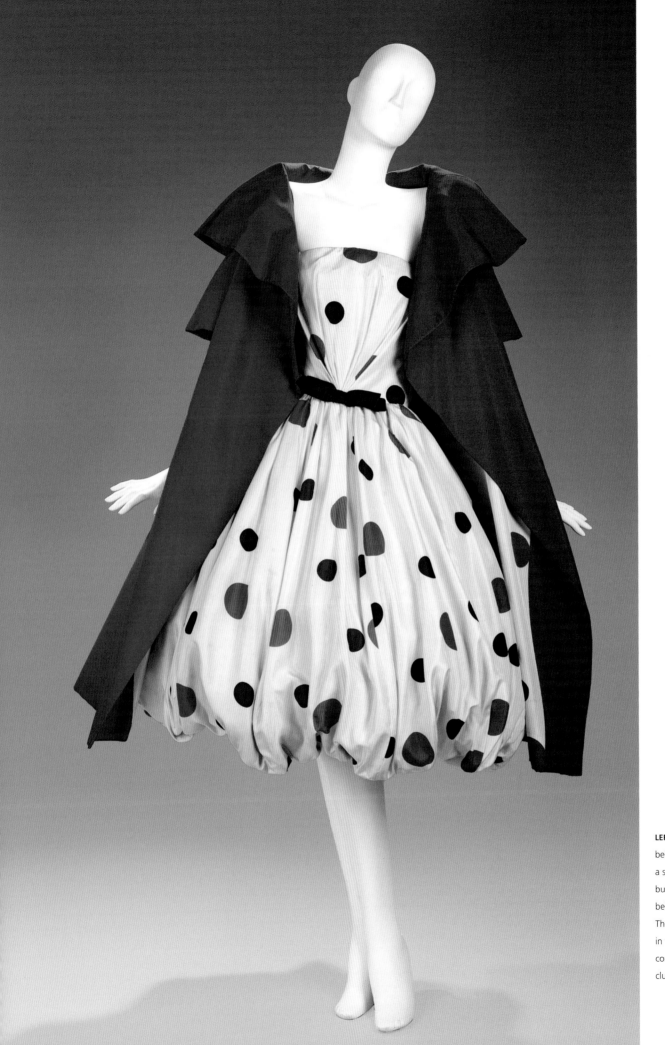

**LEFT:** In 1961, with a slender belted bow, Arnold Scaasi cinched a scattered polka dot-printed bubble dress tight to the waist, below a billowing red silk mantle. The bodice of the dress continued in folds to a fitted strapless conclusion – an echo of a tightly clutched paper bag.

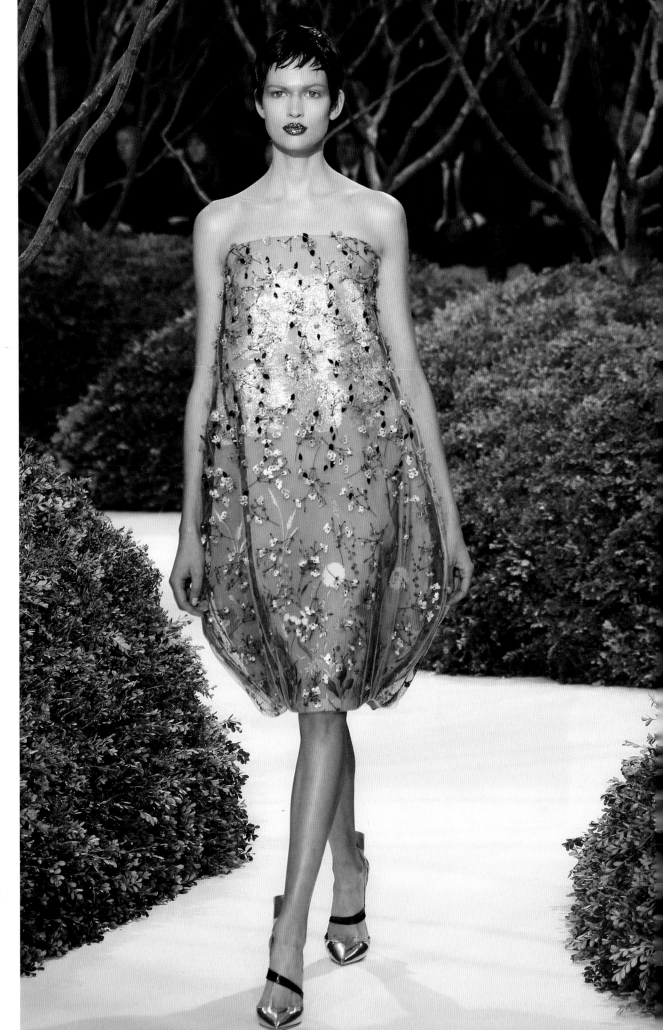

**RIGHT:** Raf Simons' inaugural couture collection for Dior in S/S 2013 was characterized by pastoral serenity, emphasizing the exquisite skills of the *petites mains* of the atelier in crafting clouds of delicate floral embroidery. This semi-transparent bubble dress aptly justifies its name by ballooning gently around the figure, festooned in silk millefleurs.

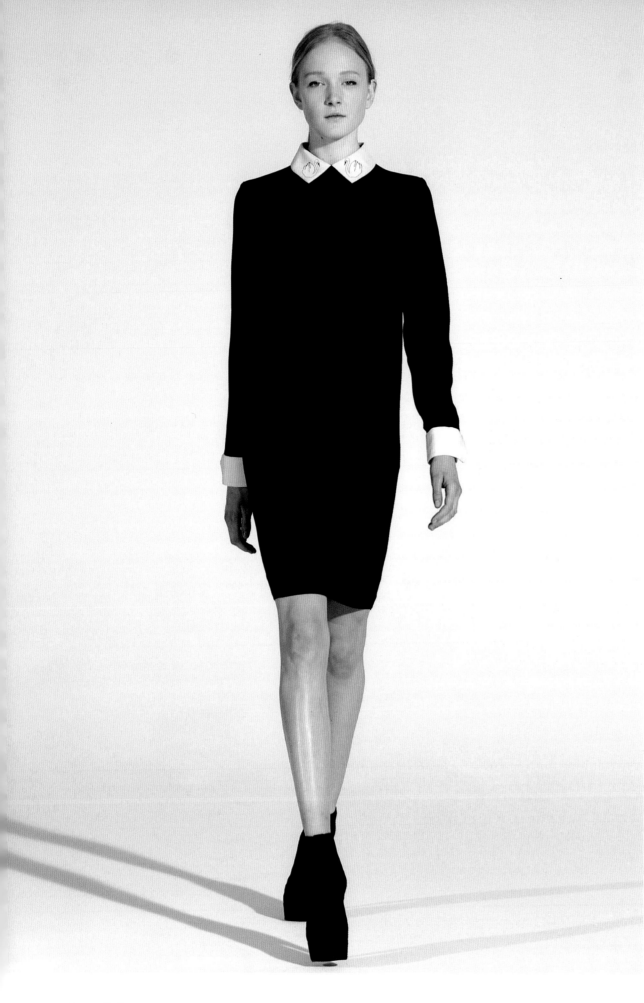

LEFT: For the second line to her signature range, "Victoria", UK-born designer Victoria Beckham negates the inherent sophistication of the Little Black Dress with the addition of a demure, white Peter Pan collar and matching cuffs.

OPPOSITE LEFT: Symbolizing her subservient status as carer to her ailing husband, Catherine Deneuve as Séverine Serizy in Luis Buñuel's *Belle de Jour* (1967) wears the archetypal maid's uniform. Nevertheless, it is imbued with a seductive sensuality.

OPPOSITE RIGHT: Part of the bohemian life of the 1920s, the Polish-born artist Tamara de Lempicka (1898–1980) used narrative elements in her images of the free, independent and bold "new woman", seen in her portrait of a *Woman in a Black Dress* (1923).

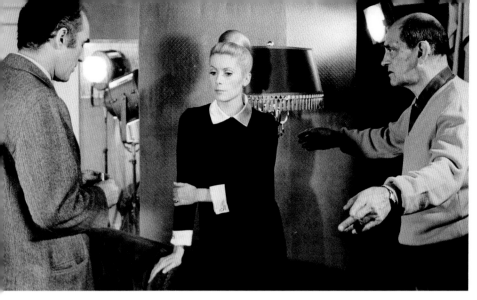

# Belle de Jour

In contrast to her role as a prostitute in Luis Buñuel's 1967 film *Belle de Jour*, the French film actress Catherine Deneuve wears clothes of apparent propriety, despite a storyline that encompasses domination, sadomasochism and bondage. The sexuality is covert, not explicit, and is only hinted at in the actress's wardrobe, designed by Yves Saint Laurent and which marked the beginning of a long-standing relationship between designer and muse.

As Séverine Serizy, the disaffected bourgeois housewife who cannot connect physically with her husband, Deneuve wears clothes of pale pink and cream in soft, undemanding fabrics such as knitted jersey and cashmere. As Belle, who spends her afternoons with clients in a luxurious Parisian brothel, Deneuve adopts a military severity with sculptured double-breasted coats in dark shades of black and brown, in tough, untouchable fabrics such as vinyl and leather.

Although 1967 marked the height of the miniskirt, Saint Laurent kept the hemlines to just above the knee, which required a flatter shoe than the then popular stiletto. French shoe designer Roger Vivier's classic Pilgrim block-heeled, round-toed pump had been designed at the request of Saint Laurent to complement his Mondrian shift dresses launched in 1965 (*see page* 208). With the appearance of the film, the shoe became an instant bestseller. Many of the typical Saint Laurent elements worn by Deneuve were already in evidence in the designer's ready-to-wear collections, such as the military-inspired coats and high-waisted shift dresses.

The turtleneck sleeveless shift dress worn by Deneuve in brown wool represents classic 1960s tailoring. Similarly, the camel-coloured wool shirtdress with the fly-front, concealing the zippered opening, is also constructed from a close-napped woollen face cloth which creates a carapace over the body, an effect emphasized by the top-stitched seams and detailing then prevalent. Given the connotations of servility – a detachable white collar and cuffs are a prerequisite of anyone performing practical tasks such as a nurse, a waitress or even the playboy bunny – the archetypal maid's uniform worn by Deneuve at the end of the film, when she is taking care of her husband, has perhaps surprisingly been re-imagined for many catwalk collections, most particularly by Victoria Beckham for her diffusion range "Victoria" of Autumn/Winter 2012–13.

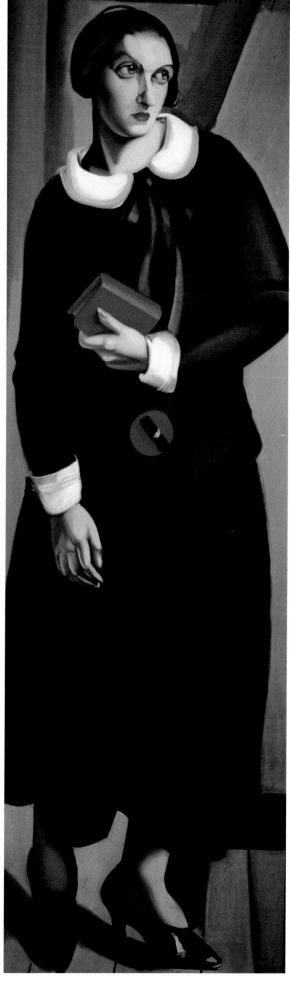

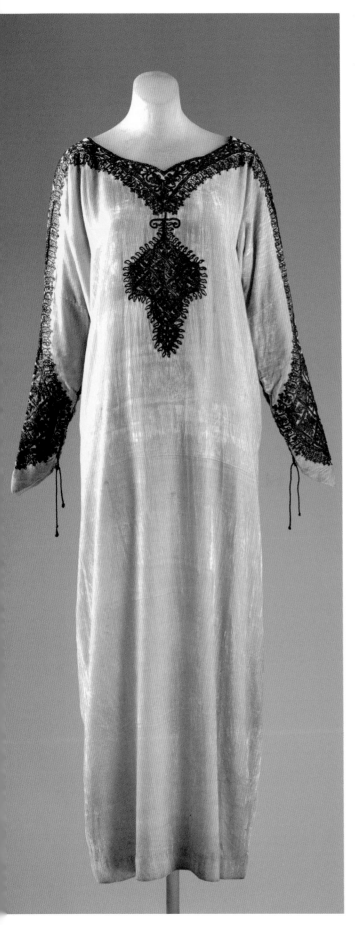

# The Kaftan

Among the many borrowings from the vernacular dress of other cultures, the kaftan remains the most ubiquitous, a simple T-shaped garment where the construction is rooted in the simplest way of utilizing the full loom width of the fabric without waste. Pulled on over the head, it generally featured various decorative embellishment concentrated at the hem, neck and sleeves, the vulnerable parts of the garment. The kaftan was first depicted in the art of ancient Persia from 600 BCE and its use spread by the thirteenth century into Eastern Europe and Russia, reaching its zenith in magnificence in the early Ottoman Empire (1299–1923).

The impact of non-Western aesthetics has been a major influence on clothing construction since the early twentieth century, when American couturière Jessie Franklin Turner's signature tea gowns in "exotic" fabrics and T-shaped silhouettes (*see page* 93) heralded the introduction of the kaftan into Western fashion. Other designers, including Parisian-based Vitaldi Babani, relied on this simple piecing together of geometric form, with a silk and metallic kaftan featuring lavish embroidery at the boat-shaped neckline and down the outside of the sleeves.

The influence of non-Western fashion diminished in the 1930s, to reappear in the "high" 1960s with the hippies, a youth sub-cult that expressed political dissatisfaction and anti-materialism with the adoption of clothes picked up on the hippie trail to India, Morocco and the Far East, including the embroidered cotton kaftan. Fashionable imitators of the hippies indulged their escapist fantasies by wearing high-end variations to be found in the collections of leading European and American designers including Emilio Pucci, Zandra Rhodes, Bill Gibb and the Algerian-born Yves Saint Laurent.

Thea Porter, one of the earliest among British fashion designers to bring hippie deluxe to high visibility, drew inspiration from her far-ranging travels and designed fantasy voluminous beaded and embroidered kaftans in Swiss chiffons, Indian handprints, silks, brocades and velvets. Emilio Pucci also transformed the simple cotton kaftan with the introduction of his signature polychromatic prints in psychedelic swirls of colour. These were favoured by the international jet-set and "the beautiful people" such as Princess Margaret, Talitha Getty and film actress Elizabeth Taylor, who was renowned for her collection of kaftans. Returning the garment to its historical magnificence, the actress accessorized these not with the beaded bracelets and macramé headbands of the hippies, but with a selection of opulent jewels.

LEFT: Founded in Paris in 1894 by Vitaldi Babani, the label Babani initially specialized in goods imported from Asia until 1919, when the designer produced clothing heavily influenced by the imported merchandise. This evening dress in silk velvet from 1925 is a reproduction of a North African embroidered robe.

OPPOSITE: From the extensive wardrobe of kaftans worn by film star Elizabeth Taylor – who favoured the all-concealing properties of the garment for her robust figure – this kaftan by British-based designer Thea Porter (1927–2000) exemplifies romantic hippie style with block-printed panels and ikat-woven sleeves.

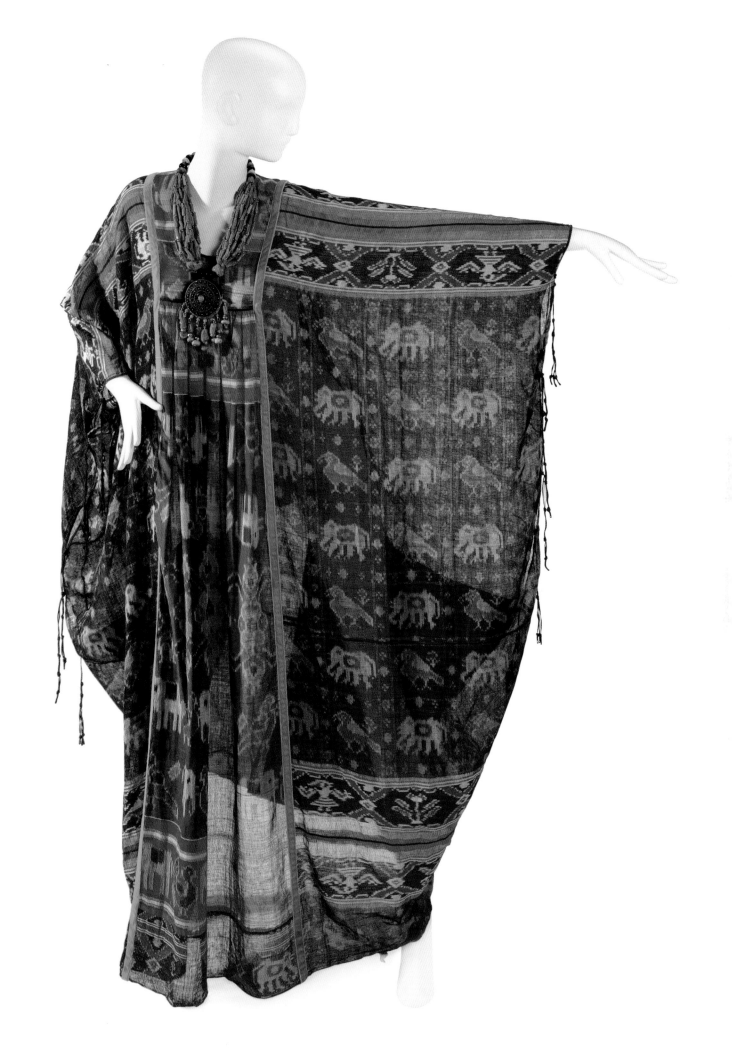

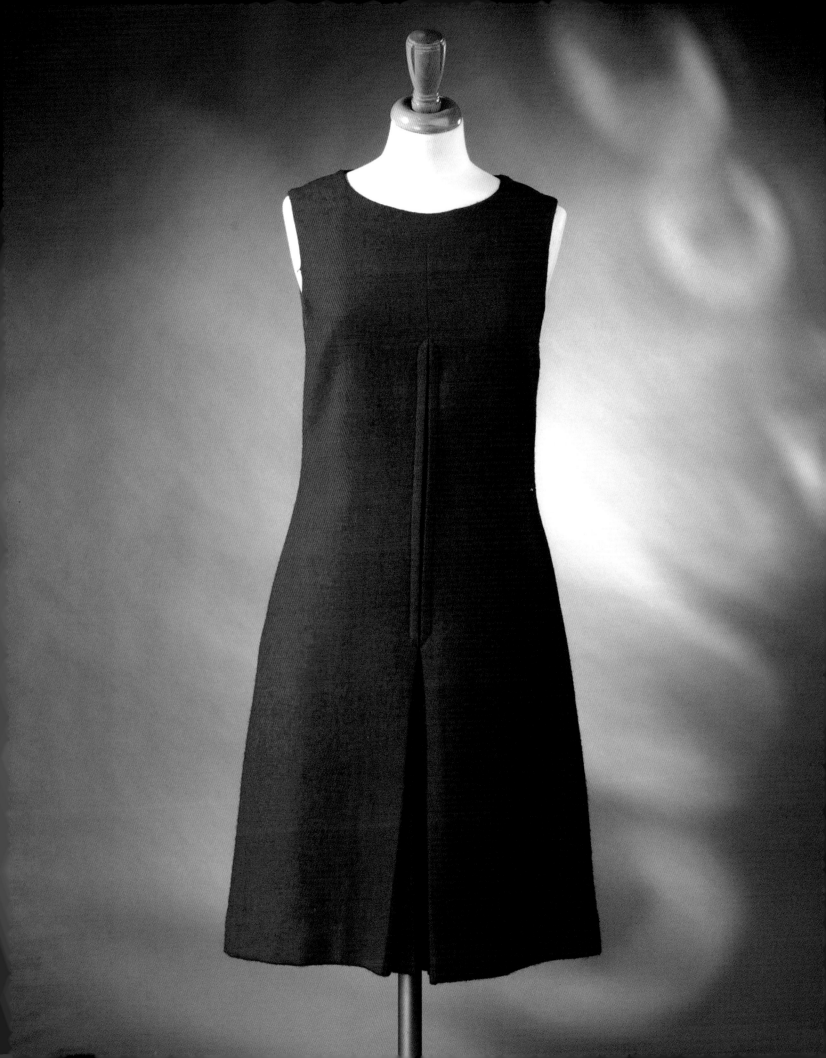

# The Mini

A potent symbol of the young, post-war teenager, the miniskirt was representative of a new social order at a time when the conservatism and hierarchies of the 1950s gave way to an era of untrammelled freedom for the newly labelled "dolly bird". In 1955 Mary Quant, the influential designer and co-founder of the boutique Bazaar, together with her husband, Alexander Plunket Greene, promulgated a streamlined silhouette typified by what Quant called "The Chelsea Look". She redefined the school uniform with skinny pinafore dresses in grey flannel or pin-striped suiting, worn with knee socks and turtle-neck skinny rib sweaters, and added elongated sports shirts as dresses and outsize V-necked cardigans, all in a subtle colour palette that eschewed the currently popular pretty pastels for ochre, plum and ginger. Initially hemlines remained resolutely on the knee until fully fashioned seamed stockings gave way to the newly developed tights, or pantyhose, at the beginning of the 1960s, with 1966 designated by fashion journalists as "the year of the leg".

Several designers were key players in the evolution of the elevated hemline. John Bates, under the label Jean Varon, was producing thigh-high skirts in innovative materials such as transparent plastic in 1962. Barbara Hulanicki of Biba claims she was responsible for the emergence of the mini on the high street as the result of a manufacturing error: double jersey had been cut while damp and, once made up into garments, it retracted into skirts measuring only ten inches. Parisian couturier André Courrèges endorsed the mini for an upmarket clientele with his "Moon Girl" collection of 1964, a modernist all-white collection of architectural simplicity that placed the hemline a few inches above the knee.

Models such as Jean Shrimpton and, later, Twiggy offered a different kind of physicality from the elegant womanly lines of the 1950s. Their waif-like proportions epitomized the new ingénue, with round shoulders, toes pointing inwards or legs splayed when sitting, a look emphasized with flat Mary Jane shoes and pale tights.

The mini re-emerged as the micro-mini in the 1980s, a wardrobe staple of the "glamazon", the woman on the move in an era of conspicuous consumption. Worn with stiletto-heeled shoes, a sharp-shouldered jacket and statement accessories, the new miniskirt represented the dress-for-success aspirations of the businesswoman rather than pre-pubescent ennui.

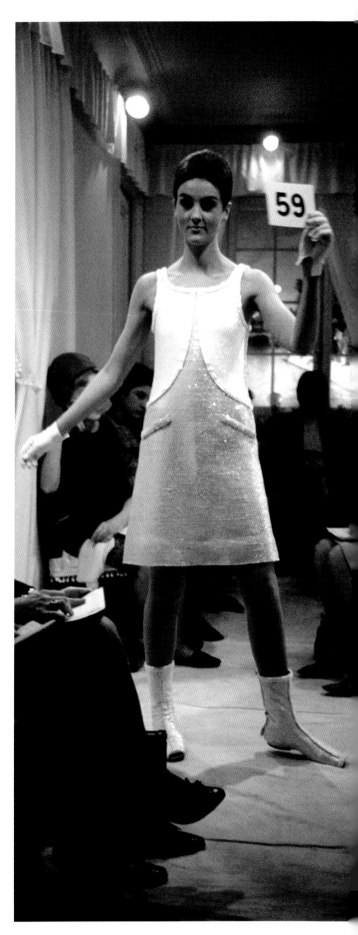

**OPPOSITE:** Promulgating the "youthquake" fashions that defined the era, Mary Quant (1934–) designed modern, simply cut clothes for the newly defined "teenager", retailing in her King's Road boutique, Bazaar. In 1965 she successfully undertook a promotional tour of the "London Look" to America.

**RIGHT:** Parisian couturier André Courrèges (1923–) produced his influential futuristic white and silver "Moon Girl" collection in 1964. Accessorized with distinctive flat, open-toed boots – much copied – signature details included the use of densely woven fabrics, which created a simple A line, cutaway sleeves and double welt seaming that added to the resistant quality of the cloth.

# Op Art

The modernist cropped shift dresses and tunics, heralding the wave of "youthquake" fashion in the 1960s, provided a minimalist canvas for Op Art, a movement that utilized bizarre perspectives to fool the eye. Canvases by artists such as Victor Vasarely and Bridget Riley, whose first purely optical work *Movement in Squares* appeared in 1961, moved Op Art off the gallery walls and into fashion. American dress manufacturer Larry Aldrich purchased works by both Riley and American abstract painter Richard Anuszkiewicz, commissioning a range of fabrics inspired by his new acquisitions – Riley famously attempted to sue a fashion house for creating a range of clothing that used one of her pieces as a dress pattern, but was unsuccessful.

Almost instantly, Op Art patterns started to appear on everything from clothes to advertisements, stationery, furnishing fabrics and even the paper dress. The trend was picked up by British designer Ossie Clark on his visit to the US with his fellow student David Hockney. The designer returned enthused about the use of the Op and Pop Art motifs he saw, and in his graduation show from London's Royal College of Art in 1964 he included an architectural and complex coat of swirling Op Art patterns that was photographed for *Vogue* by David Bailey.

The instant impact created by the dazzling black-and-white pattern was exploited when, in 1965, Anne Trehearne, former editor of the influential *Queen* magazine, asked John Bates to design a new wardrobe for Diana Rigg in her role as Emma Peel, kick-ass protagonist of the cult TV show *The Avengers*. Extensive media coverage ensured that Op Art-inspired fashion entered the mainstream, with undulating spots, stripes and checks appearing in collections by New York-based designer Betsey Johnson and British design duo Tuffin & Foale. American designer Marc Jacobs revisited the 1960s for his Spring/Summer 2013 collection for his signature line in New York, dressing lookalike style icon Edie Sedgwick of Warhol's Factory in streamlined modern graphic abstraction. Three weeks later, Jacobs continued the optic trend in Paris with his 1960s-inspired silhouettes decorated with a geometric pattern in yellow and white, the chequerboards creating an independent rhythmic surface, indicating movement.

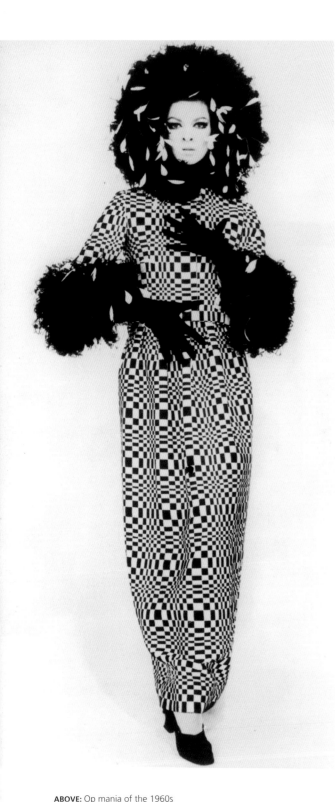

**ABOVE:** Op mania of the 1960s was reflected in the dazzling full-length sheath dress by Italian couturier Roberto Capucci (1930–), with a print inspired by *Vega*, painted in 1957 by Victor Vasarely. The distortion of the series of squares is accomplished by changes of scale and direction.

**OPPOSITE:** Superimposing exaggerated contour lines of various widths onto a second-skin nylon and spandex mesh-knit dress, Jean Paul Gaultier in 1996 creates a trompe l'oeil-effect print that redefines the female body beneath, emphasizing the breasts and hips.

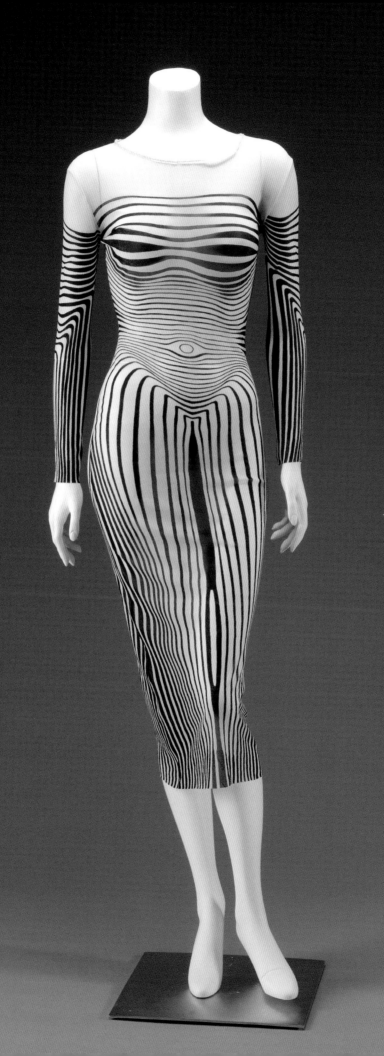

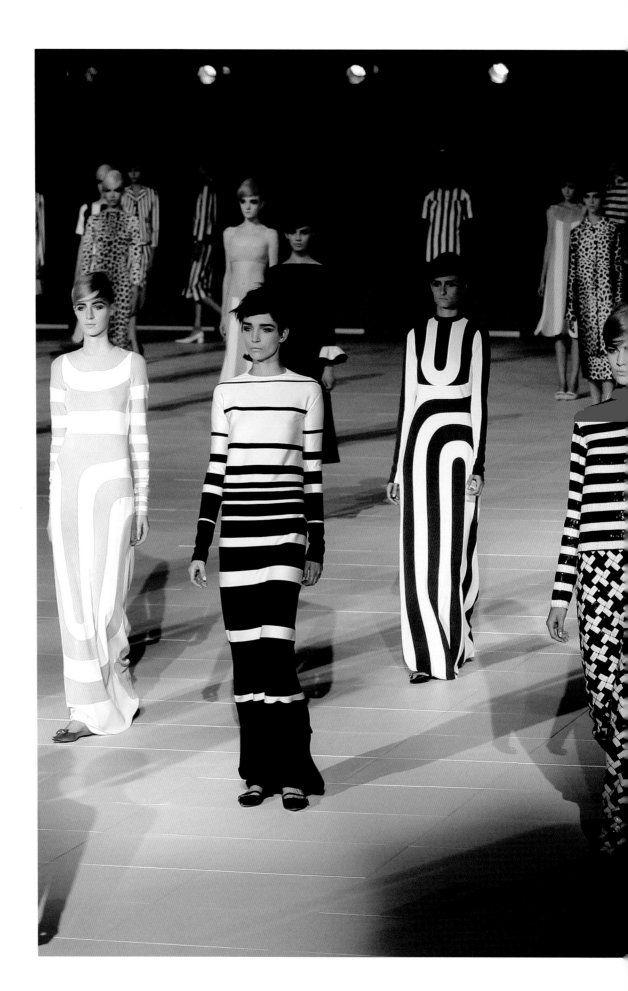

**RIGHT:** Channelling 1960s New York style icon Edie Sedgwick, Marc Jacobs' eponymous line for S/S 2013 presents expanding, contracting and undulating Op Art stripes and checks with a plethora of diagonals, horizontals and verticals that appear to move independently of the body.

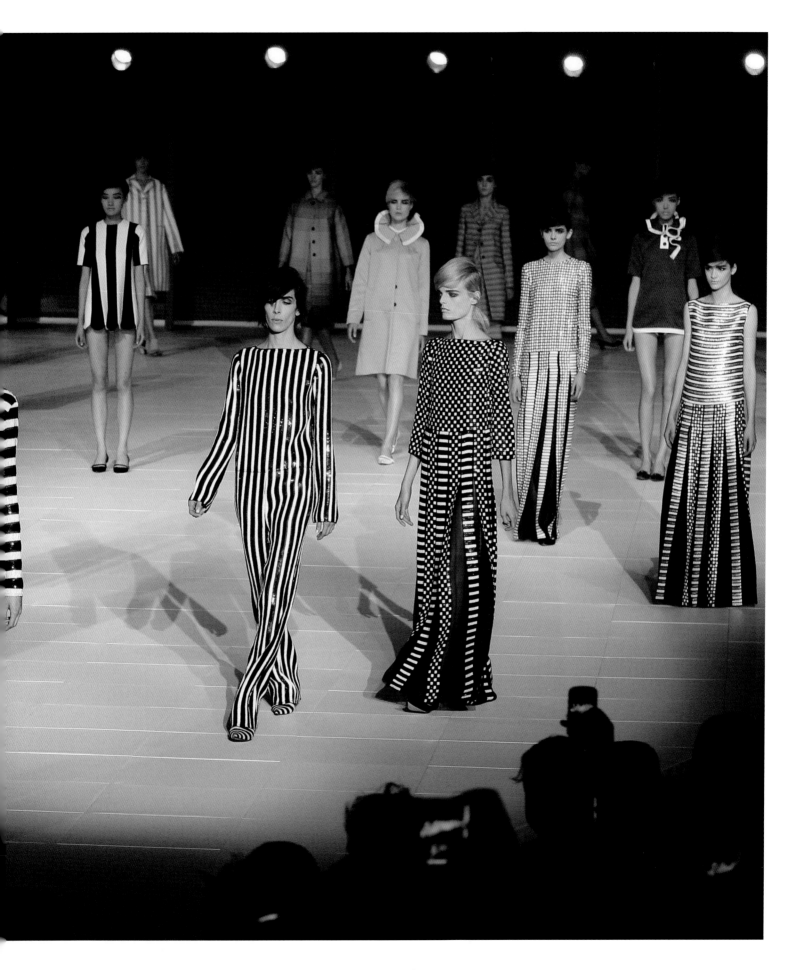

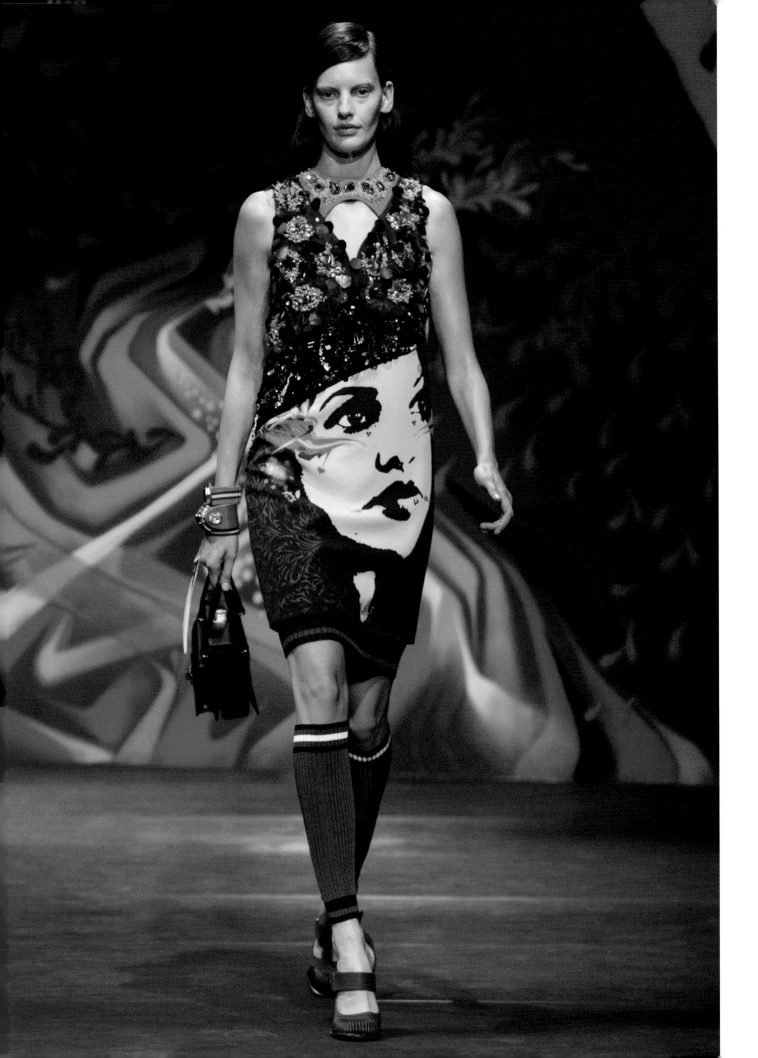

# Pop Art

A vibrant collage of stylized figurative motifs inspired by the canvases of Pop artists Andy Warhol, Roy Lichtenstein and Tom Wesselmann, Yves Saint Laurent's iconic collection of 1966 created a combination of art and fashion unseen since Schiaparelli's collaboration with the Dadaists and Surrealists of the 1930s.

Offering an aesthetic challenge to European traditions of art by the celebration of American industrial culture, Pop Art had its provenance in the late 1950s, named by British artist Richard Hamilton and the art critic Lawrence Alloway. According to their manifesto in 1957, the new art should be "popular, transient, low-cost, mass-produced, young, witty, sexy, gimmicky". Its celebration of cultural ephemera, the cult of celebrity and the appropriation of a diverse design language that included posters, packaging and images from the media all provided a lively and transgressive iconography, which continues to provide a constant source of inspiration to fashion designers.

The prolific output of Andy Warhol – Pop Art's most famous practitioner and the superstar of the New York arts and social scene in the 1960s – has since been hijacked by designers, including maverick French stylist Jean-Charles de Castelbajac. Parodying Warhol's own reproductions and his silk-screens of American icons such as Jackie Kennedy and Marilyn Monroe in 2009, Castelbajac placed an image of the artist's familiar face onto the front of a minidress, complete with a Warhol-like bleached-out candyfloss wig. Castelbajac also references Pop artist Richard Hamilton's adoption of Ben-Day dots to describe Warhol's features. This printing process originates from 1879 and is named after Benjamin Henry Day Jr, an illustrator and printer. Richard Hamilton employed this graphic texture in many of his paintings and sculptures, enlarging and exaggerating the dots.

In 1991, Gianni Versace brought into combination sensuous shapes and references to pop culture. Renowned for the exuberant decadence of his aesthetic, the Italian designer confected saturation glamour with a bejewelled all-over print, featuring portraits of Hollywood's most enduring sex goddess Marilyn Monroe and screen idol James Dean, in a long, body-skimming evening dress in 1991. In contemporary fashion, as a reaction to a period of minimalism with the emphasis on unadorned tailoring, the relationship between fashion and art is once again thriving. Graphic screen-printed portraits in the style of Warhol by illustrators such as Gabriel feature on influential Italian designer Miuccia Prada's collection for Spring/Summer 2014.

**OPPOSITE:** Miuccia Prada rehabilitates iconic female equivalents of Warhol's Che Guevara in the style of the murales artists of Latin America. Her Prada S/S 2014 collection flaunts portraits that resemble – fleetingly – Patty Hearst and Angela Davis.

**RIGHT:** JCDC, or Jean-Charles de Castelbajac, indulges in multi-layered pop irony. In his S/S 2014 collection he holds a mirror to the merchandising of graphic heroes, from Mickey Mouse to Supergirl, the latter refrocked in a spangled trompe l'oeil superhero costume in shift form.

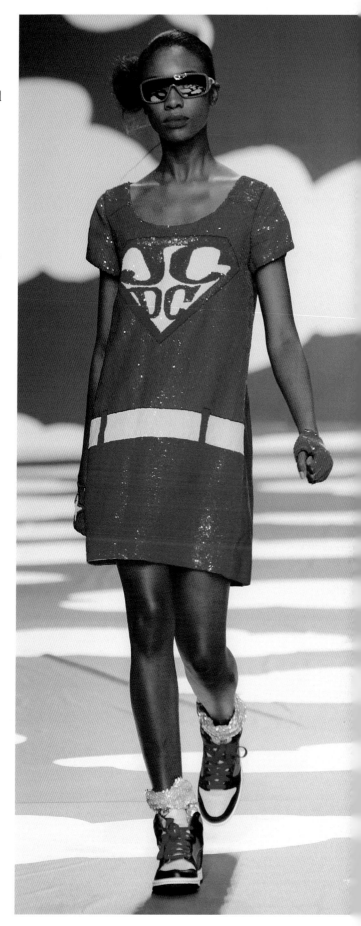

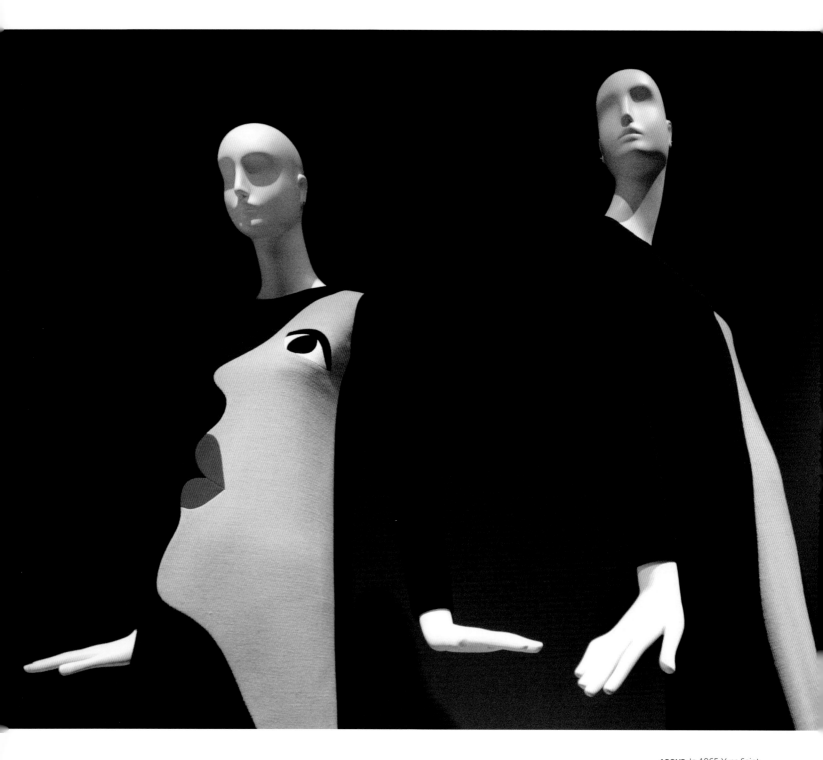

**ABOVE:** In 1965 Yves Saint Laurent achieved great success when he translated Mondrian's geometric paintings into fashion. By way of contrast, in the following year he embraced the figurative aspects of Pop Art, using enlarged fragments of female figures set, with a hint of chiaroscuro, in the dark silhouette of columnar gowns.

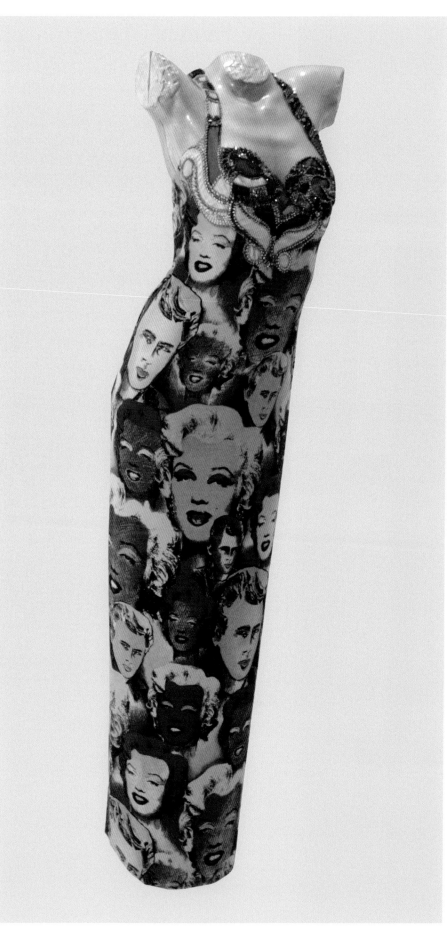

**RIGHT:** Gianni Versace's extended 15 minutes of fame was at its apogee when, in a stroke of genius, he compressed the superlatives of celebrity onto a single catwalk in 1991. Dressing the four best-known supermodels of the universe in pop imagery, directly from the Warhol lexicon, he flashily sheathed Linda Evangelista in fallen 1950s icons.

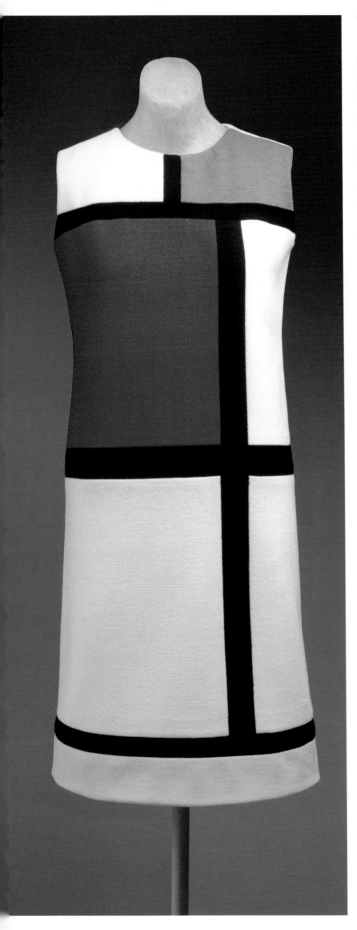

# The Painterly Dress

Certain images from art are fixtures in the visual pantheon of twentieth- and twenty-first-century fashion, from the giant red lips of Dadaist artist Man Ray – inspiration for prints from Schiaparelli to Prada – to the vibrant Pop Art motifs of Andy Warhol that are consistently appropriated by contemporary designers. Art and fashion have continued to inform each other since the 1920s, when Jean Patou produced sweaters featuring blocks of contrasting colour and horizontal stripes inspired by the work of Picasso and noted Cubist Georges Braque. At the same time, Robert and Sonia Delaunay were experimenting with colour in art and design, investigating a process called *simultanéisme* – which occurs when one colour is placed next to another and then "mixed" by the eye – seen in Sonia's first large-scale painting, *Bal Bullier*.

Increasingly intrigued by the application of these principles to design, the artist extended her practice to include clothing, and in 1924 she opened a fashion studio, the Boutique Simultanée, with couturier Jacques Heim. Blurring the line between fine and applied art, Yves Saint Laurent paid homage to the compositional rigour of Dutch-born painter Piet Mondrian's *New Plasticist* paintings of the 1930s when in 1965 the designer incorporated the grid-like pattern of primary colours seen in *Composition C (No lll) with Red, Yellow and Blue* painted in 1935 into a knee-skimming shift dress. Two decades later, the canvases of artists Braque, Matisse, van Gogh and Cocteau featured in Saint Laurent's haute couture collection, interpreted in lavish three-dimensional embroideries executed by the Lesage atelier. The free-form mark-making of Abstract Expressionism practised by American painters such as Jackson Pollock offers a dynamic surface to fashion designers and provided the inspiration for Erdem's Autumn/Winter 2011 collection, the printed surface imitating the artist's gesture of dripping or splashing the paint onto the canvas.

Periods of subdued minimalism in fashion are inevitably followed by an enthusiastic adoption of exuberant print and vibrant colour, with their provenance generally found in the work of various artists and artistic movements. Influential minimalist Phoebe Philo of Céline, adopted flashes of painterly brushstrokes in dazzling primary colours for her 2014 collection, and Karl Lagerfeld at Chanel incorporated almost the entire Pantone colour system – a favoured means of communicating accurate colour samples between designer, manufacturer, retailer and consumer, first launched in 1965 – into his Spring/Summer collection of 2014.

**LEFT:** Surpassing the use of Jasper Johns *Target* imagery in London's Mod fashions, Yves Saint Laurent went deeper into culture in Paris in 1965 for the more establishment influence of Piet Mondrian. By a strange osmosis, the YSL facsimile in dress form has acquired the same museum and critical status as the painted original.

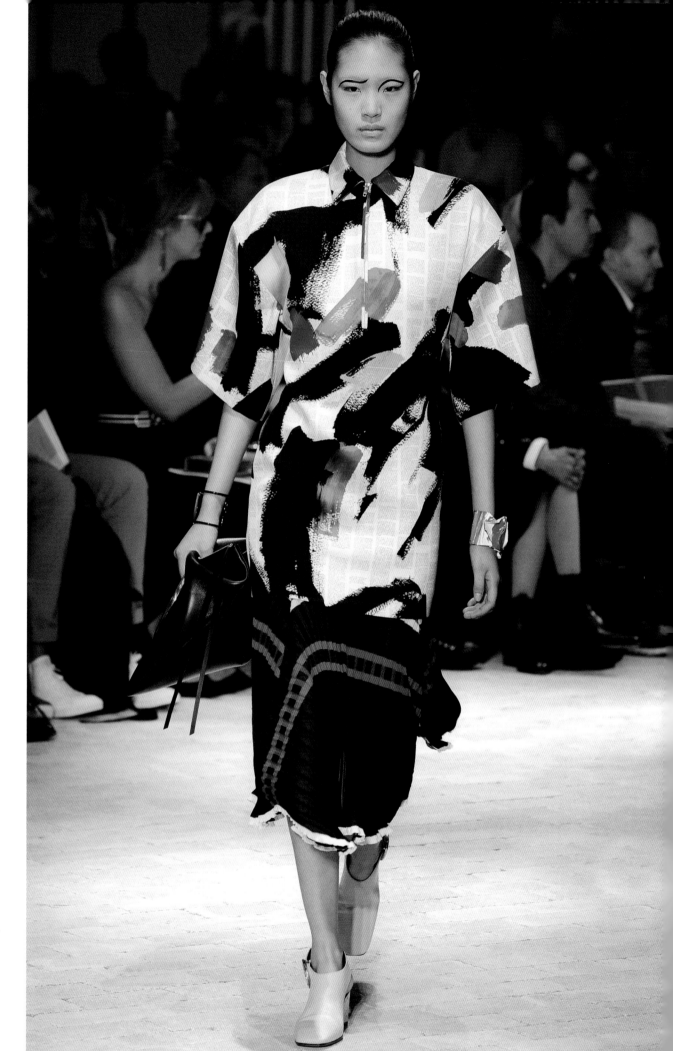

**RIGHT:** Phoebe Philo chose to amplify the flick and sway of her breezy S/S 2014 collection for Céline with both her choice of fabrics and the imagery she applied. She used dramatic gestural brushstrokes, echoing the tachisme of Pierre Soulages, the graffiti photographs of Brassaï and the chromatic abstraction of Kandinsky.

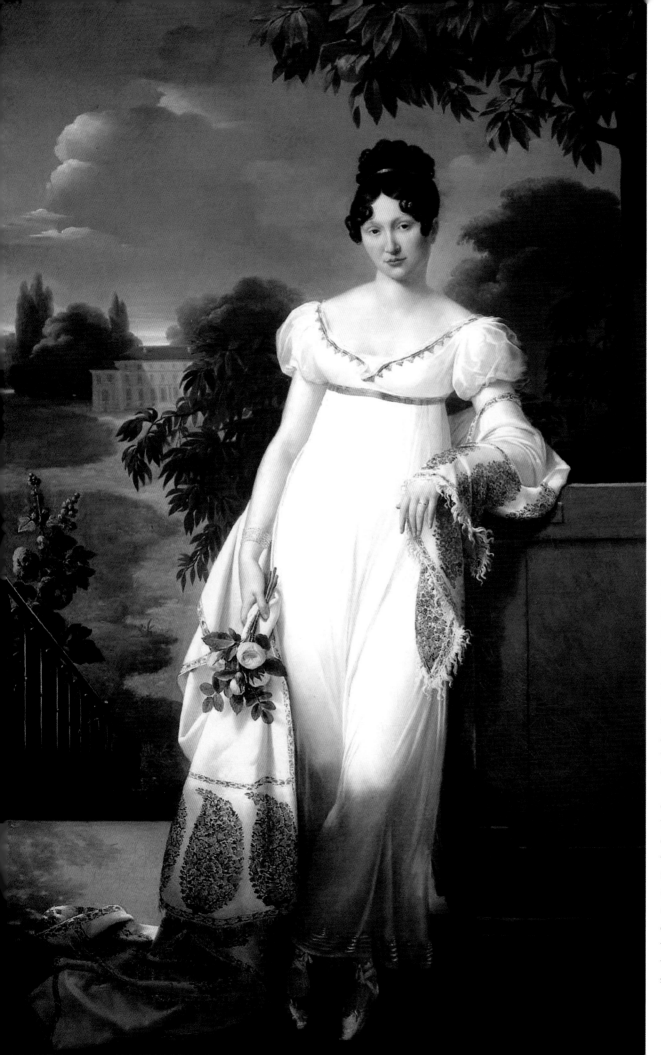

**LEFT:** The adoption of the lightweight cotton chemise dress during the neo-classical period necessitated the addition of accessories designed for warmth, including the paisley shawl. Unlike the all-over paisley design seen in the later Victorian period, the shawl, worn by Félicité-Louise-Julie-Constance de Durfort, features only a border of the cone-shaped motif.

**OPPOSITE:** Italian-born, New York-based Giorgio di Sant'Angelo (1933–89) was an early adopter of found objects, incorporating old braids, shells, ribbons and feathers into free-floating garments that reflected the hippie culture of the early 1970s. The paisley print of the handkerchief skirt is anchored to a chamois bodice, whip-stitched into place.

# The Paisley Motif

The paisley motif is one of the most enduring of images, providing inspiration for fashion designers from Matthew Williamson to luxury Italian label Etro. The origins of the motif are ambiguous, thought by some to be the mark made by curling the hand into a fist and printing with the little finger downwards into the cloth. The comma-shaped cone, known as *boteh*, or the Paisley pine, is also thought to be a seedpod and as such a symbol of life and fertility.

The characteristic teardrop pattern was a feature of shawls woven in Kashmir. Sought after by the French, Russian and British aristocracy, they were imported into Britain by the East India Company at the end of the seventeenth century. The shawls proved so popular that demand exceeded supply, and the design was copied by the artisan silk weavers in the Scottish town of Paisley. When the shawls were no longer fashionable, the pattern remained in use under the generic name of paisley. Arthur Lasenby Liberty sold the shawls while working at the Farmer & Rogers' Great Shawl and Cloak Emporium, and once he had established his own retail emporium, the paisley design continued to feature extensively in the company's textiles. Patterns originating in the 1900s were updated in the 1960s by the London store by changing the coloration and scale of the motif, and also utilizing it for Tana lawn, a lightweight dress fabric.

The extravagantly patterned free-flowing form of paisley was particularly adaptable to psychedelic interpretations and was eagerly appropriated by the counter culture. American designer Giorgio di Sant'Angelo produced a maxi-dress featuring a vibrant paisley pattern in 1973, with a chamois empire bodice, confirmation of the motif's hippie-luxe connotations.

Designers over the ages have exaggerated and distorted the basic scroll-shaped unit, varying the length of the "fruit" and "stalk" and introducing extraordinary colourways to make it their own. Inspired by a trip to India, Gerolamo "Gimmo" Etro, the founder of the luxury label Etro, introduced a paisley collection in 1981 into his home furnishings range, which was subsequently used for men's and women's accessory lines. Once the company launched a ready-to-wear range in 1994, the swirling Indian motif appeared for the first time on the label's garments.

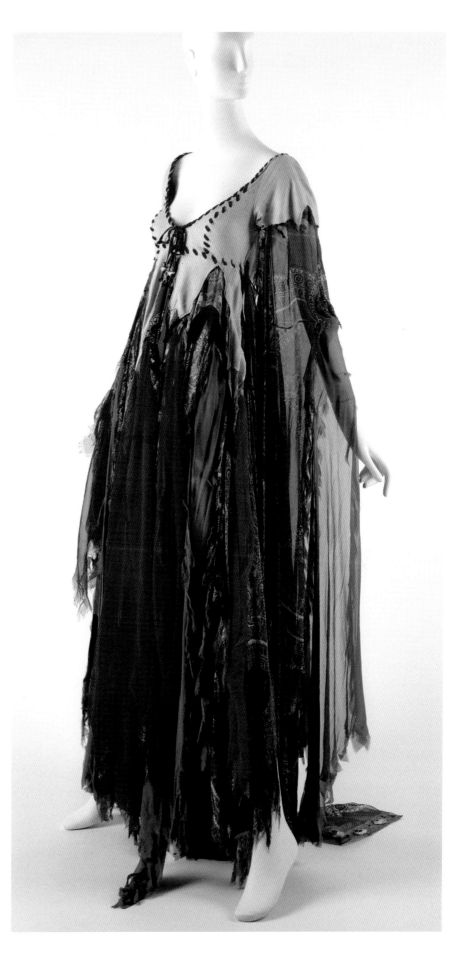

# The Pinafore

The appeal of the pinafore dress lies in its association with the simplicity and practicality of what was originally a garment worn by children, so called because it was "pinned afore" to the front of a dress to provide protective covering. Originating in the late eighteenth century, the pinafore featured a bib front and shoulder straps with an opening at the back. Daily pinafores were made from cotton or calico, with Sunday best a mere gesture towards utility, being made from organdie, a sheer lawn fabric, with ruffles on the shoulder straps. The twentieth-century schoolgirl gymslip in dark serviceable colours such as maroon, brown and navy serge owes its provenance to the pinafore, although it had a closed back, with box pleats falling from a high-waisted yoke.

During the 1960s in the UK, young style-savvy Mods sourced vintage gymslips to wear, until "youthquake" designer Mary Quant popularized her version of the pinafore dress in school uniform grey flannel, with "kick" pleats or godets at the knees, worn with coloured stockings and boots. The style was disseminated through Quant's Ginger Group, a lower-priced line that offered bonded wool jersey pinafore dresses and A-line tunics, with V-necks in the fashionable colours of mustard, prune and ginger. Skimming the outlines of the body, high-waisted and with cutaway sleeves, with straps or a deep scooped neckline, the pinafore dress, worn alone or over a striped skinny rib sweater, resonated with the boyish prepubescent silhouette of the era.

Rural imagery in fashionable dress has frequently included the adoption of the pinafore along with the smock, worn as decoration rather than for any practical reasons, evidenced by the success of the Laura Ashley label in the 1970s. The Welsh designer tapped into the pastoral nostalgia of the era and the "back-to-nature" ethos then prevalent and created garments of milkmaid innocence from archive prints of sprigged cotton. In contrast, the simple lines of Diane von Furstenberg's iconic wrap dress of the same era can easily be traced to the one-piece wraparound pinafore in floral printed cretonne, usually edged in a contrast bias binding worn by the working-class housewife. Complex seaming elevates the pinafore dress to high-fashion status in the debut collection by Victoria Beckham for her eponymous second line. Incorporating bust and waist darts into two vertical seams either side of a high-seamed waist, the dress in textured grey wool has all the ingénue appeal of the gymslip overridden by razor-sharp tailoring.

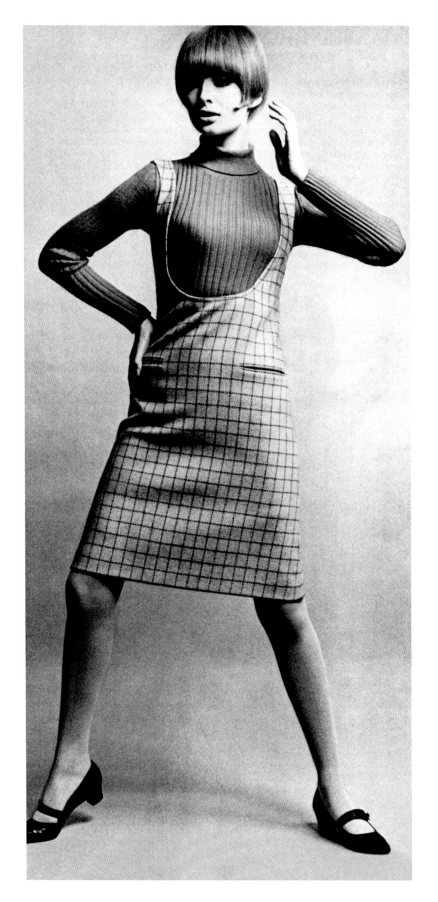

OPPOSITE: The scoop-necked pinafore dress in a window-pane check worn over a skinny rib sweater by Mary Quant became an essential outfit for every mod young girl. The designer launched the Ginger Group in 1963, a lower-priced line sold through department stores, which made her designs accessible to all.

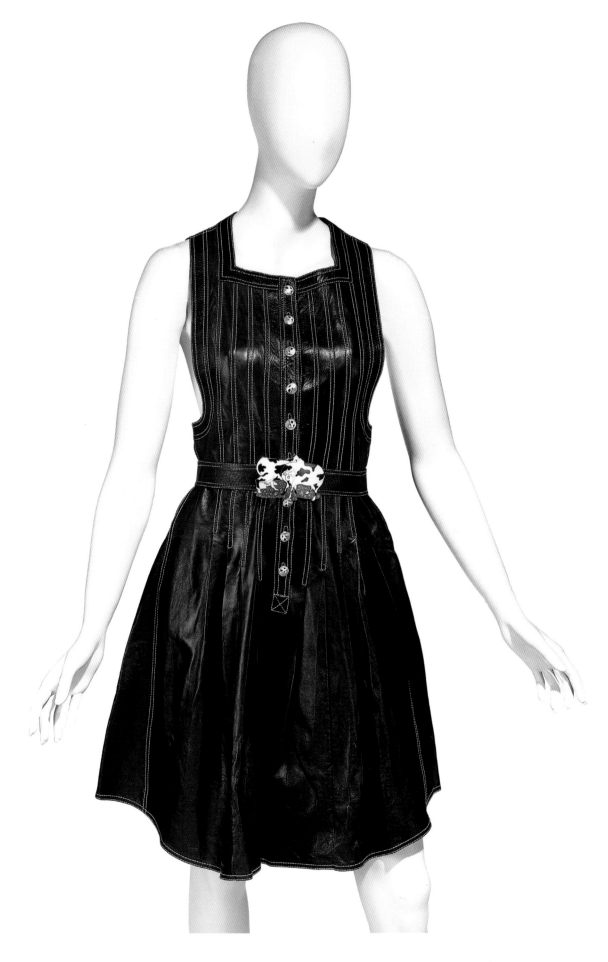

RIGHT: Renowned for the simplicity of her designs, and the use of fluid fabrics such as Hurel jersey, suede and soft leather, Scottish-born, London-based designer Jean Muir launched her label in 1966. The navy leather pinafore dress from the 1970s features her signature top-stitching of seams and pin-tucking detail.

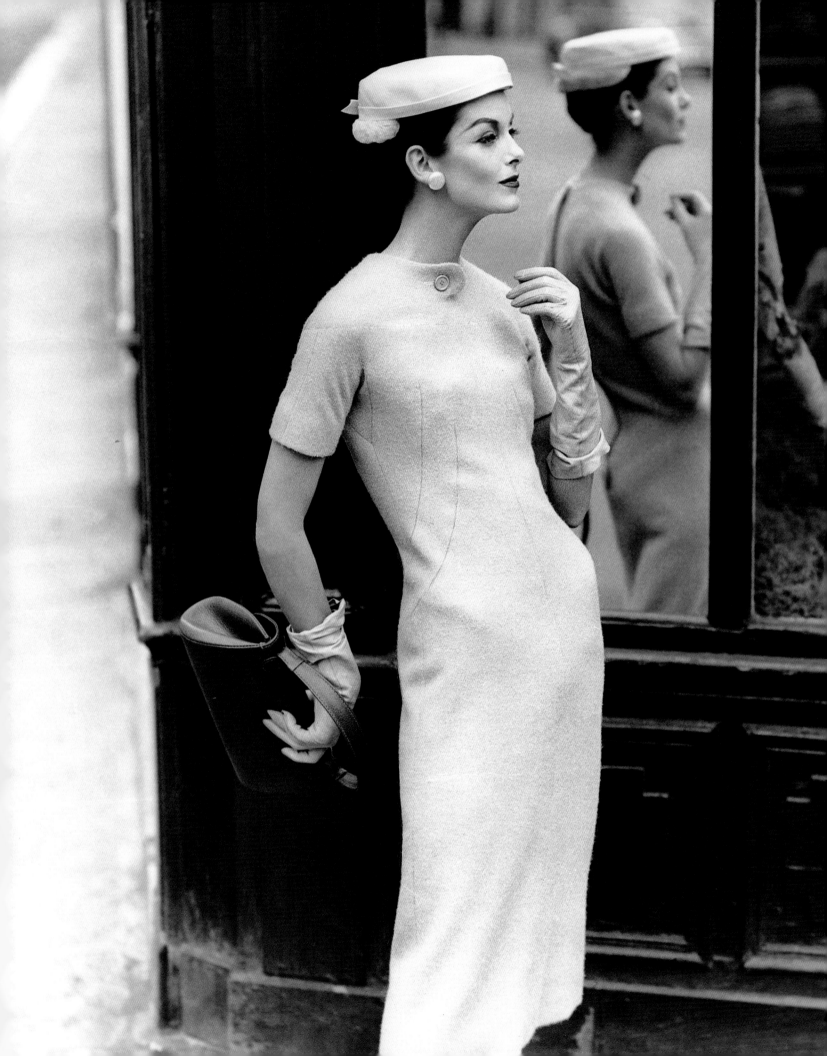

# The Sheath

Form-fitting but loose enough for comfort, the linen *kalasiris* worn by women in ancient Egypt was a type of sheath dress, a style that has recurred throughout fashion history when the silhouette has not been distorted by the addition of infrastructures such as the farthingale or crinoline, and when the waist has remained in its natural place. Named for the way it fits – a close-fitting covering or case – the design of the sheath dress, unlike the tubular chemise of the 1920s or the shapely New Look of the 1950s, acknowledged the silhouette without emphasizing any particular area of the body. Generally sleeveless and with a narrow A-line or straight skirt falling to the knee or to mid-calf providing room for easy movement, it was worn for both formal and informal occasions, depending on the fabric.

The sheath dress was modified in the 1950s by the introduction of shaping darts at the waist, which nevertheless remained unmarked by a belt, seam or waistband, creating a flattering silhouette that was generally constructed from a plain, textured material such as a wool bouclé for day – a popular fabric of the era – or brocade for evening. Unadorned by extraneous frills, flounces, pleats, draping, fancy sleeves or fussy necklines, buttons or bows, the sheath dress represented modern dressing following the voluminous and weighty amount of fabric used in post-war fashion.

Together with the Sack dress introduced in 1957 (*see page* 30), the striking simplicity of the sheath dress, a democratic garment, was readily available from mass-market manufacturers. It was elevated into the realms of luxury by couturiers such as Hubert de Givenchy and Cristóbal Balenciaga, who during the late 1950s and early 1960s used the economy of the silhouette as a base for luxurious fabrics and embellishments by the Lesage embroidery atelier. Similarly, Marc Jacobs, for his Marc for Marc Jacobs line, and Prada present the contemporary sheath dress as a backdrop for exhibiting pattern. A recurring shape in the collections of both, Miuccia Prada incorporates colour-blocked prints and Swarovski-crystal embellishment on her sheath dresses for Spring/Summer 2014. Incorporating high-octane glamour into the sheath silhouette and returning it to the fitted outline of the 1950s when film stars such as Marilyn Monroe wore the more shapely style, US-based designer L'Wren Scott – whose eponymous label lasted from 2006 until her untimely death in 2014 – took the sheath almost into body-con territory, with an emphasis on primacy of fit and a narrow pencil skirt to mid-calf.

**OPPOSITE:** Technically perfect and a tour de force of tailoring, this sheath dress in wool bouclé from 1955 by Parisian couturier Hubert de Givenchy shows an inspired use of darting and seaming, to create the moulded bodice, cap sleeves and body-skimming lines.

**RIGHT:** The New York designer L'Wren Scott (1964–2014) softened her signature strict sheath dress, one of a collection entitled "Madame du Barry" after the famed mistress of Louis XV – for whom pink was reputedly a favourite colour – with a wide Peter Pan collar and cuffed, cropped sleeves.

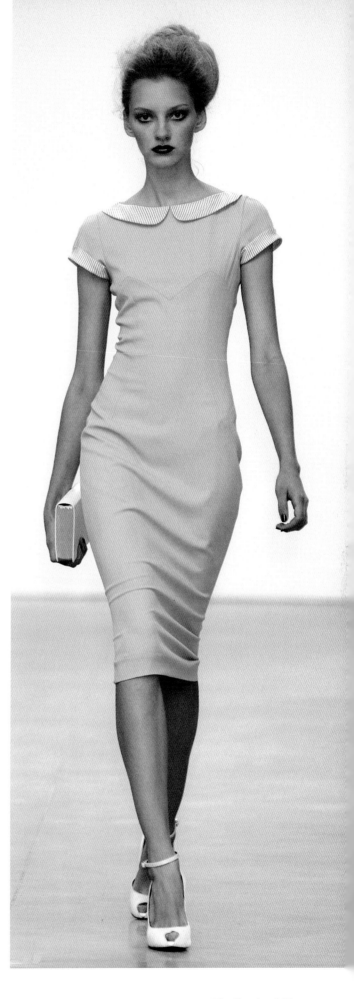

# The Paper Dress

The fleeting, transient nature of 1960s fashion was epitomized by the wear-once-and-throw-away paper dress, a simple above-the-knee chemise featuring various bold, printed designs. The first of these was credited to the Scott Paper Company of Philadelphia in 1966. Sold by mail order, the Paper Caper dress was made of Dura-Weve, a product patented in 1958, and featured a black-and-white Op Art print and a red bandana print. Constructed from bonded cellulose fibre reinforced with rayon or nylon, the dresses provided a useful canvas for do-it-yourself designs with paints and crayons and could easily be shortened with a pair of scissors.

Other dresses referenced the prevailing popularity of Pop Art imagery, particularly Andy Warhol's screen prints. Paper dresses were also manufactured and sold by Campbell's Soup Company – the Souper Dress – inspired by Warhol's 1962 artwork *Campbell's Soup Cans*. Mars Manufacturing Company also invented a wide range of paper dresses, from a basic A-line style and a paper evening dress to a full paper wedding gown, and the 28 stores of the West Coast's Joseph Magnin Co. carried paper dresses in their News Stand boutiques.

The ephemeral nature of the paper dress and the ease of construction of the simple A-line shape appealed to the new young designers working in London. Sylvia Ayton and Zandra Rhodes produced paper dresses for the influential 21 Shop at Woollands department store, and Celia Birtwell designed a floral border for a paper dress designed by partner Ossie Clark. The disposable dress by Diane Meyersohn and Joanne Silverstein from 1967 encapsulates the moment when the hard-edged motifs of modernism and the geometric shapes associated with the space-age gave way to nostalgia for the past. The paper dress recognizes both the simple fashion silhouette of the early 1960s and the planned obsolescence of the era – described by industrial designer Brooks Stevens in 1954 – while introducing the historical revivalism that was to take its place with its printed pattern of swirling, free-flowing forms of Art Nouveau. Although promoted as the ultimate in convenience, the paper dress was uncomfortable, impractical and prone to tearing. However, the cellulose fabric did provide a lightweight material for disposable garments for factory and hospital workers.

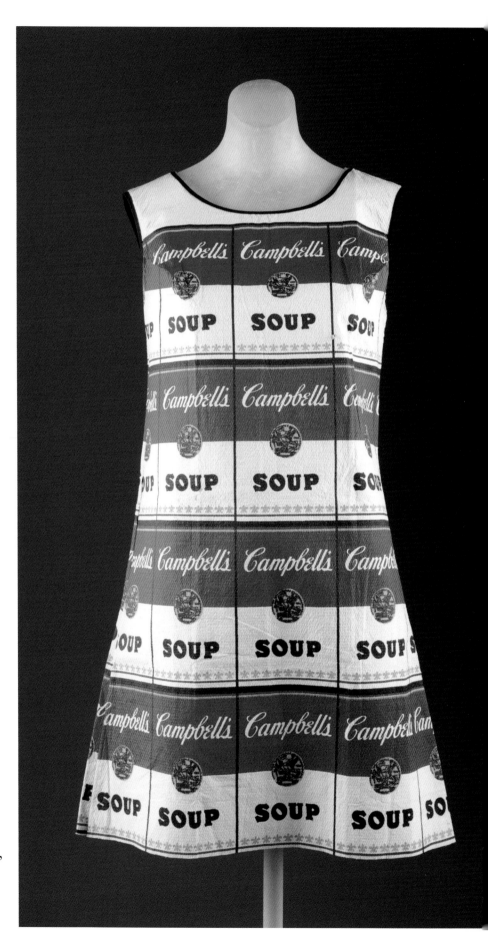

**OPPOSITE:** The Souper Dress was a successful marketing ploy. Manufactured and sold by the Campbell Soup Company in 1966, the screen-printed dress exploited the notoriety inspired by New York artist Andy Warhol's infamous 1962 artwork titled *Campbell's Soup Cans*.

**RIGHT:** Renowned fashion collaborators Ossie Clark (1942–96) and Celia Birtwell (1941–), he the master cutter, she the textile designer, utilized a bonded textile fibre for a short-sleeved shift dress featuring Birtwell's Happy Bubble design, created for UK textile company Ascher in 1966.

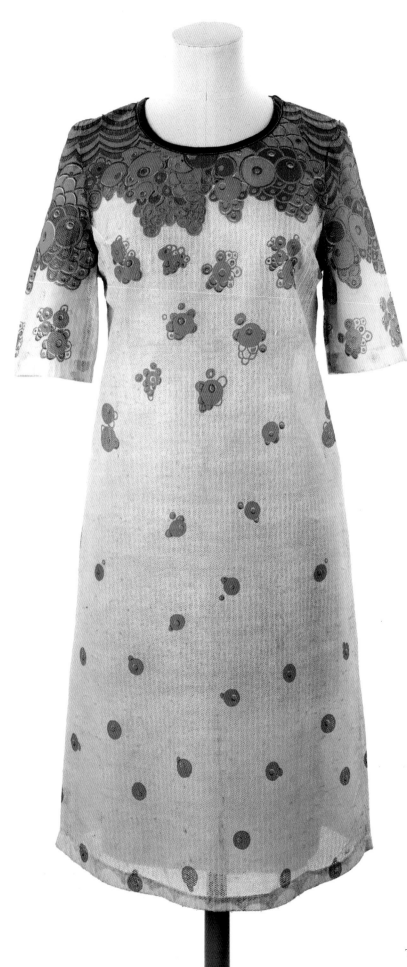

# The Topless Dress

Exposing the breasts in fashion is usually commensurate with the relinquishing of structured undergarments such as the corset. "Undress" was the prerogative of the most elevated members of the Stuart court of Charles II in the seventeenth century, when a loose one-piece coat, which later formed the basis for the mantua, was worn over a voluminous white chemise for a *déshabillé* effect. The high-waisted, clinging dresses of the *Merveilleuses* of the French Directoire (1795–99) also appeared in very low-cut necklines that, tantalizingly, almost completely revealed the breasts.

The exaggerated female form of the corseted Victorian era emphasized the breasts and hips, but these remained covered with weighty fabrics, although in contrast, eveningwear was extremely décolleté. Although the fashions of the 1920s offered a new ease with the free-floating chemise, exposed legs were the prevailing focal point and it was not until mid-century that the cantilevered bosom became the feminine ideal, with maximum uplift achieved by underwiring or circular stitched cups.

It took radical West Coast fashion designer Rudi Gernreich to free the breasts and reveal them in their natural form. Misunderstood by a prurient press, the three knitted dresses for New York Company Harmon Knitwear were never an act of provocation but one aspect of the designer's intention to change social attitudes to the naked body. The dresses were a natural progression from Gernreich's deconstruction of the swimsuit – which at the time was boned and seamed along the lines of a restrictive corset – when, in 1952, he introduced the knitted maillot, one of the first post-war garments to acknowledge the natural shape of the body. In 1964 Gernreich presented the monokini – the topless swimsuit – to the buyers and the press, modelled by Peggy Moffitt, Gernreich's favourite model, and photographed by her husband, the photographer William Claxton. The same year Gernreich designed the "No-bra Bra", manufactured in a neutral coloured jersey without padding or boning and in which the breasts were no longer moulded into points but allowed to assume their natural shape. The body stocking followed, a stretch nylon all-in-one that obviated the need for a brassière that could be worn beneath transparent dresses. The topless dresses and the monokini presaged the changing attitudes to nudity during the 1960s, but although contemporary fashion includes tantalizing glimpses of the side-boob or dresses with judiciously placed cut-outs, in high fashion breasts generally remain covered.

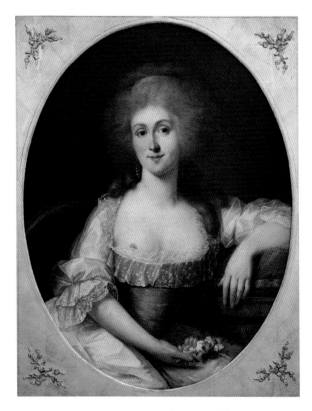

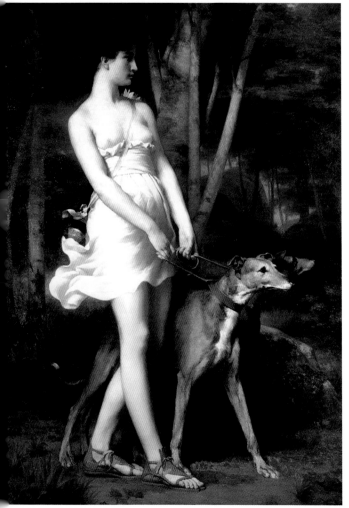

**ABOVE LEFT:** An intimate of Marie Antoinette, Marie-Thérèse-Louise de Savoie-Carignan, Princesse de Lamballe, painted in the late eighteenth century by Joseph-Siffred Duplessis (1725–1802), adopted the provocative chemise. Initially a female undergarment and a form of *déshabillé*, it was popularized by the French queen.

**LEFT:** Owing to her mythological status, the near-naked figure of Diana the huntress, the virgin goddess of the hunt and the subject of a painting by Gaston Casimir Saint-Pierre (1833–1916), was acceptable to nineteenth-century notions of propriety.

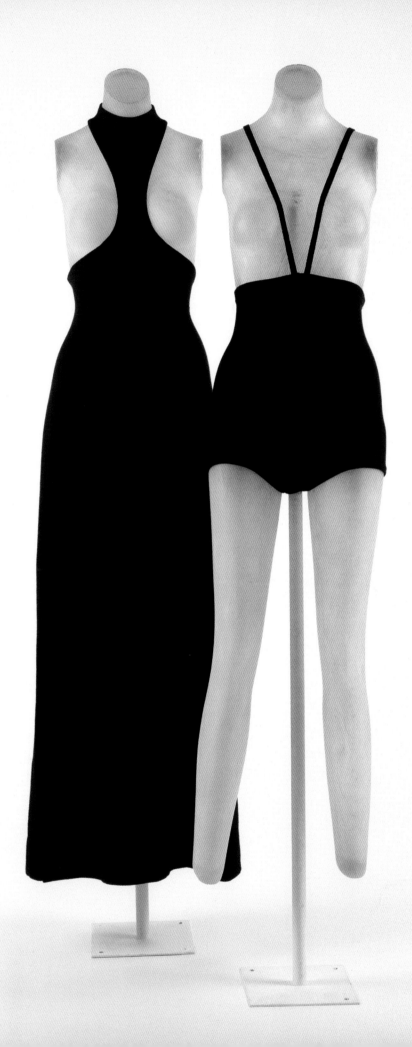

**RIGHT:** Fashion iconoclast Rudi Gernreich (1922–85) introduced his taboo-breaking topless garments in an attempt to liberate the body from the conventional structures that were then inherent in fashion and to promulgate the notion of unisex clothing – the monokini was also intended to be worn by men.

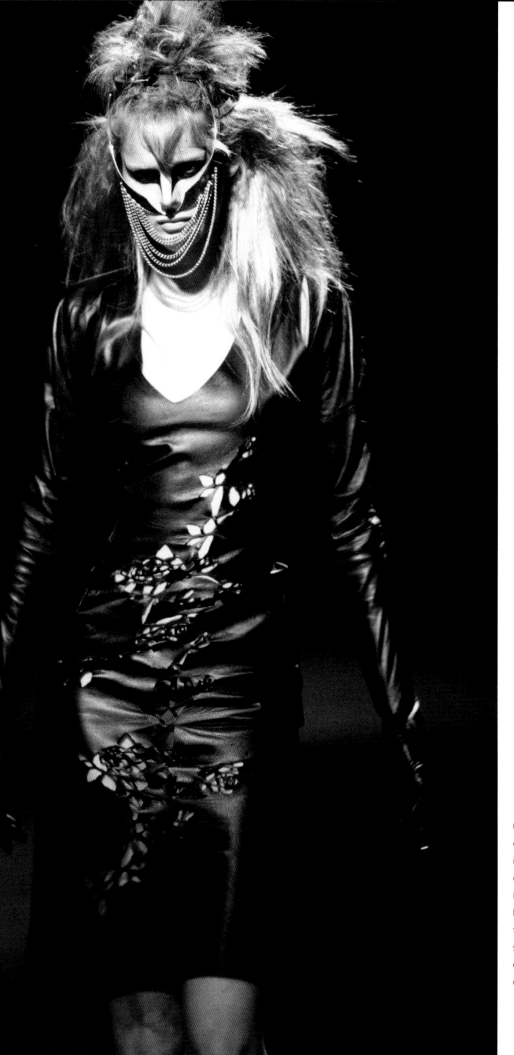

**LEFT:** Alexander McQueen's nexus of animal and human is most clear in his "It's a Jungle Out There" collection for A/W 1997–98. Enveloping the body in animal hide has an immediate resonance: to integrate opera gloves of the same second-hand skin into a dress reanimates the fore limbs of the original owner.

# The Leather Dress

The form of clothing has evolved along two principal paths: the wrapping and draping of rectangular panels of woven cloth and the conversion of the natural shape of animal hides and pelts to fit the body by cutting, tying and latterly by sewing. The culture of cloth has underpinned the development of civilization, while the earlier process of the adaptation of skins has retained overtones of animalistic primitivism, even of species primacy. This latent power endures into contemporary fashion and has gained further connotations through the wider usage of leather over millennia in a variety of functions – from harnesses to restraints, work wear and armour.

Contemporary designers often reference the crudity of some of the early construction techniques in an attempt to evoke the notion of a primitive sensibility, seen in the 1960s, when the use of leather and suede by the hippies aped the fringed buckskin worn by America's First Nation. American designer Giorgio di Sant'Angelo offered the luxe version with crudely shaped pieces of suede, whip-stitched together, to create a fringed one-shouldered minidress decorated with beads and tassels. British designer Alexander McQueen harnessed the power of animal skins for his Autumn/Winter 1997–98 collection "It's a Jungle Out There", which explored the relationship between predator and prey with a series of leather jackets and dresses styled with animalistic masks and threatening animal horns.

Chief exponent of razor-sharp tailoring for the 1980s phenomena, the glamazon, British designer Antony Price presented model Jerry Hall as a sexual predator and a fashion Valkyrie in his zipped and studded black biker dress, its rigid armature a sexual taunt. Long exiled from mainstream fashion, leather as fetish is no longer solely in the subculture of fetishist pornography and the practices of sadomasochism. When Italian designer Gianni Versace presented his bondage collection for Autumn/Winter 1992–93 of full-skirted evening dresses of pieced-together leather skins with the straps and buckles of bondage worn by an array of supermodels including Linda Evangelista, Naomi Campbell and Christy Turlington, fetish entered the fashion mainstream.

Animal skins are also capable of being crafted into a supple, fluid surface that can be treated in the same way as any other textile – embroidered, printed, and laser-cut and fashioned into garments with all the pliancy of the softest silk. American designer Donna Karan's diffusion line, DKNY, offers a racer-back snowball sleeveless dress of overstitched leather pieces juxtaposed with areas of coated mesh, combining flirty femininity with sports luxe.

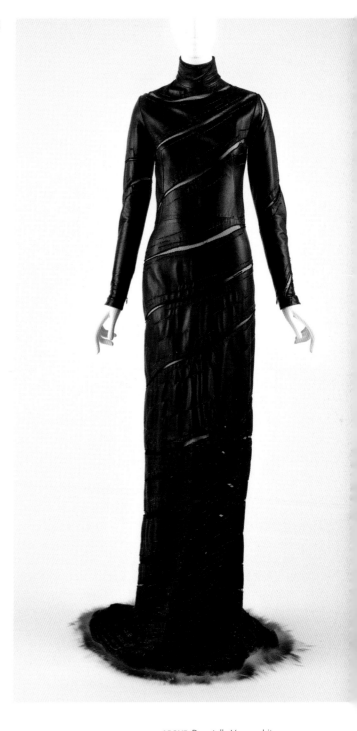

**ABOVE:** Donatella Versace hit the right leather note to ensnare Madonna with this 1999 columnar, fur-hemmed, gothic gown. A spiralling, beaded and top-stitched rent offers tantalizing glimpses of flesh through invisible gauze.

# Punk and Pins

With her signature combination of bold prints engineered to individual garments, Zandra Rhodes had, by the mid-1970s, become an established if bohemian figure in the elite circle of British designers. The upheaval of the punk explosion of 1976 created a fault line unlike any other in the relationship between disenchanted youth culture and the commercial imperatives of mainstream and designer fashion. To the chagrin of many young punk protagonists, Rhodes ventured to bridge the chasm by adopting the chain and safety pin adjuncts of punk self-expression and putting them to antithetical decorative effect in her 1977 "Conceptual Chic" collection of lacerated jersey dresses in black and pink rayon. While the utility and humility of the safety pin sat eloquently within the nihilist lexicon of original proto-punks such as the American musician and poet Richard Hell of the Neon Boys, Rhodes chose to defuse any aggressive overtones by glamorizing the safety pin with the insinuation of diamanté beads. By this curious inversion – subverting the subversive – she created a shorthand that signified the possibility of embracing alternative philosophies or lifestyles while still projecting luxury and glamour with an undercurrent of sensualism. The characteristic behaviour of rayon jersey is a weighty fluidity of movement that amplifies the natural oscillations of the body, which it also delineates closely. Latterly hailed as the "Princess of Punk", Zandra Rhodes had set a precedent for the evocation of edgy decadence by the simple act of an upgraded reference to the iconography of punk – with pins, chains and judiciously placed tears thereafter permanently embedded in the rock 'n' roll wardrobe, ready for sporadic exploitation over the subsequent decades.

In 1994, Gianni Versace secured saturation media visibility for film actress Liz Hurley when she wore his slashed and gold-pinned silk and lycra dress in black to the premiere of *Four Weddings and a Funeral*. In due course, the gown came to be known as "That Dress", which has remained an emblem of the Versace style, and a paradigm of how to create a career with a single appearence in a showstopping dress. Pop diva Lady Gaga took on the mantle in 2012 by wearing a facsimile of the original and a revised shorter version of the pin-and-gap confection, also by Versace.

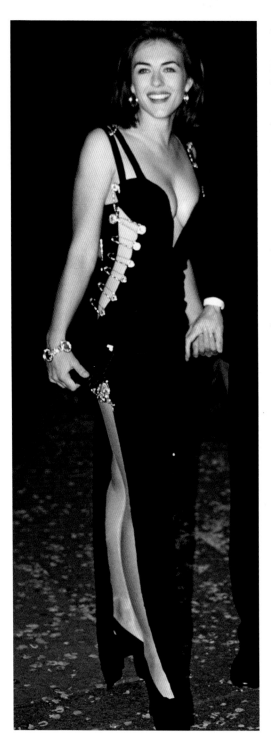

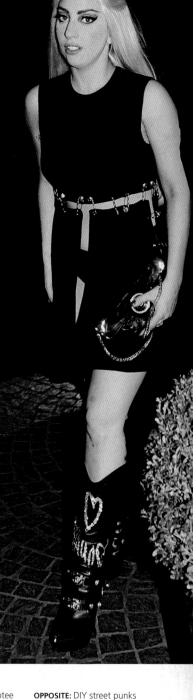

**ABOVE LEFT:** Versace avidly rejected good taste. The kitsch sexuality of the punk-inspired gown with plunging neckline worn by actress Elizabeth Hurley in 1994 propelled the actress onto the front page of every national newspaper and resolutely placed the dress as one of the most important in fashion history.

**ABOVE RIGHT:** As a noted devotee of exposure, Lady Gaga becomes a fitting vehicle for a bespoke Versace 2012 outfit, co-promoted by Donatella Versace. The three-piece of black sports bra, matching knickers and skirt pieces dangle by haute-couture punk safety pins, to consolidate the impression of a dress.

**OPPOSITE:** DIY street punks inflicted random distress to garments of various sorts, then chaotically employed safety pins to sustain them. In contrast, Zandra Rhodes withdrew the haphazard nihilism of the original and used her established compositional finesse to place tears, pins and chains with calligraphic precision.

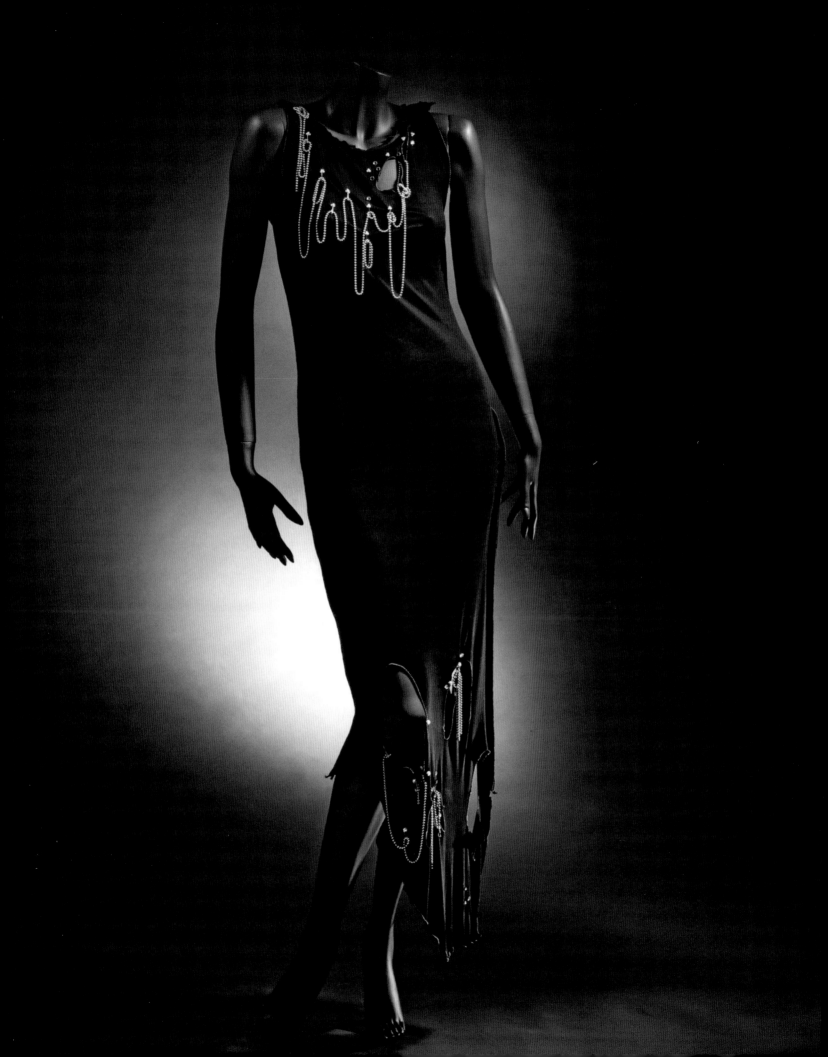

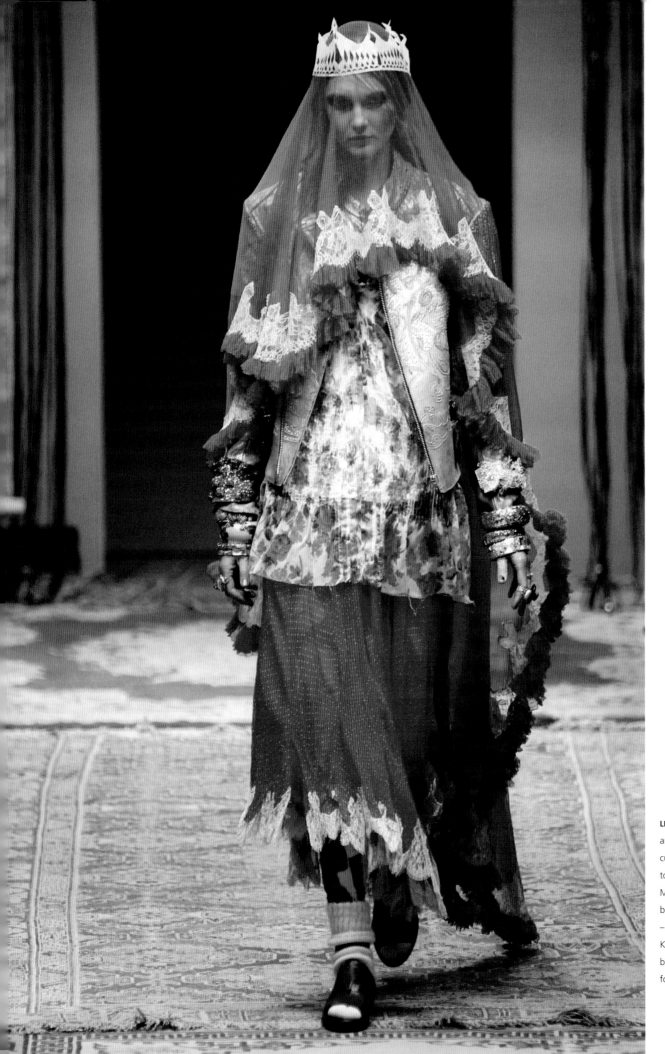

**LEFT:** Trawling through the history and accoutrements of Roma culture, from India through to Spain, British-born Edward Meadham (1979–) and French-born Benjamin Kirchhoff (1978–) – the duo behind Meadham Kirchhoff – present a neon-bright Rajasthani Indian bride for A/W 2010–11.

# Gypsy Style

Although subject to considerable prejudice, the Roma have historically been seen in a poetic light, living a nomadic life loosely concerned with pastoral pastimes. This romanticized view has given rise to the adoption of the so-called "gypsy" style in fashion from the eighteenth century onwards, leading to the contemporary version of boho, or bohemian, style.

The Roma migrated into Eastern and Western Europe in the fourteenth century through Persia en route from India, since when they have always lived as a minority group in another country, wearing clothing that reflects their religion and ethnicity. The Eastern European Roma is the one most closely associated with what is generally considered traditional "gypsy" dress: a brightly patterned calf-length skirt, frilled at the hem, a puffed-sleeved blouse with a drawstring neckline and a *dilko*, a headscarf tied at the back.

Wealth was often converted into jewellery or gold coins – *galbi* – traditionally woven into a woman's hair or sewn into her clothing. Fascination with generic gypsy culture has always resonated with fashion "outsiders", including Dorelia McNeill, mistress of Welsh-born artist Augustus John. The artist and his muse spent time travelling in gypsy caravans throughout Britain, finally creating a bohemian commune in Dorset. Dorelia adopted the uncorseted Roma style in an attempt to distance herself from the conventional moralities of the early twentieth century, setting the paradigm for picturesque fashion with her uncorseted dresses in vibrant colours.

One of the most significant and influential designers, Yves Saint Laurent devoted his 1970 *prêt-à-porter* collection to Roma style, with scooped-necked drawstring blouses, ruffled skirts and wide, tasselled belts – a look to which Tom Ford paid homage when, as creative head of Yves Saint Laurent in 2001, he presented fringed piano shawls tied around the waist and frilled blouses. Contemporary designers continue to be inspired by versions of Roma culture: Dolce & Gabbana, Meadham Kirchhoff and John Galliano for his eponymous label in 2004 have all presented a version of Roma style for the catwalk, interpreting the basic components in luxuriously embellished fabrics. Inspired by the seafarers of the Yemeni tribes of Western Asia, John Galliano combined an extravagantly wide crinoline with the accoutrements of a nomadic tribe. A floral headscarf is tied at the back, with a canteen of miniature pots and pans hanging amid an abundance of fake hair.

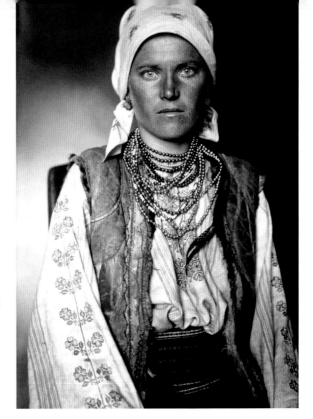

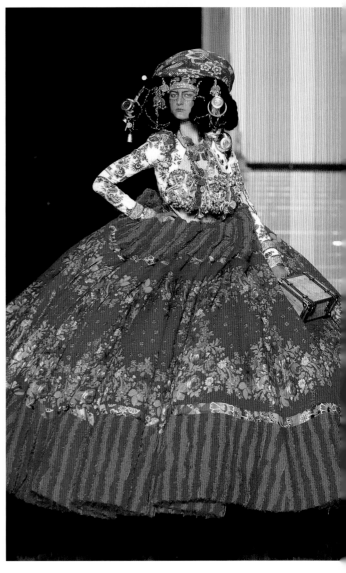

**ABOVE RIGHT:** First published in *National Geographic* in 1907 in a segment entitled "Some of Our Immigrants" and photographed by Augustus Sherman, this portrait of a young girl from Ruthenia – southwestern Ukraine – shows the costume of her origins: a *dilka*, a headscarf tied at the back, and an embroidered *rubakha*.

**RIGHT:** Constantly appropriating the traditional costumes of the indigenous population of the world and transforming them into high-end fashion, John Galliano's ethnographic imagination included his notion of "gypsy" style for A/W 2004–5, a combination of extreme embellishment with folkloric print.

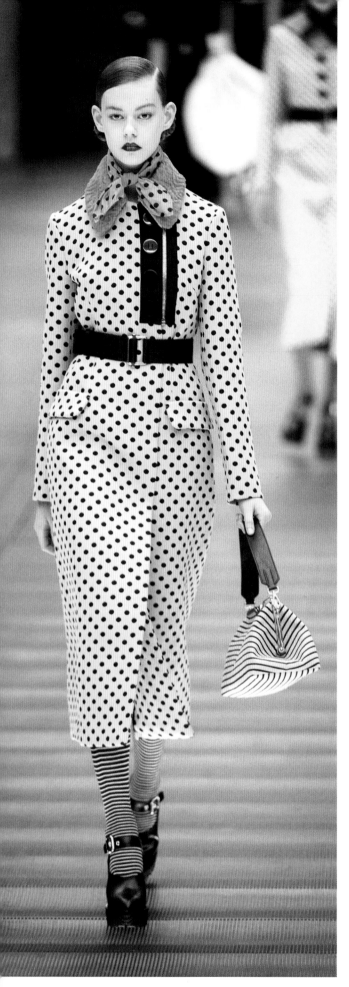

# Polka Dots

Effervescent, signifier of joie de vivre and visually compelling, the polka dot pattern has proved irresistible to those designers who wish to convey a youthful insouciance. Originally associated with swimwear – Marilyn Monroe posed in a polka dot two-piece swimsuit in 1951 and pop singer Brian Hyland famously sang *Itsy Bitsy Teenie Weenie Yellow Polka Dot Bikini* in 1961 – the polka dot captures a carefree spirit of playfulness. It is usually formed by a number of equally sized, filled circles, spaced relatively closely together in two contrasting colours, providing a visually satisfying division of positive and negative space. The pattern is multi-directional and is formed from the equidistant spacing of five spots in repeat; it is this regular repeat pattern that differentiates the polka dot from a simple design of spots.

Polka dot dresses made their cinematic debut in 1928 when Disney cartoon character Minnie Mouse was featured wearing a black-and-white dotted skirt for her role in *Steamboat Willie*. Although photographed primarily in black and white, colourful polka dots rapidly gained popularity during the 1930s. The cartoon-like aspect of the patterning was rendered elegant by the mid-nineteenth century couturiers, including Balmain, Jacques Fath and Christian Dior, who included petrol blue polka dots in his 1948 "Envoi" collection. A favourite motif of Yves Saint Laurent in the 1960s, the designer featured widely spaced coin-sized spots throughout the decade, varying the classic navy-and-white colourway to include his signature red and blue.

Obsessed with polka dots, the visionary Japanese artist Yayoi Kusama, who describes the polka dots as "*round, soft, colourful, senseless and unknowing. Polka-dots become movement... Polka dots are a way to infinity*", was asked to collaborate with Marc Jacobs on a capsule collection for French fashion house Louis Vuitton in 2012 to coincide with the Whitney Museum of American Art's new exhibition of Kusama's work. The resulting line created garments and accessories in Kusama's spotted oeuvre, which covered every item, from bags to dresses, the highlight of which was a yellow drop-waisted dress with a frill skirt. Miuccia Prada for the "little sister" label Miu Miu combines the primness of the polka dot pattern in an effective colourway of pink and black with horizontal schoolgirl stripes for a collection that emphasizes the ingénue nature of the pattern for Autumn/Winter 2013–14.

**LEFT:** With a quintessentially Parisian touch, Miuccia Prada for Miu Miu A/W 2013–14 employs small-scale polka dots in the unusual coloration of black and pink, juxtaposed with stripes and playful detailing, thus combining the buttoned-up primness of the young schoolgirl with a covert flirtatiousness.

**OPPOSITE:** In a similar spirit to the couturier Cristóbal Balenciaga, Yves Saint Laurent combined the flounces, ruffled sleeves and pompom trimmings of a Spanish flamenco costume but applied them to a baby-doll silhouette for a youthful cocktail dress in polychromatic polka dots, dating from 1964.

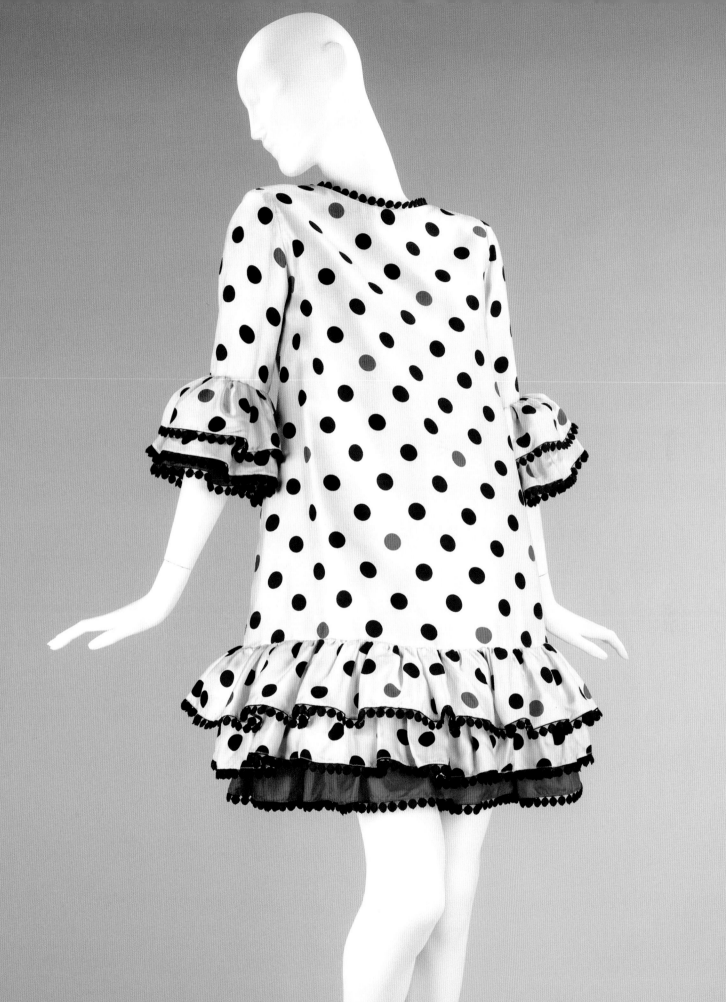

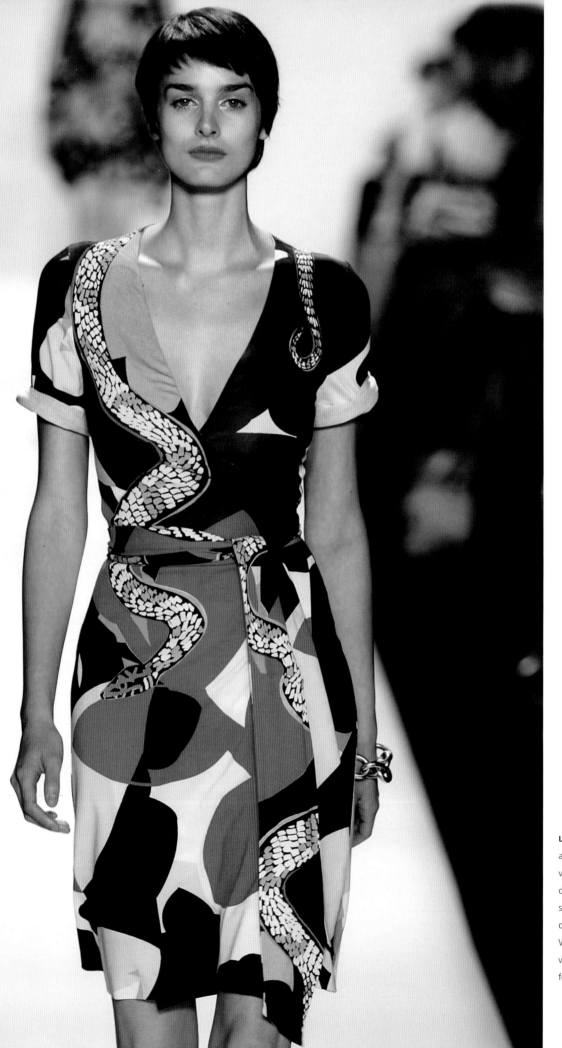

**LEFT:** A fashion phenomenon and a perennial wardrobe staple, the versatile wrap dress by American designer Diane von Furstenberg solved the "day-to-night" dilemma of the working woman. Worn with a blazer by day, the wrap could be positioned lower for the evening.

# The Wrap Dress

With exemplary timing, US designer Diane von Furstenberg launched her wrap dress at a time when women required a practical working wardrobe that was an alternative to the hippie clothes available at the tail end of the counter culture or the structured Courrèges-inspired trouser suit. Nothing less than a cultural phenomenon, the wrap dress exemplified women's freedom to be both glamorous and authoritative as the second wave of feminism directed them to the workplace and also extolled the delights of sexual freedom. With no zip fastenings, hooks-and-eyes or buttons, the dress became symbolic of women's sexual liberation – the dress was easy to put on and equally easy to take off. Von Furstenberg recounts that "a woman who chose to could be out of it in a minute". The first wrap dress was launched in 1973, a period when fashion was cut to fit close to the body, especially over the torso.

The designer was inspired to create the wrap dress by the appearance of Julie Nixon Eisenhower wearing a Diane von Furstenberg wrap top and skirt on television when she decided to combine the two pieces into one. The overwhelming success of the garment resulted in a global fashion empire built on a single style with more than five million garments sold. The slogan, "Feel like a woman, wear a dress!" appeared on every dress tag and became the registered trademark of the company. The dress had a universal appeal, von Furstenberg records in her autobiography *A Signature Life* (1998), "The wrap dress transcended generations, geographical distinctions, social and economic differences."

The wrap dress also transcended body shape. The garment was universally flattering, with a deep "V" neckline that could be adjusted to display as little or as much décolletage as required. The simple pinafore shape wrapped closely around the body at the waist and hips but the skirt flared out to allow for an unrestricted stride. Prints were integral to the soft rayon/cotton mix fabrics, most popularly animal and reptile prints, as well as small geometric abstract designs. With the fashion nostalgia for the 1970s, the demand for the wrap dress returned, and in 1997 it was successfully relaunched in von Furstenberg's signature prints but with the style adapted to contemporary taste: smaller rounded collars, a shorter length and in a silk jersey rather than cotton.

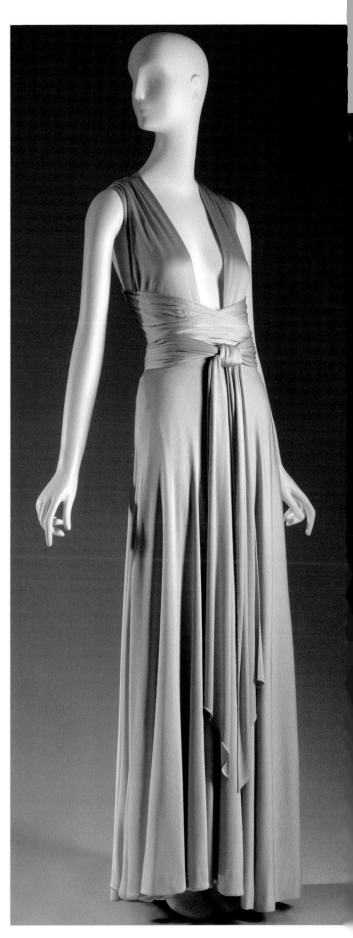

**RIGHT:** Referencing mid-twentieth-century design innovators such as Claire McCardell in his adoption of an aesthetic minimalism, Roy Halston Frowick (1932–90) created similarly versatile garments during the 1970s, as with this evening dress. Featuring long ties, it allowed the wearer to wrap them around the bodice to create different effects.

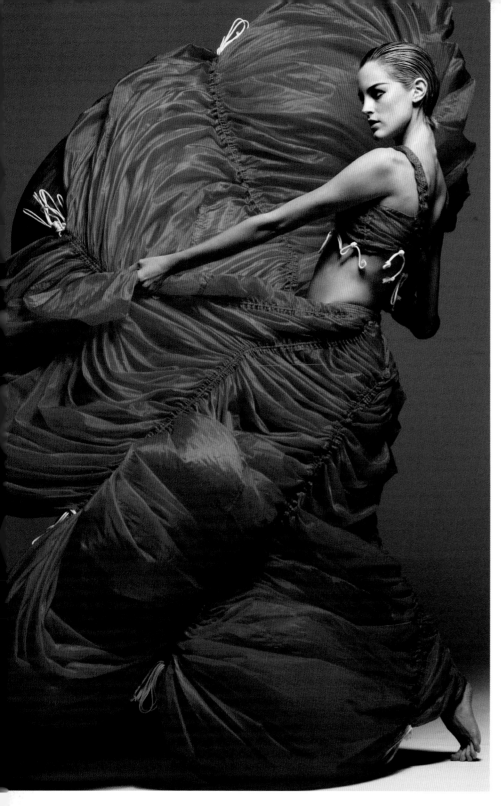

# The Parachute

Designers frequently exploit fashion detritus, such as second-hand clothing or military surplus supplies, to transform them into high-status fashion pieces. The parachute, no more than a functional device used to slow the motion of an object through the atmosphere by creating drag, would normally provide sparse inspiration for fashion garments, except in the austere times of war, when shortages of silk and nylon resulted in their usage for exceptional garments for special occasions such as a wedding.

In 1944, an American B-29 pilot, Major Claude Hensinger, deployed his parachute when his plane's engine caught fire, ejecting safely from the aircraft over Japanese-held territory. He kept his 'chute and returned home to Pennsylvania, where his prospective bride Ruth used the nylon parachute for her wedding gown. Modelled on a Walter Plunkett dress, which appeared in the 1939 historical epic *Gone with the Wind*, the skirt element used the original channelled parachute strings to foreshorten the fabric above the hem at the front, thus releasing the train effect at the back.

New York-based designer Norma Kamali, a pioneer of active sportswear, introduced her own fabled parachute dress in 1975. Renowned for her use of eclectic assemblages from found fabrics such as chenille bedspreads, mud cloth from Mali and her influential sleeping-bag coat, this prompted a colleague – Halston's creative director – to present the designer with a vintage silk parachute left over from the Korean War. Kamali produced reconfigured garments from plundered army surplus stores, then a fashionable source of clothing, ranging from duffle coats to flying jackets. Retaining the technical construction of the parachute, Kamali created a dress reliant on drawstrings enclosed in stitched seams to control the volume and fit: the airy lightness of the silk is ruched and gathered to create a billowing skirt, the length adjustable depending on tensioning of the thick cord. The designer continues to update the parachute dress by introducing new styles and colours, with variations in cut and colour. Later designs included the drawstring technique applied to bodices and sleeves, providing greater versatility in length and volume, and especially effective when fashioned into a Victorian-style wedding dress complete with fitted bodice and a train.

**ABOVE:** Norma Kamali updated the parachute dress in International Orange in 1974. Silk was replaced by a more durable and water-repellent nylon. With a low porosity to air, it commonly weighed below two ounces per square yard. The inherent ability to catch the wind is an attraction in the context of exuberant dress.

**OPPOSITE:** The use of illicit supplies of parachute silk for intimate items of the World War II boudoir was a staple of wartime rationing-fired humour. The Smithsonian Institute has conserved a more practical parachute relic in the antebellum-styled wedding dress of the bride of Major Claude Hensinger, whose life the parachute had preserved.

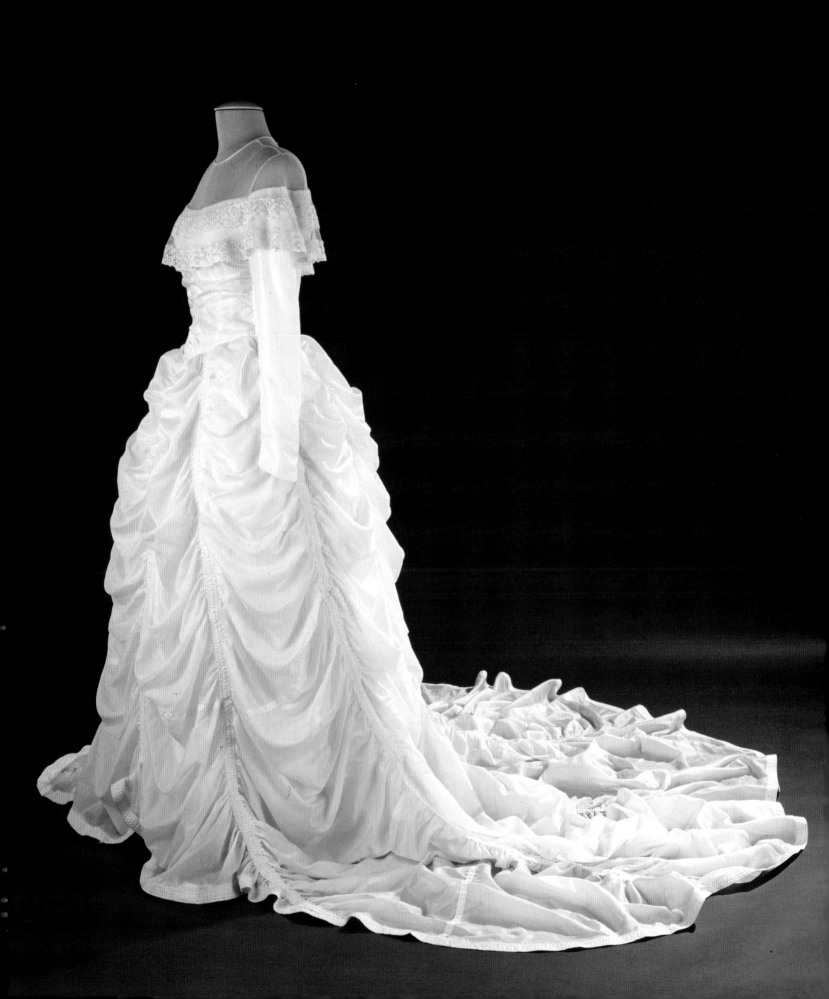

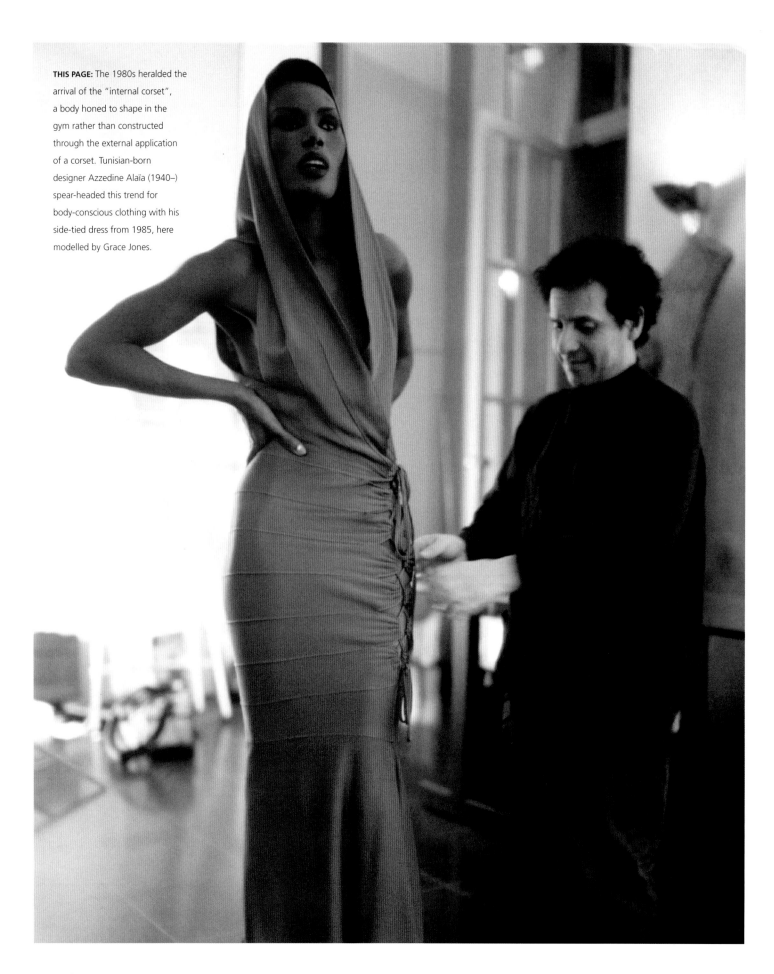

**THIS PAGE:** The 1980s heralded the arrival of the "internal corset", a body honed to shape in the gym rather than constructed through the external application of a corset. Tunisian-born designer Azzedine Alaïa (1940–) spear-headed this trend for body-conscious clothing with his side-tied dress from 1985, here modelled by Grace Jones.

# The Body-Con Dress

Body-con fashion signifies show-stopping curves, a structured, sex-is-power perennial favourite of the body-confident and first seen in the 1980s when stretch in fabrics was harnessed to flatter the aerobics-honed physique. Tunisian-born designer Azzedine Alaïa, dubbed "The King of Cling" by the fashion press, was instrumental in putting stretch into mainstream fashion in 1980 with the inclusion of the body suit and the tubular mini in a collection designed entirely in black. As with his admired predecessor Madeleine Vionnet, the master cutter from the 1920s, Alaïa experimented with bias cut and also worked directly onto the body to achieve a perfect fit. Although his dresses might appear to follow the line of the body, in reality they were cut to create their own perfect shape, enhancing curves where there were none and flattening those surplus to requirements by means of stretch fabrics and complex spiral seams.

The iconic side-laced dress launched in 1985 was followed by the Mermaid evening dress in green acetate knit with a spiral zip set in a curved seam. Alaïa's overtly sexy silhouette, often accessorized by opaque black tights, was featured in Robert Palmer's iconic music video, *Addicted to Love*, directed by legendary British photographer Terence Donovan in 1986.

First seen as the finale to Hervé Léger's 1989 catwalk show, the bandage dress utilized elasticized strips of fabric sewn together to mould and shape the body from shoulder to hem. With a single vowel marking the difference between bondage and bandage, both describe the near-fetishistic effect of the bands of fabric wrapped tightly around the body to compress and control the female form. In contrast, the construction of the Galaxy dress by French designer Roland Mouret is disguised within the underpinning structure. Launched in 2005, it became a sartorial sensation, recalling 1940s Hollywood-inspired film-star glamour. Constructed from Powerflex, a tough, stretchy fabric previously used to make underwear, the dress imposed an hourglass silhouette by both suppressing and enhancing the natural curves of the body. It emphasized the breasts, smoothed stomachs, flattered the upper arms with ruched cap sleeves and extended shoulders so that hips appeared diminished. The form-following pencil skirt narrowed towards the knees, ending in a small fishtail kick.

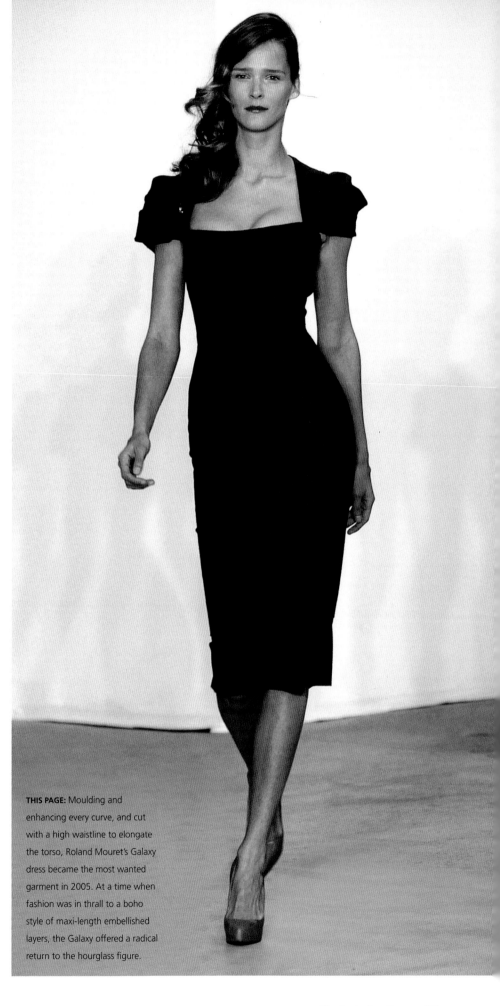

**THIS PAGE:** Moulding and enhancing every curve, and cut with a high waistline to elongate the torso, Roland Mouret's Galaxy dress became the most wanted garment in 2005. At a time when fashion was in thrall to a boho style of maxi-length embellished layers, the Galaxy offered a radical return to the hourglass figure.

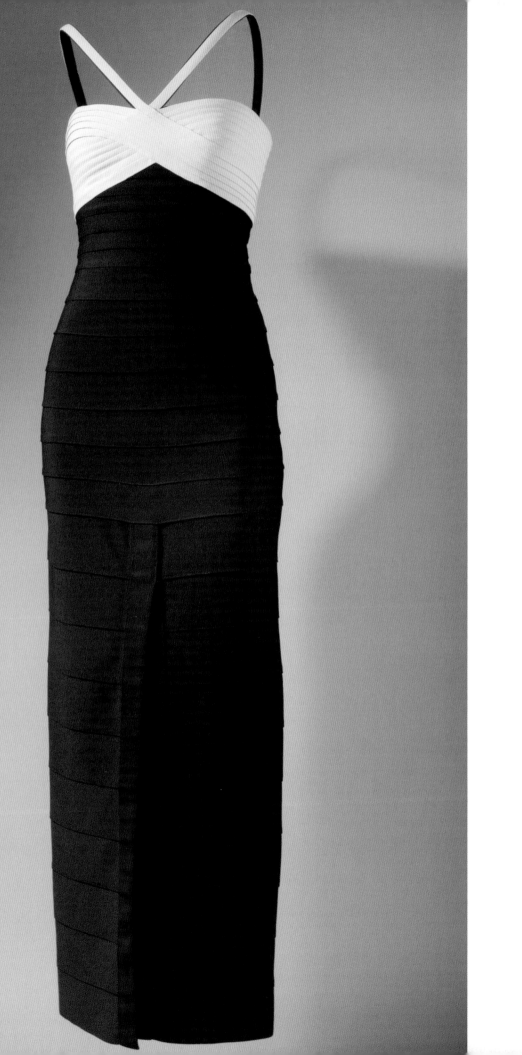

**LEFT:** French designer Hervé Peugnet – who changed his name to Hervé Léger for commercial purposes – extended the bandage-like strips of fabric to the ankle in this monochrome rayon and lycra knit evening gown from 1989.

**OPPOSITE:** The Hervé Léger label was acquired by the American group BCBG Max Azria Group in 1998. Max and Lubov Azria continue to refresh the iconic bandage dress by introducing a sports-luxe element, seen here in the strips of skin-toned rubberized mesh for Resort 2014.

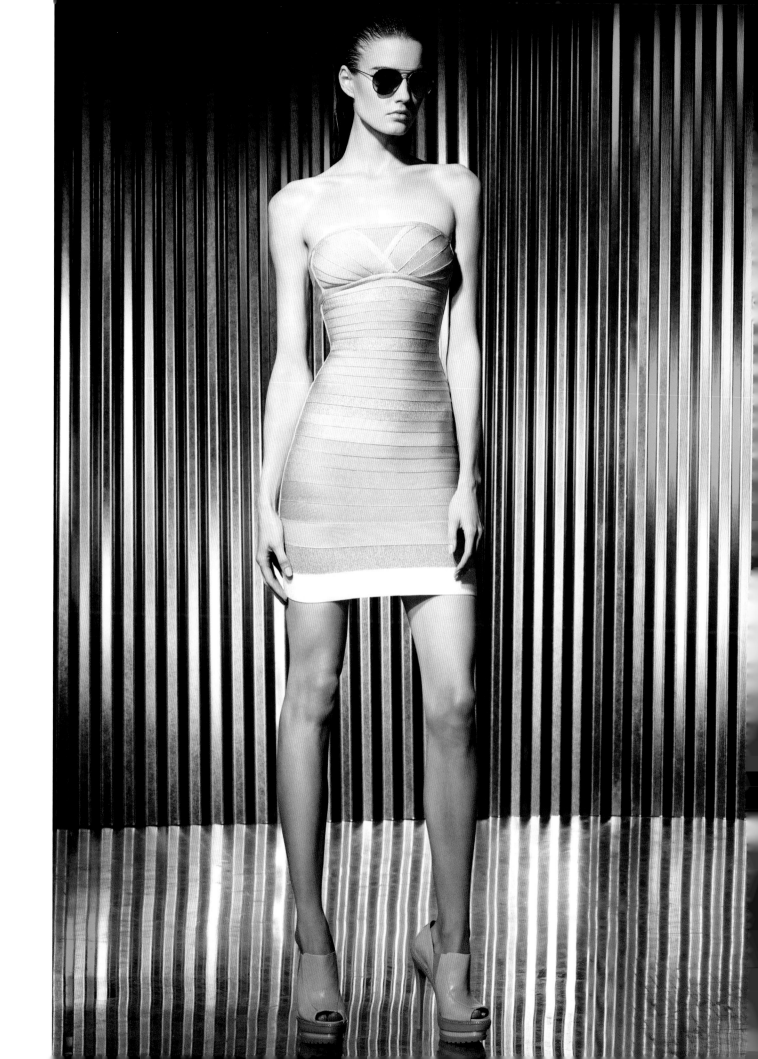

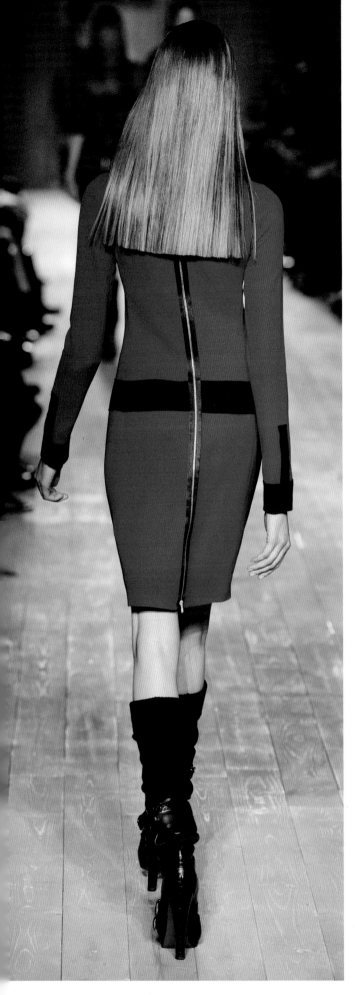

# The Zip Dress

At the beginning of the twentieth century, the economy was transformed by the manufacture and retailing of products through industrial progress and invention, including the zip fastener. Developed by a US-based Swedish engineer, Gideon Sundback, the "Hookless Fastener" – a series of closely spaced "scoops" brought together by a slider – was introduced in 1913. The zip fastener revolutionized the construction of garments; it enabled a perfect figure-enhancing fit with ease of closure and replaced a variety of buttons, hooks-and-eyes, loops, ties and bows as a means of fastening a garment.

The French heritage house, Hermès, was the first to introduce the zip into fashion. Emile-Maurice, grandson of the original founder of the company, foresaw the potential of a kind of zip used on the canvas roof of cars while on a trip to Canada, and obtained an exclusive two-year European patent on its use. The "Hermès fastener" appeared on their first leather garment, a zippered golfing jacket constructed for HRH The Prince of Wales in 1922.

The utilitarian aspects of the zip fastener were initially met with some resistance by the fashion industry and it was confined to daywear until avant-garde designer Elsa Schiaparelli daringly introduced the zip into her evening dresses. Although in common usage and lauded for its practicality and versatility in a whole range of garments throughout the twentieth and twenty-first centuries, the zipper also continues to imply easy access to the naked body, and depending on its site, offering the potential for an immediate sexual encounter. Author Aldous Huxley used zips throughout his 1923 novel *Brave New World* to describe the mechanical nature of sex in his vision for the future, a notion also propagated in the "zipless fuck" – a sexual encounter without emotional involvement – propounded by Erica Jong in her 1973 book *Fear of Flying*.

During the "youthquake" fashions of the 1960s, the zipper adorned the front of minidresses, usually featuring an oversized ring attached to the slider. The Tunisian-born designer Azzedine Alaïa (*see also page 233*), who redefined body-conscious dressing in the 1980s, introduced the zip into his Mermaid dress of 1986. Constructed in green acetate, the dress incorporates a spiral zipper set in a curved seam that attaches a hood to the dress. Left exposed, the zip fastener is a seeming declaration of availability, snaking up the back of the tourniquet-tight sheath dresses of British designer Victoria Beckham.

**LEFT:** Victoria Beckham's debut collection was launched in 2008, establishing her reputation with a range of body-conscious gowns. At couture level of fashion, the zip is hand-sewn into place to render it invisible. For A/W 2012–13 Beckham makes a statement by placing it externally, a distinguishing feature of the dress.

**OPPOSITE:** The simple lines of this archetypal minidress in wool jersey, designed in 1964 by Mary Quant, epitomize the modernity of the era, with the easy-fitting drop-waist and pleated skirt. The centre-front opening, secured by a zip, extends from hip to neck, leading to a squared-off Peter Pan collar in contrasting fabric.

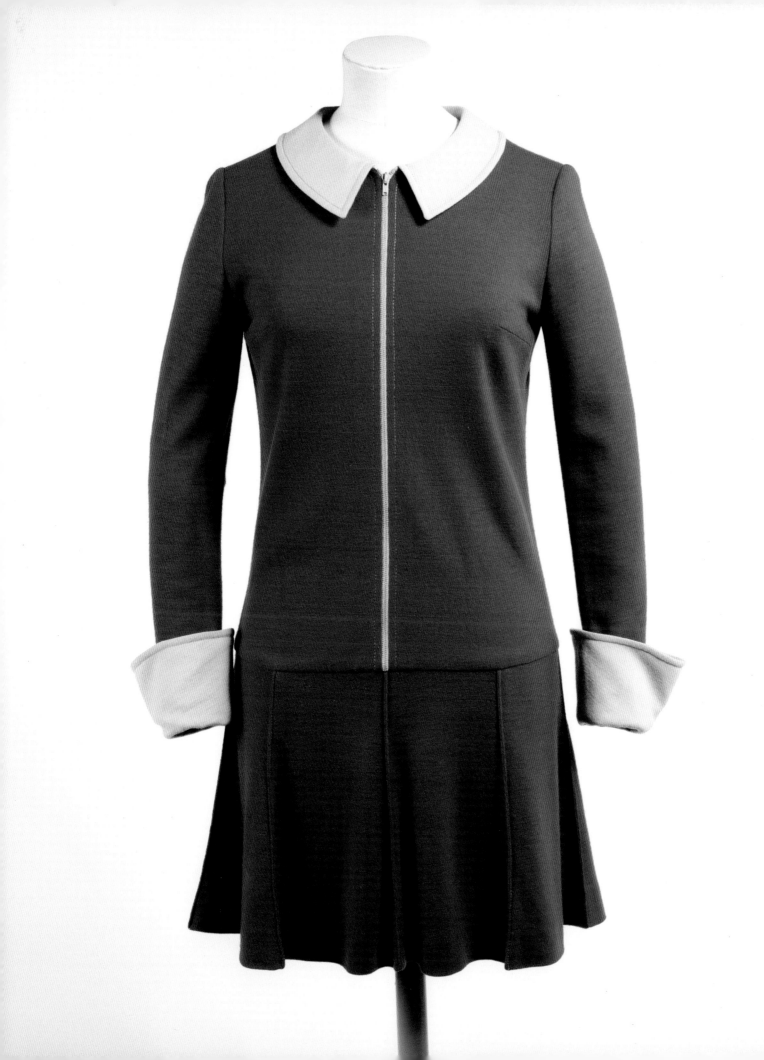

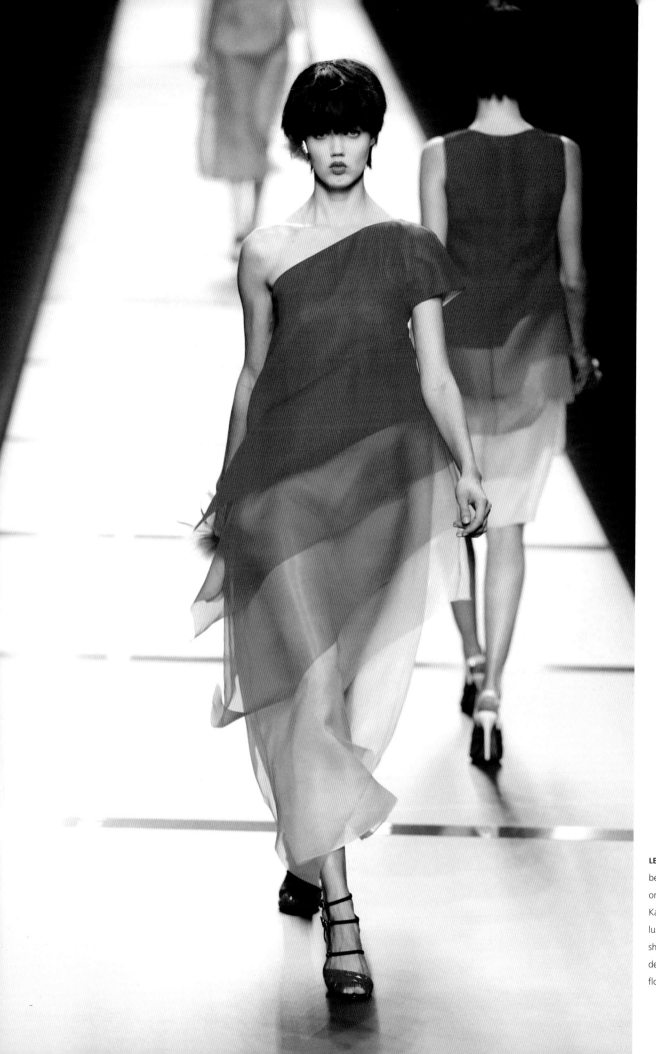

**LEFT:** Each individual colour can be adjusted by tinting, shading or toning to create different hues. Karl Lagerfeld, for the Italian luxury house Fendi S/S 2014, shades layers of red, laser-cut, destiffened organza to create floating panels of colour.

# Colourblocking

More than any other aspect of fashionable dress, colour is the first feature to attract attention, with cut, structure and texture subservient to the impact of many hues. As a major preoccupation across a range of art movements and theories in the early years of the twentieth century, the potency of abstract colour composition was inevitably incorporated into the lexicon of design for the fashionable body. As the imperative pursuit of the representational ebbed, artists and theorists grouped and realigned under the aegis of numerous *isms* as they explored the essential mechanics of perception and expression invested in colour, line and form, as with the Orphicists Robert and Sonia Delaunay who, against the backdrop of Cubism, led the avant-garde impetus to find lyrical impact in pure abstract form rendered in bright colour, which they also used to clothe the body.

By the 1920s, the fundamentals of modernism had been consolidated and were embodied in the ethos of the Bauhaus School, founded by Walter Gropius in 1919. Tutors such as Johannes Itten and Josef Albers theorized and proselytized on the foundations of abstract expression residing in codified relationships of colours and non-representational forms. This theoretical legacy has informed designers in many disciplines and periodically takes primacy in the creative output of numerous fashion designers.

Roksanda Ilincic has formed a very close linkage with the Josef & Anni Albers Foundation in her 2014 collections, producing colour-blocked dresses in direct homage to the studies by Josef Albers of 1963 on the interaction of colour. By distributing angular expanses of pure colour in counterpoint and asymmetrical balance, Ilincic is manipulating such principles as colour temperature, intensity and relativity to both animate and anchor the human figure in space. The immaculate seaming of the dresses, the saturation colour and the dense opacity of the material reinforce the hard-edge graphic, as if transposed direct from Albers' printed colour primer.

In Karl Lagerfeld's Spring/Summer 2014 collection for Fendi, chromatic dynamism has a circuitous path to implementation as the theme includes the watery evocation of the illusion of transparency through the precise layering of laser-cut organza sections. On assembly, these finally recall the power of tonal colour blocking to cause the eye to travel, with darker tones receding and consequently attenuating the figure.

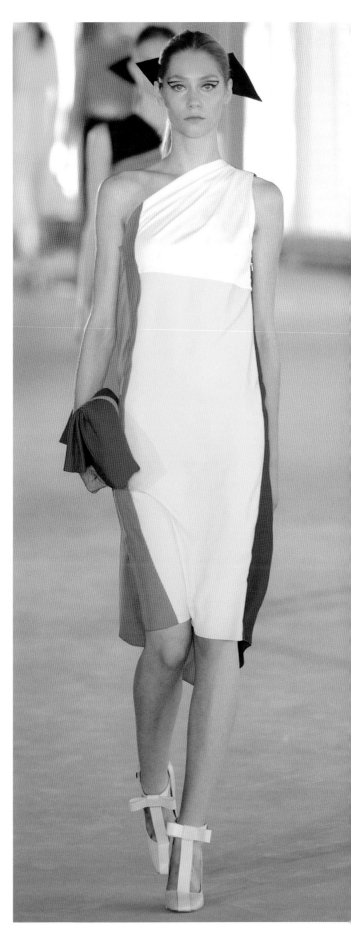

**RIGHT:** Colour blocking – the trend for wearing multiple solid colours in one outfit – was also observed in the fourteenth century with the adoption of parti-coloured clothing. Sophisticated contemporary colour blocking is the signature of Serbian-born, London-based designer Roksanda Ilincic (1970–), exemplified by her S/S 2014 collection.

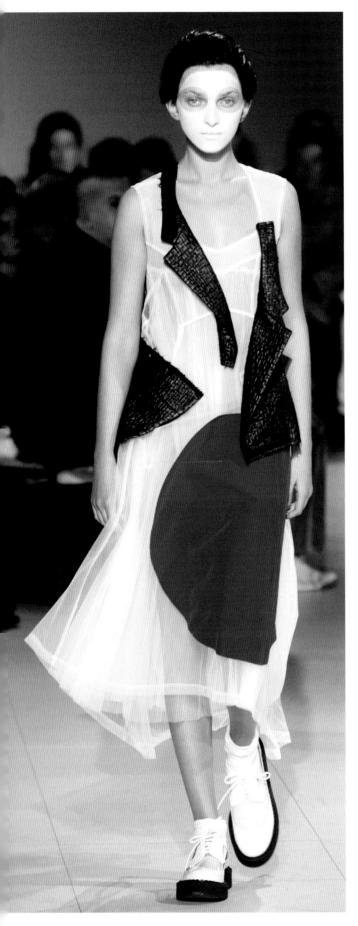

# Deconstruction

Rei Kawakubo first challenged conventional preoccupations invested in the seductive aspects of fashion through her engagement in the anti-fashion Hiroshima-chic moment of the 1980s. In taking a conceptual stance in the exploration of the relationship between humanity and apparel, Kawakubo is hailed as a pioneer of the deconstructive approach to fashion design. The philosophical theory of deconstruction originates primarily in the literary critique and semiotic analysis of Jacques Derrida and has come to be deployed with a varied degree of rigour across the creative aesthetic of areas as diverse as architecture and fashion.

At the cerebral end of the spectrum of deconstructivism, the Belgian designers, Ann Demeulemeester, Dries van Noten and Martin Margiela have been afforded the highest levels of respect from fashion commentators – with Margiela, in particular, attracting near-messianic devotion. The underlying notion is that signifiers in the complex language of fashion and clothing not only carry meaning when placed in their stereotypical physical context, but also have eloquence when rendered as deconstructed fragments, elevated from the sedimentary layers of visual culture, to be reconfigured as potent new inflections. This analytical process offers a number of tools for the confection of paradoxical re-assemblages: dislocation, economy, inversion, appropriation, reorientation and changes of scale and material.

By 2007, Rei Kawakubo for Comme des Garçons was long established as adroit in her compositional sensitivity and easy in her manipulation of the essences of cultural archaeology. Her flimsy chiffon dress from the Spring/Summer collection brought together disparate elements of both Japanese and European iconography. The strict graphic palette of red, black and white is stereotypically Japanese, as the large-scale opaque circle in red satin directly recalls the national flag, while the white mask of the geisha is recalled though bereft of lip and eye colour. In contrast, the base form of the dress in sheer fabric has the European connotations of a Victorian chemise, with structural panels delineated by the opacity of shirt seams. Dismembered and fraying components of a tailored European jacket in glossy black cloqué fabric are redistributed across the underlying dress into an abstract composition relating to the red circle.

For Spring/Summer 2009, Maison Martin Margiela also made reference to the clothing of the Victorian and Edwardian boudoir by radically rescaling the plunging bodice of a Belle Époque underdress, extending the scope for embonpoint display.

**LEFT:** For S/S 2007, Rei Kawakubo for Comme des Garçons deconstructed a Western-style tailored jacket, the pieces of which were then reconnected on a base of silk organza. These were combined with the red-on-white circle of the Japanese flag, perceived by the designer as "the purest form of design in existence".

**OPPOSITE:** Hussein Chalayan chose to return from a sabbatical with a tale of voodoo, curses and superstition in 2002. The catwalk narrative progressed from intact tailoring, through a process of time-lapsed degeneration, to final acts of deconstructive demolition. A dress of dissolving, delicately tattered layers characterizes a curse fulfilled.

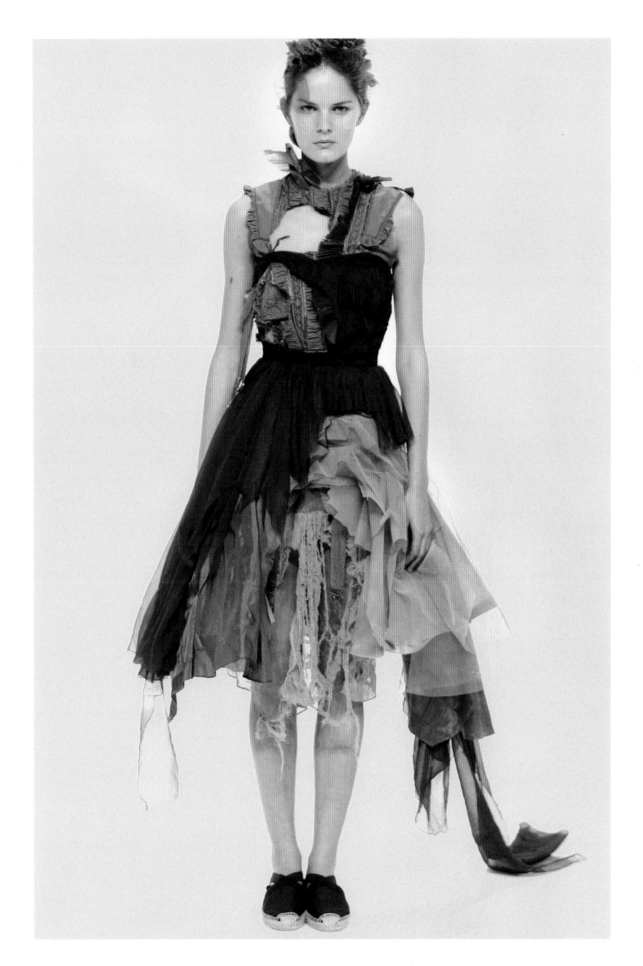

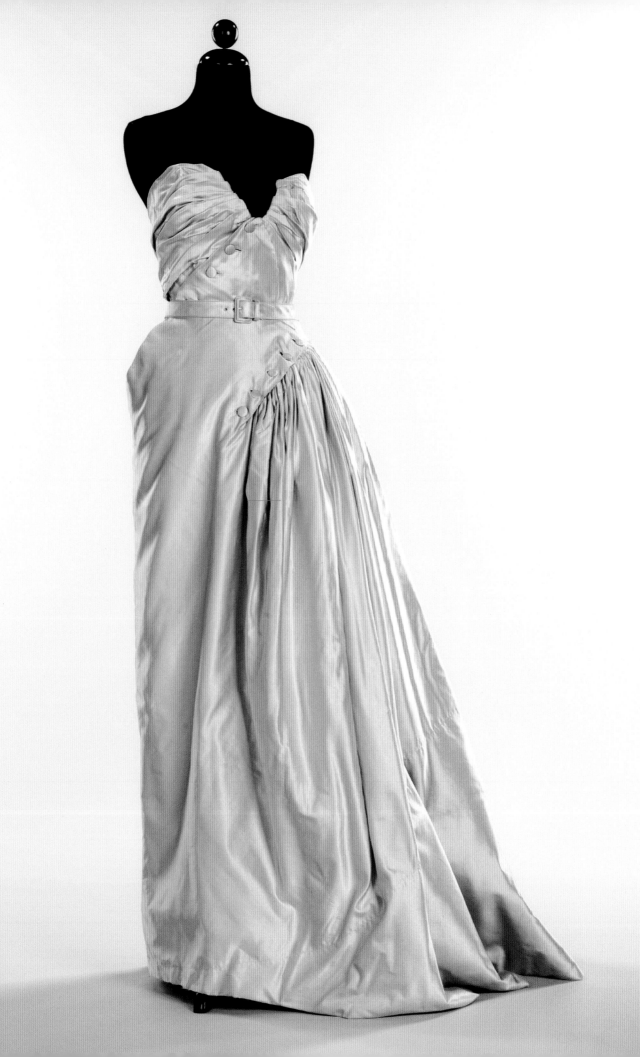

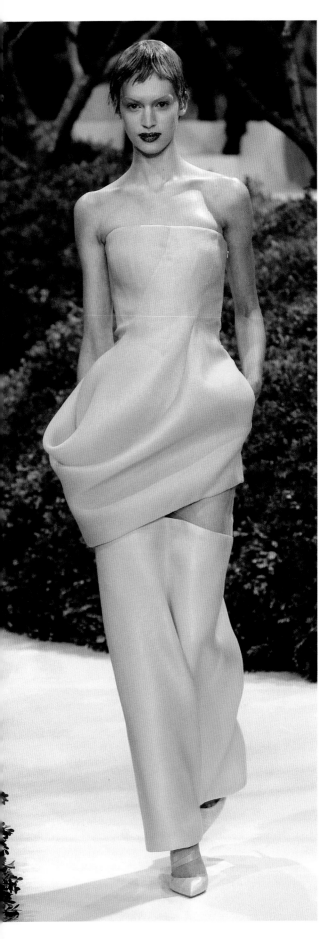

# Asymmetry

Symmetry is considered the most pleasing of notions, one that establishes both balance and harmony by the means of an exact correspondence of parts on either side of a central line. Although the Rococo period of the mid-eighteenth century had a taste for asymmetry in its woven, printed and embroidered silks which featured an asymmetrical or shell-shaped space that went under the name *cartouche*, the creation of deliberate asymmetry in garments is a twentieth-century design phenomenon.

To introduce asymmetry is to create a visual dislocation, one that disturbs the accepted norms of dress. Asymmetry was celebrated by mid-century couturier Christian Dior first with his Zig-Zag line in 1949, and the following year with his Oblique line. These included elements such as diagonal tucks swirled around bodices and skirts, asymmetrical necklines and peplums, dresses fastened or wrapped to one side, and uneven hemlines and collars extending outwards in a single exaggerated point. Most of these design details featured on Dior's long and lean etiolated line, which replaced the hourglass silhouette with which he made his name.

Asymmetrical details were particularly potent when incorporated into Dior's tailored daywear, but they were equally effective when the couturier introduced them into his eveningwear, most notably with the Gruau evening dress in ivory silk satin, named after the renowned French fashion illustrator René Gruau. The dress features two diagonal rows of self-covered buttons that form a parallelogram between the breasts and the hips, accentuating the spiral effect of the gown. Balance and harmony are restored by the ruched bodice and the gathers that fall from one hip. Belgian-born Raf Simons, in a couture collection as creative head of Dior in 2013, explored the archives of the couture house, considering every permutation of the founder, including the original asymmetry, which Simons modernized by layering a diagonally draped skirt over an underskirt. In contemporary fashion, extreme asymmetry has connotations of the avant-garde, the difficult to wear, the conceptual – more usually associated with the Japanese designers such as Comme des Garçons and Junya Watanabe. However, introducing a collection featuring asymmetrical bold forms and experimental fabrics for Spring/Summer 2013, fashion provocateur J. W. Anderson plays with various ways of draping, suspending, twisting and gathering material to create new forms and silhouettes, epitomized by the artful arrangement of three black pleather bows falling diagonally across a bodice before ending in a sweeping, ankle-length side train of minutely corrugated fabric.

**OPPOSITE:** Christian Dior named his 1949 asymmetrical gown after the renowned fashion illustrator René Gruau. Their creative collaboration began with Dior's New Look in 1947, and Gruau continued to disseminate the aesthetic of the House after Dior's untimely death.

**LEFT:** Fulfilling the ideal of women as *femmes-fleurs* while referencing Dior's totemic deployment of asymmetry, Raf Simons' second collection for the couture house in 2013 included this full-length gown with an irregular silhouette created by a swathe of fabric gathered on one hip.

# The Crystal Dress

Adding to the armoury of decorative effects for imparting fashionable glamour is the Swarovski crystal, the invention of Daniel Swarovski. Born in Bohemia – the centre of the glass industry – he developed the technique of precision grinding and polishing hundreds of paste stones in one process that has since dominated twentieth- and twenty-first century paste production. By combining lead and silica, and burnt limestone and soda at an extremely high temperature, the resulting glass has a high refractivity which can be cut and faceted like any other precious gemstone. Swarovski patented the process of applying these crystal beads onto fabric during the 1920s, an effect eagerly appropriated by designers such as Schiaparelli and Chanel in an era that celebrated the highly embellished knee-length evening dress. Along with metallic lace, sequins and paillettes, gold and silver threadwork, beading and rhinestone (a generic term applied to anything artificial that sparkles made from glass, paste or quartz crystal), the crystal added to the repertoire of light-reflecting metallic surfaces available to designers, and became a favourite of on-screen stars such as Marlene Dietrich. Her mysterious allure and covert sexuality depended on lighting effects, exotic plots and dramatic costumes of fur, feathers, lace and figure-hugging dresses, and the crystal was an invaluable tool in adding to her luminous screen presence. Together with director Josef von Sternberg – who filmed interior daytime shots at night so that her features could be drenched with light – and Hollywood costumier Travis Banton, the three of them honed Dietrich's image and set it against a background of romantic locations.

Almost inevitably associated with night-time glamour, crystal-encrusted fashion has varied in popularity depending on the prevailing vogue in eveningwear. In 2006, Swarovski presented "Runway Rocks", in which designers such as Christopher Kane, Jean Paul Gautier and Antonio Berardi were invited to exploit the versatility of the crystal, and it is frequently incorporated with embroidery and laser-cut effects to provide a complex embellished surface or to provide kinetic theatrical effects – in 2007, designer Hussein Chalayan featured a dress made with Swarovski crystals and 200 moving laser beams in *Readings*, a short film made in collaboration with fashion photographer Nick Knight. In a collection that celebrated the natural world, Alexander McQueen incorporated crystals into his "Natural Dis-Tinction, Un-Natural Selection" ready-to-wear collection for Spring/Summer 2009. The designer created cropped dresses cut like the carapace of a beetle, the surface a mosaic of black, faceted crystal.

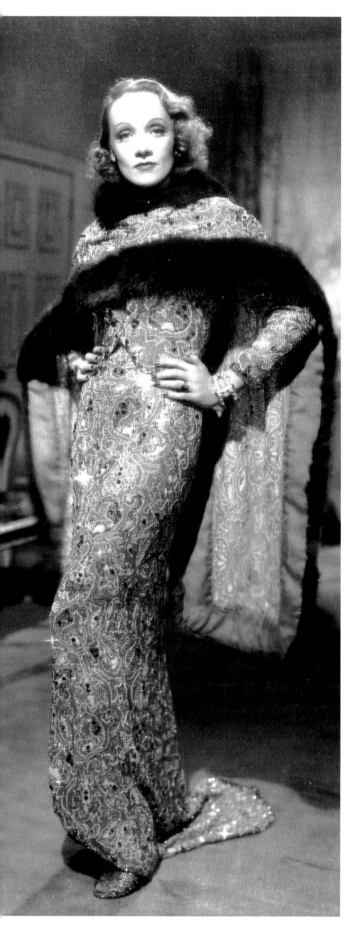

**LEFT:** In Ernst Lubitsch's romantic comedy *Angel* (1937), filmed in black and white, the impact of the light-reflecting, crystal-encrusted gown, designed by Hollywood costumier Travis Banton for actress Marlene Dietrich (1901–92), added immeasurably to the star's luminous appeal.

**OPPOSITE:** Symbolizing the negative impact of twenty-first-century evolution, and rich with detail, Alexander McQueen superimposes an hourglass silhouette of crystal embellishment over a structured beetle-like carapace for his S/S 2009 ready-to-wear collection.

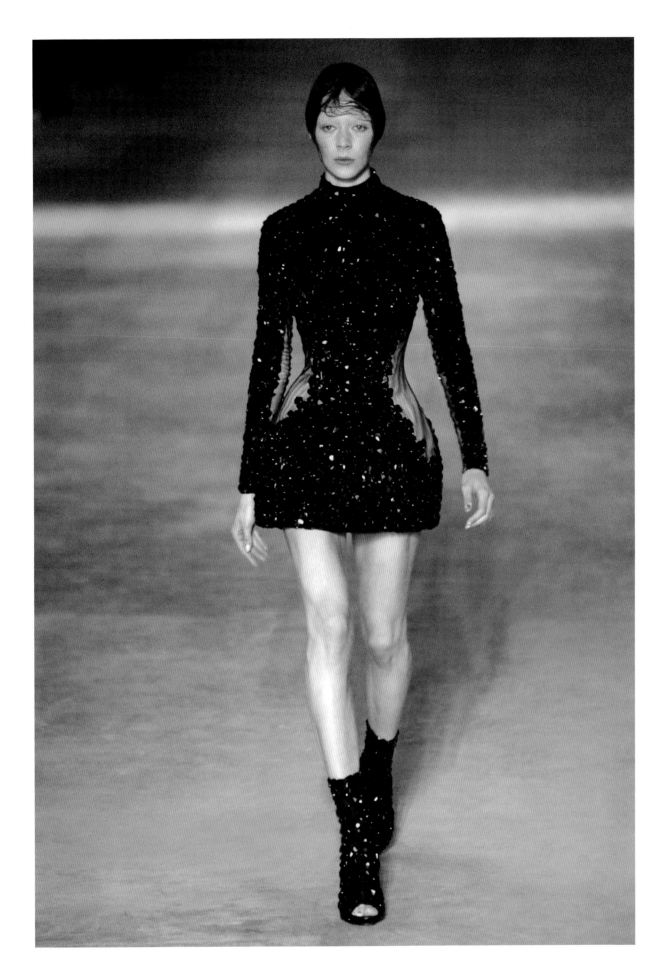

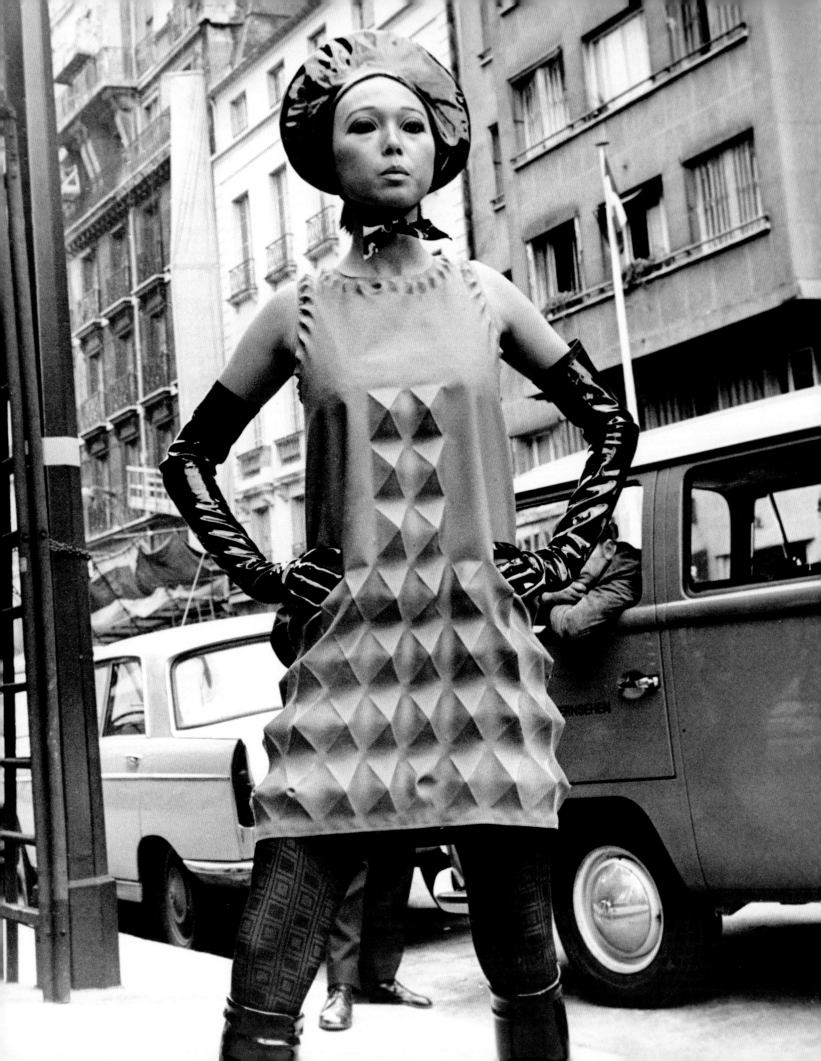

# The Sculptural Dress

The eloquence of fashion has a degree of permanent dependency on nuances of three-dimensional composition, balancing structural form, textures and colours in a compelling relationship with the figure. From time to time, designers explore these preoccupations with direct reference to the output of artists who use the rigid materials of sculpture and architecture to fabricate their vision; such cross-reference is affirmation of the immersion of apparel in the general tides of visual culture. Following his 1965 "Cosmocorps" collection in which Pierre Cardin was inspired by the exploration of space, in 1968 the designer used a patented fabric system, Cardine, produced for him in the synthetic fibre Dynel by Union Carbide, which allowed him to emboss geometric forms to stand in crisp relief away from the surface of angular shift dresses. The wider visual context of this range of designs lay in the genre of geometric abstraction with the addition or illusion of depth, as in the three-dimensional work of Victor Vasarely, Ellsworth Kelly and Frank Stella, who were among the artists in the widely influential 1965 exhibition *The Responsive Eye* at the Museum of Modern Art (MOMA), New York. Cardin's designs also made connection with open geodesic and modular constructivist sculpture and architecture of the time, typified by Erwin Hauer and Buckminster Fuller. In turn, Cardin came to represent futurism with his minimalist perforate forms, recalling the sculpted apertures of Henry Moore and Barbara Hepworth.

Tom Ford revisited this chain of connections in his Spring/Summer 2012 collection, when stark graphic dresses appeared to make allusion to the Hepworth bronze *Two Forms (Divided Circle)*. Hepworth found cohesion not through strict symmetry but by the easy distribution of masses and openings poised on the brink of instability. By a different mode of gestural expression, Ford uses a dark silhouette to ensnare the circular opposition of negative, white-banded voids, with the figure acting as an anchoring fulcrum at the centre, exploiting the curvy fit of the torso as a sensual counterpoint to the monumental abstraction of the overall outline. In 2007, Yohji Yamamoto evaded any accepted notions of seduction, gender or practicality with his densely compacted wool felt and knitted dress that shares the architectonic severity of the gargantuan curved steel installations of Richard Serra. Where Serra confronts the perceptions with outlandish scale and overbearing atavistic forms, Yamamoto invests the figure with curvilinear textile mass that carries an elemental gravity and almost monastic presence.

**OPPOSITE:** Pierre Cardin's sculpted Cardine dresses of 1968 were created in the midst of the New Brutalist tendency in architecture and sculpture, where repeated modular units were seen as consolidating mass and form and generating optical fluidity as a result of the transit of light and shade.

**BELOW:** Reflecting the contemplative atmospherics of stark abstract sculpture, Yohji Yamamoto engineers a serene, floor-length, felt pinafore, which, in profile, creates vestigial angelic wings held precisely in parallel to the cut of an elongated armhole, swept forward below the breasts. Such full-circuit compositional finesse confirms the acuity of Yamamoto's sculptural sensitivity.

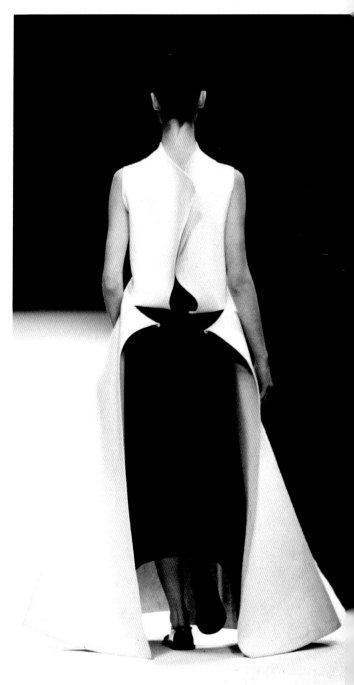

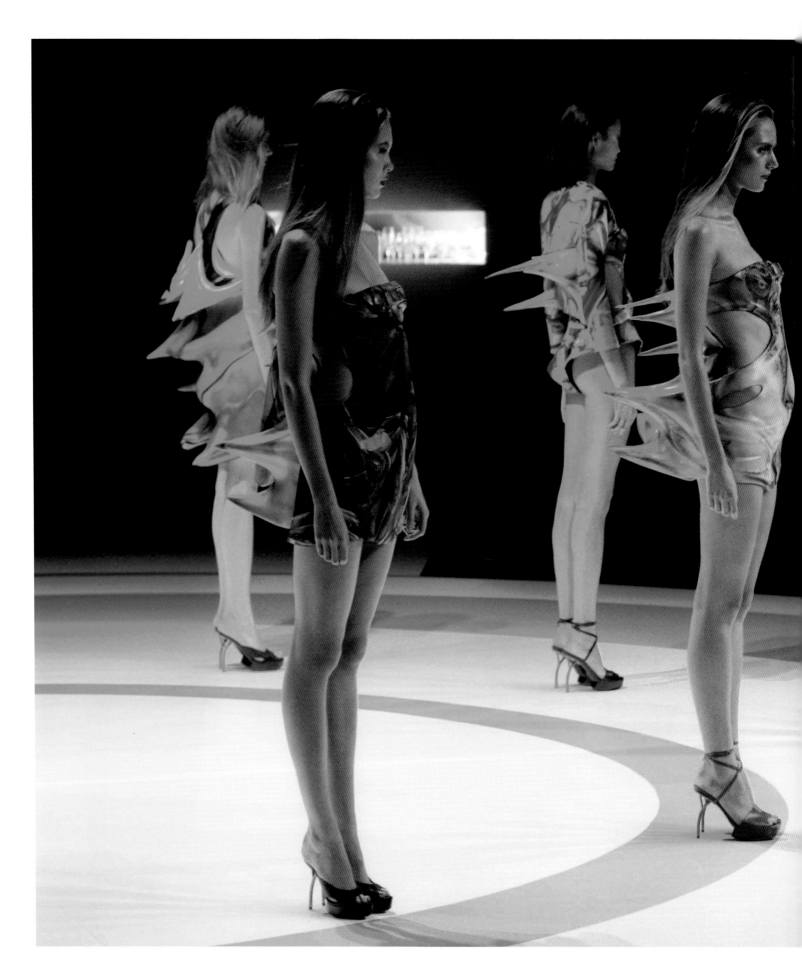

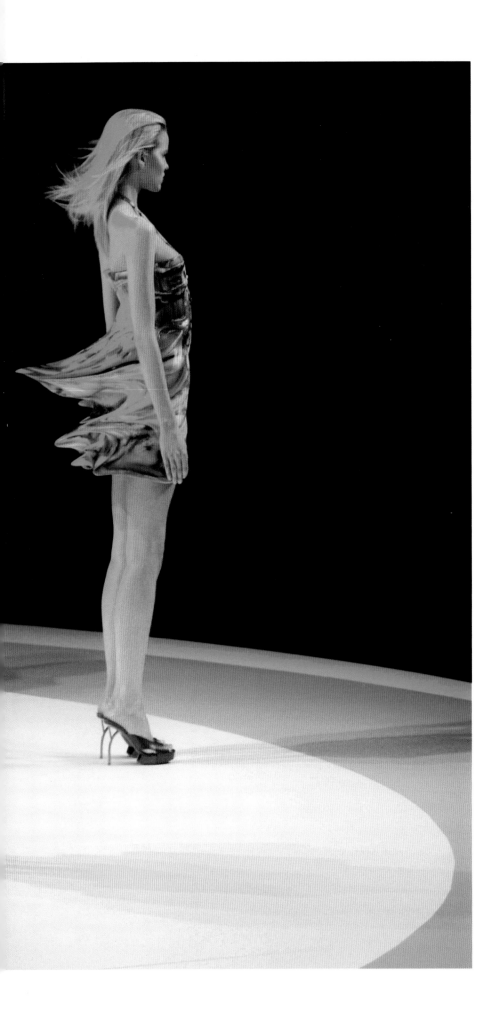

**LEFT:** With his "Inertia" collection of S/S 2009, Hussein Chalayan sought to capture frozen moments of dynamism, depicting the impact of elemental forces in sculptural form. Exemplified by airflow over static figures, his flimsy moulded dresses were held in stasis in a fleeting streamline billow.

# AUTHOR ACKNOWLEDGEMENTS

Many thanks to Lisa Dyer, Mabel Chan and Emma Copestake at Carlton Books, and to my daughter, Emily Angus.

# FURTHER READING

Baines, Barbara. *Fashion Revivals from the Elizabethan Age to the Present Day*. B.T.Batsford Ltd, London, 1981.

Blaszczyk, Regina Lee. *The Colour Revolution*. The MIT Press, Cambridge, Massachusetts and London, 2012.

Bolton, Andrew. *Wild: Fashion Untamed*. The Metropolitan Museum of Art New York, Yale University Press, New Haven, Connecticut, 2005.

Breward, Christopher. *Fashion*. Oxford University Press, Oxford, 2003.

Charles-Roux, Ednonde. *Chanel and Her World*. Weidenfeld and Nicolson, London, 1982.

Chierichetti, David. *The Life and Times of Hollywood's Celebrated Costume Designer Edith Head*. Harper Collins, New York, 2003.

Coleridge, Nicholas. *The Fashion Conspiracy: A Remarkable Journey through the Empires of Fashion*. Heinemann, London, 1988.

Dior, Christian. *Dior by Dior*. Weidenfeld & Nicolson, London, 1957.

Evans, Caroline. *Fashion at the Edge*. Yale University Press, New Haven, Connecticut, 2003.

Fogg, Marnie. *Boutique: A '60s Cultural Phenomenon*. Mitchell Beazley, London, 2003.

Hartnell, Norman. *The Silver and the Gold*. Evans Brothers Ltd, London, 1955.

Kennett, Frances. *Coco: The Life and Love of Gabrielle Chanel*. Victor Gollancz Ltd, London, 1980.

Laver, James. *Costume and Fashion: A Concise History*. Thames & Hudson, London, 1969.

Lee-Potter, Charlie. *Sportswear in Vogue Since 1910*. The Conde Nast Publications Ltd, London, 1984.

Mears, Patricia. *American Beauty: Aesthetics and Innovation in Fashion*. Yale University Press, New Haven, Connecticut, 2009.

Milbank, Caroline Rennolds. *New York Fashion: The Evolution of American Style*. Harry N. Abrams, Inc., New York, 1989.

Reeder, Jan Glier. *High Style: Masterworks from the Brooklyn Museum Costume Collection at the Metropolitan Museum of Art*. Yale University Press. New Haven, Connecticut, 2010.

Schiaparelli, Elsa. *Shocking Life*. J.M. Dent & Sons Ltd, London, 1954.

Steele, Valerie. *Fashion Italian Style*. Yale University Press, New Haven, Connecticut, 2003.

Steele, Valerie. *Fifty Years of Fashion*. Yale University Press, New Haven, Connecticut, 1997.

Von Furstenberg, Diane. *Diane, A Signature Life*. Simon & Schuster, New York, 1998.

Wilcox, Claire, Valerie Mendes & Chiara Buss. *The Art of Gianni Versace*. V&A Publications, London, 2002.

Wilcox, Claire. *The Golden Age of Couture: Paris and London 1947–1957*. V&A Publications, London, 2008.

Williams, Beryl. *Fashion Is Our Business*. John Gifford Limited, London, 1948.

# PICTURE CREDITS

The publishers would like to thank the following sources for their kind permission to reproduce the pictures in this book.

Key
t = top
b = bottom
l = left
r = right

Page 1 Massimo Listri/Corbis; 3 Helen and Kate Storey 'Spinal Column Dress from Primitive Streak' (1997), photography by Justine, modeled by Korinna @ Models 1; 4–5(t) The Metropolitan Museum of Art/Art Resource/Scala, Florence; 4–5(b) Fashion Museum, Bath and North East Somerset Council/Acquired with the assistance of The Art Fund and V&A/Purchase Grant Fund/The Bridgeman Art Library; 6 Ullstein bild/akg-images; 7 akg-images; 8 The Metropolitan Museum of Art/Art Resource/Scala, Florence; 9 Trunk Archive; 10 Fairchild Photo Service/Condé Nast/Corbis; 11(t) Ashmolean Museum, University of Oxford, UK/The Bridgeman Art Library; 11(b) Wikimedia Commons; 12 Peter Horree/Alamy; 13 The Metropolitan Museum of Art/Art Resource/Scala, Florence; 14 Rex Features; 15 Paramount Pictures/Sunset Boulevard/Corbis; 16 Fairchild Photo Service/Condé Nast/Corbis; 17 Wikimedia Commons; 18 Stephane Cardinale/People Avenue/Corbis; 19 Philippe Wojazer/Reuters/Corbis; 20 © Victoria and Albert Museum, London; 21 Gamma–Keystone/Getty Images; 22 Fairchild Photo Service/Condé Nast/Corbis; 23 Fairchild Photo Service/Condé Nast/Corbis; 24 Rex Features; 25(t) Wikimedia Commons; 25(b) Antonio de Moraes Barros/Getty Images; 26(t) © Victoria and Albert Museum, London; 26(b) The Bridgeman Art Library/Getty Images; 27 Nils Jorgensen/Rex Features; 28 Wikimedia Commons; 29(t) UPPA/Photoshot; 29(b) Antonio de Moraes Barros/Getty Images; 30 Hulton Fine Art Collection/Getty Images; 31 Yale Joel/Getty Images; 32 The Metropolitan Museum of Art/Art Resource/Scala, Florence; 33 Corbis; 34 Wikimedia Commons; 35 Zhang Yuwei/Xinhua Press/Corbis; 36 Antonio de Moraes Barros/Getty Images/Getty Images; 37 Pierre Vauthey/Sygma/Corbis; 38 De Agostini Picture Library/akg-images; 39 Patrick Kovarik/Getty Images; 40 Rex Features; 41 Museum of Fine Arts, Boston, Massachusetts, USA/The Elizabeth Day McCormick Collection/The Bridgeman Art Library; 42 De Agostini Picture Library/The Bridgeman Art Library; 43 The Metropolitan Museum of Art/Art Resource/Scala, Florence; 44(t) Private Collection/Archives Charmet/The Bridgeman Art Library; 44(b) Fairchild Photo Service/Condé Nast/Corbis; 45 Condé Nast Archive/Corbis; 46 © Victoria and Albert Museum, London; 47 The Metropolitan Museum of Art/Art Resource/Scala, Florence; 48(l) The Metropolitan Museum of Art/Art Resource/Scala, Florence; 48–49 Universal Images Group/Getty Images; 50 Kerry Taylor Auctions; 51 Wikimedia Commons; 52 Francois Guillot/AFP/Getty Images; 53(t) Scottish National Portrait Gallery, Edinburgh, Scotland/The Bridgeman Art Library; 53(b) Antonio de Moraes Barros/Getty Images; 54 Victor Virgile/Getty Images; 55 The Metropolitan Museum of Art/Art Resource/Scala, Florence; 56 First View; 57 Thierry Orban/Sygma/Corbis; 58 Ken Towner/Evening Standard/Rex Features; 59 The FIT, New York; 60 Steve Wood/Rex Features; 61(l) Fernanda Calfat/Getty Images; 61(r) David Fisher/Rex Features; 62 Bettmann/Corbis; 63 Museum of Fine Arts, Boston, Massachusetts, USA/Gift of Miss Florence Codman and Dr. Charles Austin Eager Codman/The Bridgeman Art Library; 64 Bertrand Rindoff Petroff/Getty Images; 65 Michel Arnaud/Corbis; 66 Tim Rooker/Rex Features; 67 Patrice Stable; 68(l) Victor Virgile/Getty Images; 68(r) Vittorio Zunino Celotto/Getty Images; 69 De Agostini Picture Library/The Bridgeman Art Library; 70 Rex Features; 71 Universal Group Images/Getty Images; 72 Roger-Viollet/Rex Features; 73(t) Museum of Fine Arts, Boston, Massachusetts, USA/Transferred from the William Morris Hunt Memorial Library/The Bridgeman Art Library; 73(b) Camera Press; 74 Laurent Lecat/akg-images; 75 Chateau de Fontainebleau, Seine-et-Marne, France/Giraudon/The Bridgeman Art Library; 76 Camera Press; 77 Ken Towner/Associated Newspapers/Rex Features; 78 Wikimedia Commons; 79 Pierre Verdy/Getty Images; 80 The Metropolitan Museum of Art/Art Resource/Scala, Florence; 81 The Metropolitan Museum of Art/Art Resource/Scala, Florence; 82 Alfred Eisenstaedt/Getty Images; 83 Wikimedia Commons; 84 Corbis; 85 Kim Knott; 86 Francois Guillot/Getty Images; 87 Pierre Verdy/Getty Images; 89 The Metropolitan Museum of Art/Art Resource/Scala, Florence; 89(l) Cincinnati Art Museum, Ohio, USA/Gift of Miyake Design Studio in memory of Otto C. Thieme/The Bridgeman Art Library; 89(r) © Victoria and Albert Museum, London; 90 Victoria & Albert Museum, London, UK/The Stapleton Collection/The Bridgeman Art Library; 91 Victoria & Albert Museum, London, UK/The Bridgeman Art Library; 92(t) Philadelphia Museum of Art, Pennsylvania, PA, USA/Gift of Mrs William H. Greene, 1962/The Bridgeman Art Library; 92(b) Olycom SPA/Rex Features; 93 The Metropolitan Museum of Art/Art Resource/Scala, Florence; 94 White Images/Scala, Florence; 95 Andy Lane/BodyMap; 96 Helen and Kate Storey 'Spinal Column Dress from Primitive Streak' (1997), photography by Justine, modeled by Korinna @ Models 1; 97 © Victoria and Albert Museum, London; 98 Fairchild Photo Service/Condé Nast/Corbis; 99 Gareth Cattermole/Getty Images; 100 The Metropolitan Museum of Art/Art Resource/Scala, Florence; 101 © Victoria and Albert Museum, London; 102 Les Arts Décoratifs, Paris/Patrick Gries/akg-images; 103 The Metropolitan Museum of Art/Art Resource/Scala, Florence; 104(l) Mitchell Sams/Camera Press; 104(r) Fairchild Photo Service/Condé Nast/Corbis; 105 Victor Virgile/Getty Images; 106(t) The Metropolitan Museum of Art/Art Resource/

Scala, Florence; 106(b) The Metropolitan Museum of Art/Art Resource/Scala, Florence; 107 Pascal le Segretain/Getty Images; 108 Wikimedia Commons; 109 Daniel Simon/Getty Images; 110(l) The Metropolitan Museum of Art/Art Resource/Scala, Florence; 110(r) The Metropolitan Museum of Art/Art Resource/Scala, Florence; 111 The Metropolitan Museum of Art/Art Resource/Scala, Florence; 112(t) Corbis; 112(b) Rex Features; 113 The Metropolitan Museum of Art/Art Resource/Scala, Florence; 114 Victor Virgile/Getty Images; 115 Heritage Image Partnership Ltd/Alamy; 116 Olycom SPA/Rex Features; 117 John Kobal Foundation/Getty Images; 118 The Metropolitan Museum of Art/Art Resource/Scala, Florence; 119 Camera Press; 120 Antonio de Moraes Barros/Getty Images; 121 Ken Towner/Evening Standard/Rex Features; 122 Prado, Madrid, Spain/Giraudon/The Bridgeman Art Library; 123 The Metropolitan Museum of Art/Art Resource/Scala, Florence; 124 Mondadori/Getty Images; 125 Corbis; 126 Corbis; 127 Condé Nast Archive/Corbis; 128 Condé Nast Archive/Corbis; 129 Sipa Press/Rex Features; 130 The Metropolitan Museum of Art/Art Resource/Scala, Florence; 131 Kedleston Hall, Derbyshire, UK/National Trust Photographic Library/John Hammond/The Bridgeman Art Library; 132 Rex Features; 133 Stuart Ramson/Getty; 134 Brian Ach/Getty Images; 135 Hardy Amies London/Mary Evans Picture Library; 136 Albright Knox Art Gallery, Buffalo, New York, USA/The Bridgeman Art Library; 137 Courtesy Everett Collection/Rex Features; 138 Fairchild Photo Service/Condé Nast/Corbis; 139 Venturelli/Getty Images; 140 Condé Nast Archive/Corbis; 141 Steve Granitz/Getty Images; 142 © Victoria and Albert Museum, London; 143 Press Association Images; 144 Fairchild Photo Service/Condé Nast/Corbis; 145(l) Richard Bord/Getty Images; 145(r) Victor Vigile/Getty Images; 146(l) LACMA/Art Resource NY/Scala, Florence; 146(r) J. W. Anderson; 147 Press Association Images; 148 © Victoria and Albert Museum, London; 149 Luke MacGregor/Reuters/Corbis; 150 The Metropolitan Museum of Art/Art Resource/Scala, Florence; 151 Victor Vigile/Getty Images; 152 Rex Features; 153 The Metropolitan Museum of Art/Art Resource/Scala, Florence; 154 The Metropolitan Museum of Art/Art Resource/Scala, Florence; 155 Stephane Cardinale/People Avenue/Corbis; 156 © Bristol Museum and Art Gallery, UK/The Bridgeman Art Library; 157 Erte Enterprises; 158 Everett Collection/Rex Features; 159 Francois Guillot/Getty Images; 160 Francois Deshayes/BESTI/SIPA/Rex Features; 161 Chris Moore/Catwalking/Getty Images; 162 © Les Arts Décoratifs, Paris/akg-images; 163 Julien M. Hekimian/Getty Images; 164 BPK, Bildagentur fuer Kunst, Kultur und Geschichte, Berlin/Scala, Florence; 165 Courtesy Everett Collection/Rex Features; 166 Pierre Vauthey/Sygma/Corbis; 167 © Victoria and Albert Museum, London; 168 First View; 169 Everett Collection/Rex Features; 170 Cavan Pawson/Evening Standard/Rex Features; 171 Condé Nast Archive/Corbis; 172 Condé Nast Archive/Corbis; 173 Condé Nast Archive/Corbis; 174 © The Estate of Erwin Blumenfeld; 175 Jean Yu; 176 Keystone-France/Getty Images; 177 Antonio de Moraes Barros/Getty Images; 178 The Metropolitan Museum of Art/Art Resource/Scala, Florence; 179 Sunset Boulevard/Corbis; 180 The Metropolitan Museum of Art/Art Resource/Scala, Florence; 181 The Metropolitan Museum of Art/Art Resource/

Scala, Florence; 182 Bettmann/Corbis; 183 Eliot Elisofon/Getty Images; 184 The Metropolitan Museum of Art/Art Resource/Scala, Florence; 185 Chicago History Museum/Getty Images; 186 Francois Guillot/Getty Images; 187 Massimo Listri/Corbis; 188-189 Micke Sebastien/Getty Images; 190 Missouri History Museum, St Louis; 191 Private Collection/Photo © Christie's Images/The Bridgeman Art Library; 192 The Metropolitan Museum of Art/Art Resource/Scala, Florence; 193 Julien M. Hekimian/Getty Images; 194 Peter Michael Dills/Getty Images; 195(l) Sipa Press/Rex Features; 195(r) MPortfolio/Electa/akg–images; 196 The Metropolitan Museum of Art/Art Resource/Scala, Florence; 197 ED/Christies/Camera Press; 198 © Victoria and Albert Museum, London; 199 Rex Features; 200 Keystone/Getty Images; 201 Indianapolis Museum of Art, USA/Deaccessioned Textile Fund/The Bridgeman Art Library; 202–203 Rex Features; 204 Rex Features; 205 MaxPP/epa/Corbis; 206 Robert Galbraith/Reuters/Corbis; 207 Tony Kyriacou/Rex Features; 208 The Metropolitan Museum of Art/Art Resource/Scala, Florence; 209 Fairchild Photo Service/Condé Nast Archive/Corbis; 210 Wikimedia Commons; 211 The Metropolitan Museum of Art/Art Resource/Scala, Florence; 212 Mary Evans Picture Library; 213 Private Collection/Photo © Christie's Images/The Bridgeman Art Library; 214 Condé Nast Archive/Corbis; 215 Fairchild Photo Service/Condé Nast/Corbis; 216 The Metropolitan Museum of Art/Art Resource/Scala, Florence; 217 © Victoria and Albert Museum, London; 218(t) Wikimedia Commons; 218(b) Wikimedia Commons; 219 The Metropolitan Museum of Art/Art Resource/Scala, Florence; 220 First View; 221 The Metropolitan Museum of Art/Art Resource/Scala, Florence; 222 Rex Features; 223 © Victoria and Albert Museum, London; 224 Antonio de Moraes Barros/Getty Images; 225(t) Commission of Immigration (Ellis Island, N.Y.)/National Geographic Society/Corbis; 225(b) Press Association Images; 226 Pixelformula/Sipa/Rex Features; 227 The Metropolitan Museum of Art/Art Resource/Scala, Florence; 228 Frazer Harrison/Getty Images; 229 The FIT, New York; 230 Private Collection/Photo © Christie's Images/The Bridgeman Art Library; 231 Smithsonian Institution, National Museum of American History; 232 Sharok Hatami/Rex Features; 233 Fernanda Calfat/Getty Images; 234 LACMA/Art Resource NY/Scala, Florence; 235 First view; 236 Charles Sykes/Rex Features; 237 © Victoria and Albert Museum, London; 238 Rex Features; 239 Fairchild Photo Service/Condé Nast/Corbis; 240 Anthea Simms/Camera Press; 241 Camera Press; 242 The Metropolitan Museum of Art/Art Resource/Scala, Florence; 243 Antonio de Moraes Barros/Getty Images; 244 John Kobal Collection/Getty Images; 245 Antonio de Moraes Barros/Getty Images; 246 Paul Popper/Popperfoto/Getty Images; 247 First View; 248–249 François Guillot/Getty Images; 250–251 Antonio de Moraes Barros/Getty Images; 252–253 Venturelli/Getty Images; 254–255 Philippe Wojazer/Reuters/Corbis.